Cryptography
and Data Security

Dorothy Elizabeth Robling Denning
PURDUE UNIVERSITY

ADDISON-WESLEY PUBLISHING COMPANY
Reading, Massachusetts ■ Menlo Park, California
London ■ Amsterdam ■ Don Mills, Ontario ■ Sydney

Library of Congress Cataloging in Publication Data

Denning, Dorothy E., (Dorothy Elizabeth), 1945–
  Cryptography and data security.

  Includes bibliographical references and index.
  1. Computers—Access control.   2. Cryptography.
3. Data protection.   I. Title.
QA76.9.A25D46   1982   001.64′028′9   81–15012
ISBN 0–201–10150–5   AACR2

Reprinted with corrections, January 1983

ISBN 0–201–10150–5
     HIJ–MA–8987

In memory of my Father,

Cornelius Lowell Robling

1910–1965

Preface

Electronic computers have evolved from exiguous experimental enterprises in the 1940s to prolific practical data processing systems in the 1980s. As we have come to rely on these systems to process and store data, we have also come to wonder about their ability to protect valuable data.

Data security is the science and study of methods of protecting data in computer and communication systems from unauthorized disclosure and modification. The goal of this book is to introduce the mathematical principles of data security and to show how these principles apply to operating systems, database systems, and computer networks. The book is for students and professionals seeking an introduction to these principles. There are many references for those who would like to study specific topics further.

Data security has evolved rapidly since 1975. We have seen exciting developments in cryptography: public-key encryption, digital signatures, the Data Encryption Standard (DES), key safeguarding schemes, and key distribution protocols. We have developed techniques for verifying that programs do not leak confidential data, or transmit classified data to users with lower security clearances. We have found new controls for protecting data in statistical databases—and new methods of attacking these databases. We have come to a better understanding of the theoretical and practical limitations to security.

Because the field is evolving so rapidly, it has been difficult to write a book that is both coherent and current. Even as the manuscript was in production, there were new developments in the field. Although I was able to incorporate a few of these developments, they are not as well integrated into the book as I would like. In many cases, I was only able to include references.

Some areas are still unsettled, and I was unable to treat them to my satisfaction. One such area is operating system verification; another is the integration of cryptographic controls into operating systems and database systems. I hope to cover these topics better in later editions of the book.

Data security draws heavily from mathematics and computer science. I have assumed my audience has some background in programming, data structures, operating systems, database systems, computer architecture, probability theory, and linear algebra. Because I have found most computer science students have little background in information theory and number theory, I have included self-contained tutorials on these subjects. Because complexity theory is a relatively new area, I have also summarized it.

This book is used in a one-semester graduate computer science course at Purdue University. The students are assigned exercises, programming projects, and a term project. The book is suitable for a graduate or advanced undergraduate course and for independent study. There are a few exercises at the end of each chapter, most of which are designed so the reader can recognize the right answer. I have purposely not included solutions. There is also a puzzle.

Here is a brief summary of the chapters:

- *Chapter 1, Introduction,* introduces the basic concepts of cryptography, data security, information theory, complexity theory, and number theory.
- *Chapter 2, Encryption Algorithms,* describes both classical and modern encryption algorithms, including the Data Encryption Standard (DES) and public-key algorithms.
- *Chapter 3, Cryptographic Techniques,* studies various techniques related to integrating cryptographic controls into computer systems, including key management.
- *Chapter 4, Access Controls,* describes the basic principles of mechanisms that control access by subjects (e.g., users or programs) to objects (e.g., files and records). These mechanisms regulate direct access to objects, but not what happens to the information contained in these objects.
- *Chapter 5, Information Flow Controls,* describes controls that regulate the dissemination of information. These controls are needed to prevent programs from leaking confidential data, or from disseminating classified data to users with lower security clearances.
- *Chapter 6, Inference Controls,* describes controls that protect confidential data released as statistics about subgroups of individuals.

I am deeply grateful to Jim Anderson, Bob Blakley, Peter Denning, Whit Diffie, Peter Neumann, and Rich Reitman, whose penetrating criticisms and suggestions guided me to important results and helped me focus my ideas. I am also grateful to Greg Andrews, Leland Beck, Garrett Birkhoff, Manuel Blum, David Chaum, Francis Chin, Larry Cox, Töre Dalenius, George Davida, Dave Gifford, Carl Hammer, Mike Harrison, Chris Hoffmann, Stephen Matyas, Jon Millen, Bob Morris, Glen Myers, Steve Reiss, Ron Rivest, Brian Schanning, Jan Schlörer, Gus Simmons, and Larry Snyder. These people gave generously of their time to help make this a better book.

I am thankful to the students who read the book, worked the problems, and provided numerous comments and suggestions: George Adams, Brian Beuning, Steve Booth, Steve Breese, Carl Burch, Steve Burton, Ray Ciesielski, Cliff Cockerham, Ken Dickman, James Drobina, Dave Eckert, Jeremy Epstein, Tim Field, Jack Fitch, Jim Fuss, Greg Gardner, Neil Harrison, Ching-Chih Hsiao, Teemu Kerola, Ron Krol, Meng Lee, Peter Liesenfelt, Paul Morrisett, Tim Nodes, Bhasker Parthasarathy, Steve Pauley, Alan Pieramico, Steve Raiman, Dan Reed, David Rutkin, Paul Scherf, Carl Smith, Alan Stanson, Mark Stinson, Andy Tong, and Kim Tresner. I am especially thankful to Matt Bishop for providing solutions and for grading.

The working version of the book was prepared on the department's VAX computer. I am grateful to Doug Comer, Herb Schwetman, and the many others who kept the system operational and paid careful attention to backup procedures. I am grateful to the people who helped with the publication of the book, especially Peter Gordon, Gail Goodell, Cheryl Wurzbacher, and Judith Gimple.

I am especially grateful to my husband, Peter, for his encouragement, support, advice, and help throughout.

Contents

1

Introduction

1.1 CRYPTOGRAPHY

Cryptography is the science and study of secret writing. A **cipher** is a secret method of writing, whereby **plaintext** (or **cleartext**) is transformed into **ciphertext** (sometimes called a **cryptogram**). The process of transforming plaintext into ciphertext is called **encipherment** or **encryption**; the reverse process of transforming ciphertext into plaintext is called **decipherment** or **decryption**. Both encipherment and decipherment are controlled by a cryptographic **key** or keys (see Figure 1.1).

There are two basic types of ciphers: transpositions and substitutions. **Transposition ciphers** rearrange bits or characters in the data. With a "rail-fence" cipher, for example, the letters of a plaintext message are written down in a

FIGURE 1.1 Secret writing.

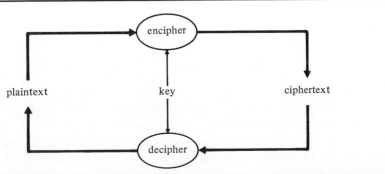

pattern resembling a rail fence, and then removed by rows. The following illustrates this pattern:

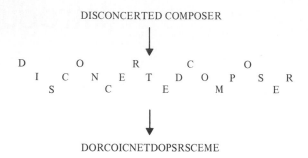

The key to the cipher is given by the depth of the fence, which in this example is 3.

   Substitution ciphers replace bits, characters, or blocks of characters with substitutes. A simple type of substitution cipher shifts each letter in the English alphabet forward by K positions (shifts past Z cycle back to A); K is the key to the cipher. The cipher is often called a **Caesar cipher** because Julius Caesar used it with $K = 3$. The following illustrates Caesar's method:

IMPATIENT WAITER
         ↓
LPSDWLHQW ZDLWHU.

   A **code** is a special type of substitution cipher that uses a "code book" as the key. Plaintext words or phrases are entered into the code book together with their ciphertext substitutes, as shown next:

Word	Code
BAKER	1701
FRETTING	5603
GUITARIST	4008
LOAFING	3790
.	.
.	.
.	.

LOAFING BAKER

↓

3790 1701

The term code is sometimes used to refer to any type of cipher.

   In computer applications, transposition is usually combined with substitution. The Data Encryption Standard (DES), for example, enciphers 64-bit blocks using a combination of transposition and substitution (see Chapter 2).

   Cryptanalysis is the science and study of methods of breaking ciphers. A cipher is **breakable** if it is possible to determine the plaintext or key from the ciphertext, or to determine the key from plaintext-ciphertext pairs. There are three basic methods of attack: ciphertext-only, known-plaintext, and chosen-plaintext.

   Under a **ciphertext-only attack**, a cryptanalyst must determine the key solely from intercepted ciphertext, though the method of encryption, the plaintext language, the subject matter of the ciphertext, and certain probable words may be known. For example, a message describing the location of a buried treasure would probably contain words such as BURIED, TREASURE, NORTH, TURN, RIGHT, MILES.

Under a **known-plaintext attack**, a cryptanalyst knows some plaintext-ciphertext pairs. As an example, suppose an enciphered message transmitted from a user's terminal to the computer is intercepted by a cryptanalyst who knows that the message begins with a standard header such as "LOGIN". As another example, the cryptanalyst may know that the *Department* field of a particular record contains the ciphertext for *Physics;* indeed, the cryptanalyst may know the *Department* field of every record in the database. In some cases, knowledge of probable words allows a close approximation to a known-plaintext attack. Encrypted programs are particularly vulnerable because of the regular appearance of keywords—e.g. **begin, end, var, procedure, if, then**. Even if the exact position of encrypted keywords is unknown, a cryptanalyst may be able to make reasonable guesses about them. Ciphers today are usually considered acceptable only if they can withstand a known-plaintext attack under the assumption that the cryptanalyst has an arbitrary amount of plaintext-ciphertext pairs.

Under a **chosen-plaintext attack**, a cryptanalyst is able to acquire the ciphertext corresponding to selected plaintext. This is the most favorable case for the cryptanalyst. A database system may be particularly vulnerable to this type of attack if users can insert elements into the database, and then observe the changes in the stored ciphertext. Bayer and Metzger [Baye76] call this the **planted record problem**.

Public-key systems (defined in Section 1.3) have introduced a fourth kind of attack: a **chosen-ciphertext attack**. Although the plaintext is not likely to be intelligible, the cryptanalyst may be able to use it to deduce the key.

A cipher is **unconditionally secure** if, no matter how much ciphertext is intercepted, there is not enough information in the ciphertext to determine the plaintext uniquely. We shall give a formal definition of an unconditionally secure cipher in Section 1.4. With one exception, all ciphers are breakable given unlimited resources, so we are more interested in ciphers that are computationally infeasible to break. A cipher is **computationally secure**, or **strong**, if it cannot be broken by systematic analysis with available resources.

The branch of knowledge embodying both cryptography and cryptanalysis is called **cryptology**.

1.2 DATA SECURITY

Classical cryptography provided secrecy for information sent over channels where eavesdropping and message interception was possible. The sender selected a cipher and encryption key, and either gave it directly to the receiver or else sent it indirectly over a slow but secure channel (typically a trusted courier). Messages and replies were transmitted over the insecure channel in ciphertext (see Figure 1.2). Classical encryption schemes are described in Chapter 2.

Modern cryptography protects data transmitted over high-speed electronic

FIGURE 1.2 Classical information channel.

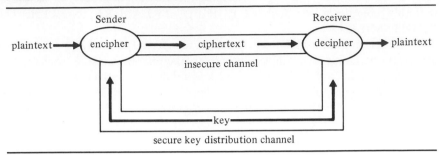

lines or stored in computer systems. There are two principal objectives: **secrecy** (or **privacy**), to prevent the unauthorized disclosure of data; and **authenticity** or **integrity**), to prevent the unauthorized modification of data.

Information transmitted over electronic lines is vulnerable to passive wiretapping, which threatens secrecy, and to active wiretapping, which threatens authenticity (see Figure 1.3). **Passive wiretapping (eavesdropping)** refers to the interception of messages, usually without detection. Although it is normally used to disclose message contents, in computer networks it can also be used to monitor traffic flow through the network to determine who is communicating with whom. Protection against disclosure of message contents is provided by enciphering transformations, which are described in Chapter 2, and by the cryptographic techniques described in Chapter 3. Protection against traffic flow analysis is provided by controlling the endpoints of encryption; this is discussed in Chapter 3.

Active wiretapping (tampering) refers to deliberate modifications made to the message stream. This can be for the purpose of making arbitrary changes to a message, or of replacing data in a message with replays of data from earlier messages (e.g., replacing the amount field of a transaction "CREDIT SMITH'S ACCOUNT WITH $10" with the amount field of an earlier transaction "CREDIT JONES'S ACCOUNT WITH $5000"). It can be for the purpose of injecting false messages, injecting replays of previous messages (e.g., to repeat a credit transaction), or deleting messages (e.g., to prevent a transaction "DEDUCT $1000 FROM SMITH'S ACCOUNT"). Encryption protects against message

FIGURE 1.3 Threats to secure communication.

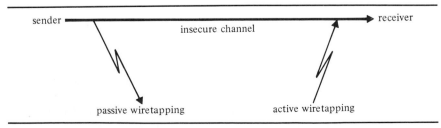

modification and injection of false messages by making it infeasible for an opponent to create ciphertext that deciphers into meaningful plaintext. Note, however, that whereas it can be used to detect message modification, it cannot prevent it.

Encryption alone does not protect against replay, because an opponent could simply replay previous ciphertext. Cryptographic techniques for protecting against this problem are discussed in Chapter 3. Although encryption cannot prevent message deletion, the cryptographic techniques discussed in Chapter 3 can detect deletions of blocks or characters within a message stream. Deletion of entire messages can be detected with communication protocols that require message acknowledgment.

FIGURE 1.4 Threats to data stored in computer systems.

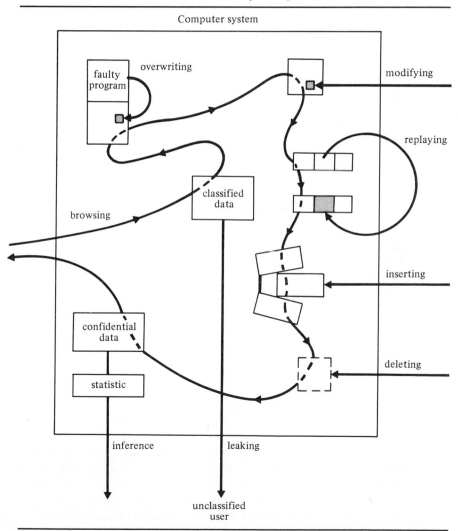

Data in computer systems is vulnerable to similar threats (see Figure 1.4). Threats to secrecy include browsing, leakage, and inference. **Browsing** refers to searching through main memory or secondary storage for information (e.g., confidential data or proprietary software programs). It is similar to eavesdropping on communication channels, but there are two important differences. On the one hand, information stored in computer systems has a longer lifetime; in this sense, browsing poses a more serious threat than eavesdropping. On the other hand, information transmitted over electronic lines is vulnerable to tapping even when access to the system is denied. Browsing is possible only if the user has access to the system and to unauthorized regions of memory. Access controls, described in Chapter 4, can prevent this.

Cryptography protects against browsing by making the information unintelligible. It can supplement access controls and is especially useful for protecting data on tapes and discs which, if stolen, can no longer be protected by the system. Cryptography cannot, however, protect data from disclosure while it is being processed in the clear. Access controls are needed for this purpose, and these controls must include procedures that clear memory between use to ensure that confidential data is not inadvertently exposed. If access is not controlled, encrypted data can also be vulnerable to **ciphertext searching** (e.g., finding employees making identical salaries by searching for records with identical ciphertext salaries); cryptographic solutions to this problem are described in Chapter 3.

Leakage refers to the transmission of data to unauthorized users by processes with legitimate access to the data. A compiler, for example, could leak a proprietary software program while it is being compiled. An income tax program could leak confidential information about a user. A file editor could leak classified military data to a user without a security clearance. Cryptography and access controls must be supplemented with information flow controls, discussed in Chapter 5, to control information dissemination.

Inference refers to the deduction of confidential data about a particular individual by correlating released statistics about groups of individuals. For example, if Smith is the only non-Ph.D. faculty member in a Physics department, Smith's salary can be deduced by correlating the average salary of all faculty in the department with the average salary of all Ph.D. faculty in the department. Although cryptography and access controls can protect the data records from browsing, they do not provide a mathematical framework for determining which statistics can be released without disclosing sensitive data. Inference controls, discussed in Chapter 6, address this problem.

Threats to authenticity include tampering and accidental destruction. **Tampering** with data in computer systems is analogous to active wiretapping on communication channels, but differs from it in the same ways browsing differs from passive wiretapping. Like active wiretapping, tampering can be for the purpose of making arbitrary changes to data (e.g., changing the *Salary* field of an employee record from $20,000 to $25,000). It can be for the purpose of replaying data stored previously in a record (e.g., to restore a previous balance in an accounting record), or replaying data stored in some other record (e.g., to make the *Salary* field of an employee record the same as that of a higher paid employee). It can also be for the purpose of overwriting data with nonsense (e.g., overwriting a cryptographic key so that encrypted data becomes inaccessible). Finally, it can be for the purpose of inserting records (e.g., adding a dummy employee record to the payroll file) or deleting files or records (e.g., to remove a bad credit report). Cryptographic techniques can help protect against these threats by making it possible to detect false or replayed ciphertext. But it cannot prevent them. Access controls are essential for the reliable operation of the system. Backup is vital for recovery.

Accidental destruction refers to the unintentional overwriting or deletion of data. Unintentional overwriting is caused by faulty software (e.g., because an array subscript is out-of-range). Cryptography cannot protect against this threat. Access controls, implemented in language processors and in hardware, provide error confinement by preventing programs from writing into the memory regions of other programs or into system tables. Unintentional deletion is caused by software or hardware failure (e.g., a disk head crash), and by user mistakes (e.g., inadvertently deleting lines of a file during an editing session). Backup is needed to recover from accidental as well as deliberate destruction. Many text editors have automatic backup facilities so that an earlier version of a file is easily recovered; some have facilities for undoing each editing command.

Computer systems are vulnerable to another problem: **masquerading**. If an intruder can gain access to a system under another user's account, then the intruder can access the user's data files and all other information permitted to the user. Similarly, if a program can spoof legitimate users logging into the system into believing that they are conversing with the system, the program might be able to obtain confidential information from these users (e.g., their login passwords). Protection against masquerading requires that the system and user be able to mutually authenticate each other. Such strategies that use encrypted passwords are described in Chapter 3. "Digital signatures" provide a more general means of authenticating users or processes; they are introduced in Section 1.3.3.

Data security is the science and study of methods of protecting data in computer and communications systems. It embodies the four kinds of controls studied in this book: cryptographic controls, access controls, information flow controls, and inference controls. It also embodies procedures for backup and recovery.

1.3 CRYPTOGRAPHIC SYSTEMS

This section describes the general requirements of all cryptographic systems, the specific properties of public-key encryption, and digital signatures.

A **cryptographic system** (or **cryptosystem** for short) has five components:

1. A **plaintext message space**, $\mathcal{M}$.
2. A **ciphertext message space**, $\mathcal{C}$.
3. A **key space**, $\mathcal{K}$.
4. A family of **enciphering transformations**, $E_K: \mathcal{M} \rightarrow \mathcal{C}$, where $K \in \mathcal{K}$.
5. A family of **deciphering transformations**, $D_K: \mathcal{C} \rightarrow \mathcal{M}$, where $K \in \mathcal{K}$.

FIGURE 1.5 Cryptographic system.

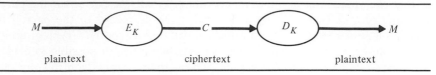

Each **enciphering transformation** E_K is defined by an **enciphering algorithm** E, which is common to every transformation in the family, and a **key** K, which distinguishes it from the other transformations. Similarly, each **deciphering transformation** D_K is defined by a **deciphering algorithm** D and a key K. For a given K, D_K is the inverse of E_K; that is, $D_K(E_K(M)) = M$ for every plaintext message M. In a given cryptographic system, the transformations E_K and D_K are described by parameters derived from K (or directly by K). The set of parameters describing E_K is called the **enciphering key,** and the set of parameters describing D_K the **deciphering key**. Figure 1.5 illustrates the enciphering and deciphering of data.

Cryptosystems must satisfy three general requirements:

1. The enciphering and deciphering transformations must be efficient for all keys.
2. The system must be easy to use.
3. The security of the system should depend only on the secrecy of the keys and not on the secrecy of the algorithms E or D.

Requirement (1) is essential for computer applications; data is usually enciphered and deciphered at the time of transmission, and these operations must not be bottlenecks. Requirement (2) implies it must be easy for the cryptographer to find a key with an invertible transformation. Requirement (3) implies the enciphering and deciphering algorithms must be inherently strong; that is, it should not be possible to break a cipher simply by knowing the method of encipherment. This requirement is needed because the algorithms may be in the public domain or known to a cryptanalyst, whence knowing K reveals E_K and D_K. Note, however, the converse need not hold; that is, knowing E_K or D_K need not reveal K. This is because the enciphering key describing E_K or the deciphering key describing D_K could be derived from K by a one-way (irreversible) transformation (see Section 1.5.3). This technique is used in public-key systems (see Section 1.3). We shall assume the algorithms E and D are public knowledge.

There are specific requirements for secrecy and authenticity. Secrecy requires that a cryptanalyst not be able to determine plaintext data from intercepted ciphertext. Formally, there are two requirements:

Secrecy requirements
1. It should be computationally infeasible for a cryptanalyst to systematically determine the deciphering transformation D_K from intercepted ciphertext C, even if the corresponding plaintext M is known.

2.   It should be computationally infeasible for a cryptanalyst to systematically
       determine plaintext M from intercepted ciphertext C.

Requirement (1) ensures that a cryptanalyst cannot systematically determine the
deciphering transformation (guessing may be possible). Thus, the cryptanalyst will
be unable to decipher C or other ciphertext enciphered under the transformation
E_K. Requirement (2) ensures that a cryptanalyst cannot systematically determine
plaintext without the deciphering transformation. Both requirements should hold
regardless of the length or number of ciphertext messages intercepted.
       Secrecy requires only that the transformation D_K (i.e., the deciphering key)
be protected. The transformation E_K can be revealed if it does not give away D_K.
Figure 1.6 illustrates. The straight line shows the intended flow through the system, while the bent line shows the undesired flow that results from successful
attacks.
       Data authenticity requires that a cryptanalyst not be able to substitute a
false ciphertext C' for a ciphertext C without detection. Formally, the two requirements are:

Authenticity requirements
1.   It should be computationally infeasible for a cryptanalyst to systematically
       determine the enciphering transformation E_K given C, even if the correspond-
       ing plaintext M is known.
2.   It should be computationally infeasible for a cryptanalyst to systematically
       find ciphertext C' such that $D_K(C')$ is valid plaintext in the set $\mathcal{M}$.

Requirement (1) ensures that a cryptanalyst cannot systematically determine the
enciphering transformation. Thus the cryptanalyst will be unable to encipher a
different plaintext message M', and substitute the false ciphertext $C' = E_K(M')$
for C. Requirement (2) ensures that a cryptanalyst cannot find ciphertext C' that
deciphers into meaningful plaintext without the enciphering transformation. Numerical data is particularly vulnerable to ciphertext substitution because all values
may be meaningful. Both requirements should hold regardless of the amount of
ciphertext intercepted.
       Authenticity requires only that the transformation E_K (i.e., the enciphering

FIGURE 1.6 Secrecy.

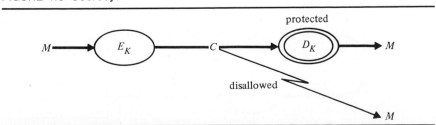

FIGURE 1.7 Authenticity.

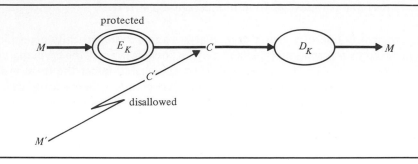

key) be protected. The transformation D_K could be revealed if it does not give away E_K. Figure 1.7 illustrates.

Simmons classifies cryptosystems as symmetric (one-key) and asymmetric (two-key) [Simm79]. In **symmetric** or **one-key** cryptosystems the enciphering and deciphering keys are the same (or easily determined from each other). Because we have assumed the general method of encryption is known, this means the transformations E_K and D_K are also easily derived from each other. Thus, if both E_K and D_K are protected, both secrecy and authenticity are achieved. Secrecy cannot be separated from authenticity, however, because making either E_K or D_K available exposes the other. Thus, all the requirements for both secrecy and authenticity must hold in one-key systems.

One-key systems provide an excellent way of enciphering users' private files. Each user A has private transformations E_A and D_A for enciphering and deciphering files (see Figure 1.8). If other users cannot access E_A and D_A, then both the secrecy and authenticity of A's data is assured.

One-key systems also provide an excellent way of protecting information transmitted over computer networks. This is the classical information channel where the sender and receiver share a secret communication key (see Figure 1.2). If both parties are mutually trustworthy, they can be assured of both the secrecy and authenticity of their communications.

Until recently, all cryptosystems were one-key systems. Thus, one-key sys-

FIGURE 1.8 Single-key encryption of private files.

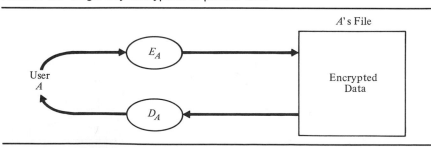

FIGURE 1.9 File encryption with separate Read/Write keys.

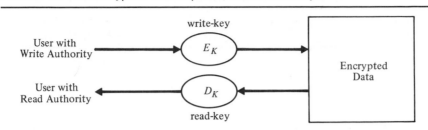

tems are also usually referred to as **conventional** (or **classical**) systems. The DES is a conventional system.

In **asymmetric** or **two-key** cryptosystems the enciphering and deciphering keys differ in such a way that at least one key is computationally infeasible to determine from the other. Thus, one of the transformations E_K or D_K can be revealed without endangering the other.

Secrecy and authenticity are provided by protecting the separate transformations—D_K for secrecy, E_K for authenticity. Figure 1.9 illustrates how this principle can be applied to databases, where some users have read-write authority to the database, while other users have read authority only. Users with read-write authority are given both D_K and E_K, so they can decipher data stored in the database or encipher new data to update the database. If E_K cannot be determined from D_K, users with read-only authority can be given D_K, so they can decipher the data but cannot update it. Thus D_K is like a **read-key**, while E_K is like a **write-key** (more precisely, the deciphering key describing D_K is the read-key, and the enciphering key describing E_K the write-key).

Note that this does not prevent a user with read-only authority (or no access authority) from destroying the data by overwriting the database with nonsense. It only prevents that user from creating valid ciphertext. To protect the data from such destruction, the system must be secured by access controls, so that no user can write into the database without the write-key E_K. The system need not, however, control read access to the data, because the data cannot be deciphered without the read-key D_K.

1.3.1. Public-Key Systems

The concept of two-key cryptosystems was introduced by Diffie and Hellman in 1976 [Diff76]. They proposed a new method of encryption called **public-key encryption**, wherein each user has both a public and private key, and two users can communicate knowing only each other's public keys.

In a public-key system, each user A has a **public enciphering transformation** E_A, which may be registered with a public directory, and a **private deciphering transformation** D_A, which is known only to that user. The private transformation D_A is described by a **private key**, and the public transformation E_A by a **public key**

FIGURE 1.10 Secrecy in public-key system.

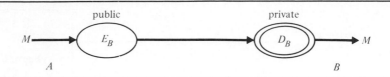

derived from the private key by a one-way transformation. It must be computationally infeasible to determine D_A from E_A (or even to find a transformation
equivalent to D_A).

In a public-key system, secrecy and authenticity are provided by the separate
transformations. Suppose user A wishes to send a message M to another user B. If
A knows B's public transformation E_B, A can transmit M to B in secrecy by
sending the ciphertext $C = E_B(M)$. On receipt, B deciphers C using B's private
transformation D_B, getting

$$D_B(C) = D_B(E_B(M)) = M .$$

(See Figure 1.10.) The preceding scheme does not provide authenticity because
any user with access to B's public transformation could substitute another message
M' for M by replacing C with $C' = E_B(M')$.

For authenticity, M must be transformed by A's own private transformation
D_A. Ignoring secrecy for the moment, A sends $C = D_A(M)$ to B. On receipt, B uses
A's public transformation E_A to compute

$$E_A(C) = E_A(D_A(M)) = M .$$

(See Figure 1.11.) Authenticity is provided because only A can apply the transformation D_A. Secrecy is not provided because any user with access to A's public
transformation can recover M.

Now, we had previously defined a transformation D_A as a function from the
ciphertext space $\mathcal{C}$ to the message space $\mathcal{M}$. To apply D_A to plaintext messages, D_A
must instead map $\mathcal{M}$ to $\mathcal{C}$. Furthermore, to restore the original message, E_A must
be the inverse of D_A; that is, E_A must be a function from $\mathcal{C}$ to $\mathcal{M}$ such that
$E_A(D_A(M)) = M$.

To use a public-key system for both secrecy and authenticity, the ciphertext
space $\mathcal{C}$ must be equivalent to the plaintext space $\mathcal{M}$ so that any pair of transformations E_A and D_A can operate on both plaintext and ciphertext messages. Furthermore, both E_A and D_A must be mutual inverses so that $E_A(D_A(M))$
$= D_A(E_A(M)) = M$. These requirements are summarized in Table 1.1.

FIGURE 1.11 Authenticity in public-key system.

TABLE 1.1 Requirements for public-key transformations.

Secrecy	Authenticity	Both
$E_A: \mathcal{M} \to \mathcal{C}$	$D_A: \mathcal{M} \to \mathcal{C}$	$E_A: \mathcal{M} \to \mathcal{M}$
$D_A: \mathcal{C} \to \mathcal{M}$	$E_A: \mathcal{C} \to \mathcal{M}$	$D_A: \mathcal{M} \to \mathcal{M}$
$D_A(E_A(M)) = M$	$E_A(D_A(M)) = M$	$D_A(E_A(M)) = M$
		$E_A(D_A(M)) = M$

To achieve both secrecy and authenticity, the sender and receiver must each apply two sets of transformations. Suppose A wishes to send a message M to B. First A's private transformation D_A is applied. Then A enciphers the result using B's public enciphering transformation E_B, and transmits the doubly transformed message $C = E_B(D_A(M))$ to B. B recovers M by first applying B's own private deciphering transformation D_B, and then applying A's public transformation E_A to validate its authenticity, getting

$$E_A(D_B(C)) = E_A\big(D_B\big(E_B\big(D_A(M)\big)\big)\big)$$
$$= E_A(D_A(M))$$
$$= M .$$

(See Figure 1.12.)

Only one of the public-key encryption methods discussed in Chapter 2 can be used for both secrecy and authenticity. This is the scheme invented by Rivest, Shamir, and Adleman of MIT (referred to as the "RSA scheme"). The RSA scheme is based on the difficulty of factoring large numbers (see Section 2.7). The schemes based on the difficulty of solving "knapsack problems" can be used for either secrecy or authenticity but not both (see Section 2.8). McEliece's [McEl78] scheme based on error correcting codes (not discussed in this book) is also restricted to secrecy.

Simmons [Simm81] shows how a public-key authenticity system can be used to verify the identity of individuals seeking entrance to secured areas (computer room, nuclear reactor site, etc.). Each individual permitted to enter the area is given an ID card containing descriptive information such as name and social security number, identifying information such as voiceprint or handprint, and access

FIGURE 1.12 Secrecy and authenticity in public-key system.

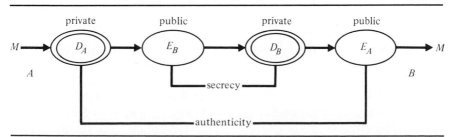

control information such as the time of day when entrance is permitted. The information is encrypted under the private key of the central authority issuing the card. The corresponding public key is distributed to all areas where entry is controlled. The individual enters the restricted area through a special facility where the identifying information is taken and checked against the information stored on the individual's card.

1.3.2 Digital Signatures

A **digital signature** is a property private to a user or process that is used for signing messages. Let B be the recipient of a message M signed by A. Then A's signature must satisfy these requirements:

1. B must be able to **validate** A's signature on M.
2. It must be impossible for anyone, including B, to **forge** A's signature.
3. In case A should disavow signing a message M, it must be possible for a judge or third party to **resolve** a dispute arising between A and B.

A digital signature, therefore, establishes **sender authenticity**; it is analogous to an ordinary written signature. By condition (2), it also establishes data authenticity.

Public-key authentication systems provide a simple scheme for implementing digital signatures. Because the transformation D_A is private to A, D_A serves as A's digital signature. The recipient B of a message M signed by A (i.e., transformed by D_A) is assured of both sender and data authenticity. It is impossible for B or anyone else to forge A's signature on another message, and impossible for A to disclaim a signed document (assuming D_A has not been lost or stolen). Because the inverse transformation E_A is public, the receiver B can readily validate the signature, and a judge can settle any disputes arising between A and B. Summarizing,

1. A signs M by computing $C = D_A(M)$.
2. B validates A's signature by checking that $E_A(C)$ restores M.
3. A judge resolves a dispute arising between A and B by checking whether $E_A(C)$ restores M in the same way as B.

Whereas conventional systems such as the DES provide data authenticity, they do not in themselves provide sender authenticity. Because the sender and receiver share the same key, the receiver could forge the sender's signature, and it would be impossible for a judge to settle a dispute.

It is possible to implement digital signatures in conventional systems using a trusted third party S. The following approach was suggested by Merkle [Merk80]. Each user A registers a pair of private transformations E_A and D_A with S, where $E_A(D_A(M)) = M$ for every message M. To send a signed message M to B, A computes $C = D_A(M)$, and transmits C to B. To check the validity of C and obtain M, B sends C to S. S computes $E_A(C) = M$ and returns M to B enciphered under

B's private transformation. (Other methods of implementing digital signatures in conventional systems are described in Rabin [Rabi78], Needham and Schroeder [Need78], Popek and Kline [Pope79], and Smid [Smid79].)

There are difficulties with both the conventional and public-key approach if signature keys are lost or stolen. This problem is addressed in Chapter 3.

There are many applications for digital signatures. For example, if customer *A*'s bank receives an electronic message requesting the withdrawal of $100,000, the bank must be certain the request came from *A*; if *A* later disavows the message, the bank must be able to prove to a third party that the message originated with *A*.

In the preceding example, secrecy is desired as well as authenticity, because the customer would like the transaction to be confidential. In some applications, sender and data authenticity are desirable in the absence of secrecy. Simmons [Simm79] describes a system developed at Sandia Laboratories for nuclear test ban treaty verification where authentication is required but secrecy cannot be tolerated. Each nation is allowed to install a seismic observatory in the other nation (the host) to determine whether it is complying with a requirement to stop all underground testing of nuclear weapons. The observatory transmits the data gathered back to a monitor in the nation owning the observatory. There are three requirements:

1. The monitor must be certain the information reported back has originated from the observatory and has not been tampered with by the host; thus both sender and data authenticity are essential.
2. The host nation must be certain the information channel is not being used for other purposes; thus it must be able to read all messages transmitted from the observatory.
3. Neither the monitor nor the host should be able to create false messages that appear to have originated from the observatory. If a dispute arises between the monitor and host about the authenticity of a message, a third party (e.g., the United Nations or NATO) must be able to resolve the dispute.

All three requirements are satisfied in a public-key authentication system, where the observatory uses a private transformation (unknown even to the host) to sign all messages transmitted to the monitor. Both the monitor and host have access to the corresponding public transformation.

Merkle [Merk80] describes two applications of signatures for software protection. The first involves distributing network software to the individual nodes of a network. If the software is signed, the nodes can check the validity of the software before execution. The second involves running privileged programs in operating systems. The system (preferably hardware) could refuse to execute any program in privileged mode that is not properly signed by a program verifier, making it impossible for someone to substitute a program that could run in privileged mode and wreak havoc in the system. This idea could be extended to all programs, with the system refusing to execute any code that has not been signed by some authority. Note that these applications do not require a method of resolving disputes. They could, therefore, be implemented in a conventional system, where the sender and receiver share a common key.

1.4 INFORMATION THEORY

In 1949, Shannon [Shan49] provided a theoretical foundation for cryptography based on his fundamental work on information theory [Shan48]. He measured the theoretical secrecy of a cipher by the uncertainty about the plaintext given the received ciphertext. If, no matter how much ciphertext is intercepted, nothing can be learned about the plaintext, the cipher achieves perfect secrecy.

With one exception, all practical ciphers leave some information about the plaintext in the ciphertext. As the length of the ciphertext increases, the uncertainty about the plaintext usually decreases, eventually reaching 0. At this point, there is enough information to determine the plaintext uniquely, and the cipher is, at least in theory, breakable.

Most ciphers are theoretically breakable with only a few hundred bits of plaintext. But this does not mean these ciphers are insecure, because the computational requirements to determine the plaintext may exceed available resources. Thus, the important question is not whether a cipher is unconditionally secure, but whether it is computationally secure in the sense of being infeasible to break.

This section reviews information theory and its application to cryptography. Information theory also applies to the problem of controlling information dissemination; this application is discussed in Chapter 5. Section 1.5 discusses computational complexity and its application to cryptography.

Information theory addresses two related problems: the "noisy channel problem" and the secrecy problem. In the noisy channel problem, a sender transmits a message M over a noisy channel to a receiver (see Figure 1.13). If a distorted message M' is received, then the receiver would like to recover M. To make this possible, the sender adds redundant bits (called error control codes) to M in such a way that transmission errors can be corrected (or at least detected so that the receiver can request retransmission).

The noisy channel problem is analogous to the secrecy problem in cryptographic systems—the noise corresponding to the enciphering transformation, the

FIGURE 1.13 Noisy channel.

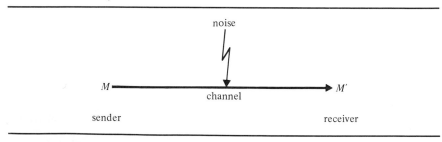

received message M' to ciphertext. Although the role of the cryptanalyst is similar to the role of the receiver in the noisy channel problem, the role of the sender is quite different because the objective is to make message recovery infeasible. (See [Simm79] for more discussion of this.)

1.4.1. Entropy and Equivocation

Information theory measures the **amount of information** in a message by the average number of bits needed to encode all possible messages in an optimal encoding. The *Sex* field in a database, for example, contains only one bit of information because it can be encoded with one bit (*Male* can be represented by "0", *Female* by "1"). If the field is represented by an ASCII character encoding of the character strings "MALE" and "FEMALE", it will take up more space, but will not contain any more information. The *Salary* field in a database, however, contains more than one bit of information, because there are more possibilities, and these possibilities cannot all be encoded with one bit. In computer systems, programs and text files are usually encoded with 8-bit ASCII codes, regardless of the amount of information in them. As we shall see shortly, text files can be compressed by about 40% without losing any information.

The amount of information in a message is formally measured by the entropy of the message. The entropy is a function of the probability distribution over the set of all possible messages. Let $X_1, \ldots, X_n$ be n possible messages occurring with probabilities $p(X_1), \ldots, p(X_n)$, where $\sum_{i=1}^{n} p(X_i) = 1$. The **entropy** of a given message is defined by the weighted average:

$$H(X) = - \sum_{i=1}^{n} p(X_i) \log_2 p(X_i) .$$

We shall write this as the sum taken over all messages X:

$$H(X) = -\sum_{X} p(X) \log_2 p(X)$$

$$= \sum_{X} p(X) \log_2 \left(\frac{1}{p(X)} \right) . \tag{1.1}$$

Example:
Suppose there are two possibilities: *Male* and *Female,* both equally likely; thus $p(Male) = p(Female) = 1/2$. Then

$$H(X) = \frac{1}{2}(\log_2 2) + \frac{1}{2}(\log_2 2)$$

$$= \frac{1}{2} + \frac{1}{2} = 1 ,$$

confirming our earlier observation that there is 1 bit of information in the *Sex* field of a database. ∎

Intuitively, each term $\log_2\left(1/p(X)\right)$ in Eq. (1.1) represents the number of bits needed to encode message X in an optimal encoding—that is, one which minimizes the expected number of bits transmitted over the channel. The weighted average $H(X)$ gives the expected number of bits in optimally encoded messages.

Because $1/p(X)$ decreases as $p(X)$ increases, an optimal encoding uses short codes for frequently occurring messages at the expense of using longer ones for infrequent messages. This principle is applied in Morse code, where the most frequently used letters are assigned the shortest codes.

"Huffman codes" [Huff52] are optimal codes assigned to characters, words, machine instructions, or phrases. Single-character Huffman codes are frequently used to compact large files. This is done by first scanning the file to determine the frequency distribution of the ASCII characters, next finding the optimal encoding of the characters, and finally replacing each character with its code. The codes are stored in a table at the beginning of the file, so the original text can be recovered. By encoding longer sequences of characters, the text can be compacted even further, but the storage requirements for the table are increased. A character encoding of the text file for this chapter using the *Compact* program on UNIX† reduced its storage requirements by 38%, which is typical for text files.‡ Machines with variable-length instruction sets use Huffman codes to assign short codes to frequently used instructions (e.g., LOAD, STORE, BRANCH).

The following examples further illustrate the application of Eq. (1.1) to determine the information content of a message.

Example:
Let $n = 3$, and let the 3 messages be the letters A, B, and C, where $p(A) = 1/2$ and $p(B) = p(C) = 1/4$. Then

$$\log_2\left(\frac{1}{p(A)}\right) = \log_2 2 = 1$$

$$\log_2\left(\frac{1}{p(B)}\right) = \log_2 4 = 2$$

$$\log_2\left(\frac{1}{p(C)}\right) = \log_2 4 = 2 ,$$

and

$$H(X) = \left(\frac{1}{2}\right)\log_2 2 + 2[\left(\frac{1}{4}\right)\log_2 4] = 0.5 + 1.0 = 1.5 .$$

An optimal encoding assigns a 1-bit code to A and 2-bit codes to B and C. For example, A can be encoded with the bit 0, while B and C can be encoded with two bits each, 10 and 11. Using this encoding, the 8-letter sequence ABAACABC is encoded as the 12-bit sequence 010001101011 as shown next:

---

†UNIX is a trademark of Bell Labs.

‡Tom Sederberg wrote a program to determine the net reduction in space for this chapter when sequences of n characters are encoded. For $n = 2$, the reduction was again about 38% (the increase in table size compensating for the decrease in text space); for $n = 3$, it dropped to about 25%.

A B   A A C   A B   C
0 10 0 0 11 0 10 11

The average number of bits per letter is $12/8 = 1.5$.

The preceding encoding is optimal; the expected number of bits per letter would be at least 1.5 with any other encoding. Note that B, for example, cannot be encoded with the single bit 1, because it would then be impossible to decode the bit sequence 11 (it could be either BB or C). Morse code avoids this problem by separating letters with spaces. Because spaces (blanks) must be encoded in computer applications, this approach in the long run requires more storage. ■

Example:
Suppose all messages are equally likely; that is, $p(X_i) = 1/n$ for $i = 1, \ldots, n$. Then

$$H(X) = n[\left(\frac{1}{n}\right)\log_2 n] = \log_2 n.$$

Thus, $\log_2 n$ bits are needed to encode each message. For $n = 2^k$, $H(X) = k$ and k bits are needed to encode each possible message. ■

Example:
Let $n = 1$ and $p(X) = 1$. Then $H(X) = \log_2 1 = 0$. There is no information because there is no choice. ■

Given n, $H(X)$ is maximal for $p(X_1) = \ldots = p(X_n) = 1/n$; that is, when all messages are equally likely (see exercises at end of chapter). $H(X)$ decreases as the distribution of messages becomes more and more skewed, reaching a minimum of $H(X) = 0$ when $p(X_i) = 1$ for some message X_i. As an example, suppose X represents a 32-bit integer variable. Then X can have at most 32 bits of information. If small values of X are more likely than larger ones (as is typical in most programs), then $H(X)$ will be less than 32, and if the exact value of X is known, $H(X)$ will be 0.

The entropy of a message measures its **uncertainty** in that it gives the number of bits of information that must be learned when the message has been distorted by a noisy channel or hidden in ciphertext. For example, if a cryptanalyst knows the ciphertext block "Z$JP7K" corresponds to either the plaintext "MALE" or the plaintext "FEMALE", the uncertainty is only one bit. The cryptanalyst need only determine one character, say the first, and because there are only two possibilities for that character, only the distinguishing bit of that character need be determined. If it is known that the block corresponds to a salary, then the uncertainty is more than one bit, but it can be no more than $\log_2 n$ bits, where n is the number of possible salaries.

Public-key systems used for secrecy only are vulnerable to a ciphertext-only attack if there is not enough uncertainty in the plaintext. To see why, consider a ciphertext $C = E_A(M)$, where E_A is a public enciphering transformation and M is a plaintext message in a set of n possible messages $M_1, \ldots, M_n$. Even if it is computationally infeasible to determine the private deciphering transformation D_A, it may be possible to determine M by computing $C_i = E_A(M_i)$ for $i = 1, 2, \ldots$ until $C = C_i$, whence $M = M_i$. This type of attack would work, for example, if M is known to be an integer salary less than \$100,000 because there would be at most 100,000 messages to try. The attack can be prevented by appending a random bit string to a short message M before enciphering; this string would be discarded on deciphering. Of course, if authenticity is used with secrecy—that is, $C = E_A(D_B(M))$, the cryptanalyst, lacking D_B, cannot search the plaintext space this way. Conventional systems are not vulnerable to this attack because the enciphering (and deciphering) key is secret.

For a given language, consider the set of all messages N characters long. The **rate of the language** for messages of length N is defined by $r = H(X)/N$; that is, the average number of bits of information in each character. For large N, estimates of r for English range from 1.0 bits/letter to 1.5 bits/letter. The **absolute rate** of the language is defined to be the maximum number of bits of information that could be encoded in each character assuming all possible sequences of characters are equally likely. If there are L characters in the language, then the absolute rate is given by $R = \log_2 L$, the maximum entropy of the individual characters. For English, $R = \log_2 26 = 4.7$ bits/letter. The actual rate of English is thus considerably less than its absolute rate. The reason is that English, like all natural languages, is highly redundant. For example, the phrase "occurring frequently" could be reduced by 58% to "crng frq" without loss of information. By deleting vowels and double letters, mst ids cn b xprsd n fwr ltrs, bt th xprnc s mst nplsnt.

Redundancy arises from the structure of the language. It is reflected in the statistical properties of English language messages in the following ways [Shan51]:

1. *Single letter frequency distributions.* Certain letters such as E, T, and A occur much more frequently than others.
2. *Digram frequency distributions.* Certain digrams (pairs of letters) such as TH and EN occur much more frequently than others. Some digrams (e.g., QZ) never occur in meaningful messages even when word boundaries are ignored (acronyms are an exception).
3. *Trigram distributions.* The proportion of meaningful sequences decreases when trigrams are considered (e.g., BB is meaningful but BBB is not). Among the meaningful trigrams, certain sequences such as THE and ING occur much more frequently than others.
4. N-*gram distributions.* As longer sequences are considered, the proportion of meaningful messages to the total number of possible letter sequences decreases. Long messages are structured not only according to letter sequences within a word but also by word sequences (e.g., the phrase PROGRAMMING LANGUAGES is much more likely than the phrase LANGUAGES PROGRAMMING).

Programming languages have a similar structure, reflected in the statistical properties of programs [Turn73]. Here there is more freedom in letter sequences (e.g., the variable name QZK is perfectly valid), but the language syntax imposes other rigid rules about the placement of keywords and delimiters.

The rate of a language (entropy per character) is determined by estimating the entropy of N-grams for increasing values of N. As N increases, the entropy per character decreases because there are fewer choices and certain choices are much more likely. The decrease is sharp at first but tapers off quickly; the rate is estimated by extrapolating for large N. (See [Shan51,Cove78].)

The **redundancy** of a language with rate r and absolute rate R is defined by $D = R - r$. For $R = 4.7$ and $r = 1$, $D = 3.7$, whence the ratio D/R shows English to be about 79% redundant; for $r = 1.5$, $D = 3.2$, implying a redundancy of 68%. We shall use the more conservative estimate $r = 1.5$ and $D = 3.2$ in our later examples.

The uncertainty of messages may be reduced given additional information. For example, let X be a 32-bit integer such that all values are equally likely; thus the entropy of X is $H(X) = 32$. Suppose it is learned that X is even. Then the entropy is reduced by one bit because the low order bit must be 0.

Given a message Y in the set $Y_1, \ldots, Y_m$, where $\sum_{i=1}^{m} p(Y_i) = 1$, let $p_Y(X)$ be the conditional probability of message X given message Y [this is sometimes written $P(X|Y)$], and let $p(X, Y)$ be the joint probability of message X and message Y; thus,

$$p(X, Y) = p_Y(X)p(Y) .$$

The **equivocation** is the conditional entropy of X given Y:

$$H_Y(X) = - \sum_{X,Y} p(X, Y) \log_2 p_Y(X) ,$$

which we shall write as

$$H_Y(X) = \sum_{X,Y} p(X, Y) \log_2 \left(\frac{1}{p_Y(X)} \right) \tag{1.2a}$$

or

$$H_Y(X) = \sum_{Y} p(Y) \sum_{X} p_Y(X) \log_2 \left(\frac{1}{p_Y(X)} \right) . \tag{1.2b}$$

Example:
Let $n = 4$ and $p(X) = 1/4$ for each message X; thus $H(X) = \log_2 4 = 2$. Similarly, let $m = 4$ and $p(Y) = 1/4$ for each message Y. Now, suppose each message Y narrows the choice of X to two of the four messages as shown next, where both messages are equally likely:

$$Y_1: X_1 \text{ or } X_2, \qquad Y_2: X_2 \text{ or } X_3$$
$$Y_3: X_3 \text{ or } X_4, \qquad Y_4: X_4 \text{ or } X_1 .$$

Then for each Y, $p_Y(X) = 1/2$ for two of the X's and $p_Y(X) = 0$ for the remaining two X's. Using Eq. (1.2b), the equivocation is thus

$$H_Y(X) = 4[\left(\tfrac{1}{4}\right) 2[\left(\tfrac{1}{2}\right) \log_2 2]] = \log_2 2 = 1 .$$

Thus knowledge of Y reduces the uncertainty of X to one bit, corresponding to the two remaining choices for X. ∎

1.4.2. Perfect Secrecy

Shannon studied the information theoretic properties of cryptographic systems in terms of three classes of information:

1. Plaintext messages M occurring with prior probabilities $p(M)$, where $\sum_M p(M) = 1$.

2. Ciphertext messages C occurring with probabilities $p(C)$, where $\sum_C p(C) = 1$.

3. Keys K chosen with prior probabilities $p(K)$, where $\sum_K p(K) = 1$.

Let $p_C(M)$ be the probability that message M was sent given that C was received (thus C is the encryption of message M). **Perfect secrecy** is defined by the condition

$$p_C(M) = p(M) ;$$

that is, intercepting the ciphertext gives a cryptanalyst no additional information.

Let $p_M(C)$ be the probability of receiving ciphertext C given that M was sent. Then $p_M(C)$ is the sum of the probabilities $p(K)$ of the keys K that encipher M as C:

$$p_M(C) = \sum_{\substack{K \\ E_K(M) = C}} p(K)$$

Usually there is at most one key K such that $E_K(M) = C$ for given M and C, but some ciphers can transform the same plaintext into the same ciphertext under different keys.

A necessary and sufficient condition for perfect secrecy is that for every C,

$$p_M(C) = p(C) \text{ for all } M .$$

This means the probability of receiving a particular ciphertext C given that M was sent (enciphered under some key) is the same as the probability of receiving C given that some other message M' was sent (enciphered under a different key). Perfect secrecy is possible using completely random keys at least as long as the messages they encipher. Figure 1.14 illustrates a perfect system with four messages, all equally likely, and four keys, also equally likely. Here $P_C(M) = P(M) = 1/4$, and $p_M(C) = p(C) = 1/4$ for all M and C. A cryptanalyst intercepting one of the ciphertext messages $C_1, C_2, C_3,$ or C_4 would have no way of

FIGURE 1.14 Perfect secrecy (adapted from [Shan49]).

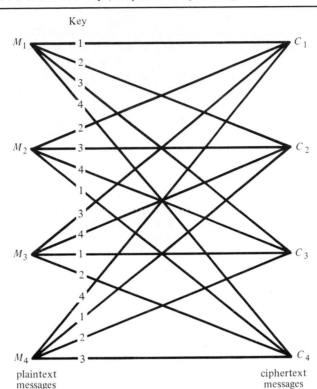

determining which of the four keys was used and, therefore, whether the correct message is M_1, M_2, M_3, or M_4.

Perfect secrecy requires that the number of keys must be at least as great as the number of possible messages. Otherwise there would be some message M such that for a given C, no K deciphers C into M, implying $P_C(M) = 0$. The cryptanalyst could thereby eliminate certain possible plaintext messages from consideration, increasing the chances of breaking the cipher.

Example:
Suppose the 31-character ciphertext

$$C = \text{LZWJWAKFGGLZWJDSFYMSYWTMLXJWFUZ}$$

was produced by a Caesar cipher (see Section 1.1), where each letter in the alphabet is shifted forward by K positions, $0 \leq K \leq 25$. Because the number of possible keys is smaller than the number of possible English sentences of length 31, perfect secrecy is not achieved. The cipher is easily broken by trying all 26 keys as shown in Figure 1.15. The plaintext message is

FIGURE 1.15 Solution of substitution cipher.

Key	Message
0:	L Z W J W A K F G G L Z W J D S F Y M S Y W T M L X J W F U Z
1:	K Y V I V Z J E F F K Y V I C R E X L R X V S L K W I V E T Y
2:	J X U H U Y I D E E J X U H B Q D W K Q W U R K J V H U D S X
3:	I W T G T X H C D D I W T G A P C V J P V T Q J I U G T C R W
4:	H V S F S W G B C C H V S F Z O B U I O U S P I H T F S B Q V
5:	G U R E R V F A B B G U R E Y N A T H N T R O H G S E R A P U
6:	F T Q D Q U E Z A A F T Q D X M Z S G M S Q N G F R D Q Z O T
7:	E S P C P T D Y Z Z E S P C W L Y R F L R P M F E Q C P Y N S
8:	D R O B O S C X Y Y D R O B V K X Q E K Q O L E D P B O X M R
9:	C Q N A N R B W X X C Q N A U J W P D J P N K D C O A N W L Q
10:	B P M Z M Q A V W W B P M Z T I V O C I O M J C B N Z M V K P
11:	A O L Y L P Z U V V A O L Y S H U N B H N L I B A M Y L U J O
12:	Z N K X K O Y T U U Z N K X R G T M A G M K H A Z L X K T I N
13:	Y M J W J N X S T T Y M J W Q F S L Z F L J G Z Y K W J S H M
14:	X L I V I M W R S S X L I V P E R K Y E K I F Y X J V I R G L
15:	W K H U H L V Q R R W K H U O D Q J X D J H E X W I U H Q F K
16:	V J G T G K U P Q Q V J G T N C P I W C I G D W V H T G P E J
17:	U I F S F J T O P P U I F S M B O H V B H F C V U G S F O D I
18:	T H E R E I S N O O T H E R L A N G U A G E B U T F R E N C H
19:	S G D Q D H R M N N S G D Q K Z M F T Z F D A T S E Q D M B G
20:	R F C P C G Q L M M R F C P J Y L E S Y E C Z S R D P C L A F
21:	Q E B O B F P K L L Q E B O I X K D R X D B Y R Q C O B K Z E
22:	P D A N A E O J K K P D A N H W J C Q W C A X Q P B N A J Y D
23:	O C Z M Z D N I J J O C Z M G V I B P V B Z W P O A M Z I X C
24:	N B Y L Y C M H I I N B Y L F U H A O U A Y V O N Z L Y H W B
25:	M A X K X B L G H H M A X K E T G Z N T Z X U N M Y K X G V A

M = THERE IS NO OTHER LANGUAGE BUT FRENCH.†

Because only one of the keys ($K = 18$) produces a meaningful message, we have:

$$p_C(M) = 1$$
$$p_C(M') = 0, \text{ for every other message } M'$$
$$p_M(C) = p(18) = \frac{1}{26}$$
$$p_{M'}(C) = 0, \text{ for every other message } M'. \quad \blacksquare$$

Example:

With a slight modification to the preceding scheme, we can create a cipher having perfect secrecy. The trick is to shift each letter by a random amount. Specifically, K is given by a stream $k_1 k_2 \ldots$, where each k_i is a random

† From S. Gorn's Compendium of Rarely Used Cliches.

integer in the range [0, 25] giving the amount of shift for the ith letter. Then the 31-character ciphertext C in the preceding example could correspond to any valid 31-character message, because each possible plaintext message is derived by some key stream. For example, the plaintext message

   THIS SPECIES HAS ALWAYS BEEN EXTINCT.†

is derived by the key stream

   18, 18, 14, 17, 4, ...

Though most of the 31-character possible plaintext messages can be ruled out as not being valid English, this much is known even without the ciphertext. Perfect secrecy is achieved because interception of the ciphertext does not reveal anything new about the plaintext message.

   The key stream must not repeat or be used to encipher another message. Otherwise, it may be possible to break the cipher by correlating two ciphertexts enciphered under the same portion of the stream (see Section 2.4.4). ■

   A cipher using a nonrepeating random key stream such as the one described in the preceding example is called a **one-time pad**. One-time pads are the only ciphers that achieve perfect secrecy. Implementation of one-time pads and approximations to one-time pads is studied in Chapters 2 and 3.

1.4.3 Unicity Distance

Shannon measured the secrecy of a cipher in terms of the **key equivocation** $H_C(K)$ of a key K for a given ciphertext C; that is, the amount of uncertainty in K given C. From Eq. (1.2b), this is

$$ H_C(K) = \sum_C p(C) \sum_K p_C(K) \log_2 \left(\frac{1}{p_C(K)} \right) \; , $$

where $p_C(K)$ is the probability of K given C. If $H_C(K)$ is 0, then there is no uncertainty, and the cipher is theoretically breakable given enough resources. As the length N of the ciphertext increases, the equivocation usually decreases.

   The **unicity distance** is the smallest N such that $H_C(K)$ is close to 0; that is, it is the amount of ciphertext needed to uniquely determine the key. A cipher is **unconditionally secure** if $H_C(K)$ never approaches 0 even for large N; that is, no matter how much ciphertext is intercepted, the key cannot be determined. (Shannon used the term "ideal secrecy" to describe systems that did not achieve perfect secrecy, but were nonetheless unbreakable because they did not give enough information to determine the key.)

   Most ciphers are too complex to determine the probabilities required to derive the unicity distance. Shannon showed, however, it is possible to approxi-

---

† Also from S. Gorn's Compendium of Rarely Used Cliches.

mate it for certain ciphers using a random cipher model. Hellman [Hell77] also derived Shannon's result using a slightly different approach.

Following Hellman, we assume each plaintext and ciphertext message comes from a finite alphabet of L symbols. Thus there are 2^{RN} possible messages of length N, where $R = \log_2 L$ is the absolute rate of the language. The 2^{RN} messages are partitioned into two subsets: a set of 2^{rN} **meaningful messages** and a set of $2^{RN} - 2^{rN}$ **meaningless messages**, where r is the rate of the language. All meaningful messages are assumed to have the same prior probability $1/2^{rN} = 2^{-rN}$, while all meaningless messages are assumed to have probability 0.

We also assume there are $2^{H(K)}$ keys, all equally likely, where $H(K)$ is the key entropy (number of bits in the key). The prior probability of all keys is $p(K) = 1/2^{H(K)} = 2^{-H(K)}$.

A **random cipher** is one in which for each key K and ciphertext C, the decipherment $D_K(C)$ is an independent random variable uniformly distributed over all 2^{RN} messages, both meaningful and not. Intuitively, this means that for a given K and C, $D_K(C)$ is as likely to produce one plaintext message as any other. Actually the decipherments are not completely independent because a given key must uniquely encipher a given message, whence $D_K(C) \neq D_K(C')$ for $C \neq C'$.

FIGURE 1.16 Random cipher model (adapted from [Hell 77]).

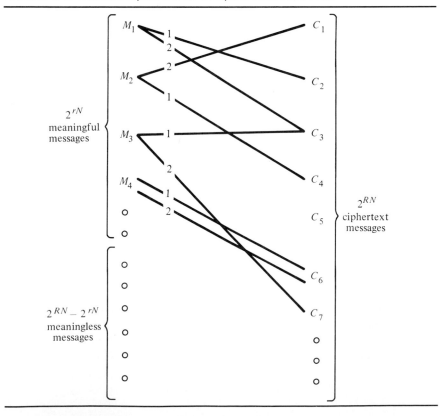

Consider the ciphertext $C = E_K(M)$ for given K and M. A **spurious key decipherment** or **false solution** arises whenever encipherment under another key K' could produce C; that is, $C = E_{K'}(M)$ for the same message M, or $C = E_{K'}(M')$ for another meaningful message M'. Figure 1.16 shows two spurious key decipherments, one from the third ciphertext and one from the sixth. A cryptanalyst intercepting one of these ciphertexts would be unable to break the cipher since there would be no way of picking the correct key. We are not concerned with decipherments that produce meaningless messages, because the cryptanalyst can immediately reject these solutions.

Now, for every correct solution to a particular ciphertext, there are $(2^{H(K)} - 1)$ remaining keys, each of which has the same probability q of yielding a spurious key decipherment. Because each plaintext message is equally likely, the probability of getting a meaningful message and, therefore, a false solution is given by

$$q = \frac{2^{rN}}{2^{RN}} = 2^{(r-R)N} = 2^{-DN},$$

where $D = R - r$ is the redundancy of the language. Letting F denote the expected number of false solutions, we have

$$F = (2^{H(K)} - 1)\, q = (2^{H(K)} - 1)\, 2^{-DN} \cong 2^{H(K)-DN}. \qquad (1.3)$$

Because of the rapid decrease in the exponential with increasing N,

$$\log_2 F = H(K) - DN = 0$$

is taken as the point where the number of false solutions is sufficiently small the cipher can be broken. Thus

$$N = \frac{H(K)}{D} \qquad (1.4)$$

is the unicity distance—the amount of text necessary to break the cipher.

If for given N, the number of possible keys is as large as the number of meaningful messages, then $H(K) = \log_2(2^{RN}) = RN$; thus

$$H(K) - DN = (R - D)N = rN \neq 0,$$

and the cipher is theoretically unbreakable. This is the principle behind the one-time pad.

Example:

Consider the DES, which enciphers 64-bit blocks (8 characters) using 56-bit keys. The DES is a reasonably close approximation to the random cipher model. Figure 1.17 shows F as a function of N for English language messages, where $H(K) = 56$ and $D = 3.2$ in Eq. (1.3). The unicity distance is thus

$$N = \frac{56}{3.2} = 17.5 \text{ characters},$$

or a little over two blocks. Doubling the key size to 112 bits would double the unicity distance to 35 characters. ■

FIGURE 1.17 Unicity distance for DES.

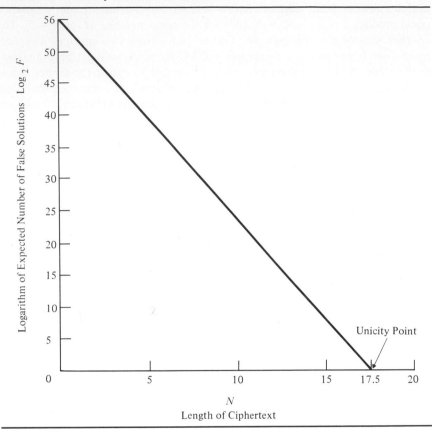

Example:
Consider a simple substitution cipher that shifts every letter in the alphabet forward by K positions, $0 \leq K \leq 25$. Then $H(K) = \log_2 26 = 4.7$ and the unicity distance is

$$N = \frac{4.7}{3.2} = 1.5 \text{ characters.}$$

This estimate does not seem plausible, however, because no substitution cipher can be solved with just one or two characters of ciphertext. There are two problems with the approximation. First, the estimate $D = 3.2$ applies only to reasonable long messages. Second, the cipher is a poor approximation to the random cipher model. This is because most ciphertexts are not produced by meaningful messages (e.g., the ciphertext QQQQ is produced only by the meaningless messages AAAA, BBBB, ..., ZZZZ), whence the decipherments are not uniformly distributed over the entire message space. Nevertheless, shifted ciphers can generally be solved with just a few characters of ciphertext. ■

The random cipher model gives a conservative estimate of the amount of ciphertext needed to break a cipher. Thus a particular cipher will have a unicity distance of at least $H(K)/D$. In practice, $H(K)/D$ is a good approximation even for simple ciphers. We shall derive the unicity distance of several ciphers in Chapter 2. The interested reader can read more about the unicity distances of classical ciphers in Deavours [Deav77].

The unicity distance gives the number of characters required to uniquely determine the key; it does not indicate the computational difficulty of finding it. A cipher may be computationally infeasible to break even if it is theoretically possible with a relatively small amount of ciphertext. Public-key systems, for example, can be theoretically broken without any ciphertext at all. The cryptanalyst, knowing the public key and the method of generating key pairs, can systematically try all possible private keys until the matching key is found (see Brassard [Bras79a, Bras80]). This strategy is computationally infeasible, however, for large key spaces (e.g., with 2^{200} keys). The DES can also be broken by exhaustive search of the key space in a known-plaintext attack (by trying all keys until one is found that enciphers the plaintext into the matching ciphertext). Nevertheless, the best known strategies for breaking the DES are extremely time-consuming. By contrast, certain substitution ciphers discussed in the next chapter use longer keys and have much greater unicity distances than DES. These ciphers are often relatively simple to solve, however, when enough ciphertext is intercepted.

Equation (1.4) shows that the unicity distance N is inversely proportional to the redundancy D. As D approaches 0, an otherwise trivial cipher becomes unbreakable. To illustrate, suppose a 6-digit integer M is enciphered as 351972 using a Caesar-type shifted substitution cipher with key K, where $0 \leq K \leq 9$, and that all possible 6-digit integers are equally likely. Then a cryptanalyst cannot determine which of the following integers is the value of M:

Key	Integer
0	351972
1	240861
2	139750
.	.
.	.
.	.
9	462083

The reason the cipher cannot be solved is that the language has no redundancy; every digit counts.

Because of the inherent redundancy of natural languages, many ciphers can be solved by statistical analysis of the ciphertext. These techniques use frequency distributions of letters and sequences of letters, ciphertext repetitions, and probable words. Although a full discussion of these techniques is beyond the scope of this book, Chapter 2 describes how a few simple ciphers can be broken using frequency distributions. (For more depth in this area, see [Konh81].)

Protection against statistical analysis can be provided by several means. One way, suggested by Shannon, is by removing some of the redundancy of the language before encryption. In computer systems, for example, Huffman codes could be used to remove redundancy by compressing a file before encryption.

Shannon also proposed two encryption techniques to thwart attacks based on statistical analysis: confusion and diffusion. **Confusion** involves substitutions that make the relationship between the key and ciphertext as complex as possible. **Diffusion** involves transformations that dissipate the statistical properties of the plaintext across the ciphertext. Many modern ciphers such as the DES and public-key schemes provide confusion and diffusion through complex enciphering transformations over large blocks of data. These ciphers can also be operated in a "chaining mode", where each ciphertext block is functionally dependent on all preceding blocks; this diffuses the plaintext across the entire ciphertext (see Chapter 3).

1.5 COMPLEXITY THEORY

Computational complexity provides a foundation for analyzing the computational requirements of cryptanalytic techniques, and for studying the inherent difficulty of solving ciphers. It also provides a foundation for studying the inherent difficulty of proving security properties about arbitrary systems (see Chapter 4), and for analyzing the computational difficulty of protecting confidential data released in the form of statistics (Chapter 6).

1.5.1 Algorithm Complexity

The strength of a cipher is determined by the computational complexity of the algorithms used to solve the cipher. The computational complexity of an algorithm is measured by its time (T) and space (S) requirements, where T and S are expressed as functions of n, and n characterizes the size of the input. A function $f(n)$ is typically expressed as an "order-of-magnitude" of the form $O(g(n))$ (called "big O" notation), where $f(n) = O(g(n))$ means there exist constants c and n_0 such that

$$f(n) \leq c \, | \, g(n) \, | \quad \text{for } n \geq n_0 \, .$$

As an example, suppose $f(n) = 17n + 10$. Then $f(n) = O(n)$ because $17n + 10 \leq 18n$ for $n \geq 10$ [i.e., $g(n) = n$, $c = 18$, and $n_0 = 10$]. If $f(n)$ is a polynomial of the form

$$f(n) = a_t n^t + a_{t-1} n^{t-1} + \cdots + a_1 n + a_0$$

for constant t, then $f(n) = O(n^t)$; that is, all constants and low-order terms are ignored.

Measuring the time and space requirements of an algorithm by its order-of-magnitude performance has the advantage of being system independent; thus, it is unnecessary to know the exact timings of different instructions or the number of bits used to represent different data types. At the same time, it allows us to see

TABLE 1.2 Classes of algorithms.

Class	Complexity	Number of operations for $n = 10^6$	Real time
Polynomial			
Constant	$O(1)$	1	1 μsec
Linear	$O(n)$	10^6	1 second
Quadratic	$O(n^2)$	10^{12}	10 days
Cubic	$O(n^3)$	10^{18}	27,397 years
Exponential	$O(2^n)$	10^{301030}	10^{301016} years

how the time and space requirements grow as the size of the input increases. For example, if $T = O(n^2)$, doubling the size of the input quadruples the running time.

It is customary to classify algorithms by their time (or space) complexities. An algorithm is **polynomial** (more precisely, polynomial time) if its running time is given by $T = O(n^t)$ for some constant t; it is **constant** if $t = 0$, **linear** if $t = 1$, **quadratic** if $t = 2$, and so forth. It is **exponential** if $T = O(t^{h(n)})$ for constant t and polynomial $h(n)$.

For large n, the complexity of an algorithm can make an enormous difference. For example, consider a machine capable of performing one instruction per microsecond (μsec); this is 10^6 instructions per second, or 8.64×10^{10} instructions per day. Table 1.2 shows the running times of different classes of algorithms for $n = 10^6$, where we have ignored all constants and rounded to 10^{11} instructions per day. At $T = O(n^3)$ execution of the algorithm becomes computationally infeasible on a sequential machine. It is conceivable, however, that a configuration with 1 million processors could complete the computation in about 10 days. For $T = O(2^n)$ execution of the algorithm is computationally infeasible even if we could have trillions of processors working in parallel.

Many ciphers can be solved by exhaustively searching the entire key space, trying each possible key to ascertain whether it deciphers into meaningful plaintext or some known plaintext. If $n = 2^{H(K)}$ is the size of the key space, then the running time of this strategy is $T = O(n) = O(2^{H(K)})$. Thus, the time is linear in the number of keys, but exponential in the key length. This is why doubling the length of the keys used for DES from 56 bits to 112 bits can have a dramatic impact on the difficulty of breaking the cipher, even though it increases the unicity distance only by a factor of 2.

1.5.2. Problem Complexity and **NP**-Completeness

Complexity theory classifies a problem according to the minimum time and space needed to solve the hardest instances of the problem on a Turing Machine (or some other abstract model of computation). A Turing Machine (TM) is a finite state machine with an infinite read-write tape (e.g., see [Gare79,Aho74,Mins67] or the description in Section 4.7.2 for details). A TM is a "realistic" model of computation in that problems that are polynomial solvable on a TM are also polynomial solvable on real systems and vice versa.

Problems that are solvable in polynomial time are called **tractable** because they can usually be solved for reasonable size inputs. Problems that cannot be systematically solved in polynomial time are called **intractable** or simply "hard", because as the size of the input increases, their solution becomes infeasible on even the fastest computers. Turing [Turi36] proved that some problems are so hard they are **undecidable** in the sense that it is impossible to write an algorithm to solve them. In particular, he showed the problem of determining whether an arbitrary TM (or program) halts is undecidable. Many other problems have been shown to be undecidable by proving that if they could be solved, then the "halting problem" could be solved (see Section 4.7.2 for an example).

Figure 1.18 shows several important complexity classes and their possible relationships (their exact relationships are unknown). The class **P** consists of all problems solvable in polynomial time.

FIGURE 1.18 Complexity classes.

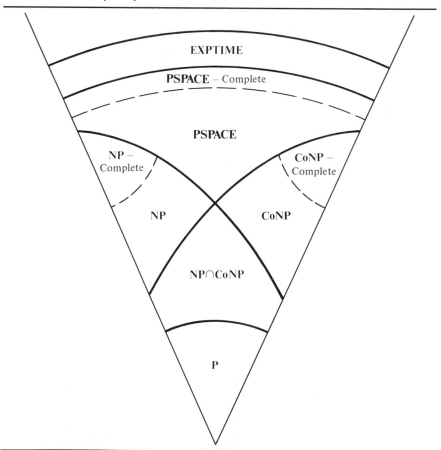

The class **NP** (nondeterministic polynomial) consists of all problems solvable in polynomial time on a nondeterministic TM. This means if the machine guesses the solution, it can check its correctness in polynomial time. Of course, this does not really "solve" the problem, because there is no guarantee the machine will guess the right answer.

To systematically (deterministically) solve certain problems in **NP** seems to require exponential time. An example of such a problem is the "knapsack problem": given a set of n integers $A = \{a_1, \ldots, a_n\}$ and an integer S, determine whether there exists a subset of A that sums to S.† The problem is clearly in **NP** because for any given subset, it is easy to check whether it sums to S. Finding a subset that sums to S is much harder, however, as there are 2^n possible subsets; trying all of them has time complexity $T = O(2^n)$. Another example of a problem that seems to have exponential time complexity is the "satisfiability problem", which is to determine whether there exists an assignment of values to a set of n boolean variables $v_1, \ldots, v_n$ such that a given set of clauses over the variables is true.

The class **NP** includes the class **P** because any problem polynomial solvable on a deterministic TM is polynomial solvable on a nondeterministic one. If all **NP** problems are polynomial solvable on a deterministic TM, we would have **P** = **NP**. Although many problems in **NP** seem much "harder" than the problems in **P** (e.g., the knapsack problem and satisfiability) no one has yet proved **P** ≠ **NP**.

Cook [Cook71] showed the satisfiability problem has the property that every other problem in **NP** can be reduced to it in polynomial time. This means that if the satisfiability problem is polynomial solvable, then every problem in **NP** is polynomial solvable, and if some problem in **NP** is intractable, then satisfiability must also be intractable. Since then, other problems (including the knapsack problem) have been shown to be equivalent to satisfiability in the preceding sense. This set of equivalent problems is called the **NP-complete** problems, and has the property that if any one of the problems is in **P**, then all **NP** problems are in **P** and **P** = **NP**. Thus, the NP-complete problems are the "hardest" problems in **NP**. The fastest known algorithms for systematically solving these problems have worst-case time complexities exponential in the size n of the problem. Finding a polynomial-time solution to one of them would be a major breakthrough in computer science.

A problem is shown to be **NP**-complete by proving it is **NP**-hard and in **NP**. A problem is **NP-hard** if it cannot be solved in polynomial time unless **P** = **NP**. To show a problem A is **NP**-hard, it is necessary to show that some **NP**-complete problem B is polynomial-time reducible to an instance of A, whence a polynomial-time algorithm for solving A would also solve B. To show A is in **NP**, it is necessary to prove that a correct solution can be proved correct in polynomial time.

The class **CoNP** consists of all problems that are the complement of some problem in **NP**. Intuitively, problems in **NP** are of the form "determine whether a

---

† The integers represent rod lengths, and the problem is to find a subset of rods that exactly fits a one-dimensional knapsack of length n.

solution exists," whereas the complementary problems in **CoNP** are of the form "show there are no solutions." It is not known whether **NP** = **CoNP**, but there are problems that fall in the intersection **NP** ∩ **CoNP**. An example of such a problem is the "composite numbers problem": given an integer n, determine whether n is composite (i.e., there exist factors p and q such that $n = pq$) or prime (i.e., there are no such factors). The problem of finding factors, however, may be harder than showing their existence.

The class **PSPACE** consists of those problems solvable in polynomial space, but not necessarily polynomial time. It includes **NP** and **CoNP**, but there are problems in **PSPACE** that are thought by some to be harder than problems in **NP** and **CoNP**. The **PSPACE**-complete problems have the property that if any one of them is in **NP**, then **PSPACE** = **NP**, or if any one is in **P**, then **PSPACE** = **P**. The class **EXPTIME** consists of those problems solvable in exponential time, and includes **PSPACE**. The interested reader is referred to [Gare79,Aho74] for a more complete treatment of complexity theory.

1.5.3. Ciphers Based on Computationally Hard Problems

In their 1976 paper, Diffie and Hellman [Diff76] suggested applying computational complexity to the design of encryption algorithms. They noted that **NP**-complete problems might make excellent candidates for ciphers because they cannot be solved in polynomial time by any known techniques. Problems that are computationally more difficult than the problems in **NP** are not suitable for encryption because the enciphering and deciphering transformations must be fast (i.e., computable in polynomial time). But this means the cryptanalyst could guess a key and check the solution in polynomial time (e.g., by enciphering known plaintext). Thus, the cryptanalytic effort to break any polynomial-time encryption algorithm must be in **NP**.

Diffie and Hellman speculated that cryptography could draw from the theory of **NP** complexity by examining ways in which **NP**-complete problems could be adapted to cryptographic use. Information could be enciphered by encoding it in an **NP**-complete problem in such a way that breaking the cipher would require solving the problem in the usual way. With the deciphering key, however, a short-cut solution would be possible.

To construct such a cipher, secret "trapdoor" information is inserted into a computationally hard problem that involves inverting a one-way function. A function f is a **one-way function** if it is easy to compute $f(x)$ for any x in the domain of f, while, for almost all y in the range of f, it is computationally infeasible to compute $f^{-1}(y)$ even if f is known. It is a **trapdoor one-way function** if it is easy to compute f^{-1} given certain additional information. This additional information is the secret deciphering key.

Public-key systems are based on this principle. The trapdoor knapsack schemes described in Section 2.8 are based on the knapsack problem. The RSA scheme described in Section 2.7 is based on factoring composite numbers.

The strength of such a cipher depends on the computational complexity of the problem on which it is based. A computationally difficult problem does not necessarily imply a strong cryptosystem, however. Shamir gives three reasons [Sham79]:

1. Complexity theory usually deals with single isolated instances of a problem. A cryptanalyst often has a large collection of statistically related problems to solve (e.g., several ciphertexts generated by the same key).
2. The computational complexity of a problem is typically measured by its worst-case or average-case behavior. To be useful as a cipher, the problem must be hard to solve in almost all cases.
3. An arbitrarily difficult problem cannot necessarily be transformed into a cryptosystem, and it must be possible to insert trapdoor information into the problem in such a way that a shortcut solution is possible with this information and only with this information.

Lempel [Lemp79] illustrates the first deficiency with a block cipher for which the problem of finding an n-bit key is **NP**-complete when the plaintext corresponding to one block of ciphertext is known. But given enough known plaintext, the problem reduces to solving n linear equations in n unknowns. The cipher is described in Section 2.8.4.

Shamir [Sham79] proposes a new complexity measure to deal with the second difficulty. Given a fraction r such that $0 \le r \le 1$, the **percentile complexity** $T(n, r)$ of a problem measures the time to solve the easiest proportion r of the problem instances of size n. For example, $T(n, 0.5)$ gives the **median complexity**; that is, at least half of the instances of size n can be solved within time $T(n, 0.5)$. The problem of deciding whether a given integer is prime has median complexity $O(1)$ because half of the numbers have 2 as a factor, and this can be tested in constant time.

With respect to the third difficulty, Brassard [Bras79b] shows it may not be possible to prove that the cryptanalytic effort to invert a trapdoor one-way function is **NP**-complete. If the function satisfies a few restrictions, then a proof of **NP**-completeness would imply **NP = CoNP**.

1.6 NUMBER THEORY

This section summarizes the concepts of number theory needed to understand the cryptographic techniques described in Chapters 2 and 3. Because we are primarily interested in the properties of modular arithmetic rather than congruences in general, we shall review the basic theorems of number theory in terms of modular arithmetic, emphasizing their computational aspects. We shall give proofs of these fascinating theorems for the benefit of readers unfamiliar with them. Readers familiar with these results can go on to the next chapter. For a comprehensive treatment of this material, see, for example [LeVe77,Nive72,Vino55].

1.6.1 Congruences and Modular Arithmetic

Given integers a, b, and $n \neq 0$, a, is **congruent** to b modulo n, written†

$$a \equiv_n b$$

if and only if

$$a - b = kn$$

for some integer k; that is n divides $(a - b)$, written

$$n \mid (a - b) .$$

For example, $17 \equiv_5 7$, because $(17 - 7) = 2 * 5$.

If $a \equiv_n b$, then b is called a **residue** of a modulo n (conversely, a is a residue of b modulo n). A set of n integers $\{r_1, \ldots, r_n\}$ is called a **complete set of residues** modulo n if, for every integer a, there is exactly one r_i in the set such that $a \equiv_n r_i$. For any modulus n, the set of integers $\{0, 1, \ldots, n - 1\}$ forms a complete set of residues modulo n.

We shall write

$$a \bmod n$$

to denote the residue r of a modulo n in the range $[0, n - 1]$. For example, 7 mod 3 = 1. Clearly,

$$a \bmod n = r \quad \text{implies} \quad a \equiv_n r,$$

but not conversely. Furthermore,

$$a \equiv_n b \quad \text{if and only if} \quad a \bmod n = b \bmod n;$$

thus, congruent integers have the same residue in the range $[0, n - 1]$.

Note that this definition of mod is somewhat different from the definition in some programming languages, such as PASCAL, where a mod n gives the remainder in dividing a by n. Whereas the range of our mod is $[0, n - 1]$, the range of PASCAL's is $[-(n - 1), n - 1]$. For example, -2 mod $26 = -2$ in PASCAL rather than 24.

Like the integers, the integers mod n with addition and multiplication form a **commutative ring**. This means the laws of associativity, commutativity, and distributivity hold. Furthermore, computing in modular arithmetic (i.e., reducing each intermediate result mod n) gives the same answer as computing in ordinary integer arithmetic and reducing the result mod n. This is because reduction mod n is a

---

† We shall reserve the more familiar notation using "mod n" for modular arithmetic.

homomorphism from the ring of integers to the ring of integers mod n as shown next:

Theorem 1.1. Principle of modular arithmetic:
Let a_1 and a_2 be integers, and let op be one of the binary operators $+$, $-$, or $*$. Then reduction mod n is a homomorphism from the integers to the integers mod n (see Figure 1.19); that is,

$$(a_1 \ op \ a_2) \bmod n = [(a_1 \bmod n) \ op \ (a_2 \bmod n)] \bmod n.$$

Proof:
We can write

$$a_1 = k_1 n + r_1$$
$$a_2 = k_2 n + r_2$$

where $r_1, r_2 \in [0, n-1]$. For addition, we have

$$
\begin{aligned}
(a_1 + a_2) \bmod n &= [(k_1 n + r_1) + (k_2 n + r_2)] \bmod n \\
&= [(k_1 + k_2)n + (r_1 + r_2)] \bmod n \\
&= [r_1 + r_2] \bmod n \\
&= [(a_1 \bmod n) + (a_2 \bmod n)] \bmod n \ .
\end{aligned}
$$

Subtraction is similar. For multiplication,

$$
\begin{aligned}
(a_1 * a_2) \bmod n &= [(k_1 n + r_1) * (k_2 n + r_2)] \bmod n \\
&[(k_1 k_2 n + r_1 k_2 + r_2 k_1)n + r_1 r_2] \bmod n \\
&[r_1 * r_2] \bmod n \\
&[(a_1 \bmod n) * (a_2 \bmod n)] \bmod n \ . \quad \blacksquare
\end{aligned}
$$

The preceding theorem shows that evaluating $(a_1 \ op \ a_2)$ in modular arithmetic gives the same result as evaluating it in ordinary integer arithmetic and reducing the result mod n.

The principle of modular arithmetic is behind the familiar principle of "casting out 9's". For an integer a, $a \bmod 9$ is the sum of the digits of a (mod 9).

FIGURE 1.19 Principle of modular arithmetic.

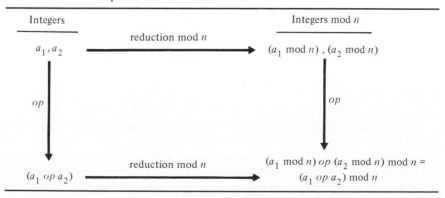

Example:

The following illustrates how this principle is applied to check the result of a computation ($135273 + 261909 + 522044$):

Integer Arithmetic	Mod 9 Arithmetic
1 3 5 2 7 3	3
2 6 1 9 0 9 $\longrightarrow$	0
+ 5 2 2 0 4 4	+ 8
9 1 9 2 2 6 $\longrightarrow$	2 . ■

Note that the principle of modular arithmetic also applies to exponentiations of the form e^t, where $0 \le t \le n - 1$; that is, computing e^t in mod n arithmetic is equivalent to computing e^t and reducing the result mod n. This is because exponentiation is equivalent to repeated multiplications:

$$e^t \bmod n = [\prod_{i=1}^{t} (e \bmod n)] \bmod n.$$

Example:

Consider the expression

$$3^5 \bmod 7.$$

This can be computed by raising 3 to the power 5 and then reducing the result mod 7 as shown next:

1.	Square 3:	$3 * 3 = 9$
2.	Square the result:	$9 * 9 = 81$
3.	Multiply by 3:	$81 * 3 = 243$
4.	Reduce mod 7:	$243 \bmod 7 = 5$,

where we have used the method of repeated squaring and multiplication to reduce the number of multiplications. Alternatively, the intermediate results of the computation can be reduced mod 7 as shown next:

1.	Square 3:	$3 * 3 \bmod 7 = 2$
2.	Square the result:	$2 * 2 \bmod 7 = 4$
3.	Multiply by 3:	$4 * 3 \bmod 7 = 5$. ■

If $t \ge n$, reducing t mod n may not give the same result; that is, $(e^{t \bmod n}) \bmod n$ may not equal $e^t \bmod n$. For example, $(2^{5 \bmod 3}) \bmod 3 = 1$, but $2^5 \bmod 3 = 2$.

Computing in modular arithmetic has the advantage of restricting the range of the intermediate values. For a k-bit modulus n (i.e., $2^{k-1} \le n < 2^k$), the value of any addition, subtraction, or multiplication will be at most $2k$ bits. This means that we can, for example, perform exponentiations of the form $a^z \bmod n$ using large numbers without generating enormous intermediate results.

Because some of the encryption algorithms discussed later in this book are

FIGURE 1.20 Fast exponentiation.

Algorithm *fastexp* (*a*, *z*, *n*)

```
begin "return x = aᶻ mod n"
    a1 := a; z1 := z;
    x := 1;
    while z1 ≠ 0 do "x(a1ᶻ¹ mod n) = aᶻ mod n"
        begin
            while z1 mod 2 = 0 do
                begin "square a1 while z1 is even"
                    z1 := z1 div 2;
                    a1 := (a1 * a1) mod n
                end;
            z1 := z1 − 1;
            x  := (x * a1) mod n "multiply"
        end;
    fastexp := x
end
```

based on exponentiation mod n, we give here a fast exponentiation algorithm. The algorithm, shown in Figure 1.20, uses repeated squaring and multiplication. The notation for this algorithm and other algorithms in this book is based on PASCAL control structures. The operator "div" denotes integer division with truncation. Because $z1 = 0$ when the algorithm terminates, the loop invariant "$x(a1^{z1} \bmod n)$ $= a^z \bmod n$" implies that $x = a^z \bmod n$. Suppose a, z, and n are k-bit integers. Letting $(z_{k-1}, \ldots, z_1, z_0)$ denote the binary representation of z, the algorithm processes the bits in the order $z_0, z_1, \ldots, z_{k-1}$ (i.e., from low order to high order), squaring when the bits are 0, and multiplying and squaring when they are 1. In a hardware implementation of the algorithm, these bits could be accessed directly, omitting the computations "$z1 \bmod 2$", "$z1 \operatorname{div} 2$", and "$z1 - 1$".

Let T be the running time of the algorithm. Because each 0-bit gives rise to one multiplication and each 1-bit gives rise to two multiplications (except for the leftmost 1-bit, which gives rise to one multiplication), the number of multiplications is bounded by

$$k + 1 \le T \le 2k + 1,$$

where $k = \lfloor \log_2 z \rfloor$ is the length of z in bits ("$\lfloor \ \rfloor$" denotes the floor—i.e., round down to nearest integer); this is linear in the length of z. The expected number of multiplications for all z of length k is $1.5k + 1$. By comparison, a naive algorithm performs $z - 1$ multiplications, which is exponential in the length of z.

1.6.2. Computing Inverses

Unlike ordinary integer arithmetic, modular arithmetic sometimes permits the computation of multiplicative inverses; that is, given an integer a in the range

[0, $n - 1$], it may be possible to find a unique integer x in the range [0, $n - 1$] such that

$$ax \bmod n = 1 .$$

For example, 3 and 7 are multiplicative inverses mod 10 because 21 mod 10 = 1. It is this capability to compute inverses that makes modular arithmetic so appealing in cryptographic applications.

We will now show that given $a \in$ [0, $n - 1$], a has a unique inverse mod n when a and n are relatively prime; that is when $gcd(a, n) = 1$, where "gcd" denotes the greatest common divisor. We first prove the following lemma:

Lemma 1.1:
If $gcd(a, n) = 1$, then ($ai \bmod n$) $\neq$ ($aj \bmod n$) for each i, j such that $0 \leq i < j < n$.

Proof:
Assume the contrary. Then $n \mid a(i - j)$. Since $gcd(a, n) = 1$, ($i - j$) must be a multiple of n. But this is impossible because both i and j are smaller than n. ∎

This property implies that each $ai \bmod n$ ($i = 0, \ldots, n - 1$) is a distinct residue mod n, and that the set $\{ai \bmod n\}_{i=0, \ldots, n-1}$ is a permutation of the complete set of residues $\{0, \ldots, n - 1\}$. For example, if $n = 5$ and $a = 3$:

$$3 * 0 \bmod 5 = 0$$
$$3 * 1 \bmod 5 = 3$$
$$3 * 2 \bmod 5 = 1$$
$$3 * 3 \bmod 5 = 4$$
$$3 * 4 \bmod 5 = 2 .$$

This property does not hold when a and n have a common factor, as shown next:

$$2 * 0 \bmod 4 = 0$$
$$2 * 1 \bmod 4 = 2$$
$$2 * 2 \bmod 4 = 0$$
$$2 * 3 \bmod 4 = 2 .$$

Lemma 1.1 implies a has a unique inverse when $gcd(a, n) = 1$:

Theorem 1.2:
If $gcd(a, n) = 1$, then there exists an integer x, $0 < x < n$, such that $ax \bmod n = 1$.

Proof:
Because the set $\{ai \bmod n\}_{i=0, \ldots, n-1}$ is a permutation of $\{0, 1, \ldots, n - 1\}$, $x = i$, where $ai \bmod n = 1$, is a solution. ∎

Theorem 1.2 shows the existence of an inverse, but does not give an algorithm for finding it. We shall now review some additional properties of congruences related to reduced residues and the Euler totient function, showing how these properties lead to the construction of an algorithm for computing inverses.

The **reduced set of residues** mod n is the subset of residues $\{0, \ldots, n-1\}$ relatively prime to n.† For example, the reduced set of residues mod 10 is $\{1, 3, 7, 9\}$. If n is prime, the reduced set of residues is the set of $n-1$ elements $\{1, 2, \ldots, n-1\}$; that is, it is the complete set of residues except for 0. Note that 0 is never included in the reduced set of residues.

The **Euler totient function** $\phi(n)$ is the number of elements in the reduced set of residues modulo n. Equivalently, $\phi(n)$ is the number of positive integers less than n that are relatively prime to n.

For a given modulus n, let $\{r_1, \ldots, r_{\phi(n)}\}$ be the reduced set of residues. The reduced set of residues has the property that every integer relatively prime to n is congruent modulo n to some member r_j of the set. Thus if $gcd(a, n) = 1$ for some integer a, then for each r_i $[1 \le i \le \phi(n)]$, $gcd(ar_i, n) = 1$ and ar_i mod $n = r_j$ for some r_j. By the same reasoning as for a complete set of residues, the set $\{ar_i$ mod $n\}_{i=1, \ldots, \phi(n)}$ is, therefore, a permutation of $\{r_1, \ldots, r_{\phi(n)}\}$.

For prime p, the number of integers less than p that are relatively prime to p is trivially given by $\phi(p) = p - 1$. For the product of two primes p and q we have:

Theorem 1.3:
For $n = pq$ and p, q prime,

$$\phi(n) = \phi(p)\phi(q) = (p-1)(q-1) .$$

Proof:
Consider the complete set of residues modulo n: $\{0, 1, \ldots, pq - 1\}$. All of these residues are relatively prime to n except for the $p - 1$ elements $\{q, 2q, \ldots, (p-1)q\}$, the $q - 1$ elements $\{p, 2p, \ldots, (q-1)p\}$, and 0. Therefore,

$$\phi(n) = pq - [(p-1) + (q-1) + 1] = pq - p - q + 1$$
$$= (p-1)(q-1) . \quad \blacksquare$$

Example:
Let $p = 3$ and $q = 5$. Then $\phi(15) = (3-1)(5-1) = 2 * 4 = 8$, and there are 8 elements in the reduced set of residues modulo 15: $\{1, 2, 4, 7, 8, 11, 13, 14\}$. $\blacksquare$

In general, for arbitrary n, $\phi(n)$ is given by

$$\phi(n) = \prod_{i=1}^{t} p_i^{e_i-1} (p_i - 1) ,$$

where

---

† Strictly speaking, any complete set of residues relatively prime to n is a reduced set of residues; here we are only interested in the set of residues in the range $[1, n-1]$.

$$n = p_1^{e_1} p_2^{e_2} \cdots p_t^{e_t}$$

is the prime factorization of n (i.e., the p_i are distinct primes, and e_i gives the number of occurrences of p_i).

Example:
For $n = 24 = 2^3 3^1$,

$$\phi(24) = 2^2(2 - 1)3^0(3 - 1) = 8;$$

the reduced set of residues is $\{1, 5, 7, 11, 13, 17, 19, 23\}$. ■

The following are two important results of number theory:

Theorem 1.4. Fermat's Theorem:
Let p be prime. Then for every a such that $gcd(a, p) = 1$,

$$a^{p-1} \bmod p = 1 .$$

The proof follows from Euler's generalization: ■

Theorem 1.5. Euler's Generalization:
For every a and n such that $gcd(a, n) = 1$,

$$a^{\phi(n)} \bmod n = 1 .$$

Proof:
Let $\{r_1, \ldots, r_{\phi(n)}\}$ be the reduced set of residues modulo n such that $0 < r_i < n$ for $1 \le i \le \phi(n)$. Then $\{ar_1 \bmod n, \ldots, ar_{\phi(n)} \bmod n\}$ is a permutation of $\{r_1, \ldots, r_{\phi(n)}\}$. Therefore,

$$\prod_{i=1}^{\phi(n)} (ar_i \bmod n) = \prod_{i=1}^{\phi(n)} r_i$$

giving

$$(a^{\phi(n)} \bmod n) \prod_{i=1}^{\phi(n)} r_i = \prod_{i=1}^{\phi(n)} r_i ,$$

which, by cancellation, implies $a^{\phi(n)} \bmod n = 1$. ■

Euler's generalization of Fermat's theorem gives us an algorithm for solving an equation

$$ax \bmod n = 1 ,$$

where $gcd(a, n) = 1$. This solution is given by

$$x = a^{\phi(n)-1} \bmod n . \tag{1.5}$$

If n is prime, this is simply

$$x = a^{(n-1)-1} \bmod n = a^{n-2} \bmod n .$$

Example:
Let $a = 3$ and $n = 7$. Then

$$x = 3^5 \bmod 7 ,$$

which we saw earlier is 5. This checks, because $3 * 5 \bmod 7 = 1$. ∎

If $\phi(n)$ is known, the inverse x of a (mod n) can be computed using Eq. (1.5) and the algorithm *fastexp* given in Figure 1.20. Alternatively, x can be computed using an extension of Euclid's algorithm for computing the greatest common divisor [Knut69]. With this approach, it is not necessary to know $\phi(n)$.

An iterative version of Euclid's algorithm is given in Figure 1.21. The algorithm is extended to solve for x as shown in Figure 1.22. The algorithm computes $gcd(a, n)$ by computing $g_{i+1} = g_{i-1} \bmod g_i$ for $i = 1, 2, \ldots$ until $g_i = 0$, where $g_0 = n$, $g_1 = a$, and "$g_i = u_i n + v_i a$" is the loop invariant. When $g_i = 0$, $g_{i-1} = gcd(a, n)$. If $gcd(a, n) = 1$, then $g_{i-1} = 1$ and $v_{i-1}a - 1 = u_{i-1}n$, giving $v_{i-1}a \equiv_n 1$. Thus, $x = v_{i-1}$ is an inverse of a mod n. Now, x will be in the range $-n < x < n$. If x is negative, $x + n$ gives the solution in the range $0 < x < n$. Knuth shows the average number of divisions performed by the algorithm is approximately $(.843 \ln(n) + 1.47)$.

Example:
The following illustrates the execution of the algorithm to solve the equation "$3x \bmod 7 = 1$":

i	g_i	u_i	v_i	y
0	7	1	0	
1	3	0	1	2
2	1	1	−2	3
3	0			

Because $v_2 = -2$ is negative, the solution is $x = -2 + 7 = 5$. ∎

Note that the implementation of the algorithm can use three local variables: *glast, g,* and *gnext* to represent g_{i-1}, g_i, and g_{i+1}, respectively, for all i (similarly for v). Note also that the variable u is not essential to the computation and, therefore, can be omitted. We have presented the algorithm in the preceding form for clarity.

The algorithm is easily extended to find solutions to general equations

$$ax \bmod n = b$$

when $gcd(a, n) = 1$. First, the solution x_0 to "$ax \bmod n = 1$" is found. Now

$$ax_0 \bmod n = 1 \text{ implies } abx_0 \bmod n = b ,$$

whence

$$x = bx_0 \bmod n$$

FIGURE 1.21 Euclid's algorithm for computing the greatest common divisor.

Algorithm $gcd(a, n)$

begin
    $g_0 := n;$
    $g_1 := a;$
    $i \ := 1;$
    while $g_i \neq 0$ **do**
        begin
            $g_{i+1} := g_{i-1} \bmod g_i;$
            $i := i + 1$
        end;
    $gcd := g_{i-1}$
end

FIGURE 1.22 Euclid's algorithm extended to compute inverses.

Algorithm $inv\ (a, n)$

begin "Return x such that $ax \bmod n = 1$, where $0 < a < n$"
    $g_0 := n;\ g_1 := a;$
    $u_0 := 1;\ v_0 := 0;$
    $u_1 := 0;\ v_1 := 1;$
    $i \ := 1;$
    while $g_i \neq 0$ **do** "$g_i = u_i n + v_i a$"
        begin
            $y \ \ \ := g_{i-1} \operatorname{div} g_i;$
            $g_{i+1} := g_{i-1} - y * g_i;$
            $u_{i+1} := u_{i-1} - y * u_i;$
            $v_{i+1} := v_{i-1} - y * v_i;$
            $i \ \ \ := i + 1$
        end;
    $x := v_{i-1};$
    if $x \geq 0$ **then** $inv := x$ **else** $inv := x + n$
end

is the unique solution to "$ax \bmod n = b$" in the range $[1, n - 1]$. This leads to the formulas:
    Solve "$ax \bmod n = b$" when $gcd(a, n) = 1$:

$$x = [b * inv(a, n)] \bmod n \tag{1.6}$$
$$x = [b * fastexp(a, \phi(n) - 1, n)] \bmod n \tag{1.7}$$

If $gcd(a, n) \neq 1$, the equation "$ax \bmod n = b$" will either have no solution or will have more than one solution in the range $[1, n - 1]$ as described by the following theorem.

Theorem 1.6:

Let $g = gcd(a, n)$. If $g \mid b$ (i.e., $b \bmod g = 0$) the equation

$$ax \bmod n = b$$

will have g solutions of the form

$$x = [\left(\frac{b}{g}\right)x_0 + t\left(\frac{n}{g}\right)] \bmod n \qquad \text{for } t = 0, \ldots, g - 1,$$

where x_0 is the solution to

$$\left(\frac{a}{g}\right)x \bmod \left(\frac{n}{g}\right) = 1 ;$$

otherwise it will have no solution.

Proof:

If "$ax \bmod n = b$" has a solution in the range $[1, n - 1]$, then $n \mid (ax - b)$. Because $g \mid n$ and $g \mid ax$, it follows that $g \mid b$ must also hold. Now, the equation

$$\left(\frac{a}{g}\right)x \bmod \left(\frac{n}{g}\right) = 1$$

has a unique solution x_0 in the range $[1, (n/g) - 1]$. This implies that $x_1 = (b/g)x_0 \bmod (n/g)$ is a solution of

$$\left(\frac{a}{g}\right)x \bmod \left(\frac{n}{g}\right) = \left(\frac{b}{g}\right)$$

in the range $[1, (n/g) - 1]$. Therefore, $(a/g)x_1 - (b/g) = kn$ for some integer k. Multiplying by g we get $ax_1 - b = kn$, which implies that x_1 is a solution of "$ax \bmod n = b$". Now, any x in the range $[1, n - 1]$ such that $x \equiv_{(n/g)} x_1$ is also a solution of "$ax \bmod n = b$". Therefore, all solutions of "$ax \bmod n = b$" are given by

$$x = x_1 + t\left(\frac{n}{g}\right) , \quad t = 0, \ldots, g - 1 . \quad \blacksquare$$

Example:

Consider the equation

$$6x \bmod 10 = 4.$$

Because $g = gcd(6, 10) = 2$, and 2 divides 4, there are 2 solutions. We first compute the solution x_0 to the equation

$$\left(\frac{6}{2}\right)x \bmod \left(\frac{10}{2}\right) = 1,$$

that is,

$$3x \bmod 5 = 1$$

getting $x_0 = 2$. This gives

$$x_1 = \left(\frac{4}{2}\right)2 \bmod \left(\frac{10}{2}\right) = 4 \bmod 5 = 4 .$$

The solutions are thus:

$t = 0: x = 4$

$t = 1: x = [4 + \left(\frac{10}{2}\right)] \bmod 10 = 9 .$ ■

Figure 1.23 gives an algorithm for printing the solutions described by Theorem 1.6. Division is denoted by "/" rather than "div" where the numerator is evenly divisible by the denominator.

An equation of the form "$ax \bmod n = b$" may also be solved using the prime factorization of n. Let

$$n = d_1 d_2 \ldots d_t$$

be the prime factorization of n, where

$$d_i = p_i^{e_i} \qquad (1 \le i \le t)$$

and the p_i are distinct primes. Thus, the d_i are pairwise relatively prime.

Let $f(x)$ be a polynomial in x. The following theorem shows that x is a solution to the equation $f(x) \bmod n = 0$ if and only if x is a common solution to the set of equations $f(x) \bmod d_i = 0$ for $i = 1, \ldots, t$.

Theorem 1.7:
Let $d_1, \ldots, d_t$ be pairwise relatively prime, and let $n = d_1 d_2 \ldots d_t$. Then

FIGURE 1.23 Solve linear equations.

Algorithm *solve* (a, n, b)

---

begin "print all solutions x to $ax \bmod n = b$"
   $g := gcd(a, n)$;
   if $(b \bmod g) = 0$
     then begin
       print$(g,$ "solutions follow"$)$;
       $n0 := n/g$;
       $x0 := inv(a/g, n0)$;
       $x1 := \left((b/g) * x0\right) \bmod n$;
       for $t := 0$ **to** $g - 1$ **do**
         begin
           $x := (x1 + t * n0) \bmod n$;
           print(x)
         end
     end
     else print("no solutions exist")
end

$$f(x) \bmod n = 0 \qquad \text{if and only if}$$
$$f(x) \bmod d_i = 0 \qquad (1 \le i \le t) \ .$$

Proof:
Because the d_i are pairwise relatively prime, $n \mid f(x)$ if and only if $d_i \mid f(x)$ for $i = 1, \ldots, t$. ■

We can apply this result to solve equations of the form

$$ax \bmod n = b.$$

Writing this as $(ax - b) \bmod n = 0$, we find a common solution to the equations $(ax - b) \bmod d_i = 0$ or, equivalently, to the equations

$$ax \bmod d_i = b \bmod d_i \qquad (1 \le i \le t) \ .$$

We can construct a common solution x to $f(x) \bmod d_i = 0$ ($1 \le i \le t$) from a set of independent solutions $x_1, \ldots, x_t$, where x_i is a solution to $f(x) \bmod d_i = 0$. Observe that every x congruent to x_i modulo d_i is a solution to $f(x) \bmod d_i = 0$. Therefore, x is a solution to $f(x) \bmod n = 0$ if $x \bmod d_i = x_i$ for $i = 1, \ldots, t$. The Chinese Remainder Theorem shows how a common solution x to the preceding system of equations can be computed.

Theorem 1.8. Chinese Remainder Theorem:
Let $d_1, \ldots, d_t$ be pairwise relatively prime, and let $n = d_1 d_2 \ldots d_t$. Then the system of equations

$$(x \bmod d_i) = x_i \qquad (i = 1, \ldots, t)$$

has a common solution x in the range $[0, n - 1]$.

Proof:
Now, for each $i = 1, \ldots, t$, $gcd(d_i, n/d_i) = 1$. Therefore, there exist y_i such that $(n/d_i)y_i \bmod d_i = 1$. Furthermore, $(n/d_i)y_i \bmod d_j = 0$ for $j \ne i$ because d_j is a factor of (n/d_i). Let

$$x = [\sum_{i=1}^{t} \left(\frac{n}{d_i}\right) y_i x_i] \bmod n \ .$$

Then x is a solution of "$x \bmod d_i = x_i$" ($1 \le i \le t$) because

$$x \bmod d_i = \left(\frac{n}{d_i}\right) y_i x_i \bmod d_i = x_i \ . \quad ■$$

Example:
We shall show how the Chinese Remainder Theorem can be used to solve the equation "$3x \bmod 10 = 1$". We observe that $10 = 2 * 5$, so $d_1 = 2$ and $d_2 = 5$. We first find solutions x_1 and x_2, respectively, to the equations:

FIGURE 1.24 Find solution to system of equations using the
            Chinese Remainder Theorem.

Algorithm $crt(n, d_1, \ldots, d_t, x_1, \ldots, x_t)$

---

begin "return $x \in [0, n - 1]$ such that $x \bmod d_i = x_i \, (1 \leq i \leq t)$"
   for $i := 1$ **to** t **do**
     $y_i := inv \left((n/d_i) \bmod d_i, d_i\right);$
   $x := 0;$
   for $i := 1$ **to** t **do**
     $x := [x + (n/d_i) * y_i * x_i] \bmod n;$
   $crt := x$
end

$$3x \bmod 2 = 1$$
$$3x \bmod 5 = 1 \, .$$

This gives us $x_1 = 1$ and $x_2 = 2$. We then apply the Chinese Remainder Theorem to find a common solution x to the equations:

$$x \bmod 2 = x_1 = 1$$
$$x \bmod 5 = x_2 = 2 \, .$$

We find y_1 and y_2 such that

$$\left(\frac{10}{2}\right)y_1 \bmod 2 = 1, \text{ and}$$

$$\left(\frac{10}{5}\right)y_2 \bmod 5 = 1,$$

getting $y_1 = 1$ and $y_2 = 3$. We then have

$$x = [\left(\frac{10}{2}\right)y_1 x_1 + \left(\frac{10}{5}\right)y_2 x_2] \bmod 10$$
$$= [5 * 1 * 1 + 2 * 3 * 2] \bmod 10 = 7$$

Thus 7 is the inverse of 3 (mod 10). ■

An algorithm that computes the solution given by the Chinese Remainder Theorem is given in Figure 1.24. Note that an implementation of the algorithm can combine the two **for** loops and use a single local variable to represent the y_i. We have presented the algorithm this way to show its relation to the proof of Theorem 1.8.

1.6.3 Computing in Galois Fields

When the modulus is a prime p, every integer $a \in [1, p - 1]$ is relatively prime to p and, therefore, has a unique multiplicative inverse mod p. This means the set of integers mod p, together with the arithmetic operations, is a **finite field** †, called the **Galois field GF(p)** after their discoverer Evariste Galois. Because division is possible, arithmetic mod p is more powerful than ordinary integer arithmetic. Real arithmetic is not generally applicable to cryptography because information is lost through round-off errors (the same holds for integer division, where information is lost through truncation). Many of the ciphers developed in recent years are based on arithmetic in **GF(p)**, where p is a large prime.

Another type of Galois field with applications in cryptography is based on arithmetic mod q over polynomials of degree n. These fields, denoted **GF(q^n)**, have elements that are polynomials of degree $n - 1$ (or lower) of the form

$$a = a_{n-1}x^{n-1} + \cdots + a_1 x + a_0 ,$$

where the coefficients a_i are integers mod q. Each element a is a residue mod $p(x)$, where $p(x)$ is an irreducible polynomial of degree n (i.e., p cannot be factored into polynomials of degree less than n).

Arithmetic on the coefficients of the polynomials is done mod q. For example, the coefficients c_i in the sum $c = a + b$ are given by $c_i = (a_i + b_i) \bmod q$ $(0 \leq i < n)$. Because a and b are of degree $n - 1$, the sum $a + b$ is a polynomial of degree at most $n - 1$, whence it is already reduced mod $p(x)$. The product $a * b$ could be of degree greater than $n - 1$ (but at most $2n - 2$), however, so it must be reduced mod $p(x)$; this is done by dividing by $p(x)$ and taking the remainder.

Of particular interest in computer applications are the fields **GF (2^n)**. Here the coefficients of the polynomials are the binary digits 0 and 1. Thus, an element a can be represented as a bit vector $(a_{n-1}, \ldots, a_1, a_0)$ of length n, and each of the possible 2^n bit vectors of length n corresponds to a different element in **GF(2^n)**. For example, the bit vector 11001‡ corresponds to the polynomial $(x^4 + x^3 + 1)$ in **GF(2^5)**. To avoid confusion with the notation **GF(p)**, where p is a prime number, we shall not write **GF(32)** for **GF(2^5)**, for example, even though 32 is not prime.

Computing in **GF(2^n)** is more efficient in both space and time than computing in **GF(p)**. Let p be a prime number such that $2^{n-1} < p < 2^n$, whence the elements of **GF(p)** are also represented as bit vectors of length n (using the standard binary representation of the positive integers; e.g., 11001 corresponds to the integer $2^4 + 2^3 + 1 = 25$). We first observe that whereas all 2^n bit vectors correspond to elements of **GF(2^n)**, this is not true for **GF(p)**; in particular, the bit vectors representing the integers in the range $[p, 2^n - 1]$ are not elements of **GF(p)**. Thus it is possible to represent more elements (up to twice as many!) in **GF(2^n)** than in **GF(p)** using the same amount of space. This can be important in cryptography applications, where the strength of a scheme usually depends on the size of the field. For comparable levels of security, **GF(2^n)** is more efficient in terms of space than **GF(p)**.

We next observe that arithmetic is more efficient in **GF(2^n)** than in **GF(p)**.

---

† A field is any integral domain in which every element besides 0 has a multiplicative inverse; the rational numbers form an infinite field.

‡ To simplify our notation, we shall write bit vectors as strings here and elsewhere in the book.

To see why, we shall briefly describe how the arithmetic operations are implemented in $GF(2^n)$. We assume the reader has a basic understanding of integer arithmetic in digital computers.

We first consider operations over the binary coefficients of the polynomials. Recall that these operations are performed mod 2. Let u and v be binary digits. Then u and v can be added simply by taking the "exclusive-or" $u \oplus v$; that is,

$$(u + v) \bmod 2 = u \oplus v = \begin{cases} 0 & \text{if } u = v \text{ (both bits the same)} \\ 1 & \text{if } u \neq v. \end{cases}$$

Subtraction is the same:

$$(u - v) \bmod 2 = (u + v - 2) \bmod 2 = (u + v) \bmod 2$$
$$= u \oplus v.$$

The bits u and v can be multiplied by taking the boolean "and":

$$u * v = u \text{ and } v.$$

Now, let a and b be the bit vectors $a = (a_{n-1}, \ldots, a_0)$ and $b = (b_{n-1}, \ldots, b_0)$. In $GF(2^n)$, a and b are added (or subtracted) by taking the $\oplus$ of each pair of bits. Letting $c = a + b$ (or $a - b$), we have $c = (c_{n-1}, \ldots, c_0)$, where

$$c_i = a_i \oplus b_i \quad \text{for } i = 0, \ldots, n - 1.$$

The operator $\oplus$ is extended pairwise to bit strings, so we can also write $c = a \oplus b$ to denote the sum (or difference) of a and b.

Example:
Let $a = 10101$ and $b = 01100$. In $GF(2^5)$, $c = a + b$ is computed as follows:

$$a = 1\,0\,1\,0\,1$$
$$b = 0\,1\,1\,0\,0$$
$$c = \overline{1\,1\,0\,0\,1}.$$

By contrast, if we add the bit vectors a and b in $GF(p)$ for $p = 31$, we must perform carries during the addition, and then divide to reduce the result mod 31:

Step 1. Add a and b:

$$a = \quad 1\,0\,1\,0\,1 \quad (21)$$
$$b = \quad \ \ 0\,1\,1\,0\,0 \quad (12)$$
$$c = 1\,\overline{0\,0\,0\,0\,1} \quad (33)$$

Step 2. Divide by 31 and keep the remainder:

$$c = \quad 0\,0\,0\,1\,0 \quad (\ 2). \quad \blacksquare$$

Multiplication of a and b in $GF(2^n)$ is also easier than in $GF(p)$. Here, however, the product $a * b$ must be divided by the irreducible polynomial $p(x)$ associated with the field. The product $d = a * b$ is represented by the polynomial sum:

$$d = \sum_{i=0}^{n-1} (a_i * b)x^i \bmod p(x),$$

where

$$a_i * b = \begin{cases} b = b_{n-1}x^{n-1} + \cdots + b_0 & \text{if } a_i = 1 \\ 0 & \text{otherwise}. \end{cases}$$

Example:
Let $a = 101$. If a is squared in $\mathbf{GF}(2^3)$ with irreducible polynomial $p(x) = x^3 + x + 1$ (1011 in binary), the product $d = a * a$ is computed as follows:

Step 1. Multiply $a * a$:

```
  1 0 1
  1 0 1
  1 0 1
0 0 0
1 0 1
1 0 0 0 1
```

Step 2. Divide by $p(x) = 1011$:

```
              1 0
1 0 1 1 ) 1 0 0 0 1
          1 0 1 1
            1 1 1 = d .
```

If a is squared in $\mathbf{GF}(p)$ for $p = 7$, the computation is similar, except the additions and subtractions in the multiply and divide steps require carries. ∎

Example:
Let $a = 111$ and $b = 100$. The product $d = a * b$ is computed in $\mathbf{GF}(2^3)$ with irreducible polynomial $p(x) = 1011$ ($x^3 + x + 1$) as follows:

Step 1. Multiply $a * b$:

```
  1 1 1
  1 0 0
  0 0 0
0 0 0
1 1 1
1 1 1 0 0
```

Step 2. Divide by $p(x) = 1011$:

```
                1 1
1 0 1 1 ) 1 1 1 0 0
          1 0 1 1
            1 0 1 0
            1 0 1 1
                  1 = d .
```

Thus, $111 * 100$ mod $1011 = 001$, so 111 and 100 are inverses mod 1011 in $\mathbf{GF}(2^3)$. ∎

To divide b by a in $\mathbf{GF}(2^n)$ with modulus $p(x)$, we compute the inverse of a mod $p(x)$, denoted a^{-1}, and multiply b by a^{-1}. Because the algorithms developed in the preceding section for computing inverses apply to any finite field, we can apply them to compute inverses in $\mathbf{GF}(2^n)$. To do this, we observe that every bit vector of length n except for the 0-vector is relatively prime to $p(x)$ regardless of the irreducible polynomial $p(x)$. Thus, the number of residues relatively prime to $p(x)$ is given by $\phi(p(x)) = 2^n - 1$, where we have extended the meaning of the Euler totient function ϕ to polynomials. We can then use Eq. (1.5) to compute a^{-1}, where $a * a^{-1}$ mod $p(x) = 1$, getting

$$a^{-1} = a^{\phi(p(x))-1} \bmod p(x) = a^{2^n-2} \bmod p(x) .$$

Alternatively, we can compute a^{-1} using the extended version of Euclid's algorithm shown in Figure 1.22:

$$a^{-1} = inv(a, p(x)) ,$$

where arithmetic is done in $\mathbf{GF}(2^n)$.

Example:
Let $a = 100$ (x^2) and $p(x) = 1011$ in $\mathbf{GF}(2^3)$.
The reader should verify that

$$a^{-1} = 100^{2^3-2} \bmod 1011 = 100^6 \bmod 1011$$
$$= 111 ,$$

and

$$a^{-1} = inv(100, 1011)$$
$$= 111 . \blacksquare$$

(Davida [Davi72] describes an algorithm for computing inverses that is suitable for parallel implementation.)

To summarize, polynomial arithmetic in $\mathbf{GF}(2^n)$ is more efficient than integer arithmetic in $\mathbf{GF}(p)$ because there are no carries, and division by the modulus is never needed for addition or subtraction.

The cost of hardware (or software) to compute in $\mathbf{GF}(2^n)$ depends somewhat on the choice of modulus. Blakley (Blak80) shows how multiplication can be efficiently implemented in $\mathbf{GF}(2^n)$ with an irreducible trinomial of the form

$$p(x) = x^n + x + 1 .$$

The polynomial $p(x) = x^3 + x + 1$ in our examples is of this form. Most such trinomials are not irreducible; the following is a list of all irreducible ones through $n = 127$:

$n = 1, 3, 4, 6, 7, 9, 15, 22, 28, 30, 46, 60, 63, 127.$

(See, for example, [Zier68,Zier69] for a list of irreducible trinomials for $n > 127$.)

   Multiplication is efficient when $p(x)$ is of this form, because the long string of 0's in $p(x)$ simplifies the reduction mod $p(x)$. To see how this works, let $d = a * b$, where $a = (a_{n-1}, \ldots, a_0)$ and $b = (b_{n-1}, \ldots, b_0)$. Before reduction mod $p(x)$, the product is given by the $(2n - 1)$-bit vector

$$(s_{n-1}, \ldots, s_2, s_1, c_{n-1}, \ldots, c_1, c_0),$$

where:

$$c_i = a_0 * b_i \oplus a_1 * b_{i-1} \oplus \ldots \oplus a_i * b_0, \qquad i = 0, \ldots, n - 1$$

$$s_i = a_i * b_{n-1} \oplus a_{i+1} * b_{n-2} \oplus \ldots \oplus a_{n-1} * b_i, \qquad i = 1, \ldots, n - 1.$$

This is illustrated next:

$$
\begin{array}{ccccc}
 & b_{n-1} & \cdots & b_1 & b_0 \\
 & a_{n-1} & \cdots & a_1 & a_0 \\
\hline
 & a_0 b_{n-1} & \cdots & a_0 b_1 & a_0 b_0 \\
 a_1 b_{n-1} & a_1 b_{n-2} & \cdots & a_1 b_0 & \\
 a_2 b_{n-1} & a_2 b_{n-2} & a_2 b_{n-3} & \cdots & \\
 \cdot & \cdot & \cdot & \cdot & \cdot \\
 \cdot & \cdot & \cdot & \cdot & \cdot \\
a_{n-1} b_{n-1} \cdots & a_{n-1} b_2 & a_{n-1} b_1 & a_{n-1} b_0 & \\
\hline
s_{n-1} & \cdots & s_2 & s_1 & c_{n-1} \cdots c_1 \; c_0 \; .
\end{array}
$$

Reducing by $p(x)$, we see that if bit $s_{n-1} = 1$, bit c_{n-1} and c_{n-2} are complemented; if bit $s_{n-2} = 1$, bits c_{n-2} and c_{n-3} are complemented; and so forth, giving the reduced product

$$d = (d_{n-1}, \ldots, d_0)$$

where:

$$d_{n-1} = c_{n-1} \oplus s_{n-1}$$

$$d_i = c_i \oplus s_i \oplus s_{i+1} \quad (0 < i < n-1)$$

$$d_0 = c_0 \oplus s_1 .$$

Berkovits, Kowalchuk, and Schanning [Berk79] have developed a fast implementation of $GF(2^{127})$ arithmetic using the previous approach with $p(x) = x^{127} + x + 1$.

   The fields $GF(2^n)$ are used in many error correcting codes, including "Hamming codes". These codes can be efficiently implemented using shift registers with feedback. (For more information on coding theory, see [Hamm80,Berl68, MacW78,Pete72,McEl77].) A cryptographic application for shift registers is described in Chapter 3.

EXERCISES

1.1   Decipher the following Caesar cipher using $K = 3$:

VRVRVHDPVWUHVV .

1.2   Let X be an integer variable represented with 32 bits. Suppose that the probability is $1/2$ that X is in the range $[0, 2^8 - 1]$, with all such values being equally likely, and $1/2$ that X is in the range $[2^8, 2^{32} - 1]$, with all such values being equally likely. Compute $H(X)$.

1.3   Let X be one of the six messages: A, B, C, D, E, F, where:

$$p(A) = p(B) = p(C) = \frac{1}{4}$$

$$p(D) = \frac{1}{8}$$

$$p(E) = p(F) = \frac{1}{16} .$$

Compute $H(X)$ and find an optimal binary encoding of the messages.

1.4   Prove that for $n = 2$, $H(X)$ is maximal for $p_1 = p_2 = 1/2$.

1.5   Prove that for any n, $H(X)$ is maximal for $p_i = 1/n$ ($1 \leq i \leq n$).

1.6   Show that $H(X, Y) \leq H(X) + H(Y)$, where

$$H(X, Y) = \sum_{X, Y} p(X, Y) \log_2 \left(\frac{1}{p(X, Y)}\right) .$$

[Hint: $p(X) = \sum_Y p(X, Y)$, $p(Y) = \sum_X p(X, Y)$, and $p(X)p(Y) \leq p(X, Y)$, equality holding only when X and Y are independent.]

1.7   Show that $H(X, Y) = H_Y(X) + H(Y)$. Combine this with the result in the previous problem to show that $H_Y(X) \leq H(X)$; thus, the uncertainty about X cannot increase with the additional information Y. [Hint: $p(X, Y) = p_Y(X)p(Y)$.]

1.8   Let M be a secret message revealing the recipient of a scholarship. Suppose there was one female applicant, Anne, and three male applicants, Bob, Doug, and John. The probability of each applicant receiving the scholarship is given by: $p(Anne) = 1/2$ $p(Bob) = p(Doug) = p(John) = 1/6$. Compute $H(M)$. Letting S denote a message revealing the sex of the recipient, compute $H_S(M)$.

1.9   Let M be a 6-digit number in the range $[0, 10^6 - 1]$ enciphered with a Caesar-type shifted substitution cipher with key K, $0 \leq K \leq 9$. For example, if $K = 1$, $M = 123456$ is enciphered as 234567. Compute $H(M)$, $H(C)$, $H(K)$, $H_C(M)$, and $H_C(K)$, assuming all values of M and K are equally likely.

1.10 Consider the following ciphertexts:

XXXXX

VWXYZ
RKTIC
JZQAT

Which of the these ciphertexts could result from enciphering five-letter words of English using:

a.   A substitution cipher, where each letter is replaced with some other letter, but the letters are not necessarily shifted as in the Caesar cipher (thus A could be replaced with K, B with W, etc.).
b.   Any transposition cipher.

1.11 Suppose plaintext messages are 100 letters long and that keys are specified by sequences of letters. Explain why perfect secrecy can be achieved with keys fewer than 100 letters long. How long must the keys be for perfect secrecy?

1.12 Compare the redundancy of programs written in different languages (e.g., PASCAL, APL, and COBOL). Suggest ways in which the redundancy can be reduced (and later recovered) from a program.

1.13 Show that the cancellation law does not hold over the integers mod n with multiplication when n is not prime by showing there exist integers x and y such that $x * y \bmod n = 0$, but neither x nor y is 0.

1.14 Let n be an integer represented in base 10 as a sequence of t decimal digits $d_1 d_2 \ldots d_t$. Prove that

$$n \bmod 9 = \left(\sum_{i=1}^{t} d_i \right) \bmod 9 .$$

1.15 For each equation of the form ($ax \bmod n = b$) that follows, solve for x in the range $[0, n - 1]$.

a. $5x \bmod 17 = 1$
b. $19x \bmod 26 = 1$
c. $17x \bmod 100 = 1$
d. $17x \bmod 100 = 10$

1.16 Find all solutions to the equation

$$15x \bmod 25 = 10$$

in the range $[0, 24]$.

1.17 Apply algorithm *crt* in Figure 1.24 to find an $x \in [0, 59]$ such that

$$x \bmod 4 = 3$$
$$x \bmod 3 = 2$$
$$x \bmod 5 = 4 .$$

1.18 Find a solution to the equation

$$13x \bmod 70 = 1$$

by finding x_1, x_2, and x_3 such that

$$13x_1 \bmod 2 = 1$$
$$13x_2 \bmod 5 = 1$$
$$13x_3 \bmod 7 = 1$$

and then applying algorithm *crt*.

1.19 Let $a = 100$ (x^2) in $\mathbf{GF}(2^3)$ with modulus $p(x) = 1011$ $(x^3 + x + 1)$. Divide 1000000000000 by 1011 to show that

$$a^{-1} = 100^6 \bmod 1011 = 111 .$$

Using algorithm *inv*, show that

$$a^{-1} = inv(100, 1011) = 111 .$$

1.20 Find the inverse of $a = 011$ $(x + 1)$ in $\mathbf{GF}(2^3)$ with $p(x) = 1011$.

REFERENCES

Aho74. Aho, A., Hopcroft, J., and Ullman, J., *The Design and Analysis of Computer Algorithms,* Addison-Wesley, Reading, Mass. (1974).

Baye76. Bayer, R. and Metzger, J. K., "On the Encipherment of Search Trees and Random Access Files," *ACM Trans. On Database Syst.* Vol. 1(1) pp. 37–52 (Mar. 1976).

Berk79. Berkovits, S., Kowalchuk, J., and Schanning, B., "Implementing Public Key Schemes," *IEEE Comm. Soc. Mag.* Vol. 17(3) pp. 2–3 (May 1979).

Berl68. Berlekamp, E. R., *Algebraic Coding Theory,* McGraw-Hill, New York (1968).

Blak80. Blakley, G. R., "One-Time Pads are Key Safeguarding Schemes, Not Cryptosystems," *Proc. 1980 Symp. on Security and Privacy,* IEEE Computer Society, pp. 108–113 (Apr. 1980).

Bras79a. Brassard, G., "Relativized Cryptography," *Proc. IEEE 20th Annual Symp. on Found. of Comp. Sci.,* pp. 383–391 (Oct. 1979).

Bras79b. Brassard, G., "A Note on the Complexity of Cryptography," *IEEE Trans. on Inform. Theory* Vol. IT-25(2) pp. 232–233 (Mar. 1979).

Bras80. Brassard, G., "A Time-Luck Tradeoff in Cryptography," *Proc. IEEE 21st Annual Symp. on Found. of Comp. Sci.,* pp. 380–386 (Oct. 1980).

Cook71. Cook, S. A., "The Complexity of Theorem-Proving Procedures," *Proc. 3rd Annual ACM Symp. on the Theory of Computing,* pp. 151–158 (1971).

Cove78. Cover, T. M. and King, R. C., "A Convergent Gambling Estimate of the Entropy of English," *IEEE Trans. on Infor. Theory* Vol. IT-24 pp. 413–421 (Aug. 1978).

Davi72. Davida, G. I., "Inverse of Elements of a Galois Field," *Electronics Letters* Vol. 8(21) (Oct. 19, 1972).

Deav77. Deavours, C. A., "Unicity Points in Cryptanalysis," *Cryptologia* Vol. 1(1) pp. 46–68 (Jan. 1977).

Diff76. Diffie, W. and Hellman, M., "New Directions in Cryptography," *IEEE Trans. on Info. Theory* Vol. IT-22(6) pp. 644–654 (Nov. 1976).

Gare79. Garey, M. R. and Johnson, D. S., *Computers and Intractability, A Guide to the Theory of NP-Completeness,* W. H. Freeman and Co., San Francisco, Calif. (1979).

Hamm80. Hamming, R. W., *Coding and Information Theory,* Prentice-Hall, Englewood Cliffs, N.J. (1980).

Hell77. Hellman, M. E., "An Extension of the Shannon Theory Approach to Cryptography," *IEEE Trans. on Info. Theory* Vol. IT-23 pp. 289–294 (May 1977).

Huff52. Huffman, D., "A Method for the Construction of Minimum-Redundancy Codes," *Proc. IRE* Vol. 40 pp. 1098–1101 (1952).

Knut69. Knuth, D., *The Art of Computer Programming; Vol. 2, Seminumerical Algorithms,* Addison-Wesley, Reading, Mass. (1969). (Exercise 4.5.2.15.)

Konh81. Konheim, A. G., *Cryptography: A Primer,* John Wiley & Sons, New York (1981).

Lemp79. Lempel, A., "Cryptology in Transition," *Computing Surveys* Vol. 11(4) pp. 285–303 (Dec. 1979).

LeVe77. LeVeque, W. J., *Fundamentals of Number Theory,* Addison-Wesley, Reading, Mass. (1977).

MacW78. MacWilliams, F. J. and Sloane, N. J. A., *The Theory of Error Correcting Codes,* North-Holland, New York (1978).

McEl77. McEliece, R., *The Theory of Information and Coding,* Addison-Wesley, Reading, Mass. (1977).

McEl78. McEliece, R., "A Public Key Cryptosystem Based on Algebraic Coding Theory," DSN Progress Rep. 42–44, Jet Propulsion Lab Calif. Inst. of Tech., Pasadena, Ca. (Jan., Feb. 1978).

Merk80. Merkle, R. C., "Protocols for Public Key Cryptosystems," pp. 122–133 in *Proc. 1980 Symp. on Security and Privacy,* IEEE Computer Society (Apr. 1980).

Mins67. Minsky, M., *Computation: Finite and Infinite Machines,* Prentice-Hall, Englewood Cliffs, N.J. (1967).

Need78. Needham, R. M. and Schroeder, M., "Using Encryption for Authentication in Large Networks of Computers," *Comm. ACM* Vol. 21(12) pp. 993–999 (Dec. 1978).

Nive72. Niven, I. and Zuckerman, H. A., *An Introduction to the Theory of Numbers,* John Wiley & Sons, New York (1972).

Pete72. Peterson, W. W. and Weldon, E. J., *Error Correcting Codes,* MIT Press, Cambridge, Mass. (1972).

Pope79. Popek, G. J. and Kline, C. S., "Encryption and Secure Computer Networks," *Computing Surveys* Vol. 11(4) pp. 331–356 (Dec. 1979).

Rabi78. Rabin, M., "Digitalized Signatures," pp. 155–166 in *Foundations of Secure Computation,* ed. R. A. DeMillo et al., Academic Press, New York (1978).

Sham79. Shamir, A., "On the Cryptocomplexity of Knapsack Systems," *Proc. 11th Annual ACM Symp. on the Theory of Computing,* pp. 118–129 (May 1979).

Shan48. Shannon, C. E., "A Mathematical Theory of Communication," *Bell Syst. Tech. J.* Vol. 27 pp. 379–423 (July), 623–656 (Oct.) (1948).

Shan49. Shannon, C. E., "Communication Theory of Secrecy Systems," *Bell Syst. Tech. J.* Vol. 28 pp. 656–715 (Oct. 1949).

Shan51. Shannon, C. E., "Predilection and Entropy of Printed English," *Bell Syst. Tech. J.,* Vol. 30 pp. 50–64 (Jan. 1951).

Simm79. Simmons, G. J., "Symmetric and Asymmetric Encryption," *Computing Surveys* Vol. 11(4) pp. 305–330 (Dec. 1979).

Simm81. Simmons, G. J., "Half a Loaf is Better Than None: Some Novel Message Integrity Problems," *Proc. 1981 Symp. on Security and Privacy,* IEEE Computer Society pp. 65–69, (April 1981).

Smid79. Smid, M., "A Key Notarization System for Computer Networks," NBS Special Pub. 500–54, National Bureau of Standards Washington, D.C. (Oct. 1979).

Turi36. Turing, A., "On Computable Numbers, with an Application to the Entscheidungsproblem," *Proc. London Math. Soc. Ser. 2* Vol. 42, pp. 230–265 and Vol. 43, pp. 544–546 (1936).

Turn73. Turn, R., "Privacy Transformations for Databank Systems," pp. 589–600 in *Proc. NCC,* Vol. 42, AFIPS Press, Montvale, N.J. (1973).

Vino55. Vinogradov, I. M., *An Introduction to the Theory of Numbers,* Pergamon Press, Elmsford, N.Y. (1955).

Zier68. Zierler, N. and Brillhart, J., "On Primitive Trinomials (Mod 2)," *Info. and Control* Vol. 13 pp. 541–554 (1968).

Zier69. Zierler, N. and Brillhart, J., "On Primitive Trinomials (Mod 2)," *Info. and Control* Vol. 14 pp. 566–569 (1969).

Encryption Algorithms

2.1. TRANSPOSITION CIPHERS

Transposition ciphers rearrange characters according to some scheme. This rearrangement was classically done with the aid of some type of geometric figure. Encipherment proceeded in two steps as shown next:

$$\text{plaintext} \xrightarrow[\text{write} - \text{in}]{} \text{figure} \xrightarrow[\text{take} - \text{off}]{} \text{ciphertext}$$

First, the plaintext was written into the figure according to some "write-in" path. Second, the ciphertext was taken off the figure according to some "take-off" path. The key consisted of the figure together with the write-in and take-off paths.

The geometrical figure was often a 2-dimensional array (matrix). In **columnar transposition** the plaintext was written into a matrix by rows. The ciphertext was obtained by taking off the columns in some order.

Example:
Suppose that the plaintext RENAISSANCE is written into a 3 × 4 matrix by rows as follows:

$$
\begin{array}{cccc}
1 & 2 & 3 & 4 \\
\hline
R & E & N & A \\
I & S & S & A \\
N & C & E &
\end{array}
$$

If the columns are taken off in the order 2–4–1–3, the resulting ciphertext is ESCAARINNSE. ■

(See Mellen [Mell73] for a generalization of this technique to n-dimensional arrays.)

Many transposition ciphers permute the characters of the plaintext with a **fixed period** d. Let $\mathbf{Z}_d$ be the integers 1 through d, and let $f{:}\mathbf{Z}_d \rightarrow \mathbf{Z}_d$ be a permutation over $\mathbf{Z}_d$. The key for the cipher is given by the pair $K = (d, f)$. Successive blocks of d characters are enciphered by permuting the characters according to f. Thus, a plaintext message

$$M = m_1 \ldots m_d \; m_{d+1} \ldots m_{2d} \ldots$$

is enciphered as

$$E_K(M) = m_{f(1)} \ldots m_{f(d)} \; m_{d+f(1)} \ldots m_{d+f(d)} \ldots .$$

Decipherment uses the inverse permutation.

> **Example:**
> Suppose that $d = 4$ and f gives the permutation:
>
> $$i : 1\ 2\ 3\ 4$$
> $$f(i): 2\ 4\ 1\ 3 ;$$
>
> thus, the first plaintext character is moved to the third position in the cipher-text, the second plaintext character to the first position, and so forth. The plaintext RENAISSANCE is enciphered as:
>
> $$M \quad = \text{RENA ISSA NCE}$$
> $$E_K(M) = \text{EARN SAIS CNE} .$$
>
> The preceding ciphertext is broken into groups of four letters only for clarity; the actual ciphertext would be transmitted as a continuous stream of characters to hide the period. The short block at the end is enciphered by moving the characters to their relative positions in the permutation. ■

Like columnar transposition, periodic permutation ciphers can be viewed as transpositions of the columns of a matrix in which the plaintext is written in by rows. With periodic permutations, however, the ciphertext is also taken off by rows. This is more efficient for computer applications, because each row (block) can be enciphered and deciphered independently. With columnar transposition, the entire matrix must be generated for encipherment and decipherment.

The cryptanalyst can easily recognize whether a cipher is a transposition cipher because the relative frequencies of the letters in the ciphertext will closely match the expected frequencies for plaintext. The ciphers are broken by **anagramming**—the process of restoring a disarranged set of letters into their original positions (e.g., see [Sink66,Gain56]). This is facilitated with tables of frequency distributions for digrams (double-letter combinations) and for trigrams (triple-letter combinations). Figure 2.1 shows the frequency distribution of digrams in a file containing 67,375 letters (all letters were converted to uppercase). The file contained the preface of this book and other documents†. Note that the digrams TH and HE, which occur in the word THE, are in the highest group.

---

†Six ACM President's Letters and a grant proposal.

FIGURE 2.1 Frequency distribution of digrams.

	A	B	C	D	E	F	G	H	I	J	K	L	M	N	O	P	Q	R	S	T	U	V	W	X	Y	Z
A	•	−	−	−	•	•	−	•	−	•	•	+	−	*	•	−	•	+	+	*	•	−	•	•	•	•
B	•	•	•		−			•	•	•		−	•		−	•			•	•	•	•	•	•		−
C	+	•	•	•	+	•	•	+	+	•	•	•	•	•	+	•	•	−	•	−	−		•		•	
D	−	•	•	•	+	•	•	•	+	•	•	•	•	−	•	•	•	−	−	−	−	•	•	•	•	
E	+	−	+	+	−	−	−	−	•	•	−	•	•	+	+	*	−	*	*	+	•	−	−	−	•	•
F	−	•	•	•	•	−	−	•	•		•	•	•	•	+	•	•	•	•	•	−	•	•	•	•	•
G	−	•	•	•	−	•	•	•	•		•	•	•	•	•	•	•	•	•	−	•	•	•	•	•	•
H	+	•	•	•	*	•	•	•	•	−		•	•	•	−	•	•	•	•	•	•	+	•	•	•	•
I	−	•	+	−	+	−	−	•	•		•	−	−	*	+	•	•	−	+	+		−	•	•		•
J	•			•	•			•						•				•		•						
K	•	•	•		−	•	•	•	•			•	•	•	•	•		•	•	•	•	•	•		•	
L	−	•	•	−	+	•	•	•	−		•	+	•	•	−	•	•	•	−	−	−	•	•	•	•	−
M	+	•	•	•	+	•	•	•	−			•	•	−	•	−	•	+	•	•	•	•	•	•	•	•
N	−	•	+	+	+	−	+	•	−	•	•	•	•	•	+	•	•	•	+	*	•	•	•	•	•	•
O	−	−	−	−	•	+	−	•	•	•	•	−	+	*	−	−	•	+	−	−	+	−	−	•	•	•
P	−		•	•	•	•	•	−	•	•	•	−	•	•	−	−		+	•	−	−		•		•	•
Q																					−					
R	+	•	−	−	*	•	•	•	+	•	•	•	•	−	•	+	•	•	•	•	+	+	•	•	−	•
S	+	−	+	•	+	−	•	−	+	•	•	•	•	−	•	+	−	•	•	−	•	*	−	•	−	−
T	+	•	•	•	*	•	•	*	*	•	•	•	•	•	+	•	•	−	+	−	−	•	−			−
U	−	•	−	•	−	•	•	•	•		•	−	•	−	•	•		−	−	−		•	•	•		
V	•				+				−				•	•		•			•						•	
W	−	•	•	•	−	•	−	−	•	•	•	•	•	−	•			•	•	•	•		•		•	•
X	•	•	•		•	•		•	•		•		•		•	−		•	•	•	•		•			
Y	−	•	•	•	•	•		•	•	•	•	•	•	−	•	•		•	•	−	−	•	•		•	•
Z	•			•				•				•						•								•

Maximum digram frequency = 2.31 % of the digrams

Key: * High: more than 1.15 % of the digrams
 + Medium: more than 0.46 % of the digrams
 − Low: more than 0.12 % of the digrams
 · Rare: more than 0.00 % of the digrams
 blank: no occurrences

To determine the expected number of characters required to break a permutation cipher with period d, observe that there are $d!$ possible arrangements of d characters. Assuming all keys (i.e., arrangements) are equally likely, the entropy of the key is thus $H(K) = \log_2 d!$ Using Eq. (1.4), the unicity distance is thus:

$$N = \frac{H(K)}{D} = \frac{\log_2 d!}{D}.$$

Using Sterling's approximation for $d!$, we get

$$N \cong \frac{d \log_2\left(\frac{d}{e}\right)}{3.2}$$

$$= .3d \log_2\left(\frac{d}{e}\right)$$

taking $D = 3.2$ bits/letter as the redundancy of English.

Example:
If the period is $d = 27$, then $d/e \cong 10$ and $\log_2 (d/e) \cong 3.2$, so $N \cong 27$.   ∎

2.2 SIMPLE SUBSTITUTION CIPHERS

There are four types of substitution ciphers: simple substitution, homophonic substitution, polyalphabetic substitution, and polygram substitution. Simple substitution ciphers replace each character of plaintext with a corresponding character of ciphertext; a single one-to-one mapping from plaintext to ciphertext characters is used to encipher an entire message. Homophonic substitution ciphers are similar, except the mapping is one-to-many, and each plaintext character is enciphered with a variety of ciphertext characters. Polyalphabetic substitution ciphers use multiple mappings from plaintext to ciphertext characters; the mappings are usually one-to-one as in simple substitution. Polygram substitution ciphers are the most general, permitting arbitrary substitutions for groups of characters.

A **simple substitution cipher** replaces each character of an ordered **plaintext alphabet**, denoted $\mathcal{A}$, with the corresponding character of an ordered **cipher alphabet**, denoted C (typically C is a simple rearrangement of the lexicographic order of the characters in $\mathcal{A}$). Let $\mathcal{A}$ be an n-character alphabet $\{a_0, a_1, \ldots, a_{n-1}\}$. Then C is an n-character alphabet $\{f(a_0), f(a_1), \ldots, f(a_{n-1})\}$, where $f: \mathcal{A} \to C$ is a one-to-one mapping of each character of $\mathcal{A}$ to the corresponding character of C. The key to the cipher is given by C or, equivalently, by the function f.

To encipher, a plaintext message $M = m_1 m_2 \ldots$ is written as the ciphertext message:

$$E_K(M) = f(m_1)f(m_2) \ldots .$$

Example:
Suppose that f maps the standard English alphabet $\mathcal{A} = \{A, B, \ldots, Z\}$ into the cipher alphabet C shown next:

$\mathcal{A}$: A B C D E F G H I J K L M N O P Q R S T U V W X Y Z
C: H A R P S I C O D B E F G J K L M N Q T U V W X Y Z .

Then the plaintext RENAISSANCE is enciphered as:

$$M = RENAISSANCE$$
$$E_K(M) = NSJHDQQHJRS. \quad \blacksquare$$

The preceding example uses a **keyword mixed alphabet**: the cipher alphabet is constructed by first listing the letters of a keyword (in this case HARPSI-CHORD), omitting duplicates, and then listing the remaining letters of the alphabet in order.

Ciphers based on **shifted alphabets** (sometimes called "direct standard alphabets" [Sink66]) shift the letters of the alphabet to the right by k positions, modulo the size of the alphabet. Formally,

$$f(a) = (a + k) \bmod n ,$$

where n is the size of the alphabet $\mathcal{A}$, and "a" denotes both a letter of $\mathcal{A}$ and its position in $\mathcal{A}$. For the standard English alphabet, $n = 26$ and the positions of the letters are as follows:

0 – A	7 – H	13 – N	20 – U
1 – B	8 – I	14 – O	21 – V
2 – C	9 – J	15 – P	22 – W
3 – D	10 – K	16 – Q	23 – X
4 – E	11 – L	17 – R	24 – Y
5 – F	12 – M	18 – S	25 – Z
6 – G		19 – T	

We noted in Chapter 1 that this type of cipher is called a **Caesar cipher**, because Julius Caesar used it with $k = 3$. Under the Caesar cipher, our plaintext RENAISSANCE is enciphered as

$$M = RENAISSANCE$$
$$E_K(M) = UHQDLVVDQFH.$$

More complex transformations of the plaintext alphabet are possible. Ciphers based on multiplications (sometimes called "decimations" [Sink66]) of the standard alphabet multiply each character by a key k; that is,

$$f(a) = ak \bmod n ,$$

where k and n are relatively prime so that the letters of the alphabet produce a complete set of residues (see Section 1.6.2).

Example:
If $k = 9$ and $\mathcal{A}$ is the standard English alphabet, we have

$$\mathcal{A} = ABC \ DEF \ GHI \ JKL \ MNO \ PQR \ STU \ VWX \ YZ$$
$$\mathcal{C} = AJS \ BKT \ CLU \ DMV \ ENW \ FOX \ GPY \ HQZ \ IR ,$$

whence

$$M = RENAISSANCE$$
$$E_K(M) = XKNAUGGANSK. \quad \blacksquare$$

FIGURE 2.2 Churchyard cipher.

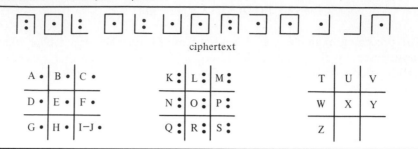

If k and n are not relatively prime, several plaintext letters will encipher to the same ciphertext letter, and not all letters will appear in the ciphertext alphabet. For example, if $n = 26$ and $k = 13$,

$$f(A) = f(C) = f(E) = \cdots = f(Y) = A\ (0)$$
$$f(B) = f(D) = f(F) = \cdots = f(Z) = N\ (13)\ .$$

Addition (shifting) and multiplication can be combined to give an **affine transformation** (linear plus a constant):

$$f(a) = (ak_1 + k_0) \bmod n\ ,$$

where k_1 and n are relatively prime.

Higher-order transformations are obtained with **polynomial transformations** of degree t:

$$f(a) = (a^t k_t + a^{t-1} k_{t-1} + \cdots + ak_1 + k_0) \bmod n\ .$$

Caesar ciphers are polynomial transformations of degree 0, while affine transformations are of degree 1.

Some substitution ciphers use nonstandard ciphertext alphabets. For example, the Churchyard cipher shown in Figure 2.2 was engraved on a tombstone in Trinity Churchyard, New York, in 1794 [Kruh77]. The key to the cipher is given by the "tic-tac-toe" diagrams. The solution is left as an exercise to the reader. A similar cipher was also engraved on a tombstone in St. Paul's Churchyard, New York, in 1796. The first published solution to the ciphers appeared in the *New York Herald* in 1896—over 100 years later.

Messages have also been encoded in musical symbols [Sam79]. A common method was a simple substitution of individual notes for letters. Several composers used such schemes to encode the names of people into their works, and then build themes around the encoding. Bach, for example, incorporated his own name (which in German usage can be written $B^\flat$-A-C-B) into the "Musical Offering" and the "Art of the Fugue".

Let us now calculate the number of letters needed to break general substitution alphabets of size n. Observe that the number of possible keys is $n!$—the number of ways of arranging the n letters of the alphabet. If all keys are equally likely, the unicity distance is

$$N \simeq \frac{H(K)}{D} = \frac{\log_2 n!}{D} .$$

For English, $N \simeq \log_2 26!/3.2 \simeq 88.4/3.2 \simeq 27.6$. Thus, approximately 27 or 28 letters are needed to break these ciphers by frequency analysis. This explains the difficulty in solving the Churchyard ciphers, which contained only 15 characters. In practice, ciphers with at least 25 characters representing a "sensible" message in English can be readily solved [Frie67].

Ciphers based on polynomial transformations have smaller unicity distances and are easier to solve. For shifted alphabets, the number of possible keys is only 26; the unicity distance, derived in Section 1.4.3; is:

$$N \simeq \frac{\log_2 26}{3.2} \simeq 1.5 .$$

FIGURE 2.3 Frequency distribution of letters.

Char	Expected	Actual %	
A	8.0	7.5	***************
B	1.5	1.4	***
C	3.0	4.1	********
D	4.0	3.2	******
E	13.0	12.7	*************************
F	2.0	2.3	*****
G	1.5	1.9	****
H	6.0	3.8	********
I	6.5	7.7	***************
J	0.5	0.2	
K	0.5	0.4	*
L	3.5	3.8	********
M	3.0	3.0	******
N	7.0	7.0	**************
O	8.0	7.5	***************
P	2.0	3.0	******
Q	0.2	0.2	
R	6.5	6.7	*************
S	6.0	7.3	***************
T	9.0	9.2	******************
U	3.0	2.8	******
V	1.0	1.0	**
W	1.5	1.4	***
X	0.5	0.3	*
Y	2.0	1.6	***
Z	0.2	0.1	

Each * represents 0.5 percent.
Number of Letters = 67375

2.2.1 Single-Letter Frequency Analysis

Simple substitution ciphers are generally easy to break in a ciphertext-only attack using single-letter frequency distributions. Figure 2.3 shows the frequency distribution of the letters in the file used previously for Figure 2.1. The letters had a slightly different distribution than expected based on other sources; for comparison, the percentages in a commonly used table described in Kahn [Kahn67] are shown alongside the actual percentages.

Kahn partitions the letters into subsets of high, medium, low, and rare frequency of usage as shown in Figure 2.4. Other sources give slightly different frequency distributions, but the letters fall into these same general categories. Except for H (which was too low) and P (which was too high), our letters also fell into these categories.

Computer files may have a frequency distribution quite different from that of English text. Figure 2.5 shows the distribution of ASCII characters in the Pascal program that computed the frequency distributions. Note the large number of blanks.

By comparing the letter frequencies in a given ciphertext with the expected frequencies, a cryptanalyst can match the ciphertext letters with the plaintext letters. Digram and trigram distributions are also helpful.

Ciphers based on shifted alphabets are usually easy to solve, because each ciphertext letter is a constant distance from its corresponding plaintext letter.

Ciphers based on affine transformations of the form

$$f(a) = (ak_1 + k_0) \bmod n$$

are somewhat trickier [Sink66]. If a set of t correspondences (or suspected correspondences) between plaintext letters m_i and ciphertext letters c_i ($1 \leq i \leq t$), then it may be possible to determine the multiplier k_1 and shift factor k_0 by solving the system of equations:

$$(m_1 k_1 + k_0) \bmod n = c_1$$
$$\vdots$$
$$(m_t k_1 + k_0) \bmod n = c_t .$$

Example:
Consider the following plaintext-ciphertext letter correspondences (the numbers in parentheses are the numerical equivalents):

FIGURE 2.4 Partitioning of letters by frequency.

high:	E T A O N I R S H
medium:	D L U C M
low:	P F Y W G B V
rare:	J K Q X Z

Plaintext	Ciphertext
E (4)	K (10)
J (9)	T (19)
N (13)	U (20)

This gives the three equations:

$$(4k_1 + k_0) \bmod 26 = 10 \quad (1)$$
$$(9k_1 + k_0) \bmod 26 = 19 \quad (2)$$
$$(13k_1 + k_0) \bmod 26 = 20 \quad (3)$$

Subtracting Eq. (1) from Eq. (2), we get

$$5k_1 \bmod 26 = 9 \ .$$

We can solve for k_1 using Eq. (1.6) (see Section 1.6.2), getting

$$k_1 = [9 * inv(5, 26)] \bmod 26$$
$$= (9 * 21) \bmod 26$$
$$= 7 \ .$$

Substituting in Eq. (1) gives

$$(28 + k_0) \bmod 26 = 10 \ ,$$

whence

$$k_0 = -18 \bmod 26 = 8 \ .$$

Note that we did not need Eq. (3) to solve for k_1 and k_0. We must, however, check that the solution satisfies Eq. (3). If it does not, then at least one of the three plaintext-ciphertext correspondences is incorrect (or else the cipher is not an affinc transformation). In this case, the key does satisfy Eq. (3). ∎

In general, we may need more than two equations to solve for k_0 and k_1. This is because equations of the form "$ak \bmod 26 = c$" have multiple solutions when a divides 26 (see Section 1.6.2).

Peleg and Rosenfeld [Pele79] describe a relaxation algorithm for solving general substitution ciphers. For each plaintext letter a and ciphertext letter b, an initial probability $Pr[f(a) = b]$ is computed based on single-letter frequencies, where $Pr[f(a) = b]$ is the probability that plaintext letter a is enciphered as b. These probabilities are then iteratively updated using trigram frequencies until the algorithm converges to a solution (set of high probability pairings).

2.3 HOMOPHONIC SUBSTITUTION CIPHERS

A **homophonic substitution cipher** maps each character a of the plaintext alphabet into a set of ciphertext elements $f(a)$ called **homophones**. Thus the mapping f from plaintext to ciphertext is of the form $f: \mathcal{A} \rightarrow 2^C$. A plaintext message $M = m_1m_2$ . . . is enciphered as $C = c_1c_2$ . . . , where each c_i is picked at random from the set of homophones $f(m_i)$.

FIGURE 2.5 Distribution of ASCII characters in frequency analysis program.

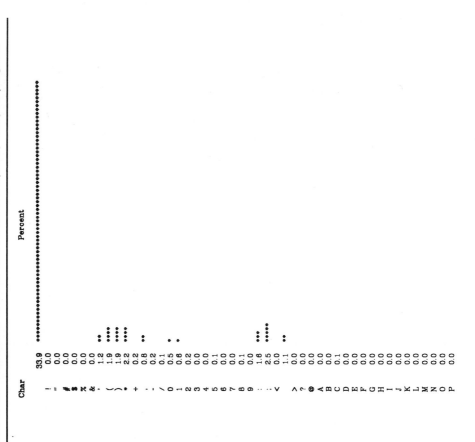

68

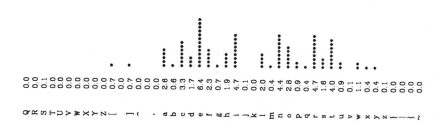

Number of Characters in Sequence = 2449

Index of Coincidence = .13393

Example:
Suppose that the English letters are enciphered as integers between 0 and 99, where the number of integers assigned to a letter is proportional to the relative frequency of the letter, and no integer is assigned to more than one letter. The following illustrates a possible assignment of integers to the letters in the message PLAIN PILOT (for brevity, integer assignments for the remaining letters of the alphabet are not given):

Letter	Homophones
A	17 19 34 41 56 60 67 83
I	08 22 53 65 88 90
L	03 44 76
N	02 09 15 27 32 40 59
O	01 11 23 28 42 54 70 80
P	33 91
T	05 10 20 29 45 58 64 78 99

One possible encipherment of the message is:

$$M = \text{P L A I N P I L O T}$$
$$C = \text{91 44 56 65 59 33 08 76 28 78} \quad . \quad \blacksquare$$

Kahn [Kahn67] notes the first known Western use of a homophonic cipher appears in correspondence between the Duchy of Mantua and Simeone de Crema in 1401. Multiple substitutions were assigned only to vowels; consonants were assigned single substitutions.

Homophonic ciphers can be much more difficult to solve than simple substitution ciphers, especially when the number of homophones assigned to a letter is proportional to the relative frequency of the letter. This is because the relative distribution of the ciphertext symbols will be nearly flat, confounding frequency analysis. A homophonic cipher may still be breakable, however, if other statistical properties of the plaintext (e.g., digram distributions) are apparent in the ciphertext (e.g., see [Prat42,Stah73]).

Clearly, the more ciphertext symbols available to distribute among the plaintext letters, the easier it is to construct a strong cipher. In the limiting case where each letter of plaintext enciphers into a unique ciphertext symbol, the cipher can be unbreakable.

2.3.1 Beale Ciphers

For over a century amateur cryptanalysts have been trying to solve a cipher purported to point to a treasure buried in Virginia around 1820 by a party of adventurers led by Thomas Jefferson Beale. The cipher is the first of three ciphers left by Beale. The second cipher, solved by James Ward [Ward85] in the 1880s, describes the alleged treasure and states that the first cipher contains directions for finding it. The treasure consists of gold, silver, and jewels worth millions of

FIGURE 2.6 Declaration of Independence (first 107 words).

---

 (1) When, in the course of human events, it becomes necessary
(11) for one people to dissolve the political bands which have
(21) connected them with another, and to assume among the Powers
(31) of the earth the separate and equal station to which
(41) the Laws of Nature and of Nature's God entitle them,
(51) a decent respect to the opinions of mankind requires that
(61) they should declare the causes which impel them to the
(71) separation. We hold these truths to be self-evident; that
(81) all men are created equal, that they are endowed by
(91) their Creator with certain unalienable rights; that among
(99) these are Life, Liberty, and the pursuit of Happiness.

---

dollars today. The third cipher is supposed to list the next of kin of the adventurers.

The second cipher (B2) is an interesting example of a homophonic substitution cipher. The key is the Declaration of Independence (DOI). The words of the DOI are numbered consecutively as shown in Figure 2.6.

Beale enciphered each letter in the plaintext message by substituting the number of some word which started with that letter. The letter W, for example, was enciphered with the numbers 1, 19, 40, 66, 72, 290, and 459. The cipher begins

   115 73 24 818 37 52 49 17 31 62 657 22 7 15 ,

which deciphers to "I have deposited . . .".

The first cipher (B1) has been "solved"—allegedly—by several persons, using techniques for solving homophonics plus anagramming to make the "solution" fit. No one admits having found the treasure, however, and there is considerable speculation that the whole thing is a hoax. Gillogly [Gill80] found a strange anomaly in B1, which he believes supports the hoax hypothesis. He deciphered B1 using the initial letters of the DOI, and discovered the sequence

   ABFDEFGHIIJKLMMNOHPP

in the middle of the plaintext. Gillogly observed that the first F is encrypted as 195 and that word 194 begins with a C; similarly, the last H is encrypted as 301 and word 302 begins with an O. Hammer [Hamm79] found 23 encrypting errors in B1, so it is possible the F (for C) and H (for O) were "typos", and the original plaintext sequence was ABCDEFGHIIJKLMMNOOPP. Perhaps the sequence is a clue that the DOI is the key—not to abundant riches—but to a gigantic practical joke.

Meanwhile, members of the Beale Cipher Association pool their findings, hoping to either locate the treasure or simply solve the riddle. More information about these fascinating ciphers may also be found in [Beal78,Hamm71].

2.3.2 Higher-Order Homophonics

Given enough ciphertext C, most ciphers are theoretically breakable (in the Shannon sense—doing so may be computationally infeasible). This is because there will be a single key K that deciphers C into meaningful plaintext; all other keys will produce meaningless sequences of letters. Hammer [Hamm81] shows it is possible to construct higher-order homophonic ciphers such that any intercepted ciphertext will decipher into more than one meaningful message under different keys. For example, a ciphertext could decipher into the following two messages under different keys:

THE TREASURE IS BURIED IN GOOSE CREEK

THE BEALE CIPHERS ARE A GIGANTIC HOAX.

To construct a second-order homophonic cipher (one in which each ciphertext has two possible plaintext messages), the numbers 1 through n^2 are randomly inserted into an $n \times n$ matrix K whose rows and columns correspond to the characters of the plaintext alphabet $\mathcal{A}$. For each plaintext character a, row a of K defines one set of homophones $f_1(a)$ and column a defines another set of homophones $f_2(a)$. The set of rows thus corresponds to one key (mapping) f_1 and the set of columns to a second key f_2. A plaintext message $M = m_1 m_2 \ldots$ is enciphered along with a dummy message $X = x_1 x_2 \ldots$ to get ciphertext $C = c_1 c_2 \ldots$, where

$$c_i = K[m_i, x_i] \quad i = 1, 2, \ldots .$$

Each ciphertext element c_i is thus selected from the intersection of the sets $f_1(m_i)$ and $f_2(x_i)$ and, therefore, deciphers to either m_i (under key f_1) or x_i (under f_2). A cryptanalyst cannot deduce the correct message from the ciphertext C because both M and X are equally likely. The intended recipient of the message can, however, decipher C knowing K.

Example:
Let $n = 5$. The following illustrates a 5×5 matrix for the plaintext alphabet $\{E, I, L, M, S\}$:

	E	I	L	M	S
E	10	22	18	02	11
I	12	01	25	05	20
L	19	06	23	13	07
M	03	16	08	24	15
S	17	09	21	14	04

The message SMILE is enciphered with the dummy message LIMES as follows:

$$
\begin{aligned}
M &= S \quad M \quad I \quad L \quad E \\
X &= L \quad I \quad M \quad E \quad S \\
C &= 21 \quad 16 \quad 05 \quad 19 \quad 11 \; . \quad \blacksquare
\end{aligned}
$$

Hammer investigated the possibility of B1 being a second-order homophonic. Beale might have enciphered messages M and X using two documents—for example, the DOI for M and the Magna Carta (MC) for X. Each ciphertext element c_i would then be some number j such that the jth word of the DOI begins with m_i and the jth word of the MC begins with x_i. Hammer deduced, however, that Beale had probably not used this method.

2.4 POLYALPHABETIC SUBSTITUTION CIPHERS

Because simple substitution ciphers use a single mapping from plaintext to ciphertext letters, the single-letter frequency distribution of the plaintext letters is preserved in the ciphertext. Homophonic substitutions conceal this distribution by defining multiple ciphertext elements for each plaintext letter. **Polyalphabetic substitution ciphers** conceal it by using multiple substitutions.

FIGURE 2.7 Cipher disk.

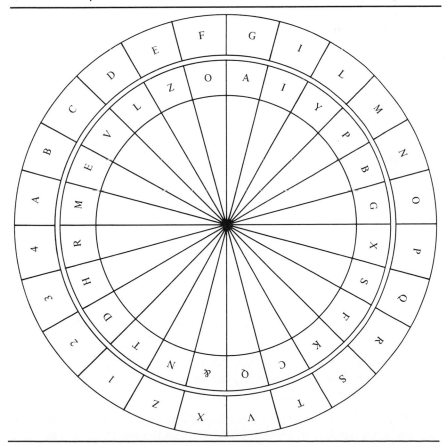

The development of polyalphabetic ciphers began with Leon Battista Alberti, the father of Western cryptography [Kahn67]. In 1568, Alberti published a manuscript describing a cipher disk that defined multiple substitutions (see Figure 2.7). In the outer circle Alberti placed 20 plaintext letters (H, K, and Y were not used and J, U, and W were not part of the Latin alphabet) and the numbers 1–4 (for special codes). In the movable inner circle he randomly placed the letters of the Latin alphabet plus "&". The disk thus defined 24 possible substitutions from the plaintext letters in the outer ring to the ciphertext letters in the inner ring, depending on the position of the disks. Alberti's important insight was his realization that the substitution could be changed during encipherment by turning the inner disk.

Most polyalphabetic ciphers are **periodic substitution ciphers** based on a period d. Given d cipher alphabets $C_1, \ldots, C_d$, let $f_i : A \rightarrow C_i$ be a mapping from the plaintext alphabet A to the ith cipher alphabet C_i ($1 \leq i \leq d$). A plaintext message

$$M = m_1 \ldots m_d \, m_{d+1} \ldots m_{2d} \ldots$$

is enciphered by repeating the sequence of mappings $f_1, \ldots, f_d$ every d characters:

$$E_K(M) = f_1(m_1) \ldots f_d(m_d) \, f_1(m_{d+1}) \ldots f_d(m_{2d}) \ldots .$$

For the special case $d = 1$, the cipher is **monoalphabetic** and equivalent to simple substitution.

2.4.1 Vigenère and Beaufort Ciphers

A popular form of periodic substitution cipher based on shifted alphabets is the **Vigenère cipher**. As noted by Kahn [Kahn67], this cipher has been falsely attributed to the 16th Century French cryptologist Blaise de Vigenère. The key K is specified by a sequence of letters:

$$K = k_1 \ldots k_d \, ,$$

where k_i ($i = 1, \ldots, d$) gives the amount of shift in the ith alphabet; that is,

$$f_i(a) = (a + k_i) \bmod n .$$

Example:
The encipherment of the word RENAISSANCE under the key BAND is shown next:

$$
\begin{aligned}
M \quad &= \text{RENA\ \ ISSA\ \ NCE} \\
K \quad &= \text{BAND\ \ BAND\ \ BAN} \\
E_K(M) &= \text{SEAD\ \ \ JSFD\ \ OCR} .
\end{aligned}
$$

In this example, the first letter of each four-letter group is shifted (mod 26) by 1, the second by 0, the third by 13, and the fourth by 3. ■

TABLE 2.1 Vigenère Tableau.

Plaintext

	A	B	C	D	E	F	G	H	I	J	K	L	M	N	O	P	Q	R	S	T	U	V	W	X	Y	Z
A	A	B	C	D	E	F	G	H	I	J	K	L	M	N	O	P	Q	R	S	T	U	V	W	X	Y	Z
B	B	C	D	E	F	G	H	I	J	K	L	M	N	O	P	Q	R	S	T	U	V	W	X	Y	Z	A
C	C	D	E	F	G	H	I	J	K	L	M	N	O	P	Q	R	S	T	U	V	W	X	Y	Z	A	B
D	D	E	F	G	H	I	J	K	L	M	N	O	P	Q	R	S	T	U	V	W	X	Y	Z	A	B	C
E	E	F	G	H	I	J	K	L	M	N	O	P	Q	R	S	T	U	V	W	X	Y	Z	A	B	C	D
F	F	G	H	I	J	K	L	M	N	O	P	Q	R	S	T	U	V	W	X	Y	Z	A	B	C	D	E
G	G	H	I	J	K	L	M	N	O	P	Q	R	S	T	U	V	W	X	Y	Z	A	B	C	D	E	F
H	H	I	J	K	L	M	N	O	P	Q	R	S	T	U	V	W	X	Y	Z	A	B	C	D	E	F	G
I	I	J	K	L	M	N	O	P	Q	R	S	T	U	V	W	X	Y	Z	A	B	C	D	E	F	G	H
J	J	K	L	M	N	O	P	Q	R	S	T	U	V	W	X	Y	Z	A	B	C	D	E	F	G	H	I
K	K	L	M	N	O	P	Q	R	S	T	U	V	W	X	Y	Z	A	B	C	D	E	F	G	H	I	J
L	L	M	N	O	P	Q	R	S	T	U	V	W	X	Y	Z	A	B	C	D	E	F	G	H	I	J	K
Key M	M	N	O	P	Q	R	S	T	U	V	W	X	Y	Z	A	B	C	D	E	F	G	H	I	J	K	L
N	N	O	P	Q	R	S	T	U	V	W	X	Y	Z	A	B	C	D	E	F	G	H	I	J	K	L	M
O	O	P	Q	R	S	T	U	V	W	X	Y	Z	A	B	C	D	E	F	G	H	I	J	K	L	M	N
P	P	Q	R	S	T	U	V	W	X	Y	Z	A	B	C	D	E	F	G	H	I	J	K	L	M	N	O
Q	Q	R	S	T	U	V	W	X	Y	Z	A	B	C	D	E	F	G	H	I	J	K	L	M	N	O	P
R	R	S	T	U	V	W	X	Y	Z	A	B	C	D	E	F	G	H	I	J	K	L	M	N	O	P	Q
S	S	T	U	V	W	X	Y	Z	A	B	C	D	E	F	G	H	I	J	K	L	M	N	O	P	Q	R
T	T	U	V	W	X	Y	Z	A	B	C	D	E	F	G	H	I	J	K	L	M	N	O	P	Q	R	S
U	U	V	W	X	Y	Z	A	B	C	D	E	F	G	H	I	J	K	L	M	N	O	P	Q	R	S	T
V	V	W	X	Y	Z	A	B	C	D	E	F	G	H	I	J	K	L	M	N	O	P	Q	R	S	T	U
W	W	X	Y	Z	A	B	C	D	E	F	G	H	I	J	K	L	M	N	O	P	Q	R	S	T	U	V
X	X	Y	Z	A	B	C	D	E	F	G	H	I	J	K	L	M	N	O	P	Q	R	S	T	U	V	W
Y	Y	Z	A	B	C	D	E	F	G	H	I	J	K	L	M	N	O	P	Q	R	S	T	U	V	W	X
Z	Z	A	B	C	D	E	F	G	H	I	J	K	L	M	N	O	P	Q	R	S	T	U	V	W	X	Y

The Vigenère Tableau facilitated encryption and decryption (see Table 2.1). For plaintext letter a and key letter k, the ciphertext c is the letter in column a of row k. For ciphertext c, the plaintext a is the column containing c in row k.

The **Beaufort cipher** is similar, using the substitution

$$f_i(a) = (k_i - a) \bmod n.$$

Note that the same function can be used to decipher; that is, for ciphertext letter c,

$$f_i^{-1}(c) = (k_i - c) \bmod n.$$

The Beaufort cipher reverses the letters in the alphabet, and then shifts them to the right by $(k_i + 1)$ positions. This can be seen by rewriting f_i as follows:

$$f_i(a) = [(n - 1) - a + (k_i + 1)] \bmod n.$$

Example:
If $k_i = $ D, the mapping from plaintext to ciphertext letters is given by $f_i(a) = (D - a) \bmod 26$ as shown next:

$$\mathcal{A}: \text{A B C D E F G H I J K L M N O P Q R S T U V W X Y Z}$$

$$\mathcal{C}: \text{D C B A Z Y X W V U T S R Q P O N M L K J I H G F E .} \quad \blacksquare$$

The Vigenère Tableau can be used to encipher and decipher. For plaintext letter a, the ciphertext letter c is the row containing the key k in column a. For ciphertext letter c, the plaintext letter a is the column containing k in row c. The Beaufort cipher is named after the English admiral Sir Francis Beaufort, although it was first proposed by the Italian Giovanni Sestri in 1710 [Kahn67].

The **Variant Beaufort cipher** uses the substitution

$$f_i(a) = (a - k_i) \bmod n.$$

Because

$$(a - k_i) \bmod n = (a + (n - k_i)) \bmod n,$$

the Variant Beaufort cipher is equivalent to a Vigenère cipher with key character $(n - k_i)$.

The Variant Beaufort cipher is also the inverse of the Vigenère cipher; thus if one is used to encipher, the other is used to decipher.

The unicity distance for periodic substitution ciphers is easy to calculate from the individual substitution ciphers. If there are s possible keys for each simple substitution, then there are s^d possible keys if d substitutions are used. The unicity distance is thus

$$N \cong \frac{H(K)}{D} = \frac{\log_2(s^d)}{D} = \frac{\log_2 s}{D} d.$$

If N ciphertext characters are required to break the individual substitution ciphers, then dN characters are required to break the complete cipher. For a Vigenère cipher with period d, $s = 26$, giving

$$N \cong \frac{4.7}{3.2}d \cong 1.5d .$$

To solve a periodic substitution cipher, the cryptanalyst must first determine the period of the cipher. Two tools are helpful: the index of coincidence and the Kasiski method.

2.4.2 Index of Coincidence

The **index of coincidence** (*IC*), introduced in the 1920s by William Friedman [Frie20] (see also [Kahn67]), measures the variation in the frequencies of the letters in the ciphertext. If the period of the cipher is 1 (i.e., simple substitution is used), there will be considerable variation in the letter frequencies and the *IC* will be high. As the period increases, the variation is gradually eliminated (due to diffusion) and the *IC* will be low.

Following Sinkov [Sink66], we shall derive the *IC* by first defining a **measure of roughness** (*MR*), which gives the variation of the frequencies of individual characters relative to a uniform distribution:

$$MR = \sum_{i=0}^{n-1} \left(p_i - \frac{1}{n} \right)^2 ,$$

where p_i is the probability that an arbitrarily chosen character in a random ciphertext is the *i*th character a_i in the alphabet ($i = 0, \ldots, n - 1$), and

$$\sum_{i=0}^{n-1} p_i = 1 .$$

For the English letters we have

$$MR = \sum_{i=0}^{25} \left(p_i - \frac{1}{26} \right)^2$$

$$= \sum_{i=0}^{25} p_i^2 - \frac{2}{26} \sum_{i=0}^{25} p_i + 26 \left(\frac{1}{26} \right)^2$$

$$= \sum_{i=0}^{25} p_i^2 - \frac{2}{26} + \frac{1}{26}$$

$$= \sum_{i=0}^{25} p_i^2 - .038 .$$

Because the period and, therefore, the probabilities are unknown, it is not possible to compute MR. But it is possible to estimate MR using the distribution of letter frequencies in the ciphertext. Observe that

$$MR + .038 = \sum_{i=0}^{25} p_i^2$$

is the probability that two arbitrarily chosen letters from a random ciphertext are the same. Now, the total number of pairs of letters that can be chosen from a given ciphertext of length N is $\binom{N}{2} = N(N-1)/2$. Let F_i be the frequency of the ith letter of English ($i = 0, \ldots, 25$) in the ciphertext; thus, $\sum_{i=0}^{25} F_i = N$. The number of pairs containing just the ith letter is

$$\frac{F_i(F_i - 1)}{2} .$$

The IC is defined to be the probability that two letters chosen at random from the given ciphertext are alike:

$$IC = \frac{\sum_{i=0}^{25} F_i(F_i - 1)}{N(N-1)} .$$

Because this is an estimate of $\sum_{i=0}^{25} p_i^2$, the IC is an estimate of $MR + .038$. But unlike MR, IC can be computed from the ciphertext.

Now, MR ranges from 0 for a flat distribution (infinite period) to .028 for English and ciphers with period 1. Thus, IC varies from .038 for an infinite period to .066 for a period of 1. For a cipher of period d, the expected value of IC is:

$$\left(\frac{1}{d}\right)\frac{N-d}{N-1}(.066) + \left(\frac{d-1}{d}\right)\frac{N}{N-1}(.038) .$$

Table 2.2 shows the expected value of IC for several values of d.

To estimate the period of a given cipher, the cryptanalyst measures the frequencies of the letters in the ciphertext, computes IC using Eq. (2.1), and

TABLE 2.2 Expected index of coincidence.

d	IC
1	.066
2	.052
3	.047
4	.045
5	.044
10	.041
large	.038

finally compares this with the expected values shown in Table 2.2. Because *IC* is statistical in nature, it does not necessarily reveal the period exactly. Nevertheless, it may provide a clue as to whether the cipher is monoalphabetic, polyalphabetic with small period, or polyalphabetic with large period.

2.4.3 Kasiski Method

The **Kasiski method**, introduced in 1863 by the Prussian military officer Friedrich W. Kasiski [Kasi63], analyzes repetitions in the ciphertext to determine the exact period (see also [Kahn67,Gain56]). For example, suppose the plaintext TO BE OR NOT TO BE is enciphered with a Vigenère cipher using key HAM as shown next:

$$M \quad = \text{T O B E O R N O T T O B E}$$
$$K \quad = \text{H A M H A M H A M H A M H}$$
$$E_K(M) = \text{A O N L O D U O F A O N L}$$

Notice that the ciphertext contains two occurrences of the cipher sequence AONL, 9 characters apart.

Repetitions in the ciphertext occur when a plaintext pattern repeats at a distance equal to a multiple of the key length. Repetitions more than two cipher characters long are unlikely to occur by pure chance. If m ciphertext repetitions are found at intervals I_j ($1 \le j \le m$), the period is likely to be some number that divides most of the m intervals. The preceding example has an interval $I_1 = 9$, suggesting a period of 1, 3, or 9 (in fact it is 3).

The *IC* is useful for confirming a period d found by the Kasiski method or by exhaustive search (whereas this would be tedious and time-consuming by hand, a computer can systematically try $d = 1, 2, 3, \ldots$ until the period is found). Letting $c_1 c_2 \ldots$ denote the ciphertext, the *IC* is computed for each of the sequences:

$$1: c_1 \ c_{d+1} \ c_{2d+1} \ \cdots$$
$$2: c_2 \ c_{d+2} \ c_{2d+2} \ \cdots$$
$$\cdot$$
$$\cdot$$
$$\cdot$$
$$d: c_d \ c_{2d} \ \ c_{3d} \ \ \cdots$$

If each sequence is enciphered with one key, each will have an *IC* close to .066. Once the period is determined, each cipher alphabet is separately analyzed as for simple substitution.

Example:
We shall now apply the index of coincidence and Kasiski method to analyze the ciphertext shown in Figure 2.8. Figure 2.9 shows that the frequency distribution of the letters in the ciphertext is flatter than normal, and that the *IC* is .0434; this suggests a polyalphabetic substitution cipher with a period of about 5.

FIGURE 2.8 Sample ciphertext.

```
ZHYME ZVELK OJUBW CEYIN CUSML RAVSR YARNH CEARI UJPGP VARDU
QZCGR NNCAW JALUH GJPJR YGEGQ FULUS QFFPV EYEDQ GOLKA LVOSJ
TFRTR YEJZS RVNCI HYJNM ZDCRO DKHCR MMLNR FFLFN QGOLK ALVOS
JWMIK QKUBP SAYOJ RRQYI NRNYC YQZSY EDNCA LEILX RCHUG IEBKO
YTHGV VCKHC JEQGO LKALV OSJED WEAKS GJHYC LLFTY IGSVT FVPMZ
NRZOL CYUZS FKOQR YRYAR ZFGKI QKRSV IRCEY USKVT MKHCR MYQIL
XRCRL GQARZ OLKHY KSNFN RRNCZ TWUOC JNMKC MDEZP IRJEJ W
```

FIGURE 2.9 Frequency distribution of ciphertext in Figure 2.8.

Char	Percent
A	4.0 ********
B	0.9 **
C	6.1 ************
D	2.0 ****
E	4.9 **********
F	3.5 *******
G	4.0 ********
H	3.2 ******
I	3.5 *******
J	4.6 *********
K	5.2 **********
L	5.8 ************
M	3.2 ******
N	4.6 *********
O	4.0 ********
P	2.0 ****
Q	3.8 ********
R	8.7 *****************
S	4.3 *********
T	2.0 ****
U	3.5 *******
V	4.0 ********
W	1.7 ***
X	0.6 *
Y	6.1 ************
Z	3.8 ********

Number of Characters = 346
Index of Coincidence = .0434

To determine the exact period, we observe there are three occurrences of the 11-character sequence QGOLKALVOSJ (see Figure 2.8), the first two separated by a distance of 51 characters, and the second two by 72 characters. Because 3 is the only common divisor of 51 and 72, the period is almost certain to be 3, even though the IC predicted a somewhat larger period.

Figure 2.10 shows the IC and frequency distribution for each of the sequences.

1: $c_1 \, c_4 \, c_7 \ldots$
2: $c_2 \, c_5 \, c_8 \ldots$
3: $c_3 \, c_6 \, c_9 \ldots$.

Each ciphertext alphabet has an IC near or above .66, confirming the hypothesis that the period is 3.

FIGURE 2.10 Frequency distributions for separate sequences.

Frequency Analysis for Sequence 1			Frequency Analysis for Sequence 2			Frequency Analysis for Sequence 3		
Char	Percent		Char	Percent		Char	Percent	
A	0.0		A	9.6	*********************	A	2.6	*****
B	0.0		B	0.9	**	B	1.7	***
C	6.0	************	C	1.7	***	C	10.4	*********************
D	1.7	***	D	2.6	*****	D	1.7	***
E	4.3	*********	E	10.4	**********************	E	0.0	
F	5.2	**********	F	2.6	*****	F	2.6	*****
G	2.6	*****	G	2.6	*****	G	7.0	**************
H	0.9	**	H	8.7	******************	H	0.0	
I	5.2	**********	I	5.2	**********	I	0.0	
J	8.6	*****************	J	0.0		J	5.2	**********
K	13.8	****************************	K	0.9	**	K	0.9	**
L	1.7	***	L	1.7	***	L	13.9	****************************
M	0.9	**	M	1.7	***	M	7.0	**************
N	0.9	**	N	9.6	*******************	N	3.5	*******
O	0.0		O	12.2	*************************	O	0.0	
P	2.6	*****	P	1.7	***	P	1.7	***
Q	1.7	***	Q	0.0		Q	9.6	*******************
R	9.5	*******************	R	4.3	*********	R	12.2	*************************
S	0.0		S	8.7	******************	S	4.3	*********
T	0.9	**	T	5.2	**********	T	0.0	
U	5.2	**********	U	4.3	*********	U	0.9	**
V	11.2	**********************	V	0.9	**	V	0.0	
W	1.7	***	W	0.9	**	W	2.6	*****
X	1.7	***	X	0.0		X	0.0	
Y	4.3	*********	Y	3.5	*******	Y	10.4	*********************
Z	9.5	*******************	Z	0.0		Z	1.7	***

Number of Characters in Sequence = 116

Index of Coincidence = .06747

Number of Characters in Sequence = 115

Index of Coincidence = .06499

Number of Characters in Sequence = 115

Index of Coincidence = .07597

To determine the type of cipher, we might first consider a simple Vigenère or Beaufort cipher. Looking at the second alphabet, we see a surprising similarity between this distribution and the expected distribution for English letters (see Figure 2.3). This suggests a Vigenère cipher with an A as the second key character, whence the letters c_2, c_5, . . . are already in plaintext. We leave finding the first and third characters and deciphering the text as an exercise for the reader. The plaintext is one of Raymond Smullyan's† gems. ■

2.4.4 Running-Key Ciphers

The security of a substitution cipher generally increases with the key length. In a **running-key cipher**, the key is as long as the plaintext message, foiling a Kasiski attack (assuming the key does not repeat). One method uses the text in a book (or any other document) as a key sequence in a substitution cipher based on shifted alphabets (i.e., a nonperiodic Vigenère cipher). The key is specified by the title of the book and starting position (section, paragraph, etc.).

Example:
Given the starting key: "*Cryptography and Data Security,* Section 2.3.1, paragraph 2," the plaintext message "THE TREASURE IS BURIED . . ." is enciphered as

$$
\begin{aligned}
M &= \text{THETREASURE I SBURIED...} \\
K &= \text{THESECONDC I PHERISAN...} \\
E_K(M) &= \text{MO I LVGOFXTMXZFLZAEQ...}
\end{aligned}
$$

(the string "(B2)" in the text was omitted from the key sequence because some of the characters are not letters). ■

Because perfect secrecy is possible using key sequences as long as the messages they encipher, one might expect a running key cipher to be unbreakable. This is not so. If the key has redundancy (as with English text), the cipher may be breakable using Friedman's methods [Frie18] (see also [Kahn67,Diff79]). Friedman's approach is based on the observation that a large proportion of letters in the ciphertext will correspond to encipherments where both the plaintext and key letters fall in the high frequency category (see Figure 2.4).

Example:
In our earlier example, 12 of the 19 ciphertext letters came from such pairs, as noted next:

$$
\begin{aligned}
M &= \text{THETREASUREISBURIED ...} \\
K &= \text{THESECONDCIPHERISAN .... }
\end{aligned}
$$

---

† R. Smullyan, *This Book Needs No Title,* Prentice-Hall, Englewood Cliffs, N.J., 1980.

Of the remaining 7 pairs, either the plaintext or key letter belongs to the high frequency category in 6 of the pairs, and both belong to the medium category in the remaining pair. ■

Friedman recommends starting with the assumption that all ciphertext letters correspond to high frequency pairs, thus reducing the number of initial possibilities for each plaintext and key letter. The initial guesses are then related to digram and trigram distributions (and possibly probable words) to determine the actual pairings.

Example:
Consider the first three ciphertext letters MOI in the preceding example. There are 26 possible plaintext-key letter pairings for each ciphertext letter (assuming a shifted substitution). Examining the possible pairs for M, we see there are only three pairs where both the plaintext and key character fall in the high frequency category:

plaintext letter: A B C D E F G H I J K L M N O P Q R S T U V W X Y Z
key letter: M L K J I H G F E D C B A Z Y X W V U T S R Q P O N

ciphertext letter: M M M M M M M M M M M M M M M M M M M M M M M M M M

The high frequency pairs for all three letters are:

M	O	I
E–I	A–O	A–I
I–E	O–A	I–A
T–T	H–H	E–E
		R–R

Now, there are 3 * 3 * 4 = 36 possible combinations of the preceding pairs:

```
plaintext:   EAA  EAI  ... THE ... THR
key:         IOI  IOA  ... THE ... THR
ciphertext:  MOI  MOI  ... MOI ... MOI .
```

Many of the trigrams for either the plaintext or key are very unlikely (e.g., EAA and IOI in the first combination). The trigram THE occurring simultaneously in both the plaintext and key is the most likely, and a cryptanalyst making this choice will have correctly guessed the first word of both the plaintext and key. ■

2.4.5 Rotor and Hagelin Machines

Rotor and Hagelin machines implement polyalphabetic substitution ciphers with a long period.

A rotor machine consists of a bank of t rotors or wired wheels. The perimeter of each rotor R_i has 26 electrical contacts (one for each letter of the alphabet) on both its front and rear faces. Each contact on the front face is wired to a contact on the rear face to implement a mapping f_i from plaintext to ciphertext letters. R_i can rotate into 26 positions, and each position alters the mapping. When R_i is in position j_i, the mapping is defined by

$$F_i(a) = (f_i(a - j_i) \bmod 26 + j_i) \bmod 26 .$$

A plaintext letter (signal) enters the bank of rotors at one end, travels through the rotors in succession, and emerges as ciphertext at the other end. A machine with t rotors effectively implements a substitution cipher composed of F_1, $\ldots$, F_t. The ith plaintext letter m_i of a message $M = m_1 m_2 \ldots$ is enciphered as

$$E_{k_i}(m_i) = F_t \circ \ldots \circ F_1(a) ,$$

where k_i consists of the wired mappings $f_1, \ldots, f_t$ and the positions $j_1, \ldots, j_t$ of the rotors.

The wirings plus initial positions of the rotors determine the starting key. As each plaintext letter is enciphered, one or more of the rotors moves to a new position, changing the key. A machine with t rotors does not return to its starting position until after 26^t successive encipherments; a machine with 4 rotors, for example, thus has a period of $26^4 = 456{,}976$ letters; one with 5 rotors has a period of 11,881,376 letters. The Enigma, invented by Arthur Scherbius and used by the Germans up through World War II, uses an odometer rotor motion. The first rotor advances to the next position after each character is enciphered. After it has made a complete rotation, the second rotor advances to its next position. Similarly, after the second rotor has made a complete rotation, the third advances, and so on until all rotors have moved through all positions. (See [Diff79,Kahn67,Konh81, Deav80a,Deav80b] for additional information about these machines, including methods used to break them.)

The Hagelin machines, invented by Boris Hagelin [Kahn67] in the 1920s and 1930s, use keywheels with pins. There are t wheels, and each wheel has p_i pins ($1 \le i \le t$), where the p_i are relatively prime. The Hagelin C-48, for example, has 6 wheels with 17, 19, 21, 23, 25, and 26 pins, respectively. The pins can be pushed either left or right, and the combined setting of the pins and positions of the wheels determine a key. Letting k_i be the key when the ith plaintext character m_i is enciphered, m_i is enciphered as in a Beaufort substitution:

$$E_{k_i}(m_i) = (k_i - m_i) \bmod 26$$

(deciphering is the same). After each ciphertext character is enciphered, all t wheels are rotated one position forward. Because the p_i do not have any common factors, the wheels do not return to their starting position until after $\prod_{i=1}^{t} p_i$ encipherments. The C-48, for example, has a period of over 100 million. Hagelin machines were used extensively during World War II, and are still used today. (See also [Diff79,Kahn67,Bark77,Rive81]).

Although rotor and Hagelin machines generate long key streams, they are not as random as they might seem, and the machines are vulnerable to cryptanalysis (see preceding references). Techniques for generating key streams that seem less vulnerable are described in Chapter 3.

2.4.6 Vernam Cipher and One-Time Pads

If the key to a substitution cipher is a random sequence of characters and is not repeated, there is not enough information to break the cipher. Such a cipher is called a **one-time pad**, as it is only used once.

   The implementation of one-time pads in computer systems is based on an ingenious device designed by Gilbert Vernam in 1917 [Kahn67]. An employee of American Telephone and Telegraph Company (A. T. & T.), Vernam designed a cryptographic device for telegraphic communications based on the 32-character Baudot code of the new teletypewriters developed at A. T. & T. Each character is represented as a combination of five marks and spaces, corresponding to the bits 1 and 0 in digital computers. A nonrepeating random sequence of key characters is punched on paper tape, and each plaintext bit is added modulo 2 to the next key bit. Letting $M = m_1 m_2 \ldots$ denote a plaintext bit stream and $K = k_1 k_2 \ldots$ a key bit stream, the **Vernam cipher** generates a ciphertext bit stream $C = E_K(M) = c_1 c_2$, ..., where

$$c_i = (m_i + k_i) \bmod 2 , \quad i = 1, 2, \ldots .$$

The cipher is thus like a Vigenère cipher over the binary alphabet $\{0, 1\}$.

   The Vernam cipher is efficiently implemented in microelectronics by taking the "exclusive-or" of each plaintext/key pair (see Section 1.6.3):

$$c_i = m_i \oplus k_i .$$

Because $k_i \oplus k_i = 0$ for $k_i = 0$ or 1, deciphering is performed with the same operation:

$$\begin{aligned} c_i \oplus k_i &= m_i \oplus k_i \oplus k_i \\ &= m_i . \end{aligned}$$

Example:
If the plaintext character A (11000 in Baudot) is added to the key character D (10010 in Baudot), the result is:

$$\begin{aligned} M \quad &= 1\ 1\ 0\ 0\ 0 \\ K \quad &= 1\ 0\ 0\ 1\ 0 \\ E_K(M) \quad &= 0\ 1\ 0\ 1\ 0 . \quad \blacksquare \end{aligned}$$

Army cryptologist Major Joseph Mauborgne suggested the one-time use of each key tape, and thus the most formidable cipher of all was born. The only drawback of the cipher is that it requires a long key sequence; we shall return to this problem in the next chapter.

   If the key to a Vernam cipher is repeated, the cipher is equivalent to a running-key cipher with a text as key. To see why, suppose two plaintext streams M and M' are enciphered with a key stream K, generating ciphertext streams C and C', respectively. Then

$$c_i = m_i \oplus k_i,$$
$$c_i' = m_i' \oplus k_i,$$

for $i = 1, 2, \ldots$. Let C'' be a stream formed by taking the $\oplus$ of C and C'; then

$$\begin{aligned} c_i'' &= c_i \oplus c_i' \\ &= m_i \oplus k_i \oplus m_i' \oplus k_i \\ &= m_i \oplus m_i' , \end{aligned}$$

for $i = 1, 2, \ldots$. The stream C'' is thus equivalent to a stream generated by the encipherment of message M with message (key) M' and is no longer unbreakable. Note that this ciphertext is broken by finding the plaintext rather than the key. Of course, once the plaintext is known, the key is easily computed (each $k_i = c_i \oplus m_i$).

2.5 POLYGRAM SUBSTITUTION CIPHERS

All of the preceding substitution ciphers encipher a single letter of plaintext at a time. By enciphering larger blocks of letters, **polygram substitution ciphers** make cryptanalysis harder by destroying the significance of single-letter frequencies.

2.5.1 Playfair Cipher

The **Playfair cipher** is a digram substitution cipher named after the English scientist Lyon Playfair; the cipher was actually invented in 1854 by Playfair's friend, Charles Wheatstone, and was used by the British during World War I [Kahn67]. The key is given by a 5 × 5 matrix of 25 letters (J was not used), such as the one shown in Figure 2.11. Each pair of plaintext letters $m_1 m_2$ is enciphered according to the following rules:

1. If m_1 and m_2 are in the same row, then c_1 and c_2 are the two characters to the right of m_1 and m_2, respectively, where the first column is considered to be to the right of the last column.
2. If m_1 and m_2 are in the same column, then c_1 and c_2 are the two characters

FIGURE 2.11 Key for Playfair cipher.

H	A	R	P	S
I	C	O	D	B
E	F	G	K	L
M	N	Q	T	U
V	W	X	Y	Z

below m_1 and m_2, respectively, where the first row is considered to be below the last row.

3. If m_1 and m_2 are in different rows and columns, then c_1 and c_2 are the other two corners of the rectangle having m_1 and m_2 as corners, where c_1 is in m_1's row and c_2 is in m_2's row.

4. If $m_1 = m_2$, a null letter (e.g., X) is inserted into the plaintext between m_1 and m_2 to eliminate the double.

5. If the plaintext has an odd number of characters, a null letter is appended to the end of the plaintext.

Example:

To encipher the first two letters of RENAISSANCE, observe that R and E are two corners of the rectangle

$$
\begin{array}{ccc}
H & A & R \\
I & C & O \\
E & F & G
\end{array}
$$

They are thus enciphered as the other two corners, H and G. The entire plaintext is enciphered as:

$$
\begin{aligned}
M \quad &= \text{RE NA IS SA NC EX} \\
E_K(M) &= \text{HG WC BH HR WF GV} \quad \blacksquare
\end{aligned}
$$

2.5.2 Hill Cipher

The **Hill cipher** [Hill29] performs a linear transformation on d plaintext characters to get d ciphertext characters. Suppose $d = 2$, and let $M = m_1 m_2$. M is enciphered as $C = E_K(M) = c_1 c_2$, where

$$
\begin{aligned}
c_1 &= (k_{11}m_1 + k_{12}m_2) \bmod n \\
c_2 &= (k_{21}m_1 + k_{22}m_2) \bmod n .
\end{aligned}
$$

Expressing M and C as the column vectors $M = (m_1, m_2)$ and $C = (c_1, c_2)$, this can be written as

$$
C = E_K(M) = KM \bmod n ,
$$

where K is the matrix of coefficients:

$$
\begin{pmatrix} k_{11} & k_{12} \\ k_{21} & k_{22} \end{pmatrix} . \quad \blacksquare
$$

That is,

$$
\begin{pmatrix} c_1 \\ c_2 \end{pmatrix} = \begin{pmatrix} k_{11} & k_{12} \\ k_{21} & k_{22} \end{pmatrix} \begin{pmatrix} m_1 \\ m_2 \end{pmatrix} \bmod n .
$$

Deciphering is done using the inverse matrix K^{-1}:

$$D_K(C) = K^{-1}C \bmod n$$
$$= K^{-1}KM \bmod n$$
$$= M \ ,$$

where $KK^{-1} \bmod n = I$, and I is the 2×2 identity matrix.

Example:
Let n be 26 and let K and K^{-1} be as follows:

$$
\begin{matrix}
K & K^{-1} & & I \\
\begin{pmatrix} 3 & 2 \\ 3 & 5 \end{pmatrix} & \begin{pmatrix} 15 & 20 \\ 17 & 9 \end{pmatrix} \bmod 26 = & & \begin{pmatrix} 1 & 0 \\ 0 & 1 \end{pmatrix} .
\end{matrix}
$$

Suppose we wish to encipher the plaintext message EG, which corresponds to the column vector (4, 6). We compute

$$\begin{pmatrix} c_1 \\ c_2 \end{pmatrix} = \begin{pmatrix} 3 & 2 \\ 3 & 5 \end{pmatrix} \begin{pmatrix} 4 \\ 6 \end{pmatrix} \bmod 26$$
$$= \begin{pmatrix} 24 \\ 16 \end{pmatrix} ,$$

getting the ciphertext $C = (24, 16)$ or YQ. To decipher, we compute

$$\begin{pmatrix} 15 & 20 \\ 17 & 9 \end{pmatrix} \begin{pmatrix} 24 \\ 16 \end{pmatrix} \bmod 26 = \begin{pmatrix} 4 \\ 6 \end{pmatrix} . \quad \blacksquare$$

Because the enciphering transformation is linear, it may be possible to solve for the key with just a few characters of known plaintext. Suppose $d = 2$, and the cryptanalyst has the following correspondences of plaintext and ciphertext:

$$M_1 = (m_1, m_2), \ C_1 = (c_1, c_2)$$
$$M_2 = (m_3, m_4), \ C_2 = (c_3, c_4) \ .$$

Let M and C be the following matrices of column vectors:

$$M = (M_1, M_2) = \begin{pmatrix} m_1 & m_3 \\ m_2 & m_4 \end{pmatrix}$$
$$C = (C_1, C_2) = \begin{pmatrix} c_1 & c_3 \\ c_2 & c_4 \end{pmatrix} .$$

We have

$$C = KM \bmod n \ .$$

If M is nonsingular, the cryptanalyst can compute its inverse and solve for K:

$$K = CM^{-1} \bmod n \ .$$

This strategy can be applied for any d, and requires only $O(d^3)$ operations to compute the inverse.

2.6 PRODUCT CIPHERS

A **product cipher** E is the composition of t functions (ciphers) $F_1, \ldots, F_t$, where each F_i may be a substitution or transposition. Rotor machines are product ciphers, where F_i is implemented by rotor R_i $(1 \leq i \leq t)$.

2.6.1 Substitution-Permutation Ciphers

Shannon [Shan49] proposed composing different kinds of functions to create "mixing transformations", which randomly distribute the meaningful messages uniformly over the set of all possible ciphertext messages. Mixing transformations could be created, for example, by applying a transposition followed by an alternating sequence of substitutions and simple linear operations.

This approach is embodied in the LUCIFER cipher, designed at IBM by Feistel [Feis73]. LUCIFER uses a transformation that alternately applies substitutions and transpositions.

Figure 2.12 illustrates how the basic principle is applied to 12-bit blocks (in practice, longer blocks should be used). The cipher alternatively applies substitutions S_i and permutations P_i, giving

$$C = E_K(M) = S_t \circ P_{t-1} \circ \ldots \circ S_2 \circ P_1 \circ S_1(M) \ ,$$

where each S_i is a function of the key K. The substitutions S_i are broken into 4 smaller substitutions $S_{i1}, \ldots, S_{i4}$, each operating on a 3-bit subblock to reduce the complexity of the microelectronic circuits. Because the permutations P_i shuffle all

FIGURE 2.12 Substitution-permutation cipher.

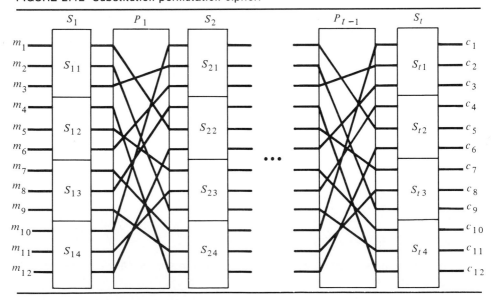

FIGURE 2.13 DES enciphering algorithm.

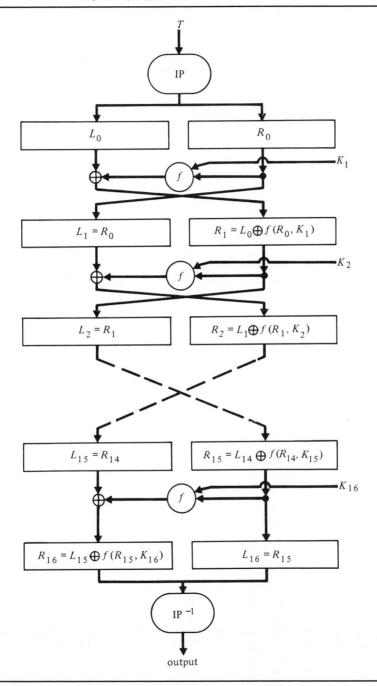

12-bits, each bit of plaintext can conceivably affect each bit of ciphertext. (See [Feis70,Feis75,Kam78] for details on the design of substitution-permutation ciphers.)

2.6.2 The Data Encryption Standard (DES)

In 1977 the National Bureau of Standards announced a Data Encryption Standard to be used in unclassified U.S. Government applications [NBS77]. The encryption algorithm was developed at IBM, and was the outgrowth of LUCIFER.

DES enciphers 64-bit blocks of data with a 56-bit key. There is disagreement over whether a 56-bit key is sufficiently strong; we shall discuss this controversy after describing the algorithm.

The algorithm—which is used both to encipher and to decipher—is summarized in Figure 2.13. An input block T is first transposed under an initial permutation IP, giving $T_0 = IP(T)$. After it has passed through 16 iterations of a function f, it is transposed under the inverse permutation IP^{-1} to give the final result. The permutations IP and IP^{-1} are given in Tables 2.3(a) and 2.3(b), respectively. These tables (as well as the other permutation tables described later) should be read left-to-right, top-to-bottom. For example, IP transposes $T = t_1 t_2 \ldots t_{64}$ into $T_0 = t_{58} t_{50} \ldots t_7$. All tables are fixed.

Between the initial and final transpositions, the algorithm performs 16 iterations of a function f that combines substitution and transposition. Let T_i denote the result of the ith iteration, and let L_i and R_i denote the left and right halves of T_i, respectively; that is, $T_i = L_i R_i$, where

$$L_i = t_1 \ldots t_{32}$$
$$R_i = t_{33} \ldots t_{64} .$$

Then

$$L_i = R_{i-1}$$
$$R_i = L_{i-1} \oplus f(R_{i-1}, K_i)$$

where "$\oplus$" is the exclusive-or operation and K_i is a 48-bit key described later. Note that after the last iteration, the left and right halves are not exchanged; instead the

TABLE 2.3(a) Initial permutation IP.

58	50	42	34	26	18	10	2
60	52	44	36	28	20	12	4
62	54	46	38	30	22	14	6
64	56	48	40	32	24	16	8
57	49	41	33	25	17	9	1
59	51	43	35	27	19	11	3
61	53	45	37	29	21	13	5
63	55	47	39	31	23	15	7

TABLE 2.3(b) Final permutation IP^{-1}.

40	8	48	16	56	24	64	32
39	7	47	15	55	23	63	31
38	6	46	14	54	22	62	30
37	5	45	13	53	21	61	29
36	4	44	12	52	20	60	28
35	3	43	11	51	19	59	27
34	2	42	10	50	18	58	26
33	1	41	9	49	17	57	25

FIGURE 2.14 Calculation of $f(R_{i-1}, K_i)$.

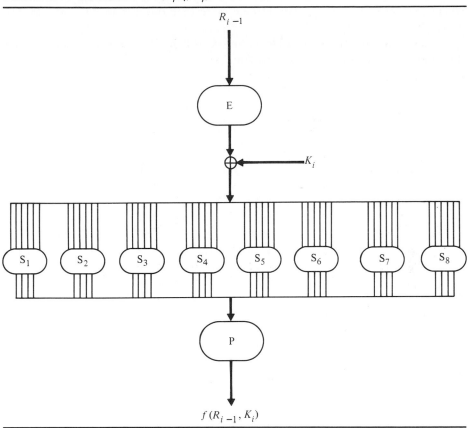

$$f(R_{i-1}, K_i)$$

concatenated block $R_{16}L_{16}$ is input to the final permutation IP^{-1}. This is necessary in order that the algorithm can be used both to encipher and to decipher.

The function f *and S-boxes.*   Figure 2.14 shows a sketch of the function $f(R_{i-1}, K_i)$. First, R_{i-1} is expanded to a 48-bit block $E(R_{i-1})$ using the bit-selection table E

TABLE 2.4 Bit-selection Table E.

32	1	2	3	4	5
4	5	6	7	8	9
8	9	10	11	12	13
12	13	14	15	16	17
16	17	18	19	20	21
20	21	22	23	24	25
24	25	26	27	28	29
28	29	30	31	32	1

TABLE 2.5 Permutation P.

16	7	20	21
29	12	28	17
1	15	23	26
5	18	31	10
2	8	24	14
32	27	3	9
19	13	30	6
22	11	4	25

shown in Table 2.4. This table is used in the same way as the permutation tables, except that some bits of R_{i-1} are selected more than once; thus, given $R_{i-1} = r_1 r_2 \ldots r_{32}$, $E(R_{i-1}) = r_{32} r_1 r_2 \ldots r_{32} r_1$.

Next, the exclusive-or of $E(R_{i-1})$ and K_i is calculated and the result broken into eight 6-bit blocks $B_1, \ldots, B_8$, where

$$E(R_{i-1}) \oplus K_i = B_1 B_2 \ldots B_8 .$$

TABLE 2.6 Selection functions (S-boxes).

Row	0	1	2	3	4	5	6	7	8	9	10	11	12	13	14	15	
									Column								
0	14	4	13	1	2	15	11	8	3	10	6	12	5	9	0	7	
1	0	15	7	4	14	2	13	1	10	6	12	11	9	5	3	8	S_1
2	4	1	14	8	13	6	2	11	15	12	9	7	3	10	5	0	
3	15	12	8	2	4	9	1	7	5	11	3	14	10	0	6	13	
0	15	1	8	14	6	11	3	4	9	7	2	13	12	0	5	10	
1	3	13	4	7	15	2	8	14	12	0	1	10	6	9	11	5	S_2
2	0	14	7	11	10	4	13	1	5	8	12	6	9	3	2	15	
3	13	8	10	1	3	15	4	2	11	6	7	12	0	5	14	9	
0	10	0	9	14	6	3	15	5	1	13	12	7	11	4	2	8	
1	13	7	0	9	3	4	6	10	2	8	5	14	12	11	15	1	S_3
2	13	6	4	9	8	15	3	0	11	1	2	12	5	10	14	7	
3	1	10	13	0	6	9	8	7	4	15	14	3	11	5	2	12	
0	7	13	14	3	0	6	9	10	1	2	8	5	11	12	4	15	
1	13	8	11	5	6	15	0	3	4	7	2	12	1	10	14	9	S_4
2	10	6	9	0	12	11	7	13	15	1	3	14	5	2	8	4	
3	3	15	0	6	10	1	13	8	9	4	5	11	12	7	2	14	
0	2	12	4	1	7	10	11	6	8	5	3	15	13	0	14	9	
1	14	11	2	12	4	7	13	1	5	0	15	10	3	9	8	6	S_5
2	4	2	1	11	10	13	7	8	15	9	12	5	6	3	0	14	
3	11	8	12	7	1	14	2	13	6	15	0	9	10	4	5	3	
0	12	1	10	15	9	2	6	8	0	13	3	4	14	7	5	11	
1	10	15	4	2	7	12	9	5	6	1	13	14	0	11	3	8	S_6
2	9	14	15	5	2	8	12	3	7	0	4	10	1	13	11	6	
3	4	3	2	12	9	5	15	10	11	14	1	7	6	0	8	13	
0	4	11	2	14	15	0	8	13	3	12	9	7	5	10	6	1	
1	13	0	11	7	4	9	1	10	14	3	5	12	2	15	8	6	S_7
2	1	4	11	13	12	3	7	14	10	15	6	8	0	5	9	2	
3	6	11	13	8	1	4	10	7	9	5	0	15	14	2	3	12	
0	13	2	8	4	6	15	11	1	10	9	3	14	5	0	12	7	
1	1	15	13	8	10	3	7	4	12	5	6	11	0	14	9	2	S_8
2	7	11	4	1	9	12	14	2	0	6	10	13	15	3	5	8	
3	2	1	14	7	4	10	8	13	15	12	9	0	3	5	6	11	

Each 6-bit block B_j is then used as input to a selection (substitution) function
(**S-box**) S_j, which returns a 4-bit block $S_j(B_j)$. These blocks are concatenated
together, and the resulting 32-bit block is transposed by the permutation **P** shown
in Table 2.5. Thus, the block returned by $f(R_{i-1}, K_i)$ is

  $P(S_1(B_1) \ldots S_8(B_8))$.

Each S-box S_j maps a 6-bit block $B_j = b_1 b_2 b_3 b_4 b_5 b_6$ into a 4-bit block as defined in

FIGURE 2.15 Key schedule calculation.

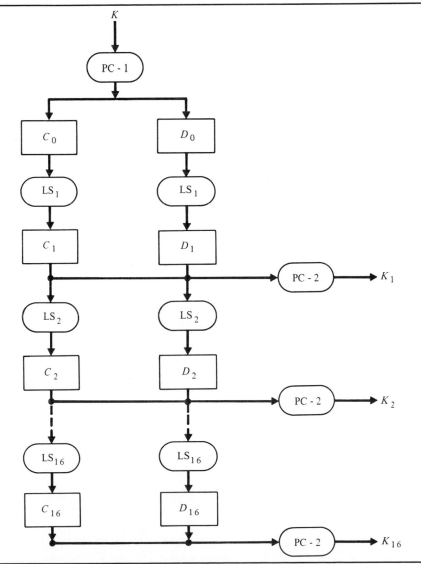

Table 2.6. This is done as follows: The integer corresponding to b_1b_6 selects a row in the table, while the integer corresponding to $b_2b_3b_4b_5$ selects a column. The value of $S_j(B_j)$ is then the 4-bit representation of the integer in that row and column.

> **Example:**
> If $B_1 = 010011$, then S_1 returns the value in row 1, column 9; this is 6, which is represented as 0110. ∎

Key calculation.   Each iteration i uses a different 48-bit key K_i derived from the initial key K. Figure 2.15 illustrates how this is done. K is input as a 64-bit block, with 8 parity bits in positions 8, 16, ..., 64. The permutation PC-1 (permuted choice 1) discards the parity bits and transposes the remaining 56 bits as shown in Table 2.7. The result PC-1(K) is then split into two halves C and D of 28 bits each. The blocks C and D are then successively shifted left to derive each key K_i. Letting C_i and D_i denote the values of C and D used to derive K_i, we have

$$C_i = LS_i(C_{i-1}), \quad D_i = LS_i(D_{i-1}),$$

where LS_i is a left circular shift by the number of positions shown in Table 2.8, and C_0 and D_0 are the initial values of C and D. Key K_i is then given by

$$K_i = PC\text{-}2(C_i D_i), \text{ where}$$

PC-2 is the permutation shown in Table 2.9.

Deciphering.   Deciphering is performed using the same algorithm, except that K_{16} is used in the first iteration, K_{15} in the second, and so on, with K_1 used in the

TABLE 2.7 Key permutation PC-1.

57	49	41	33	25	17	9
1	58	50	42	34	26	18
10	2	59	51	43	35	27
19	11	3	60	52	44	36
63	55	47	39	31	23	15
7	62	54	46	38	30	22
14	6	61	53	45	37	29
21	13	5	28	20	12	4

TABLE 2.8 Key schedule of left shifts LS.

Iteration i	Number of Left Shifts
1	1
2	1
3	2
4	2
5	2
6	2
7	2
8	2
9	1
10	2
11	2
12	2
13	2
14	2
15	2
16	1

TABLE 2.9 Key permutation PC-2.

14	17	11	24	1	5
3	28	15	6	21	10
23	19	12	4	26	8
16	7	27	20	13	2
41	52	31	37	47	55
30	40	51	45	33	48
44	49	39	56	34	53
46	42	50	36	29	32

16th iteration. This is because the final permutation IP^{-1} is the inverse of the initial permutation IP, and

$$R_{i-1} = L_i$$
$$L_{i-1} = R_i \oplus f(L_i, K_i) .$$

Note that whereas the order of the keys is reversed, the algorithm itself is not.

Implementation.   DES has been implemented both in software and in hardware. Hardware implementations achieve encryption rates of several million bps (bits per second).

In 1976 (before DES was adopted), the National Bureau of Standards held two workshops to evaluate the proposed standard. At that time, Diffie and Hellman, and others, were concerned about possible weaknesses (see [Hell76, Diff77]. After the second workshop, Morris, Sloane, and Wyner [Morr77] reported that they believed the DES had two major weaknesses:

1. *Key size:* 56 bits may not provide adequate security.
2. *S-boxes:* The S-boxes may have hidden trapdoors.

Diffie and Hellman argue that with 56-bit keys, DES may be broken under a known-plaintext attack by exhaustive search. In [Diff77] they show that a special-purpose machine consisting of a million LSI chips could try all $2^{56} \cong 7 \times 10^{16}$ keys in 1 day. Each chip would check one key per μsec or 8.64×10^{10} keys per day. Whereas it would take almost 10^6 days for one chip to check all keys, 10^6 chips can check the entire key space in 1 day. The cost of such a machine would be about $20 million. Amortized over 5 years, the cost per day would be about $10,000. Because on the average only half the key space would have to be searched, the average search time would be half a day, making the cost per solution only $5,000. More recently, Diffie [Diff81] has increased this estimate to a 2-day average search time on a $50M machine (using 1980 technology). But he and Hellman [Hell79] both predict the cost of building a special-purpose DES search machine will drop substantially by 1990.

Hellman [Hell80] has also shown that it is possible to speed up the searching process by trading time for memory in a chosen-plaintext attack (see following section). The cost per solution would be $10 on a $5M machine. Because the

FIGURE 2.16 Multiple encipherment with DES.

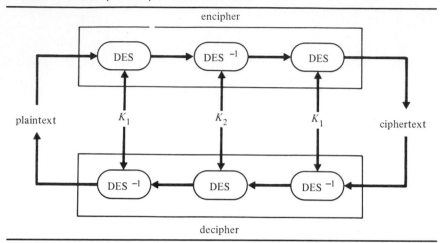

attack can be thwarted with techniques such as cipher block chaining (see Chapter 3), the search strategy itself does not pose a real threat.

Hellman and others argue that the key size should be doubled (112 bits). Tuchman [Tuch79] claims that the same level of security can be obtained with 56-bit keys, using a multiple encryption scheme invented by Matyas and Meyer. Let DES_K denote the encipering transformation for key K, and DES_K^{-1} the correspond-ing deciphering transformation. A plaintext message M is enciphered as

$$C = DES_{K_1}\left(DES_{K_2}^{-1}(DES_{K_1}(M))\right);$$

that is, it is successively enciphered, deciphered, and then enciphered again, using one key (K_1) for the encipherments and another (K_2) for the decipherment (see Figure 2.16). The message M is restored by reversing the process and applying the inverse transformations:

$$DES_{K_1}^{-1}\left(DES_{K_2}(DES_{K_1}^{-1}(C))\right) = M.$$

Merkle and Hellman [Merk81] believe this approach may be less secure than using a single 112-bit key (or even using 3 separate keys in a triple-encryption scheme), showing that it can be theoretically broken under a chosen-plaintext attack using about 2^{56} operations and 2^{56} keys stored on 4 billion tapes.

Hellman and others have also questioned whether the S-boxes are secure (the analysis behind their design is presently classified). They believe that the design should be unclassified so that it may be publicly evaluated. (See [Suga79, Hell79,Davi79,Bran79,Tuch79] for a debate on these issues.)

2.6.3 Time-Memory Tradeoff

There are two naive approaches to breaking a cipher with n keys: exhaustive search and table lookup. **Exhaustive search** uses a known-plaintext attack: Given ciphertext C, the known plaintext M is enciphered with each key K until $E_K(M)$ = C. The time complexity is $T = O(n)$ and the space complexity is $S = O(1)$. We saw earlier that if one key can be tested in 1 μsec on a special-purpose chip, then n = $2^{56} \cong 7 \times 10^{16}$ keys can be checked in $T = 10^6$ days, and 1 million chips can search the entire key space in parallel in approximately 1 day.

Table lookup uses a chosen-plaintext attack: For chosen plaintext M_0, the ciphertexts $C_i = E_{K_i}(M_0)$ are precomputed for $i = 1, \ldots, n$. The keys K_i are arranged in a table so that C_i gives the index of K_i. Thus, for a given ciphertext, the corresponding key K can be found in time $T = O(1)$, though the space complexity is $S = O(n)$. For 56-bit keys, the space requirements are $S = 56(2^{56}) \cong 56 \times 7 \times 10^{16} \cong 4 \times 10^{18}$ bits. This would require about 4 billion magnetic tapes (at about 10^9 bits per tape), costing about \$80 billion (at \$20 per tape).

Hellman's **time-memory tradeoff** technique is a hybrid approach that trades time for space in a chosen-plaintext attack [Hell80]. Like table lookup, it requires the precomputation and storage of a table. For the time-memory tradeoff technique, however, the table size is only $S = O(n^{2/3})$. Like exhaustive search, the technique also requires searching. Here again, however, the search time is only $T = O(n^{2/3})$.

Define

$$f(K) = R(E_K(M_0))$$

for chosen plaintext M_0, where R is a function that reduces a 64-bit block to a 56-bit block (by discarding 8 bits). For a given ciphertext $C_0 = E_K(M_0)$, the objective (of cryptanalysis) is to find the inverse K of f; that is,

$$K = f^{-1}(R(C_0)) .$$

For the precomputation, m starting points $SP_1, \ldots, SP_m$ are randomly chosen from the key space. The following values are computed for some integer t and i = $1, \ldots, m$:

$$X_{i0} = SP_i$$
$$X_{ij} = f(X_{i,j-1}) \quad (1 \leq j \leq t)$$

(see Table 2.10). The ending points EP_i of the computation can thus be expressed: $EP_i = f^t(SP_i)$ $(1 \leq i \leq m)$. The m pairs of values (SP_i, EP_i) are stored in a table sorted by the EP_i. The storage requirements for the table are $S = O(m)$, and the precomputation time is $T_p = O(mt)$.

Given an intercepted ciphertext $C_0 = E_K(M_0)$, the search for K proceeds by first looking for K in column $t - 1$, of the X's (see Table 2.10). If this fails, the remaining columns are searched in the order $t - 2, t - 3, \ldots, 0$. Because the X's are not stored in the table, they must be computed from the starting points as described earlier.

To begin, $Y_1 = R(C_0)$ is computed in order to reduce C_0 to 56 bits. Next, if Y_1 = EP_i for some i $(1 \leq i \leq m)$, then $Y_1 = f(X_{i,t-1})$. This implies that either K = $X_{i,t-1}$ or that f has more than one inverse. This latter event is called a "false alarm." To determine whether $X_{i,t-1}$ is correct, it is used to encipher the chosen plaintext M_0; $K = X_{i,t-1}$ if and only if $E_{X_{i,t-1}}(M_0) = C_0$.

TABLE 2.10 Time-memory tradeoff table.

Starting Points							Ending Points

$$SP_1 = X_{10} \xrightarrow{f} X_{11} \xrightarrow{f} X_{12} \xrightarrow{f} \ldots \xrightarrow{f} X_{1,t-2} \xrightarrow{f} X_{1,t-1} \xrightarrow{f} X_{1t} = EP_1$$

$$SP_i = X_{i0} \rightarrow X_{i1} \rightarrow X_{i2} \rightarrow \ldots \rightarrow X_{i,t-2} \rightarrow X_{i,t-1} \rightarrow X_{it} = EP_i$$

$$SP_m = X_{m0} \rightarrow X_{m1} \rightarrow X_{m2} \rightarrow \ldots \rightarrow X_{m,t-2} \rightarrow X_{m,t-1} \rightarrow X_{mt} = EP_m$$

If K is not found in column $t - 1$ of the X's, column $t - 2$ is searched next. This is done by setting $Y_2 = f(Y_1)$. $K = X_{i,t-2}$ for some i if and only if $Y_2 = EP_i$ and $E_{X_{i,t-2}}(M_0) = C_0$. The remaining columns are searched by computing $Y_j = f(Y_{j-1})$ for $j = 3, \ldots, t$. $K = X_{i,t-j}$ for some i if and only if $Y_j = EP_i$ and $E_{X_{i,t-j}}(M_0) = C_0$.

Assuming false alarms are rare, the time to search one table is $T = O(t)$. If all mt values of X represented by the table are randomly chosen and different, then the probability of finding a random key K in the table is $p = mt/n$. Allowing for overlap, Hellman shows that if $mt^2 = n$, the probability of success has the approximate lower bound of:

$$p \geq .8 \frac{mt}{n} \cong \frac{mt}{n}.$$

Let $m = t = n^{1/3}$. Then the storage requirements are $S = O(m) = O(n^{1/3})$, the precomputation time is $T_p = O(mt) = O(n^{2/3})$, and the search time is $T_s = O(t) = O(n^{1/3})$. The probability of success, however, is only approximately $n^{-1/3}$. For $n = 10^{17}$, this is a little better than 10^{-6}, which is not good. If $t = n^{1/3}$ tables are precomputed and searched instead, then the probability of success is quite high. The total storage requirements then become $S = O(tm) = O(n^{2/3})$, while the total precomputation time becomes $T_p = O(tmt) = O(n)$ and the total search time becomes $T_s = O(tt) = O(n^{2/3})$. The real time can be reduced by precomputing and searching some (or all) of the tables in parallel.

Rivest has observed that the search time can be reduced by forcing each endpoint EP_i to satisfy some easily tested syntactic property (e.g., begins with a fixed number of 0's) that is expected to hold after t encipherments of the starting point SP_i (so the expected number of entries represented by a table of m starting and ending points is still mt). Thus, instead of precomputing $EP_i = f^t(SP_i)$ for a fixed t, SP_i would be successively reenciphered until it satisfied the chosen property.

Hellman suggests a hardware implementation using $m = 10^5$, $t = 10^6$, and 10^6 tables. Because each table entry contains a 56-bit starting point SP and a 56-

bit ending point *EP*, the total storage requirements are thus $10^{11} \times 112$ bits or about 10^{13} bits, which can be stored on 10,000 tapes (assuming 10^9 bits per tape). These can be read and searched in 1 day with 100 tape drives. Each tape drive would have a 10^7 bit semiconductor memory for storing one table. Each memory would have 100 DES chips searching for 100 different keys in parallel. The machine would also be capable of doing the precomputation; with all 10,000 DES units operating in parallel, this would take about 1.1 years (using a DES chip operating at 4 μsec per encipherment).

The total parts would cost about \$3.6M using 1980 technology. Depreciated over 5 years, this is about \$2500 per day, or \$25 per solution. With decreasing hardware costs, the cost per solution could drop to \$1.

To break a cipher using time-memory tradeoff, it must be possible to perform a chosen-plaintext attack. This is possible when plaintext messages are known to contain commonly occurring sequences (e.g., blanks) or standard headers (e.g., "LOGIN:"), and each block is separately enciphered. Techniques such as cipher block chaining (see Section 3.4.1) protect against this type of attack. The proposed Federal standards suggest taking such precautions.

2.7 EXPONENTIATION CIPHERS

In 1978, Pohlig and Hellman [Pohl78a] published an encryption scheme based on computing exponentials over a finite field. At about the same time, Rivest, Shamir, and Adleman [Rive78a] published a similar scheme, but with a slight twist— a twist that gave the MIT group a method for realizing public-key encryption as put forth by Diffie and Hellman [Diff76]. In *Scientific American,* Martin Gardner [Gard77] described the RSA scheme as "A New Kind of Cipher That Would Take Millions of Years to Break." Oddly enough, just 60 years earlier in 1917, the same journal published an article touting the Vigenère ciphers as "impossible of translation" [Kahn67].

The Pohlig-Hellman and RSA schemes both encipher a message block $M \epsilon$ $[0, n - 1]$ by computing the exponential

$$C = M^e \bmod n \ , \tag{2.2}$$

where e and n are the key to the enciphering transformation. M is restored by the same operation, but using a different exponent d for the key:

$$M = C^d \bmod n \ . \tag{2.3}$$

Enciphering and deciphering can be implemented using the fast exponentiation algorithm shown in Figure 1.20 (see Section 1.6.1):

$$C = fastexp(M, e, n)$$
$$M = fastexp(C, d, n) \ .$$

The enciphering and deciphering transformations are based on Euler's generalization of Fermat's Theorem (see Theorem 1.5 in Section 1.6.2), which states that for every M relatively prime to n,

$M^{\phi(n)} \bmod n = 1$.

This property implies that if e and d satisfy the relation

$$ed \bmod \phi(n) = 1 \ , \tag{2.4}$$

then Eq. (2.3) is the inverse of Eq. (2.2), so that deciphering restores the original plaintext message. This result is proved in the following theorem:

Theorem 2.1:
Given e and d satisfying Eq. (2.4) and a message $M \ \epsilon \ [0, n - 1]$ such that $gcd(M, n) = 1$,

$(M^e \bmod n)^d \bmod n = M$.

Proof:
We have

$(M^e \bmod n)^d \bmod n = M^{ed} \bmod n$.

Now, $ed \bmod \phi(n) = 1$ implies that $ed = t\phi(n) + 1$ for some integer t. Thus,

$$\begin{aligned} M^{ed} \bmod n &= M^{t\phi(n)+1} \bmod n \\ &= MM^{t\phi(n)} \bmod n \\ &= M(M^{t\phi(n)} \bmod n) \bmod n \ , \end{aligned}$$

where:

$$\begin{aligned} M^{t\phi(n)} \bmod n &= (M^{\phi(n)} \bmod n)^t \bmod n \\ &= 1^t \bmod n \\ &= 1 \ . \end{aligned}$$

Thus,

$$\begin{aligned} M^{ed} \bmod n &= (M * 1) \bmod n \\ &= M \ . \ \blacksquare \end{aligned}$$

By symmetry, enciphering and deciphering are commutative and mutual inverses; thus,

$(M^d \bmod n)^e \bmod n = M^{de} \bmod n = M$.

It is because of this symmetry that the RSA scheme can be used for secrecy and authenticity in a public-key system.

Given $\phi(n)$, it is easy to generate a pair (e, d) satisfying Eq. (2.4). This is done by first choosing d relatively prime to $\phi(n)$, and then using the extended version of Euclid's algorithm (see Figure 1.22 in Section 1.6.2) to compute its inverse:

$$e = inv(d, \phi(n)) \ . \tag{2.5}$$

[Because e and d are symmetric, we could also pick e and compute $d = inv(e, \phi(n))$.]

Given e, it is easy to compute d (or vice versa) if $\phi(n)$ is known. But if e and n can be released without giving away $\phi(n)$ or d, then the deciphering transformation can be kept secret, while the enciphering transformation is made public. It is the ability to hide $\phi(n)$ that distinguishes the RSA scheme from the Pohlig-Hellman scheme.

2.7.1 Pohlig-Hellman Scheme

In the Pohlig-Hellman scheme, the modulus is chosen to be a large prime p. The enciphering and deciphering functions are thus given by

$C = M^e \bmod p$
$M = C^d \bmod p$,

where all arithmetic is done in the Galois field $\mathbf{GF}(p)$ (see Section 1.6.3). Because p is prime, $\phi(p) = p - 1$ (see Section 1.6.2), which is trivially derived from p. Thus the scheme can only be used for conventional encryption, where e and d are both kept secret.

Example:
Let $p = 11$, whence $\phi(p) = p - 1 = 10$. Choose $d = 7$ and compute $e = inv(7, 10) = 3$. Suppose $M = 5$. Then M is enciphered as:

$C = M^e \bmod p = 5^3 \bmod 11 = 4$.

Similarly, C is deciphered as:

$M = C^d \bmod p = 4^7 \bmod 11 = 5$. ■

The security of the scheme rests on the complexity of computing discrete logarithms in $\mathbf{GF}(p)$. This is because under a known-plaintext attack, a cryptanalyst can compute e (and thereby d) given a pair (M, C):

$e = \log_M C$ in $\mathbf{GF}(p)$

(p may be deduced by observing the sizes of plaintext and ciphertext blocks). Pohlig and Hellman show that if $(p - 1)$ has only small prime factors, it is possible to compute the logarithm in $O(\log^2 p)$ time, which is unsatisfactory even for large values of p. They recommend picking $p = 2p' + 1$, where p' is also a large prime.
Now, the fastest known algorithm for computing the discrete logarithm in $\mathbf{GF}(p)$, due to Adleman [Adle79], takes approximately

$$T = \exp\left(\operatorname{sqrt}\left(\ln(p)\ln(\ln(p))\right)\right) \tag{2.6}$$

steps, where "ln" denotes the natural logarithm and "exp" its inverse). If p is 200 bits long, Eq. (2.6) evaluates to

$T = 2.7 \times 10^{11}$.

Assuming 10^{11} steps can be performed per day (i.e., about 1 step per μsec), the entire computation would take only a few days. But if p is 664 bits long (200 decimal digits),

$$T = 1.2 \times 10^{23},$$

which would take about 10^{12} days or several billion years. Figure 2.17 shows a graph of $\log_{10} T$ as a function of the length of p in bits. Techniques for picking large primes are described in the next section.

Pohlig and Hellman also note that their scheme could be implemented in the Galois Field $\mathbf{GF}(2^n)$, where $2^n - 1$ is a large prime (called a Mersenne prime—e.g., see [Knut69]). Such an implementation would be efficient and have the advantage that all messages would be exactly n bits; furthermore, every element in the range $[1, 2^n - 2]$ could be used as a key.

2.7.2 Rivest-Shamir-Adleman (RSA) Scheme

In the RSA scheme, the modulus n is the product of two large primes p and q:

$$n = pq .$$

Thus

$$\phi(n) = (p - 1) (q - 1)$$

(see Theorem 1.3 in Section 1.6.2). The enciphering and deciphering functions are given by Eq. (2.2) and (2.3). Rivest, Shamir, and Adleman recommend picking d relatively prime to $\phi(n)$ in the interval $[\max (p, q) + 1, n - 1]$ (any prime in the interval will do); e is computed using Eq. (2.5). If $inv(d, \phi(n))$ returns e such that $e < \log_2 n$, then a new value of d should be picked to ensure that every encrypted message undergoes some wrap-around (reduction modulo n).

Example:
Let $p = 5$ and $q = 7$, whence $n = pq = 35$ and $\phi(n) = (5 - 1) (7 - 1) = 24$. Pick $d = 11$. Then $e = inv(11, 24) = 11$ (in fact, e and d will always be the same for $p = 5$ and $q = 7$—see exercises at end of chapter). Suppose $M = 2$. Then

$$C = M^e \bmod n = 2^{11} \bmod 35 = 2048 \bmod 35 = 18 ,$$

and

$$C^d \bmod n = 18^{11} \bmod 35 = 2 = M . \quad \blacksquare$$

Example:
Let $p = 53$ and $q = 61$, whence $n = 53 * 61 = 3233$ and $\phi(n) = 52 * 60 = 3120$. Letting $d = 791$, we get $e = 71$. To encipher the message $M = $ RENAISSANCE, we break it into blocks of 4 digits each, where A $= 00$, B $= 01, \ldots,$ Z $= 25$, and blank $= 26$ (in practice, characters would be represented by their 8-bit ASCII codes). We thus get

FIGURE 2.17 Time to compute discrete logarithm or to factor.

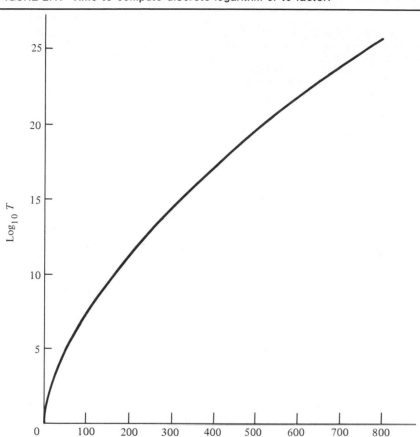

$$M = \text{R E N A I S SA NC E}$$
$$= 1704\ 1300\ 0818\ 1800\ 1302\ 0426\ .$$

The first block is enciphered as $1704^{71} = 3106$. The entire message is enciphered as

$$C = 3106\ 0100\ 0931\ 2691\ 1984\ 2927\ .\quad ∎$$

Because $\phi(n)$ cannot be determined without knowing the prime factors p and q, it is possible to keep d secret even if e and n are made public. This means that the RSA scheme can be used for public-key encryption, where the enciphering transformation is made public and the deciphering transformation is kept secret.

The security of the system depends on the difficulty of factoring n into p and q. The fastest known factoring algorithm, due to Schroeppel (unpublished), takes

$$T = \exp\left(\text{sqrt}\left(\ln(n)\ln(\ln(n))\right)\right)$$

FIGURE 2.18 Evaluate Jacobi symbol.

Algorithm $J(a, b)$: "Evaluate $\left(\dfrac{a}{b}\right)$"

---

if $a = 1$ **then** $J := 1$
else if $a \bmod 2 = 0$ **then begin**
  if $(b * b - 1)/8 \bmod 2 = 0$
    then $J := J(a/2, b)$ **else** $J := -J(a/2, b)$ **end**

else if $(a - 1) * (b - 1)/4 \bmod 2 = 0$
    then $J := J(b \bmod a, a)$ **else** $J := -J(b \bmod a, a)$

---

steps. This is the same number of steps required to compute the discrete logarithm in $GF(n)$ when n is prime [see Eq. (2.6) and Figure 2.17]. Rivest, Shamir, and Adleman suggest using 100-digit numbers for p and q; then n is 200 digits, and factoring would take several billion years at the rate of one step per microsecond.

    The security of the system also depends on using carefully selected primes p and q. If n is 200 digits, then p and q should be large primes of approximately 100 digits each. To find a 100-digit prime p, Rivest, Shamir, and Adleman recommend randomly generating numbers until a number b is found that is "probably" prime. To test b for primality, 100 random numbers $a \in [1, b - 1]$ are generated. Then b is almost certain to be prime if the following test (due to Solovay and Strassen [Solo77]) is satisfied for each a:

$$gcd(a, b) = 1 \text{ and } \left(\frac{a}{b}\right) \bmod b = a^{(b-1)/2} \bmod b \text{ ,} \qquad (2.7)$$

where $\left(\dfrac{a}{b}\right)$ is the Jacobi symbol (see [LeVe77,Nive72,Vino55] and discussion in following section). When $gcd(a, b) = 1$, the Jacobi symbol can be efficiently evaluated using the recursive function $J(a, b)$ shown in Figure 2.18. If b is prime, then Eq. (2.7) is true for all $a \in [1, b - 1]$. If b is not prime, Eq. (2.7) is true with probability at most $1/2$ for each such a, and at most $1/2^{100}$ for 100 such a's.

    For better protection against factoring, additional precautions should be taken in selecting p and q:

1. p and q should differ in length by a few digits.
2.   Both $p - 1$ and $q - 1$ should contain large prime factors.
3. $gcd(p - 1, q - 1)$ should be small.

To find a prime p such that $p - 1$ has a large prime factor, first generate a large random prime p'. Then generate

$$p = i * p' + 1 , \quad \text{for } i = 2, 4, 6, \ldots \qquad (2.8)$$

until p is prime. Further protection may be obtained by picking p' such that $p' - 1$ has a large prime factor.

    Simmons and Norris [Simm77] showed the scheme may be broken without factoring if p and q are not carefully chosen. They found that for certain keys, reenciphering a ciphertext message a small number of times restored the original plaintext message. Thus, given ciphertext $C_0 = M^e \bmod n$ and the public key (e, n), a cryptanalyst may be able to determine M by computing

$$C_i = C_{i-1}^e \bmod n , \quad \text{for } i = 1, 2, \ldots$$

until C_i is a meaningful message. Clearly, this type of attack is worthwhile only if the plaintext is restored within a reasonably small number of steps (e.g., a million). Rivest [Rive78b] showed that if each prime p is chosen so that $p - 1$ has a large prime factor p', where $p' - 1$ has a large prime factor p'', then the probability of this type of attack succeeding is extremely small. For primes larger than 10^{90}, this probability is at most 10^{-90}.

Blakley and Blakley [Blak78] and Blakley and Borosh [Blak79] show that for any choice of keys, at least nine plaintext messages will not be concealed by encipherment; that is, for any e and n, $M^e \bmod n = M$ for at least nine M. Although the probability of picking one out of nine such messages is small if messages are 200 digits long, a poor choice of keys will conceal less than 50% of all possible messages. They argue that the system will be more resistant to this type of attack and sophisticated factoring algorithms if safe primes are selected; a prime p is **safe** if

$$p = 2p' + 1, \quad \text{where } p' \text{ is an odd prime}$$

(every prime but 2 is odd). This represents a restriction on the form of Eq. (2.8) suggested by Rivest, Shamir, and Adleman. We observed earlier that Pohlig and Hellman also suggested using safe primes in their scheme.

Breaking the RSA scheme can be no more difficult than factoring, because a fast factoring algorithm automatically gives an efficient cryptanalytic procedure. This does not, however, rule out finding an efficient algorithm for cryptanalysis without finding a corresponding algorithm for factoring. Rabin [Rabi79] and Williams [Will80] have devised variants of the RSA scheme where the cryptanalytic effort is equivalent to factorization. There is, however, a drawback to these schemes arising from the constructive nature of the proofs. Rivest has observed that any cryptosystem for which there exists a constructive proof of equivalence of the cryptanalytic effort with factorization is vulnerable to a chosen-ciphertext attack (see [Will80]). Upon obtaining the deciphered message for a selected ciphertext message, a cryptanalyst can factor the modulus and break the cipher.

If n, d, and e are each 200 decimal digits (664 bits), the storage requirements per user are about 2,000 bits. Since both e and n must be made public, the public storage requirements are thus about 1.3 kilobits per user. By comparison, the DES requires only 56 bits (or 112 bits if longer keys or multiple encryption is used).

The time requirements are also considerably greater than for the DES. To encipher or decipher a 664-bit number requires 1–2 multiplications in modular arithmetic per bit, or about 1,000 multiplications total. Rivest has designed a special-purpose chip that will run at a few thousand bps [Rive80]. Although this is fast enough to support real-time communication over telephone lines, it is too slow for communication links capable of higher bit rates. Rabin's scheme [Rabi70] has a faster enciphering algorithm (requiring only one addition, one multiplication, and one division by the modulus—see exercises); the deciphering algorithm is comparable to the RSA algorithm.

Because the enciphering and deciphering functions are mutual inverses, the RSA scheme can be used for secrecy and authenticity. Each user A obtains a modulus n_A and enciphering and deciphering exponents e_A and d_A. A registers e_A and n_A with a public directory, thus making A's enciphering transformation E_A public. A keeps d_A and, therefore, the deciphering transformation D_A secret.

User B can send a secret message M to A by obtaining A's public transformation E_A and transmitting

$$E_A(M) = M^{e_A} \bmod n_A ,$$

which A deciphers using A's secret transformation D_A:

$$D_A(E_A(M)) = M^{e_A d_A} \bmod n_A = M .$$

Alternatively, A can send a signed message M to B by transmitting

$$D_A(M) = M^{d_A} \bmod n_A ,$$

which B authenticates using A's public transformation E_A:

$$E_A(D_A(M)) = M^{d_A e_A} \bmod n_A = M .$$

Because only A can apply D_A, it cannot be forged, and a judge can settle any dispute arising between A and B.

A slight difficulty arises when both secrecy and authenticity are desired, because it is necessary to apply successive transformations with different moduli. For example, in order for A to send a signed, secret message to B, A must transmit:

$$C = E_B(D_A(M)) .$$

If $n_A > n_B$, the blocks comprising $D_A(M)$ might not be in the range $[0, n_B - 1]$ of B's transformation. Reducing them modulo n_B does not solve the problem, because it would then be impossible to recover the original message. One solution is to re-block $D_A(M)$. Rivest, Shamir, and Adleman show that reblocking can be avoided using a **threshold** value h (e.g., $h = 10^{99}$). Each user has two sets of transformations: (E_{A1}, D_{A1}) for signatures and (E_{A2}, D_{A2}) for secrecy, where $n_{A1} < h < n_{A2}$. To send a signed, secret message to B, A, transmits

$$C = E_{B2}(D_{A1}(M)) ,$$

which is computable because $n_{A1} < h < n_{B2}$. User B recovers M and checks A's signature by computing

$$\begin{aligned} E_{A1}(D_{B2}(C)) &= E_{A1}(D_{B2}(E_{B2}(D_{A1}(M)))) \\ &= E_{A1}(D_{A1}(M)) \\ &= M . \end{aligned}$$

Kohnfelder [Konf78] suggests another approach, pointing out that if $C = E_B(D_A(M))$ is not computable because $n_A > n_B$, then $C' = D_A(E_B(M))$ is computable. User B, knowing both n_A and n_B, can recover M by computing either of the following:

Case 1: $n_A < n_B$
$$
\begin{aligned}
E_A(D_B(C)) &= E_A(D_B(E_B(D_A(M)))) \\
&= E_A(D_A(M)) \\
&= M .
\end{aligned}
$$

Case 2: $n_A > n_B$
$$
\begin{aligned}
D_B(E_A(C')) &= D_B(E_A(D_A(E_B(M)))) \\
&= D_B(E_B(M)) \\
&= M .
\end{aligned}
$$

If a dispute arises between A and B on the authenticity of A's signature, a judge must be able to ascertain that M originated with A. If $n_A < n_B$, B applies B's private transformation to C and presents the judge with $X = D_B(C)$ and M. The judge computes

$$ M' = E_A(X) $$

using A's public transformation, and verifies that $M' = M$. If $n_A > n_B$, another approach is needed because D_B must be applied after E_A, and B may not want to give D_B to the judge. The solution is for B to present the judge with C' and M. The judge computes

$$
\begin{aligned}
X &= E_B(M) \\
X' &= E_A(C') = E_A(D_A(E_B(M)))
\end{aligned}
$$

using both A's and B's public transformations, and verifies that $X = X'$. Table 2.11 summarizes.

In the above approach, the storage requirements for a signed message are the same as for the unsigned message. Thus, in applications where the unsigned message is stored in the clear or as ciphertext encrypted by some other method, the total storage requirements are twice that of the unsigned message alone. An alternative, described by Davies and Price [Davs80], is to compress a message into a "digest" by hashing, and then sign the digest. This reduces the storage requirements for a signed message to a fixed size block.

TABLE 2.11 Secrecy and authenticity in RSA scheme.

	$n_A < n_B$	$n_A > n_B$
A transmits	$C = E_B(D_A(M))$	$C' = D_A(E_B(M))$
B computes	$M = E_A(D_B(C))$	$M = D_B(E_A(C'))$
B gives judge	$M, X = D_B(C)$	M, C'
Judge computes	$M' = E_A(X)$	$X = E_B(M)$, $X' = E_A(C')$,
Judge tests	$M' = M$	$X = X'$

2.7.3 Mental Poker

Shamir, Rivest, and Adleman [Sham80a] show how any commutative cipher can be used to play a fair game of "mental poker". The scheme is easily implemented with an exponentiation cipher, where the players share a common modulus n.

Mental poker is played like ordinary poker but without cards and without verbal communication; all exchanges between the players must be accomplished using messages. Any player may try to cheat. The requirements for a fair game are as follows:

1. The game must begin with a "fair deal". Assuming the players have exchanged a sequence of messages to accomplish this, then

    a. The players should know the cards in their own hand but not the others.
    b. All hands must be disjoint.
    c. All possible hands must be equally likely for each player.

2. During the game, players may want to draw additional cards from the remaining deck; these must also be dealt fairly as described in (1). Players must also be able to reveal cards to their opponents without compromising the security of their remaining cards.

3. At the end of the game, the players must be able to check that the game was played fairly, and that their opponents did not cheat.

For simplicity, assume there are two players Alice and Bob, and each has a secret key. The keys are not revealed until the end of the game.

Let E_A and D_A denote Alice's secret transformations, and let E_B and D_B denote Bob's. The enciphering transformations must commute; that is, for any message M:

$$E_A(E_B(M)) = E_B(E_A(M)) .$$

The 52 cards are represented by messages:

M_1:   "two of clubs"
M_2:   "three of clubs"

.

.

.

M_{52}:   "ace of spades" .

Bob is the dealer. The protocol for a fair deal is as follows:

1. Bob enciphers the 52 messages, getting 52 encrypted messages:

    $$E_B(M_i) , \qquad i = 1, \ldots, 52 .$$

    He then randomly shuffles the encrypted deck and sends it to Alice.

2.   Alice randomly selects 5 encrypted messages and returns them to Bob. Bob
      deciphers them to determine his hand.
3.   Alice randomly selects 5 more encrypted messages, $C_1, \ldots, C_5$. She enci-
      phers them with her key, getting

$$C_i' = E_A(C_i) , \qquad i = 1, \ldots, 5 .$$

She then sends the doubly enciphered messages $C_1', \ldots, C_5'$ to Bob.
5.   Bob deciphers each message C_i' with his key, getting

$$\begin{aligned} D_B(C_i') &= D_B\big(E_A(E_B(M_j))\big) \\ &= D_B\big(E_B(E_A(M_j))\big) \\ &= E_A(M_j) \end{aligned}$$

for some message M_j. He returns these to Alice. She then deciphers them
with her key to determine her hand.

During the game, additional cards may be dealt by repeating the preceding procedure. At the end of the game, both players reveal their keys to prove they did not
cheat.

      Because exponentiation in modular arithmetic is commutative, mental poker
may be implemented with an exponentiation cipher. Bob and Alice agree on a
large modulus n with corresponding $\phi(n)$. Alice picks a secret key (e_A, d_A) such
that $e_A d_A \bmod \phi(n) = 1$ and uses the transformations:

$$E_A(M) = M^{e_A} \bmod n$$
$$D_A(C) = C^{d_A} \bmod n .$$

Similarly, Bob picks a secret key (e_B, d_B) and uses the transformations:

$$E_B(M) = M^{e_B} \bmod n$$
$$D_B(C) = C^{d_B} \bmod n .$$

      Lipton [Lipt79a] shows that it may be possible to cheat using this encryption
method. One way uses quadratic residues. A number a is a **quadratic residue**
modulo n if $gcd(a, n) = 1$ and there exists an x such that

$$x^2 \equiv_n a,$$

or, equivalently,

$$x^2 \bmod n = a \bmod n ;$$

otherwise, it is a **quadratic nonresidue** modulo n. Any x satisfying the preceding
equations is a **square root** of a modulo n. Let R_2 denote the set of quadratic
residues modulo n. For any message $M = a$, enciphering (or deciphering) M
preserves its membership in R_2 as shown by the following theorem:

      Theorem 2.2:
      Given a, $0 < a < n$, $a \in R_2$ if and only if $E_K(a) = a^e \bmod n \in R_2$, where
      $K = (e, n)$.

Proof:

First, suppose $a \epsilon R_2$. Then $x^2 \bmod n = a$ for some x. Because

$$E_K(a) = a^e \bmod n = (x^2)^e \bmod n = (x^e)^2 \bmod n,$$

$E_K(a)$ is in R_2.

Now, suppose $E_K(a) \epsilon R_2$. Because deciphering is the same operation as enciphering but with exponent d, $(E_K(a))^d \bmod n = a$ must also be in R_2. ■

Example:

Let $n = 11$. Then 3 is a quadratic residue modulo 11 because $5^2 \bmod 11 = 3$. Suppose $e = 4$. Then $3^4 \bmod 11 = 4$ is also a quadratic residue because

$$2^2 \bmod 11 = 4. ■$$

Alice can exploit this result by noting which cards have messages in R_2. After Bob has encrypted and shuffled these messages, she still cannot decipher them. She can tell, however, which correspond to those in R_2. If the modulus n is a prime p (as in the Pohlig-Hellman scheme), the probability of a message being in R_2 is $1/2$; this gives her one bit of information per card which could help her to win. For example, if she observes that the plaintext messages for all four aces are quadratic residues, she could select quadratic residues for her hand and quadratic nonresidues for Bob's.

For prime p, half the numbers in the range $[1, p - 1]$ are in R_2 and half are not. To prove this result, we first prove that the equation $x^2 \bmod p = a$ has either two solutions or no solutions. (See also [LeVe77,Nive72,Vino55].)

Theorem 2.3:

For prime $p > 2$ and $0 < a < p$,

$$x^2 \bmod p = a$$

has two solutions if $a \epsilon R_2$ and no solutions otherwise.

Proof:

If $a \epsilon R_2$, there is at least one solution x_1. But then $p - x_1$ must also be a solution because

$$(p - x_1)^2 \bmod p = (p^2 - 2px_1 + x_1^2) \bmod p$$
$$= x_1^2 \bmod p = a .$$

Furthermore, the solutions are distinct because $p - x_1 = x_1$ is possible only if 2 divides p. ■

Theorem 2.4:

For prime $p > 2$, there are $(p - 1)/2$ quadratic residues modulo p and $(p - 1)/2$ quadratic nonresidues.

Proof:
Clearly the $(p - 1)/2$ residues

$$1^2, 2^2, \ldots, \left(\frac{p - 1}{2}\right)^2 \bmod p$$

are quadratic residues. There can be no additional quadratic residues because for every $a \in R_2$, at least one of its roots x_1 or $p - x_1$ must fall in the range $[1, (p - 1)/2]$. ■

Example:
For $p = 7$, the quadratic residues are

$$1^2 \bmod 7 = 1$$
$$2^2 \bmod 7 = 4$$
$$3^2 \bmod 7 = 2 . ■$$

Now, if $gcd(a, p) = 1$, it is simple to determine whether $a \in R_2$ by computing $a^{(p - 1)/2} \bmod p$. Theorem 2.5 shows the result will be congruent to 1 if $a \in R_2$ and to -1 otherwise.

Theorem 2.5:
For prime $p > 2$ and $0 < a < p$,

$$a^{(p-1)/2} \bmod p = \begin{cases} 1 & \text{if } a \in R_2 \\ p - 1 & \text{otherwise} \end{cases} \tag{2.9}$$

Proof:
By Fermat's Theorem,

$$(a^{p-1} - 1) \bmod p = 0 .$$

Because p is odd, we can factor $a^{p-1} - 1$, getting

$$(a^{(p-1)/2} + 1) (a^{(p-1)/2} - 1) \bmod p = 0 .$$

This implies that p must divide either $a^{(p-1)/2} + 1$ or $a^{(p-1)/2} - 1$. (It cannot divide both because this would imply that p divides their difference, which is 2.) We thus have

$$a^{(p-1)/2} \equiv_p \pm 1 .$$

Now, if $a \in R_2$, then there exists an x such that $a = x^2 \bmod p$, which implies

$$a^{(p-1)/2} \bmod p = (x^2)^{(p-1)/2} \bmod p$$
$$= x^{p-1} \bmod p$$
$$= 1 .$$

Thus, the $(p-1)/2$ quadratic residues are solutions of

$$a^{(p-1)/2} \bmod p = 1 .$$

There can be no additional solutions because the equation, being of degree $(p-1)/2$, can have no more than $(p-1)/2$ solutions. Thus, the $(p-1)/2$ quadratic nonresidues must be solutions of

$$a^{(p-1)/2} \bmod p = p - 1 . \quad \blacksquare$$

Example:
We saw earlier that 1, 2, and 4 are quadratic residues modulo $p = 7$. We can verify this by computing $a^{(7-1)/2} \bmod 7 = a^3 \bmod 7$ for $a = 1, 2, 4$:

$$1^3 \bmod 7 = 1$$
$$2^3 \bmod 7 = 1$$
$$4^3 \bmod 7 = 1 .$$

Similarly, we can verify that $a = 2, 3,$ and 5 are quadratic nonresidues by computing

$$3^3 \bmod 7 = 6$$
$$5^3 \bmod 7 = 6$$
$$6^3 \bmod 7 = 6 . \quad \blacksquare$$

Note the relationship between Eq. (2.9) and Eq. (2.7), which is used to test a number b for primality by checking whether

$$\left(\frac{a}{b}\right) \bmod b = a^{(b-1)/2} \bmod b$$

for some random a relatively prime to b. If b is a prime p, then the Jacobi symbol $\left(\frac{a}{p}\right)$ is equivalent by the **Legendre symbol**, also denoted $\left(\frac{a}{p}\right)$, which is defined by

$$\left(\frac{a}{p}\right) = \begin{cases} +1 & \text{if } a \in R_2 \\ -1 & \text{otherwise,} \end{cases}$$

when $gcd(a, p) = 1$. By Theorem 2.5, $\left(\frac{a}{p}\right) \bmod p = a^{(p-1)/2} \bmod p$. If b is not prime, let $b = p_1 p_2 \ldots p_t$ be the prime factorization of b (factors may repeat). Then the Jacobi symbol $\left(\frac{a}{b}\right)$ is defined in terms of the Legendre symbol as follows:

$$\left(\frac{a}{b}\right) = \left(\frac{a}{p_1}\right)\left(\frac{a}{p_2}\right) \cdots \left(\frac{a}{p_t}\right) .$$

Note that whereas the Jacobi symbol is always congruent to $\pm 1 \pmod{b}$, the expression $a^{(b-1)/2} \bmod b$ may not be congruent to ± 1 when b is not prime.

Example:
For $n = 9$ and $a = 2$, $2^4 \bmod 9 = 7$. $\quad \blacksquare$

Note also that whereas $\left(\frac{a}{b}\right)$ is defined by the prime factorization of b, it can be evaluated without knowing the factors. The recursive function $J(a, b)$ given in the previous section for evaluating $\left(\dfrac{a}{b}\right)$ does so by exploiting several properties of the Jacobi symbol, namely:

1. $\left(\dfrac{1}{b}\right) = 1$.

2. $\left(\dfrac{a_1 a_2}{b}\right) = \left(\dfrac{a_1}{b}\right) \left(\dfrac{a_2}{b}\right)$.

3. $\left(\dfrac{2}{b}\right) = (-1)^{(b^2-1)/8}$.

4. $\left(\dfrac{b}{a}\right) = \left(\dfrac{b \bmod a}{a}\right)$.

5. $\left(\dfrac{a}{b}\right) \left(\dfrac{b}{a}\right) = (-1)^{(a-1)\,(b-1)/4}$ if $gcd(a, b) = 1$.

Returning to mental poker, we see that enciphering function may preserve other properties about a message $M = a$ as well. For example, let R_t be the set of elements congruent to $x^t \bmod n$ for some x. Then $a \in R_t$ if and only if $a^e \bmod n \in R_t$.

Lipton proposes two modifications to the exponential method, each of which forces all messages (plaintext and ciphertext) to be quadratic residues [Lipt79b]. The first method appends extra low-order bits to each message M, set to make the extended message a quadratic residue. The original message is recovered by discarding the extra bits. The second method multiplies nonresidue messages by a fixed nonresidue w (the product of two nonresidues is a quadratic residue). The original message is recovered by multiplying by w^{-1}, where w^{-1} is the inverse of w (mod n).

These results show that for some applications, an encryption algorithm must be more than just computationally strong. This particular application requires an algorithm that conceals not only the messages but their mathematical properties.

2.7.4 Oblivious Transfer

Rabin has devised a protocol whereby Alice can transfer a secret to Bob with probability $1/2$. Thus, Bob has a 50% chance of receiving the secret and a 50% chance of receiving nothing. On the other hand, Bob will know whether he has received the secret; Alice will not. Clearly, the uncertainty must be agreeable to both Alice and Bob, or one of them would refuse to cooperate. Called the "oblivious transfer", the protocol is described by Blum [Blum81a] as follows:

Oblivious transfer protocol
1. Alice sends to Bob the product n of two distinct odd primes p and q. The primes p and q represent her secret. They may, for example, be the secret parameters to an RSA deciphering transformation.

2.   Bob picks a number x at random, where $0 < x < n$ and $gcd(x, n) = 1$, and
      sends to Alice

$$a = x^2 \bmod n \ . \tag{2.10}$$

3.   Alice, knowing p and q, computes the four roots of a: x, $n - x$, y, $n - y$ (see
      discussion following). She picks one of these roots at random and sends it to
      Bob.

4.   If Bob receives y or $n - y$, he can determine p and q from x and y by
      computing

$$gcd(x + y, n) = p \text{ or } q$$

(see exercises at end of chapter). If he receives x or $n - x$, he learns nothing.

Equation (2.10) has four roots because n has two distinct prime factors. By
Theorem 1.7, we know that any solution x of Eq. (2.10) must be a common
solution of

$$x^2 \bmod p = a \bmod p \tag{2.11}$$
$$x^2 \bmod q = a \bmod q \ . \tag{2.12}$$

By Theorem 2.3, Eq. (2.11) has two solutions: x_1 and $p - x_1$, and Eq. (2.12) has
two solutions: x_2 and $q - x_2$. The four solutions of Eq. (2.10) are thus obtained
using the Chinese Remainder Theorem (Theorem 1.8).

Now, finding the solutions of Eq. (2.11) and (2.12) is particularly easy if
$p + 1$ and $q + 1$ are divisible by 4. Observe that

$$(a^{(p+1)/4})^2 = a^{(p+1)/2} \bmod p = a(a^{(p-1)/2}) \bmod p = a \ .$$

The last equality holds because a is a quadratic residue modulo p; thus, by Theorem 2.5, $a^{(p-1)/2} \bmod p = 1$. This gives us the two solutions:

$$x_1 = a^{(p+1)/4} \bmod p$$
$$x_2 = a^{(q+1)/4} \bmod q \ .$$

Note that Bob cannot find the root y of Eq. (2.10) without knowing p and q. If he
accidentally picks an x that is a multiple of p or q, he can compute $gcd(x, n) = p$
or q, but the probability of this happening is small for large p and q.

Example:
Let $p = 3$ and $q = 7$. Then $n = pq = 21$. Suppose Bob picks $x = 5$ and sends
to Alice

$$a = 5^2 \bmod 21 = 4 \ .$$

Alice computes the roots

$$x_1 = 4^{(3+1)/4} \bmod 3 = 1$$
$$x_2 = 4^{(7+1)/4} \bmod 7 = 2 \ .$$

Applying algorithm *crt* of Figure 1.24, Alice then computes

$$z_1 = crt(n, p, q, x_1, x_2) = 16$$
$$z_2 = crt(n, p, q, x_1, q - x_2) = 19$$
$$z_3 = crt(n, p, q, p - x_1, x_2) = 2$$
$$z_4 = crt(n, p, q, p - x_1, q - x_2) = 5 .$$

Note that $z_4 = x$, the number Bob picked. Let $y = z_2 = 19$. Then $z_3 = n - y$ and $z_1 = n - x$ (whence they can be determined from x and y directly rather than by the Chinese Remainder Theorem—see exercises at end of chapter).

Suppose now that Alice sends the root y to Bob. Bob, using x, computes p and q as follows:

$$gcd(x + y, n) = gcd(5 + 19, 21)$$
$$= gcd(24, 21) = 3 = p .$$
$$q = \frac{n}{p} = \frac{21}{3} = 7 . \quad \blacksquare$$

The oblivious transfer protocol can be used to flip coins by telephone, exchange secrets, and send certified mail [Blum81a,Rabi81,Blum81b]. We shall describe the protocol for coin flipping by telephone. The problem here is to devise a scheme whereby Bob can call HEADS or TAILS and Alice can flip in such a way that each has a 50% chance of winning. Flipping a real coin over the telephone is clearly unsatisfactory because if Bob calls HEADS, Alice can simply say "Sorry, TAILS." The solution given by Blum [Blum81a] is as follows:

Coin flipping protocol
1. Alice selects two large primes p and q and sends $n = pq$ to Bob.
2. Bob checks if n is prime, a prime power, or even; if so, Alice cheated and loses. Bob picks an x and sends $a = x^2$ mod n to Alice.
3. Alice computes the four roots of a, picks one at random, and sends it to Bob.
4. Bob wins if he can factor n.

2.8 KNAPSACK CIPHERS

We shall describe three public-key encryption schemes based on the **NP**-complete knapsack problem. The first two can be used for secrecy, but not authentication. The reason is that the enciphering transformation does not map the entire message space back onto itself; thus, it is not possible to take an arbitrary message and sign it by applying the deciphering transformation. By contrast, the third scheme can be used for authentication but not secrecy. The problem here is just the opposite: although the deciphering algorithm can be applied to all messages, the enciphering algorithm cannot.

Shamir [Sham79] studied the feasibility of constructing a knapsack system for both secrecy and authentication. In order to use a secrecy knapsack system for authentication, the system must be sufficiently dense that most messages can be signed. The interesting result is that any knapsack system with this property is polynomial solvable; thus a single knapsack system cannot be used for both secrecy and signatures.

2.8.1 Merkle-Hellman Knapsacks

Merkle and Hellman [Merk78] proposed a scheme whose security depends on the difficulty of solving the following 0−1 knapsack problem:

Given a positive integer C and a vector $A = (a_1, \ldots, a_n)$ of positive integers, find a subset of the elements of A that sum to C; that is, find a binary vector $M = (m_1, \ldots, m_n)$ such that $C = AM$, or

$$C = \sum_{i=1}^{n} a_i m_i \ . \tag{2.13}$$

This knapsack problem is adapted from Karp's knapsack problem [Karp72], which is to determine simply whether a solution M exists.

Example:
Let $n = 5$, $C = 14$, and $A = (1, 10, 5, 22, 3)$. Then $M = (1, 1, 0, 0, 1)$ is a solution. ∎

The knapsack problem is an **NP**-complete problem. The best known algorithms for solving arbitrary instances of size n require $O(2^{n/2})$ time and $O(2^{n/4})$ space [Schr79]. There is, however, a special class of knapsack problems, referred to as **simple knapsacks**, that can be solved in linear time. In a simple knapsack, the elements a_i $(i = 1, \ldots, n)$ are **super increasing** so that

$$a_i > \sum_{j=1}^{i-1} a_j$$

for $i = 2, \ldots, n$. This implies that

$$m_n = 1 \quad \text{iff} \quad C \geq a_n$$

and, for $i = n - 1, n - 2, \ldots, 1,$

$$(C - \sum_{j=i+1}^{n} m_j a_j) \geq a_i \ .$$

An algorithm for solving simple knapsacks is shown in Figure 2.19.

FIGURE 2.19 Solution to simple knapsack.

Algorithm *snap* (C, A): "Simple Knapsack Solution"
for $i := n$ **downto** 1 **do**
  begin
    if $C \geq a_i$ **then** $m_i := 1$ **else** $m_i := 0$;
    $C := C - a_i * m_i$
  end;
if $C = 0$ **then** *snap* $:= M$ **else** "no solution exists"

Example:

Rearranging the elements of the vector in the preceding example to give A' = (1, 3, 5, 10, 22) shows that A' is a simple knapsack vector, whence $snap(14, A')$ gives the solution (1, 1, 0, 1, 0). ∎

Merkle and Hellman show how to convert a simple knapsack into a **trapdoor knapsack** that is hard to solve without additional information. First, a simple knapsack vector $A' = (a'_1, \ldots, a'_n)$ is selected. This allows an easy solution to a problem $C' = A'M$. Next, an integer u is chosen such that

$$u > 2a'_n > \sum_{i=1}^{n} a'_i .$$

Then an integer w is chosen such that $gcd(u, w) = 1$, and the inverse w^{-1} of w mod u is computed using $w^{-1} = inv(w, u)$ (see Section 1.6.2). Finally, the vector A' is transformed into a hard knapsack vector $A = wA'$ mod u; that is,

$a_i = w * a'_i$ mod u .

Now, solving $C = AM$ is difficult, but with knowledge of the trapdoor information w^{-1} and u, the problem can be transformed into the easy problem:

$$
\begin{aligned}
C' &= w^{-1}C \text{ mod } u \\
   &= w^{-1}AM \text{ mod } u \\
   &= w^{-1}(wA')M \text{ mod } u \\
   &= A'M \text{ mod } u \\
   &= A'M .
\end{aligned}
$$

To apply the trapdoor knapsack problem to public-key encryption, let the public key be the hard knapsack vector A, and let the secret key be the simple knapsack vector A' together with the trapdoor information u and w^{-1} (actually A' can be computed from A, u, and w^{-1} by $A' = w^{-1}A$ mod u). Let E_A denote the enciphering transformation using the public key A, and let D_A denote the deciphering transformation using the secret key (A', u, w^{-1}).

To encipher, the plaintext is broken into blocks $M = (m_1, \ldots, m_n)$ of n bits each. Each block M is then enciphered as

$C = E_A(M) = AM$.

C is deciphered by computing

$D_A(C) = snap(w^{-1}C \text{ mod } u, A') = M$.

Example:

Let $A' = (1, 3, 5, 10)$, $u = 20$, and $w = 7$. Then $w^{-1} = 3$. The simple vector A' is transformed into the "hard" vector

$$
\begin{aligned}
A &= (7 * 1 \text{ mod } 20, 7 * 3 \text{ mod } 20, 7 * 5 \text{ mod } 20, 7 * 10 \text{ mod } 20) \\
  &= (7, 1, 15, 10) .
\end{aligned}
$$

Let $M = 13$, which is the binary vector (1, 1, 0, 1).

Then

$$C = E_A(M) = 7 + 1 + 10 = 18 ,$$

and

$$D_A(C) = D_A(18)$$
$$= snap(3 * 18 \bmod 20, A') = snap(14, A')$$
$$= (1, 1, 0, 1)$$
$$= 13 . \ \blacksquare$$

Merkle and Hellman originally suggested using $n = 100$ or more. Schroeppel and Shamir [Schr79], however, have developed an algorithm that can solve knapsacks of this size. By trading time for space, their method can solve the knapsack problem in time $T = O(2^{n/2})$ and space $S = O(2^{n/4})$. For $n = 100$, $2^{50} \cong 10^{15}$; thus, a single processor could find a solution in about 11,574 days, and 1000 processors could find a solution in about 12 days (ignoring constants and figuring 8.64×10^{10} instructions per day). But if $n = 200$, $2^{100} \cong 10^{30}$, whence the algorithm is computationally infeasible.

Merkle and Hellman suggest choosing several pairs (u, w) and iterating the transformation $A = wA' \bmod u$ to obscure the transformation. Indeed, Shamir and Zippel [Sham80a] show that if this extra precaution is not taken, the scheme is highly vulnerable to cryptanalysis when u is known.

Although the (hard) knapsack problem is **NP**-complete, this does not imply that the trapdoor knapsack problem is also **NP**-complete. It could be that the peculiar structure of the system provides a shortcut solution. No faster solution has yet been found.

Pohlig [Pohl78a] has shown that if a hard knapsack has large simple subsets, it may be feasible to find a solution in a much shorter period of time. The probability of an arbitrary knapsack having large simple subsets is extremely small, however, so this does not seem to be a serious threat.

For $n = 200$, the a_i' are chosen from the range $[(2^{i-1} - 1) 2^{200} + 1, (2^{i-1})2^{200}]$. This gives 2^{200} choices for each a_i', making it difficult for a cryptanalyst to determine any one of them. Because $u > 2a_{200}'$ is required, u is chosen from the range $[2^{401} + 1, 2^{402} - 1]$ and w from the range $[2, u - 2]$. Note that this puts each a_i in the range $[1, 2^{402} - 2]$. Thus, a 200-bit plaintext message M has a ciphertext message (knapsack problem) $C = AM$ with a 410-bit representation (summing 200 402-bit values can add up to $\lceil \log_2 200 \rceil = 8$ bits to the representation, where "$\lceil \ \rceil$" denotes the ceiling function). This is why the scheme cannot be used for authentication. There will be many 410-bit knapsack problems that do not correspond to 200-bit messages, whence the deciphering transformation cannot be applied to arbitrary messages of length 410.

For $n = 200$, the storage requirements for each public vector A are approximately $200 * 400 = 80$ kilobits. In contrast, the RSA scheme uses only about 1 kilobit per public key. Shamir [Sham80b] investigated the feasibility of reducing the storage requirements by either shortening the elements a_i or reducing their number. Let t be the length (in bits) of each a_i ($t = 400$ in the implementation suggested previously). The first strategy fails because the deciphering algorithm becomes ambiguous when $t < n$, and the scheme is insecure when t is sufficiently small. To implement the second strategy, an n-bit message M is broken into d multi-bit chunks $m_1, \ldots, m_d$ such that each coefficient m_i in Eq. (2.13) is n/d bits, and only d elements a_i are needed. This strategy also fails because such "compact knapsacks" are easier to solve than 0–1 knapsacks.

Enciphering and deciphering are faster, however, than in the RSA scheme. For $n = 200$, enciphering requires at most 200 additions, while deciphering requires at most 200 subtractions plus one multiplication in modular arithmetic. In contrast, the RSA scheme requires about 1000 multiplications in modular arithmetic to encipher and decipher. Henry [Henr81] presents a fast knapsack decryption algorithm that optimizes the evaluation of

$$C' = w^{-1}C \bmod u .$$

Letting $b_{n-1}2^{n-1} + \cdots + b_0 2^0$ denote the binary expansion of C, evaluation of C' can be expressed as

$$[b_{n-1}(2^{n-1}w^{-1} \bmod u) + \cdots + b_0(2^0 w^{-1} \bmod u)] \bmod u .$$

Since the terms in parentheses are independent of C, they can be precomputed and stored in a table. Computation of C' thus reduces to a sequence of at most n table lookups and $n - 1$ additions, followed by a single reduction mod u. The reduction mod u is "easy" in that the sum can be no larger than nu.

2.8.2 Graham-Shamir Knapsacks

Graham and Shamir independently discovered a way of obscuring the super-increasing property of trapdoor knapsacks [Sham80c,Lemp79]. A Graham-Shamir trapdoor knapsack vector $A' = (a_1', \ldots, a_n')$ has the property that each a_j' has the following binary representation:

$$a_j' = (R_j, I_j, S_j)$$

where R_j and S_j are long random bit strings, and I_j is a bit string of length n such that the jth high-order bit is 1 and the remaining $n - 1$ bits are 0. Each random bit string S_j has $\log_2 n$ 0's in its high-order bit positions so that summing does not cause them to overflow into the area of the I_j's. Thus a sum $C' = A'M$ has the binary representation:

$$C' = (R, M, S) ,$$

where $R = \sum_{j=1}^{n} R_j m_j$ and $S = \sum_{j=1}^{n} S_j m_j$. Notice that the vector of bit strings $((I_n, S_n), \ldots, (I_1, S_1))$ (i.e., the elements a_j listed in reverse order and without the R_j's) is a simple knapsack vector. The R_j's are added to obscure this property. These knapsacks are even easier to solve than Merkle-Hellman trapdoor knapsacks, however, because M can be extracted directly from the binary representation of C'.

Example:

Let $n = 5$ where A' is given by

j	R_j	I_j	S_j	
1	011010	10000	000101	$= a'_1$
2	001001	01000	000011	$= a'_2$
3	010010	00100	000100	$= a'_3$
4	011000	00010	000111	$= a'_4$
5	000110	00001	000001	$= a'_5$

Let $M = (0, 1, 0, 0, 1)$. Then

$$
\begin{aligned}
C' &= A'M \\
&= a_2 + a_5 \\
&= (R_2 + R_5, I_2 + I_5, S_2 + S_5) \\
&= 001111 \quad 01001 \quad 000100 . \quad \blacksquare
\end{aligned}
$$

A trapdoor knapsack vector A' is converted to a hard knapsack vector A as in the Merkle-Hellman scheme; that is, by picking u and w and computing $A = wA'$ mod u. Similarly, a message M is enciphered as in the Merkle-Hellman scheme, whence $C = E_A(M) = AM$. C is deciphered by computing $C' = w^{-1}C$ mod u and extracting from C' the bits representing M. Shamir and Zippel [Sham80c] believe this variant is safer, faster, and simpler to implement than the original scheme proposed by Merkle and Hellman.

2.8.3 Shamir Signature-Only Knapsacks

Unlike the RSA exponentiation scheme, the trapdoor knapsack schemes cannot be used for authentication. The reason is that the enciphering function is not "onto" the entire message space; thus, certain messages (indeed most!) cannot be deciphered before they are enciphered.

Shamir [Sham78a] shows how a trapdoor knapsack can be constructed to provide digital signatures. Shamir's knapsacks, however, cannot be used for secrecy. The scheme is based on the following **NP**-complete knapsack problem, which is also an extension of the one defined by Karp [Karp72].

Given integers n, M, and $A = (a_1, \ldots, a_{2k})$, find $C = (c_1, \ldots, c_{2k})$ such that $M = CA$ mod n; that is, such that

$$
M = \sum_{j=1}^{2k} c_j a_j \bmod n , \tag{2.14}
$$

where each c_j is an integer in the range $[0, \log n]$.

In a signature-only knapsack system, n is a k-bit random prime number ($k = 100$ would be appropriate). The pair (A, n) is the public key, M is a message in the range $[0, n - 1]$, and C is the signature of M. The recipient of a pair (M, C) can validate the signature by checking that

$$E_A(C) = CA \bmod n = M .$$

But the recipient cannot forge a signature for another message M' without solving the knapsack problem. The signer, however, has secret trapdoor information for generating a signature $C = D_A(M)$.

The secret trapdoor information is a $k \times 2k$ binary matrix H whose values are chosen at random. The vector A is constructed to satisfy the following system of modular linear equations:

$$\begin{pmatrix} h_{1,1} \cdots h_{1,2k} \\ h_{2,1} \cdots h_{2,2k} \\ \cdot \qquad \cdot \\ \cdot \qquad \cdot \\ \cdot \qquad \cdot \\ h_{k,1} \cdots h_{k,2k} \end{pmatrix} \begin{pmatrix} a_1 \\ a_2 \\ \cdot \\ \cdot \\ \cdot \\ a_{2k} \end{pmatrix} = \begin{pmatrix} 2^0 \\ 2^1 \\ \cdot \\ \cdot \\ \cdot \\ 2^{k-1} \end{pmatrix} \bmod n ,$$

giving

$$\sum_{j=1}^{2k} h_{ij} a_j = 2^{i-1} \bmod n \quad i = 1, \ldots, k .$$

Because there are only k equations in $2k$ unknowns, k values of A can be chosen at random, and the remaining values determined by solving the preceding system.

Let M be a message, and let $\overline{M} = (m_1, \ldots, m_k)$ be the reversal of M in binary (i.e., m_i is the ith low-order bit in M, $1 \leq i \leq k$). M is signed by computing

$$C = D_A(M) = \overline{M}H ,$$

whence

$$c_j = \sum_{i=1}^{k} m_i h_{ij} \quad (1 \leq j \leq 2k) .$$

We see C is a valid signature because

$$E_A(C) = CA \bmod n = \sum_{j=1}^{2k} c_j a_j \bmod n$$

$$= \sum_{j=1}^{2k} \left(\sum_{i=1}^{k} m_i h_{ij} \right) a_j \bmod n$$

$$= \sum_{i=1}^{k} m_i \left(\sum_{j=1}^{2k} h_{ij} a_j \right) \bmod n$$

$$= \sum_{i=1}^{k} m_i 2^{i-1} \bmod n$$

$$= M \ .$$

Example:
Let $k = 3$ and $n = 7$. This will allow us to sign messages in the range $[0, 6]$. Let H be as follows:

$$H = \begin{pmatrix} 1 & 0 & 1 & 0 & 0 & 1 \\ 0 & 1 & 1 & 1 & 0 & 1 \\ 1 & 0 & 1 & 1 & 1 & 0 \end{pmatrix}$$

and pick $a_1 = 1$, $a_2 = 2$, and $a_3 = 3$. Solving for the remaining values of A, we get $a_4 = 0$, $a_5 = 0$, and $a_6 = 4$, whence $A = (1, 2, 3, 0, 0, 4)$. Let $M = 3$; because this is 011 in binary, $\overline{M} = (1, 1, 0)$. The signature C is thus:

$$C = \overline{M}H$$

$$= (1 \ 1 \ 0) \begin{pmatrix} 1 & 0 & 1 & 0 & 0 & 1 \\ 0 & 1 & 1 & 1 & 0 & 1 \\ 1 & 0 & 1 & 1 & 1 & 0 \end{pmatrix}$$

$$= (1, 1, 2, 1, 0, 2) \ .$$

To validate C we compute

$$\begin{aligned} CA \bmod 7 &= [(1, 1, 2, 1, 0, 2) \ (1, 2, 3, 0, 0, 4)] \bmod 7 \\ &= [1 + 2 + 6 + 0 + 0 + 8] \bmod 7 \\ &= 17 \bmod 7 \\ &= 3 \ . \ \blacksquare \end{aligned}$$

The signing procedure thus far is insecure, because someone might be able to determine H by examining enough (M, C) pairs. To prevent this, messages are randomized before they are signed. This is done using a random binary vector $R = (r_1, \ldots, r_{2k})$. First,

$$M' = (M - RA) \bmod n$$

is computed; thus

$$M = (M' + RA) \bmod n \ .$$

Next, M' is signed as described previously, giving a signature C'. Finally, the signature of M is computed from C' by adding R, giving $C = C' + R$. C is a valid signature of M because

$$\begin{aligned} CA \bmod n &= (C' + R)A \bmod n \\ &= (C'A + RA) \bmod n \\ &= (M' + RA) \bmod n \\ &= M \ . \end{aligned}$$

Example:

Let k, n, H, A, and M be as before, and let $R = (1, 0, 0, 0, 1, 1)$. Then

$$
\begin{aligned}
M' &= (M - RA) \bmod n \\
&= (3 - [(1, 0, 0, 0, 1, 1) (1, 2, 3, 0, 0, 4)]) \bmod 7 \\
&= (3 - [1 + 0 + 0 + 0 + 0 + 4]) \bmod 7 \\
&= (3 - 5) \bmod 7 = -2 \bmod 7 \\
&= 5 ,
\end{aligned}
$$

and

$$
C' = \overline{M}'H \bmod n = (2, 0, 2, 1, 1, 1) .
$$

The signature of M is thus

$$
\begin{aligned}
C = C' + R &= (2, 0, 2, 1, 1, 1) + (1, 0, 0, 0, 1, 1) \\
&= (3, 0, 2, 1, 2, 2) ,
\end{aligned}
$$

which the reader should verify is also valid. ∎

Because a signature depends on the random vector R, a message M can have multiple signatures C satisfying Eq. (2.14), as illustrated in the preceding examples for $M = 3$. This explains why the scheme cannot be used for secrecy. Because D_A is one-to-many, computing $D_A(E_A(M))$ might not give back M.

The signature-only knapsack system has the advantage of being fast. But, like the other knapsack schemes, it is not known whether it is as difficult to solve as the **NP**-complete problem on which it is based.

2.8.4 A Breakable **NP**-Complete Knapsack

Lempel [Lemp79] describes a conventional (one-key) cipher derived jointly with Even and Yacobi with the peculiar property of being **NP**-complete under a chosen-plaintext attack, yet easily breakable given enough known plaintext. The cipher uses an n-bit secret key of the form $K = (k_1, \ldots, k_n)$, and a knapsack vector $A = (a_1, \ldots, a_n)$ of positive elements, assumed known to the cryptanalyst. Messages are enciphered by breaking them into t-bit blocks of the form $M = (m_1, \ldots, m_t)$, where $t = \lceil \log_2(1 + \sum_{i=1}^{n} a_i) \rceil$.

To encipher a message M, the sender generates a random n-bit vector $R = (r_1, \ldots, r_n)$ and forms the t-bit sum:

$$
S = A(K \oplus R) = \sum_{i=1}^{n} a_i(k_i \oplus r_i) .
$$

M is then enciphered as the $(t + n)$-bit vector

$$
C = (L, R), \text{ where } L = M \oplus S .
$$

Because the last n bits of C contain R, a receiver knowing K and A can compute S and exclusive-or it with L (the first t bits of C) to recover M.

A cryptanalyst, knowing A and a single (M, C) pair, can find S by computing

$$L \oplus M = (M \oplus S) \oplus M = S .$$

To determine K, the cryptanalyst must solve the knapsack problem $S = A(K \oplus R)$, which is **NP**-complete.

If, however, the cryptanalyst knows a set of n pairs $(M_i, C_i) = (M_i, L_i, R_i)$, for $i = 1, \ldots, n$, such that the n vectors $U_i = 1^n - 2R_i$ are linearly independent (1^n is a vector of n 1's), the cryptanalyst can easily solve for the key K. To see how this can be done, observe that

$$\begin{aligned} K \oplus R_i &= K + R_i - 2(K * R_i) \\ &= R_i + K * U_i , \end{aligned}$$

where multiplication ($*$) is componentwise. This leads to the system of equations

$$\begin{aligned} S_i &= A(K \oplus R_i) \\ &= A(R_i + K * U_i) \\ &= AR_i + (U_i * A)K \quad i = 1, \ldots, n . \end{aligned}$$

Letting $T_i = S_i - AR_i$, the n equations can be expressed in matrix form as

$$\begin{pmatrix} T_1 \\ T_2 \\ . \\ . \\ . \\ T_n \end{pmatrix} = \begin{pmatrix} U_1 \\ U_2 \\ . \\ . \\ . \\ U_n \end{pmatrix} \begin{pmatrix} a_1 & 0 & \ldots & 0 \\ 0 & a_2 & \ldots & 0 \\ . & . & . & . \\ . & . & . & . \\ . & . & & . \\ 0 & 0 & \ldots & a_n \end{pmatrix} \begin{pmatrix} k_1 \\ k_2 \\ . \\ . \\ . \\ k_n \end{pmatrix} .$$

Thus the system is readily solved for K when the U_i are linearly independent and the a_i positive. The probability of $N \geq n$ pairs (M_i, C_i) containing a subset of n linearly independent U_i is bounded below by approximately $1/3$ for $N = n$, and quickly approaches 1 as N increases.

This example shows that it is not enough to base a cipher on a computationally hard problem. It is necessary to show that the cipher cannot be broken under any form of attack. The weakness in the scheme is caused by the linear relationship between the plaintext and ciphertext, which does not hold in the other knapsack schemes.

EXERCISES

2.1 Decipher the Churchyard cipher shown in Figure 2.2.
2.2 Decipher the following ciphertext, which was enciphered using a Vigenère cipher with key ART:

YFN GFM IKK IXA T .

2.3 Decipher the following ciphertext, which was enciphered using a Beaufort cipher with key ART:

CDZ ORQ WRH SZA AHP .

2.4 Decipher the following ciphertext, which was enciphered using a Playfair cipher with the key shown in Figure 2.11.

AR HM CW CO KI PW .

2.5 Decipher the ciphertext LJ (11 9) using the decipher matrix

$$\begin{pmatrix} 15 & 20 \\ 17 & 9 \end{pmatrix}$$

with the Hill cipher. (The plaintext is a two-letter word of English).

2.6 Solve the cipher of Figures 2.8–2.10 by finding the remaining two key characters and deciphering the text.

2.7 Consider a linear substitution cipher that uses the transformation $f(a) = ak$ mod 26. Suppose it is suspected that the plaintext letter J (9) corresponds to the ciphertext letter P (15); i.e., $9k$ mod $26 = 15$. Break the cipher by solving for k.

2.8 Consider an affine substitution cipher using the transformation $f(a) = (ak_1 + k_0)$ mod 26. Suppose it is suspected that the plaintext letter E (4) corresponds to the ciphertext letter F (5) and that the plaintext letter H (7) corresponds to the ciphertext letter W (22). Break the cipher by solving for k_1 and k_0.

2.9 Determine the unicity distance of ciphers based on affine transformations of the form $f(a) - (ak_1 + k_0)$ mod 26. Assume the keys k_0 and k_1 generate a complete set of residues, and that all such keys are equally likely.

2.10 Consider a homophonic cipher that uses $26h$ ciphertext symbols, assigning h homophones to each letter of the English alphabet. Determine the number of possible keys (i.e., assignments of homophones), and use your result to calculate the unicity distance of the cipher.

2.11 Suppose that the keys used with DES consist only of the letters A–Z and are 8 letters long. Give an approximation of the length of time it would take to try all such keys using exhaustive search, assuming each key can be tested in one μsec. Do the same for keys 8 letters or digits long.

2.12 Let X' denote the bit-by-bit complement of a block X. Show that if $C = DES_K(M)$, then $C' = DES_{K'}(M')$. Explain how this property can be exploited in a chosen-plaintext attack to reduce the search effort by roughly 50%. (*Hint*: Obtain the ciphertext for a plaintext M and its complement M'.) (This symmetry in the DES was reported in [Hell76].)

2.13 Consider the RSA encryption scheme with public keys $n = 55$ and $e = 7$. Encipher the plaintext $M = 10$. Break the cipher by finding p, q, and d. Decipher the ciphertext $C = 35$.

2.14 Consider the Pohlig-Hellman exponentiation cipher, where

$$E_K(M) = M^e \bmod p(x)$$
$$D_K(C) = C^d \bmod p(x) \ ,$$

$e = 5$, $d = 3$, $p(x) = (x^3 + x + 1)$, and exponentiation is performed in the field $\mathbf{GF}(2^3)$. Because $\phi(p) = 7$ (see Section 1.6.3), $ed \bmod \phi(p) = 1$. Let $M = x^2 + 1 = 101$ in binary. Compute $C = E_K(M)$. Compute $D_K(C)$, showing that deciphering restores M.

2.15 Consider the RSA encryption scheme with $n = pq$, where $p = 5$ and $q = 7$. Prove that all keys d and e in the range $[0, \ \phi(n) - 1]$ must satisfy the equality $d = e$.

2.16 Consider the equations

$$x \bmod p = x_1 \text{ or } p - x_1$$
$$x \bmod q = x_2 \text{ or } q - x_2 \ ,$$

where $n = pq$ for primes p and q. There are four common solutions, given by

$$z_1 = crt(n, p, q, x_1, x_2)$$
$$z_2 = crt(n, p, q, x_1, q - x_2)$$
$$z_3 = crt(n, p, q, p - x_1, x_2)$$
$$z_4 = crt(n, p, q, p - x_1, q - x_2) \ .$$

Show that $z_4 = n - z_1$ and $z_3 = n - z_2$.

2.17 Using the result of the preceding exercise, find the 4 solutions to the equation $x^2 \bmod 77 = 4$ by first finding solutions to $x^2 \bmod 7 = 4$ and $x^2 \bmod 11 = 4$.

2.18 Let $n = pq$ for primes p and q. Given a, $0 < a < n$, let x and y be square roots of a modulo n such that $y \neq x$ and $y \neq n - x$. Show that $gcd(x + y, n) = p$ or q.

2.19 Show how coin flipping by telephone can be implemented using a scheme based on the mental poker protocol. Could either Bob or Alice have an advantage?

2.20 Rabin's public-key encryption scheme enciphers a message M as

$$C = M(M + b) \bmod n \ ,$$

where b and n are public and $n = pq$ for secret primes p and q. Give a deciphering algorithm for the case where $p + 1$ and $q + 1$ are divisible by 4. (*Hint:* compute d such that $2d \bmod n = b$. Then

$$(M + d)^2 \bmod n = (C + d^2) \bmod n \ .)$$

2.21 Suppose that the public key for a Merkle-Hellman knapsack system is given by the vector $A = (17, 34, 2, 21, 41)$, and that the ciphertext $C = 72$ resulted from enciphering some number M with A. The secret key is given by the values $u = 50$ and $w = 17$. Find M by deciphering C.

2.22 Consider Shamir's signature-only knapsack scheme, and let $n = 7$ and

$$H = \begin{pmatrix} 1 & 0 & 1 & 1 & 1 & 1 \\ 0 & 1 & 0 & 0 & 1 & 0 \\ 0 & 0 & 0 & 0 & 0 & 1 \end{pmatrix}$$

Given $a_1 = 1$, $a_2 = 2$, and $a_3 = 3$, compute a_4, a_5, and a_6. Sign the message M = 3, first without randomizing, and then using the random vector $R = (0, 1, 0, 1, 0, 1)$. Check the validity of both signatures.

2.23 *Class Computer Project:*
Teacher: Write a program to encipher a reasonably long message using a Vigenère or Beaufort cipher. (*Optional:* provide programs to compute the index of coincidence *IC* and print histograms of letter frequencies.)
Students: Break the cipher using the computer to analyze the ciphertext and to decipher the message.

2.24 *Class Computer Project:* Implement the DES.
Teacher: Write programs to convert ASCII character sequences into 64-bit blocks and vice versa. Each 64-bit block can be represented internally as a bit or character array of '1's and '0's so the bits are easily addressed; it can be represented externally as a record containing 64 characters ('1's and '0's). Create a file containing the data for the DES tables. Implement the DES, and encipher a message for the students. Give the students a skeleton of your program containing the declarations and statements used to input the DES tables.
Students: Complete the program and decipher the message.

2.25 *Class Computer Project:* Implement the RSA scheme using a 7-digit number n (this can be guaranteed by picking p and q in the range [1000, 3162]) and 6-digit data blocks.
Teacher: Write programs to convert character streams into 6-digit blocks and vice versa (assign a 2-digit number to each character).
Students: Generate keys. Exchange public keys and messages.

2.26 *Class Computer Project:* Implement one of the trapdoor knapsack encryption schemes.

REFERENCES

Adle79. Adleman, L., "A Subexponential Algorithm for the Discrete Logarithm Problem with Applications to Cryptography," *Proc. IEEE 20th Annual Symp. on Found. of Comp. Sci.,* pp. 55–60 (Oct. 1979).

Bark77. Barker, W. G., *Cryptanalysis of the Hagelin Cryptograph*, Aegean Park Press, Laguna Hill, Calif. (1977).

Beal78. "The Beale Ciphers," The Beale Cypher Assoc., Medfield, Mass. (1978).

Blak78. Blakley, B. and Blakley, G. R., "Security of Number Theoretic Public Key Cryptosystems Against Random Attack," *Cryptologia.* In three parts: Part I: Vol. 2, No. 4 (Oct. 1978), pp. 305–321; Part II: Vol. 3, No. 1 (Jan. 1979), pp. 29–42; Part III: Vol. 3, No. 2 (Apr. 1979), pp. 105–118.

Blak79. Blakley, G. R. and Borosh, I., "Rivest-Shamir-Adleman Public Key Cryptosystems Do Not Always Conceal Messages," *Comp. & Math. with Applic.* Vol. 5 pp. 169–178 (1979).

Blum81a. Blum, M., "Three Applications of the Oblivious Transfer: 1. Coin Flipping by Telephone, 2. How to Exchange Secrets, 3. How to Send Certified Electronic Mail," Dept. EECS, Univ. of California, Berkeley, Calif. (1981).

Blum81b. Blum, M. and Rabin, M. O., "How to Send Certified Electronic Mail," Dept. EECS, Univ. of California, Berkeley, Calif. (1981).

Bran79. Branstad, D., "Hellman's Data Does Not Support His Conclusion," *IEEE Spectrum* Vol. 16(7) p. 41 (July 1979).

Davi79. Davida, G. I., "Hellman's Scheme Breaks DES in its Basic Form," *IEEE Spectrum* Vol. 16(7) p. 39 (July 1979).

Davs80. Davies, D. W. and Price, W. L., "The Application of Digital Signatures Based on Public Key Cryptosystems," NPL Report DNACS 39/80, National Physical Lab., Teddington, Middlesex, England (Dec. 1980).

Deav80a. Deavours, C. A., "The Black Chamber: A Column; How the British Broke Enigma," *Cryptologia* Vol. 4(3) pp. 129–132 (July 1980).

Deav80b. Deavours, C. A., "The Black Chamber: A Column; La Methode des Batons," *Cryptologia* Vol. 4(4) pp. 240–247 (Oct. 1980).

Diff76. Diffie, W. and Hellman, M., "New Directions in Cryptography," *IEEE Trans. on Info. Theory* Vol. IT-22(6) pp. 644–654 (Nov. 1976).

Diff77. Diffie, W. and Hellman, M., "Exhaustive Cryptanalysis of the NBS Data Encryption Standard," *Computer* Vol. 10(6) pp. 74–84 (June 1977).

Diff79. Diffie, W. and Hellman, M., "Privacy and Authentication: An Introduction to Cryptography," *Proc. IEEE* Vol. 67(3) pp. 397–427 (Mar. 1979).

Diff81. Diffie, W., "Cryptographic Technology: Fifteen Year Forecast," BNR Inc., Mountain View, Calif. (Jan. 1981).

Feis70. Feistel, H., "Cryptographic Coding for Data-Bank Privacy," RC-2827, T. J. Watson Research Center, Yorktown Heights, N.Y. (Mar. 1970).

Feis73. Feistel, H., "Cryptography and Computer Privacy," *Sci. Am.* Vol. 228(5) pp. 15–23 (May 1973).

Feis75. Feistel, H., Notz, W. A., and Smith, J., "Some Cryptographic Techniques for Machine to Machine Data Communications," *Proc. IEEE* Vol. 63(11) pp. 1545–1554 (Nov. 1975).

Frie18. Friedman, W. F., "Methods for the Solution of Running-Key Ciphers," Riverbank Publication No. 16, Riverbank Labs, Geneva, Ill. (1918).

Frie20. Friedman, W. F., "The Index of Coincidence and Its Applications in Cryptography," Riverbank Publication No. 22, Riverbank Labs., Geneva, Ill. (1920).

Frie67. Friedman, W. F., "Cryptology," *Encyclopedia Britannica* Vol. 6 pp. 844–851 (1967).

Gain56. Gaines, H. F., *Cryptanalysis*, Dover, New York (1956).

Gard77. Gardner, M., "Mathematical Games," *Sci. Am.* Vol. 237(2) pp. 120–124 (Aug. 1977).

Gill80. Gillogly, J. J., "The Beale Ciphers: A Dissenting Opinion," *Cryptologia* Vol. 4(2) pp. 116–119 (Apr. 1980).

Hamm71. Hammer, C., "Signature Simulation and Certain Cryptographic Codes," *Comm. ACM* Vol. 14(1) pp. 3–14 (Jan. 1971).

Hamm79. Hammer, C., "How Did TJB Encode B2?" *Cryptologia* Vol. 3(1) pp. 9–15 (Jan. 1979).

Hamm81. Hammer, C., "High Order Homophonic Ciphers," *Cryptologia* Vol. 5(4) pp. 231–242, (Oct. 1981).

Hell76. Hellman, M., Merkle, R., Schroeppel, R., Washington, L., Diffie, W., Pohlig, S., and Schweitzer, P., "Results of an Initial Attempt to Cryptanalyze the NBS Data Encryption Standard," Information Systems Lab., Dept. of Electrical Eng., Stanford Univ. (1976).

Hell79. Hellman, M. E., "DES Will Be Totally Insecure Within Ten Years," *IEEE Spectrum* Vol. 16(7) pp. 32–39 (July 1979).

Hell80. Hellman, M. E., "A Cryptanalytic Time-Memory Tradeoff," *IEEE Trans. on Info. Theory* Vol. IT-26(4) pp. 401–406 (July 1980).

Henr81. Henry, P. S., "Fast Decryption Algorithm for the Knapsack Cryptographic System," *Bell System Tech. J.*, Vol. 60 (5) pp. 767–773 (May–June 1981).

Hill 29. Hill, L. S., "Cryptography in an Algebraic Alphabet," *Am. Math. Monthly* Vol. 36 pp. 306–312 (June–July 1929).

Kahn67. Kahn, D., *The Codebreakers*, Macmillan Co., New York (1967).

Kam78. Kam, J. B. and Davida, G. I., "A Structured Design of Substitution-Permutation Encryption Networks," pp. 95–113 in *Foundations of Secure Computation*, ed. R. A. DeMillo et al., Academic Press, New York (1978).

Karp72. Karp, R. M., "Reducibility Among Combinatorial Problems," pp. 85–104 in *Complexity of Computer Computations*, ed. R. E. Miller and J. W. Thatcher, Plenum Press, New York (1972).

Kasi63. Kasiski, F. W., *Die Geheimschriften und die Dechiffrir-kunst*, Mittler & Son (1863).

Knut69. Knuth, D., *The Art of Computer Programming; Vol. 2, Seminumerical Algorithms*, Addison-Wesley, Reading, Mass. (1969).

Konf78. Kohnfelder, L. M., "On the Signature Reblocking Problem in Public-Key Cryptosystems," *Comm. ACM* Vol. 21(2) p. 179 (Feb. 1978).

Konh81. Konheim, A. G., *Cryptography: A Primer*, John Wiley & Sons, New York (1981).

Kowa80. Kowalchuk, J., Shanning, B. P., and Powers, S. A., "Communications Privacy: Integration of Public and Secret Key Cryptography," *Proc. Nat'l. Telecommunications Conf.*, pp. 49.1.1–49.1.5 (Dec. 1980).

Kruh77. Kruh, L., "The Churchyard Ciphers," *Cryptologia* Vol. 1(4) pp. 372–375 (Oct. 1977).

Lemp79. Lempel, A., "Cryptology in Transition," *Computing Surveys* Vol. 11(4) pp. 285–303 (Dec. 1979).

LeVe77. LeVeque, W. J., *Fundamentals of Number Theory*, Addison-Wesley, Reading, Mass. (1977).

Lipt79a. Lipton, R. J., "How to Cheat at Mental Poker," Comp. Sci., Dept. Univ. of Calif., Berkeley, Calif. (Aug. 1979).

Lipt79b. Lipton, R. J., "An Improved Power Encryption Method," Comp. Sci., Dept. Univ. of Calif., Berkeley, Calif. (Aug. 1979).

Mell73. Mellen, G. E., "Cryptology, Computers, and Common Sense," pp. 569–579 in *Proc. NCC, Vol. 42*, AFIPS Press, Montvale, N.J. (1973).

Merk78. Merkle, R. C. and Hellman, M. E., "Hiding Information and Signatures in Trapdoor Knapsacks," *IEEE Trans. on Info. Theory* Vol. IT-24(5) pp. 525–530 (Sept. 1978).

Merk81. Merkle, R. C. and Hellman, M. E., "On the Security of Multiple Encryption," *Comm. ACM* Vol. 27(7) pp. 465–467 (July 1981).

Morr77. Morris, R., Sloane, N. J. A., and Wyner, A. D., "Assessment of the National Bureau of Standards Proposed Federal Data Encryption Standard," *Cryptologia* Vol. 1(3) pp. 281–291 (July 1977).

NBS77. "Data Encryption Standard," FIPS PUB 46, National Bureau of Standards, Washington, D.C. (Jan. 1977).

Nive72. Niven, I. and Zuckerman, H. S., *An Introduction to the Theory of Numbers*, John Wiley & Sons, New York (1972).

Pele79. Peleg, S. and Rosenfeld, A., "Breaking Substitution Ciphers Using a Relaxation Algorithm," *Comm. ACM* Vol. 22(11) pp. 598–605 (Nov. 1979).

Pohl78a. Pohlig, S. and Hellman, M., "An Improved Algorithm for Computing Logarithms over $GF(p)$ and its Cryptographic Significance," *IEEE Trans. on Info. Theory* Vol. IT-24(1) pp. 106–110 (Jan. 1978).

Pohl78b. Pohlig, S., "Bounds on a Class of Easily Solved Knapsacks," MIT Lincoln Lab., Lexington, Mass. (1978).

Prat42. Pratt, F., *Secret and Urgent*, Blue Ribbon Books, Garden City, N.Y. (1942).

Rabi79. Rabin, M. O., "Digitalized Signatures and Public-Key Functions as Intractable as Factorization," MIT/LCS/TR-212, MIT Lab. for Computer Science, Cambridge, Mass. (Jan. 1979).

Rabi81. Rabin, M. O., "Exchange of Secrets," Dept. of Applied Physics, Harvard Univ., Cambridge, Mass. (1981).

Rive78a. Rivest, R. L., Shamir, A., and Adleman, L., "A Method for Obtaining Digital Signatures and Public-Key Cryptosystems," *Comm. ACM* Vol. 21(2) pp. 120–126 (Feb. 1978).

Rive78b. Rivest, R. L., "Remarks on a Proposed Cryptanalytic Attack of the M.I.T. Public Key Cryptosystem," *Cryptologia* Vol. 2(1) pp. 62–65 (Jan. 1978).

Rive80. Rivest, R. L., "A Description of a Single-Chip Implementation of the RSA Cipher," *Lambda* Vol. 1(3) pp. 14–18 (1980).

Rive81. Rivest, R. L., "Statistical Analysis of the Hagelin Cryptograph," *Cryptologia* Vol. 5(1) pp. 27–32 (Jan. 1981).

Sam79. Sam, E., "Musical Cryptography," *Cryptologia* Vol. 3(4) pp. 193–201 (Oct. 1979).

Schr79. Schroeppel, R. and Shamir, A., "A $TS^2 = O(2^n)$ Time/Space Tradeoff for Certain **NP**-Complete Problems," *Proc. IEEE 20th Annual Symp. on Found. of Comp. Sci.*, (Oct. 1979).

Sham78. Shamir, A., "A Fast Signature Scheme," MIT/LCS/TM-107, MIT Lab. for Computer Science, Cambridge, Mass. (July 1978).

Sham79. Shamir, A., "On the Cryptocomplexity of Knapsack Systems," *Proc. 11th Annual ACM Symp. on the Theory of Computing*, pp. 118–129 (1979).

Sham80a. Shamir, A., Rivest, R. L., and Adleman, L. M., "Mental Poker," in *The Mathematical Gardner*, ed. D. Klarner, Prindle, Weber & Schmidt, Boston, Mass. (1980).

Sham80b. Shamir, A., "The Cryptographic Security of Compact Knapsacks (Preliminary Report)," pp. 94–99 in *Proc. 1980 Symp. on Security and Privacy*, IEEE Computer Society (Apr. 1980).

Sham80c. Shamir, A. and Zippel, R. E., "On the Security of the Merkle-Hellman Cryptographic Scheme," *IEEE Trans. on Info. Theory* Vol. IT-26(3) pp. 339–40 (May 1980).

Shan49. Shannon, C. E., "Communication Theory of Secrecy Systems," *Bell Syst. Tech. J.* Vol. 28 pp. 656–715 (Oct. 1949).

Simm77. Simmons, G. J. and Norris, J. N., "Preliminary Comments on the M.I.T. Public Key Cryptosystem," *Cryptologia* Vol. 1(4) pp. 406–414 (Oct. 1977).

Sink66. Sinkov, A., *Elementary Cryptanalysis*, Math. Assoc. Am. (1966).

Solo77. Solovay, R. and Strassen, V., "A Fast Monte-Carlo Test for Primality," *SIAM J. Computing* Vol. 6 pp. 84–85 (Mar. 1977).

Stah73. Stahl, F. A., "A Homophonic Cipher for Computational Cryptography," pp. 565–568 in *Proc. NCC*, Vol. 42, AFIPS Press, Montvale, N.J. (1973).

Suga79. Sugarman, R., "On Foiling Computer Crime," *IEEE Spectrum* Vol. 16(7) pp. 31–32 (July 1979).

Tuch79. Tuchman, W., "Hellman Presents No Shortcut Solutions to the DES," *IEEE Spectrum* Vol. 16(7) pp. 40–41 (July 1979).

Vino55. Vinogradov, I. M., *An Introduction to the Theory of Numbers*, Pergamon Press, Elmsford, N.Y. (1955).

Ward85. Ward, J. B., *The Beale Papers*, Pamphlet printed by Virginian Book and Job Print; reprinted by The Beale Cypher Assoc., Medfield, Mass. (1885).

Will80. Williams, H. C., "A Modification of the RSA Public-Key Encryption Algorithm," *IEEE Trans. on Info. Theory* Vol. IT-26(6) pp. 726–729 (Nov. 1980).

Cryptographic Techniques

3.1 BLOCK AND STREAM CIPHERS

Let M be a plaintext message. A **block cipher** breaks M into successive blocks M_1, $M_2, \ldots$, and enciphers each M_1 with the same key K; that is,

$$E_K(M) = E_K(M_1)E_K(M_2) \ldots .$$

Each block is typically several characters long. Examples of block ciphers are shown in Table 3.1. Simple substitution and homophonic substitution ciphers are block ciphers, even though the unit of encipherment is a single character. This is because the same key is used for each character. We shall return to block ciphers in Section 3.4.

A **stream cipher** breaks the message M into successive characters or bits m_1, $m_2, \ldots$, and enciphers each m_i with the ith element k_i of a **key stream** $K = k_1 k_2 \ldots$; that is,

TABLE 3.1 Block ciphers.

Cipher	Block size
Transposition with period d	d characters
Simple substitution	1 character
Homophonic substitution	1 character
Playfair	2 characters
Hill with $d \times d$ matrix	d characters
DES	64 bits
Exponentiation mod n	$\log_2 n$ bits (664 bits recommended)
Knapsacks of length n	n bits (200 bits recommended)

$$E_K(M) = E_{k_1}(m_1)E_{k_2}(m_2) \ldots .$$

A stream cipher is **periodic** if the key stream repeats after d characters, for some fixed d; otherwise, it is nonperiodic. Ciphers generated by Rotor and Hagelin machines are periodic stream ciphers. The Vernam cipher (one-time pad) and running-key ciphers are nonperiodic stream ciphers.

A periodic substitution cipher with a short period (e.g., Vigenère cipher) is normally regarded as a stream cipher because plaintext characters are enciphered one by one, and adjacent characters are enciphered with a different part of the key. But it has characteristics in common with both types of ciphers. Let $K = k_1 k_2 \ldots k_d$, where d is the period of the cipher. The cipher can be regarded as a block cipher, where each M_i is a block of d letters:

$$E_K(M) = E_K(M_1)E_K(M_2) \ldots ,$$

or as a stream cipher, where each m_i is one letter, and K is repeated in the key stream; that is, the key stream is:

$$\overbrace{k_1 \ldots k_d}^{K} \quad \overbrace{k_1 \ldots k_d}^{K} \quad \overbrace{k_1 \ldots k_d}^{K} \ldots$$

For short periods, the cipher is more like a block cipher than a stream cipher, but it is a weak block cipher because the characters are not diffused over the entire block. As the length of the period increases, the cipher becomes more like a stream cipher.

There are two different approaches to stream encryption: synchronous methods and self-synchronous methods (see Table 3.2). In a **synchronous stream cipher**, the key stream is generated independently of the message stream. This means that if a ciphertext character is lost during transmission, the sender and receiver must

TABLE 3.2 Stream ciphers.

Synchronous stream ciphers	Period
Vigenère with period d	d
Rotor machines with t rotors	26^t
Hagelin machines with t wheels, each having p_i pins	$p_1 p_2 \cdots p_t$
Running-key	—
Vernam	—
Linear Feedback Shift Registers with n-bit register	2^n
Output-block feedback mode with DES†	2^{64}
Counter method with DES	2^{64}

Self-synchronous methods
Autokey cipher
Cipher feedback mode

† It can be less; see [Hell80].

FIGURE 3.1 Propagation of error with self-synchronous stream cipher.

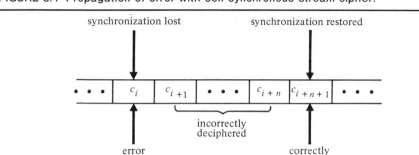

resynchronize their key generators before they can proceed further. Furthermore, this must be done in a way that ensures no part of the key stream is repeated (thus the key generator should not be reset to an earlier state). All the stream ciphers we have discussed so far are synchronous. Section 3.2 describes three methods better suited for digital computers and communications: Linear Feedback Shift Registers, output-block feedback mode, and the counter method. These ciphers are also periodic.

In a **self-synchronous stream cipher**, each key character is derived from a fixed number n of preceding ciphertext characters. Thus, if a ciphertext character is lost or altered during transmission, the error propagates forward for n characters, but the cipher resynchronizes by itself after n correct ciphertext characters have been received (see Figure 3.1). Section 3.3 describes two self-synchronous stream ciphers: autokey ciphers and cipher feedback mode. Self-synchronous stream ciphers are nonperiodic because each key character is functionally dependent on the entire preceding message stream.

Even though self-synchronous stream ciphers do not require resynchronization when errors occur, transmission errors cannot be ignored. The errors could be a sign of active wiretapping on the channel. Even if the errors are not caused by wiretapping, retransmission is necessary if the application requires recovery of lost or damaged characters.

Although protocols for recovering from transmission errors are beyond the scope of this book, we shall briefly describe the role of error detecting and correcting codes in cryptographic systems. Diffie and Hellman [Diff79] observe that if errors are propagated by the decryption algorithm, applying error detecting codes before encryption (and after decryption—see Figure 3.2) provides a mechanism for authenticity, because modifications to the ciphertext will be detected by the

FIGURE 3.2 Encryption used with error detecting codes.

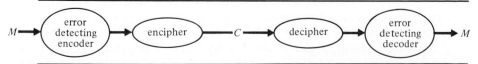

error decoder. Block ciphers and self-synchronous stream ciphers propagate errors, so this strategy is applicable for both of these modes of operation. Synchronous stream ciphers, on the other hand, do not propagate errors because each ciphertext character is independently enciphered and deciphered. If a fixed linear error detecting code is used, then an opponent could modify the ciphertext character and adjust the parity bits to match the corresponding changes in the message bits. To protect against this, a keyed or nonlinear error detecting code can be used. Error correcting codes must be applied after encryption (because of the error propagation by the decryption algorithm), but can be used with error detecting codes (applied before encryption) for authentication.

Communication protocols for initiating and terminating connections and synchronizing key streams are also beyond the scope of this book. It is worth noting, however, that such protocols must require message acknowledgement to detect deletion of messages. (For a more detailed description of the cryptography-communications interface, see [Bran75,Bran78,Feis75,Kent76,Pope79].)

All the stream ciphers discussed in this chapter use a simple exclusive-or operation for enciphering and deciphering (as in the Vernam cipher). Thus, the enciphering algorithm is given by:

$$c_i = E_{k_i}(m_i) = m_i \oplus k_i \ ,$$

where each k_i, m_i, and c_i is one bit or character. The deciphering algorithm is the same:

$$D_{k_i}(c_i) = c_i \oplus k_i$$
$$= (m_i \oplus k_i) \oplus k_i$$
$$= m_i \ .$$

3.2 SYNCHRONOUS STREAM CIPHERS

A synchronous stream cipher is one in which the key stream $K = k_1 k_2 \ldots$ is generated independently of the message stream. The algorithm that generates the stream must be deterministic so the stream can be reproduced for decipherment. (This is unnecessary if K is stored, but storing long key streams may be impractical.) Thus, any algorithm that derives the stream from some random property of the computer system is ruled out. The starting stage of the key generator is initialized by a "seed" I_0. Figure 3.3 illustrates.

We saw in Chapter 2 that stream ciphers are often breakable if the key stream repeats or has redundancy; to be unbreakable, it must be a random sequence as long as the plaintext. Intuitively, this means each element in the key alphabet should be uniformly distributed over the key stream, and there should be no long repeated subsequences or other patterns (e.g., see [Knut69,Brig76] for a discussion of criteria for judging randomness).

No finite algorithm can generate truly random sequences [Chai74]. Although this does not rule out generating acceptable keys from pseudo-random number generators, the usual congruence type generators are unacceptable.

FIGURE 3.3 Synchronous stream cipher.

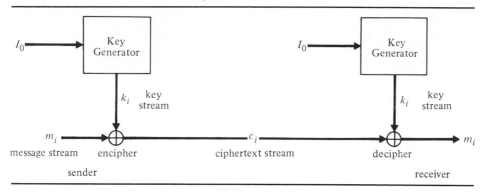

Even a good pseudo-random number generator is not always suitable for key generation. Linear Feedback Shift Registers are an example; given a relatively small amount of plaintext-ciphertext pairs, a cryptanalyst can easily derive the entire key stream. Because this technique illustrates the possible pitfalls of key generators, we shall describe it before turning to methods that appear to be much stronger.

3.2.1 Linear Feedback Shift Registers

An n-stage **Linear Feedback Shift Register** (LFSR) consists of a shift register $R = (r_n, r_{n-1}, \ldots, r_1)$ and a "tap" sequence $T = (t_n, t_{n-1}, \ldots, t_1)$, where each r_i and t_i is one binary digit. At each step, bit r_1 is appended to the key stream, bits $r_n, \ldots, r_2$ are shifted right, and a new bit derived from T and R is inserted into the left end of the register (see Figure 3.4). Letting $R' = (r'_n, r'_{n-1}, \ldots, r'_1)$ denote the next state of R, we see that the computation of R' is thus:

$$r'_i = r_{i+1} \quad i = 1, \ldots, n-1$$

$$r'_n = TR = \sum_{i=1}^{n} t_i r_i \bmod 2 = t_1 r_1 \oplus t_2 r_2 \oplus \ldots \oplus t_n r_n .$$

FIGURE 3.4 Linear Feedback Shift Register (LFSR).

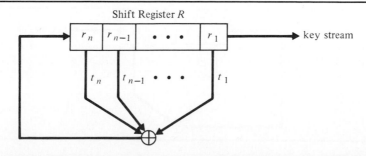

Thus,

$$R' = HR \bmod 2 \ , \qquad\qquad (3.1)$$

where H is the $n \times n$ matrix:

$$H = \begin{pmatrix} t_n & t_{n-1} & t_{n-2} & \cdots & t_3 & t_2 & t_1 \\ 1 & 0 & 0 & & 0 & 0 & 0 \\ 0 & 1 & 0 & & 0 & 0 & 0 \\ 0 & 0 & 1 & & 0 & 0 & 0 \\ & & & \cdot & & & \\ & & & \cdot & & & \\ & & & \cdot & & & \\ 0 & 0 & 0 & & 1 & 0 & 0 \\ 0 & 0 & 0 & \cdots & 0 & 1 & 0 \end{pmatrix} .$$

An n-stage LFSR can generate pseudo-random bit strings with a period of $2^n - 1$ (e.g., see [Golu67]). To achieve this, the tap sequence T must cause R to cycle through all $2^n - 1$ nonzero bit sequences before repeating. This will happen if the polynomial

$$T(x) = t_n x^n + t_{n-1} x^{n-1} + \cdots + t_1 x + 1 \ ,$$

formed from the elements in the tap sequence plus the constant 1, is primitive. A **primitive polynomial** of degree n is an irreducible polynomial that divides $x^{2^n-1} + 1$, but not $x^d + 1$ for any d that divides $2^n - 1$. Primitive trinomials of the form $T(x) = x^n + x^a + 1$ are particularly appealing, because only two stages of the feedback register need be tapped. (See [Golu67,Pete72,Zier68,Zier69] for tables of primitive polynomials.)

Example:
Figure 3.5 illustrates a 4-stage LFSR with tap sequence $T = (1, 0, 0, 1)$; thus there are "taps" on bits r_1 and r_4. The matrix H is given by

$$H = \begin{pmatrix} 1 & 0 & 0 & 1 \\ 1 & 0 & 0 & 0 \\ 0 & 1 & 0 & 0 \\ 0 & 0 & 1 & 0 \end{pmatrix} .$$

FIGURE 3.5 Four-stage LFSR.

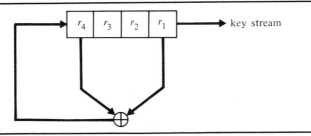

The polynomial $T(x) = x^4 + x + 1$ is primitive, so the register will cycle through all 15 nonzero bit combinations in $\mathbf{GF}(2^3)$ before repeating. Starting R in the initial state 0001, we have

```
0 0 0 1
1 0 0 0
1 1 0 0
1 1 1 0
1 1 1 1
0 1 1 1
1 0 1 1
0 1 0 1
1 0 1 0
1 1 0 1
0 1 1 0
0 0 1 1
1 0 0 1
0 1 0 0
0 0 1 0
```

The rightmost column gives the key stream $K = 100011110101100$.   ■

A binary message stream $M = m_1 m_2 \ldots$ is enciphered by computing $c_i = m_i \oplus k_i$ as the bits of the key stream are generated (see Figure 3.6). Deciphering is done in exactly the same way; that is, by regenerating the key stream and computing $c_i \oplus k_i = m_i$. The seed I_0 is used to initialize R for both encipherment and decipherment.

The feedback loop attempts to simulate a one-time pad by transforming a short key (I_0) into a long pseudo-random sequence K. Unfortunately, the result is a poor approximation of the one-time pad.

The tap sequence T is easily determined in a known-plaintext attack [Meye 73,Meye72]. Following the description in [Diff79], we shall show how this is done using just $2n$ bits of plaintext-ciphertext pairs. Let $M = m_1 \ldots m_{2n}$ be the plaintext corresponding to ciphertext $C = c_1 \ldots c_{2n}$. We can determine the key sequence $K = k_1 \ldots k_{2n}$ by computing

FIGURE 3.6 Encryption with LFSR.

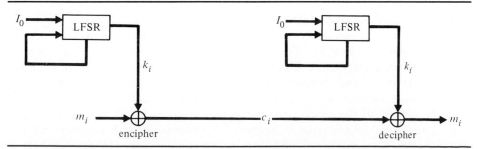

$$m_i \oplus c_i = m_i \oplus (m_i \oplus k_i) = k_i \ ,$$

for $i = 1, \ldots, 2n$.

Let R_i be a column vector representing the contents of register R during the ith step of the computation. Then

$$R_1 = (k_n, k_{n-1} \ \ldots, k_1)$$
$$R_2 = (k_{n+1}, k_n \ \ldots, k_2)$$

$$R_{n+1} = (k_{2n}, k_{2n-1} \ \ldots, k_{n+1}) \ .$$

Let X and Y be the following matrices:

$$X = (R_1, R_2, \ldots, R_n)$$
$$Y = (R_2, R_3, \ldots, R_{n+1}) \ .$$

Using Eq. (3.1), we find that X and Y are related by

$$Y = HX \bmod 2 \ .$$

Because X is always nonsingular, H can be computed from

$$H = YX^{-1} \bmod 2 \tag{3.2}$$

and T can be obtained from the first row of H. The number of operations required to compute the inverse matrix X^{-1} is on the order of n^3, whence the cipher can be broken in less than 1 day on a machine with a 1 μsec instruction time for values of n as large as 1000.

3.2.2 Output-Block Feedback Mode

The weakness of LFSRs is caused by the linearity of Eq. (3.1). A better approach is to use a nonlinear transformation. Nonlinear block ciphers such as the DES seem to be good candidates for this. Figure 3.7 illustrates an approach called **output-block feedback mode** (OFM). The feedback register R is used as input to a block encryption algorithm E_B with key B. During the ith iteration, $E_B(R)$ is computed, the low-order (rightmost) character of the output block becomes the ith key character k_i, and the entire block is fed back through R to be used as input during the next iteration. Note that each k_i is one character rather than just a single bit; this is to reduce the number of encipherments with E_B, which will be considerably more time-consuming than one iteration of a LFSR. A message stream is broken into characters and enciphered in parallel with key generation as described earlier. The technique has also been called **internal feedback** [Camp78] because the feedback is internal to the process generating the key stream; by contrast, the self-synchronous method described in Section 3.3.2 uses a feedback loop derived from the ciphertext stream. (See [Gait77] for a discussion of using DES in OFM.)

FIGURE 3.7 Synchronous stream cipher in output-block feedback mode (OFM).

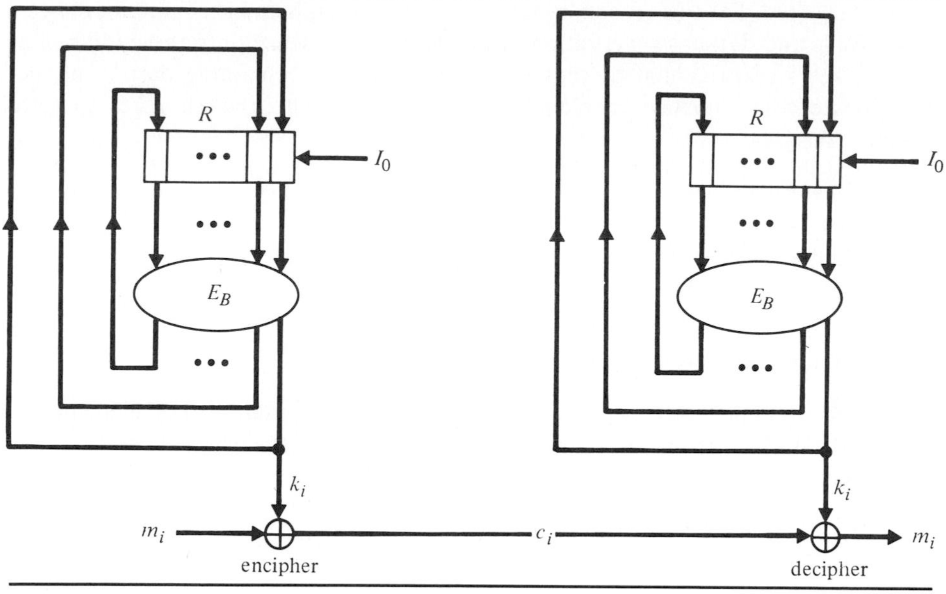

3.2.3 Counter Method

Diffie and Hellman [Diff79,Hell80] have suggested a different approach called the **counter method**. Rather than recycling the output of E_B back through E_B, successive input blocks are generated by a simple counter (see Figure 3.8).

With the counter method, it is possible to generate the ith key character k_i without generating the first $i - 1$ key characters by setting the counter to $I_0 + i - 1$. This capability is especially useful for accessing the ith character in a direct access file. With OFM, it is necessary to first compute $i - 1$ key characters.

FIGURE 3.8 Synchronous stream cipher in counter mode.

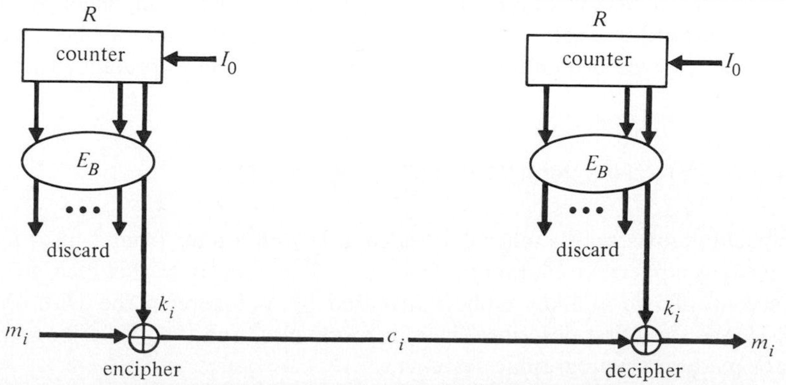

In Section 2.4.4, we saw that stream ciphers could be broken if the key stream repeated. For this reason, synchronous stream ciphers have limited applicability to file and database encryption; if an element is inserted into the middle of a file, the key stream cannot be reused to reencipher the remaining portion of the file. To see why, suppose an element m' is inserted into the file after the ith element. We have:

original plaintext: $\ldots\ m_i\ m_{i+1}\ m_{i+2}\ \ldots$
key stream: $\ldots\ k_i\ k_{i+1}\ k_{i+2}\ \ldots$
original ciphertext: $\ldots\ c_i\ c_{i+1}\ c_{i+2}\ \ldots$

updated plaintext: $\ldots\ m_i\ m'\ \ \ m_{i+1}\ \ldots$
key stream: $\ldots\ k_i\ k_{i+1}\ k_{i+2}\ \ldots$
updated ciphertext: $\ldots\ c_i\ c'_{i+1}\ c'_{i+2}\ \ldots$

Bayer and Metzger [Baye76] show that if m' is known, then all key elements k_j and plaintext elements m_j $(j > i)$ can be determined from the original and updated ciphertext:

$$k_{i+1} = c'_{i+1} \oplus m' \qquad m_{i+1} = c_{i+1} \oplus k_{i+1}$$
$$k_{i+2} = c'_{i+2} \oplus m_{i+1}, \quad m_{i+2} = c_{i+2} \oplus k_{i+2}$$
$$.$$
$$.$$
$$.$$

Note that a cryptanalyst does not need to know the position in the file where the insertion is made; this can be determined by comparing the original and updated versions of the file.

Synchronous stream ciphers protect against ciphertext searching, because identical blocks of characters in the message stream are enciphered under a different part of the key stream. They also protect against injection of false ciphertext, replay, and ciphertext deletion, because insertions or deletions in the ciphertext stream cause loss of synchronization.

Synchronous stream ciphers have the advantage of not propagating errors; a transmission error affecting one character will not affect subsequent characters. But this is also a disadvantage in that it is easier for an opponent to modify (without detection) a single ciphertext character than a block of characters. As noted earlier, a keyed or nonlinear error detecting code helps protect against this.

3.3 SELF-SYNCHRONOUS STREAM CIPHERS

A self-synchronous stream cipher derives each key character from a fixed number n of preceding ciphertext characters [Sava67]. The genesis of this idea goes back to the second of two autokey ciphers invented by Vigenère in the 16th Century [Kahn67]. We shall first describe Vigenère's schemes, and then describe a method suited for modern cryptographic systems.

3.3.1 Autokey Ciphers

An **autokey cipher** is one in which the key is derived from the message it enciphers. In Vigenère's first cipher, the key is formed by appending the plaintext $M = m_1 m_2$ ... to a "priming key" character k_1; the ith key character ($i > 1$) is thus given by $k_i = m_{i-1}$.

Example:
Given the priming key D, the plaintext RENAISSANCE is enciphered as follows, using a shifted substitution cipher (Vigenère actually used other substitutions):

$$M \quad = \text{R E N A I S S A N C E}$$
$$K \quad = \text{D R E N A I S S A N C}$$
$$E_K(M) = \text{U V R N I A K S N P G}. \quad ■$$

In Vigenère's second cipher, the key is formed by appending each character of the ciphertext to the priming key k_1; that is, $k_i = c_{i-1}$ ($i > 1$) .

Example:
Here the plaintext RENAISSANCE is enciphered with the priming key D as follows:

$$M \quad = \text{R E N A I S S A N C E}$$
$$K \quad = \text{D U Y L L T L D D Q S}$$
$$E_K(M) = \text{U Y L L T L D D Q S W}. \quad ■$$

Of course, neither of these ciphers is strong by today's standards. But Vigenère's discovery that nonrepeating key streams could be generated from the messages they encipher was a significant contribution to cryptography.

Vigenère's second autokey cipher is a self-synchronous system in the sense that each key character is computed from the preceding ciphertext character (here, the computation is a simple identity operation).

Even though each key character can be computed from its preceding ciphertext character, it is functionally dependent on all preceding characters in the message plus the priming key. Thus, each ciphertext character is functionally dependent on the entire preceding message. This phenomenon, sometimes called "garble extension", makes cryptanalysis more difficult, because the statistical properties of the plaintext are diffused across the ciphertext.

3.3.2 Cipher Feedback

Vigenère's system is weak because it exposes the key in the ciphertext stream. This problem is easily remedied by passing the ciphertext characters through a nonlinear block cipher to derive the key characters. The technique is called **cipher feed-**

FIGURE 3.9 Self-synchronous stream cipher in cipher feedback mode (CFB).

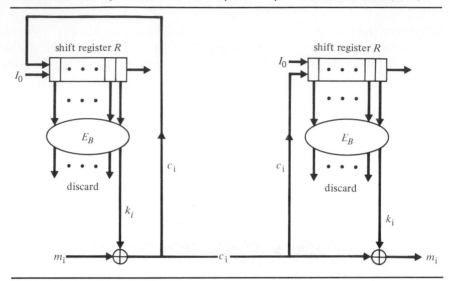

back mode (CFB) because the ciphertext characters participate in the feedback loop. It is sometimes called "chaining", because each ciphertext character is functionally dependent on (chained to) preceding ciphertext characters. This mode has been approved by the National Bureau of Standards for use with DES [GSA77].

Figure 3.9 illustrates. The feedback register R is a shift register, where each ciphertext character c_i is shifted into one end of R immediately after being generated (the character at the other end is simply discarded). As before, R is initialized to the seed I_0. During each iteration, the value of R is used as input to a block encryption algorithm E_B, and the low-order character of the output block becomes the next key character.

With CFB, transmission errors affect the feedback loop. If a ciphertext character is altered (or lost) during transmission, the receiver's shift register will differ from the transmitter's, and subsequent ciphertext will not be correctly deciphered until the erroneous character has shifted out of the register. Because the registers are synchronized after n cycles (where n is the number of characters per block), an error affects at most n characters; after that, the ciphertext is correct (see Figure 3.1).

CFB is comparable to the counter method in its ability to access data in random access files. To decipher the ith ciphertext character c_i, it suffices to load the feedback register with the n preceding ciphertext characters $c_{i-n}, \ldots, c_{i-1}$, and execute one cycle of the feedback loop to get k_i.

With CFB, it is possible to make an insertion or deletion in a file without reenciphering the entire file. It is, however, necessary to reencipher all characters after the place of insertion or deletion, or the following block of characters will not be decipherable. Reencipherment can be confined to a single record in a file by reinitializing the feedback loop for each record. Although this exposes identical records, identical records can be concealed by prefixing each record with a random block of characters, which is discarded when the record is deciphered for processing. Note that cipher feedback is not vulnerable to the insertion/deletion attack described for synchronous ciphers. This is because the key stream is automatically changed by any change in the message stream.

Self-synchronous ciphers protect against ciphertext searching because different parts of the message stream are enciphered under different parts of the key stream. They also protect against all types of authenticity threats because any change to the ciphertext affects the key stream. Indeed, the last block of ciphertext is functionally dependent on the entire message, serving as a checksum for the entire message.

A **checksum** refers to any fixed length block functionally dependent on every bit of the message, so that different messages have different checksums with high probability. Checksums are frequently appended to the end of messages for authentication. The method of computing the checksum should ensure that two messages differing by one or more bits produce the same checksum with probability only 2^{-n}, where n is the length of the checksum. CFB can be used to compute checksums for plaintext data when authenticity is required in the absence of secrecy. Although a checksum does not usually provide the same level of security as encrypting the entire message, it is adequate for many applications.

3.4 BLOCK CIPHERS

We have seen how a block encryption algorithm E can be used to generate a key stream in either synchronous or self-synchronous mode. This raises an obvious question: Is it better to use a block encryption algorithm for block encryption, or to use it for stream encryption? Although the answer to this question depends on the requirements of the particular application, we can make some general observations about the efficiency and security of the different approaches.

Using block encryption directly is somewhat faster than either stream mode, because there will be only one execution of the encryption algorithm per n characters rather than n executions. This may not be an important factor, however, when the algorithm is implemented in special-purpose hardware capable of encrypting several million bits per second (as for some DES implementations). Such data rates are well beyond the capabilities of slow-speed telecommunications lines. Furthermore, block encryption is not inherently faster than stream encryption; stream encryption can be speeded up by using a faster generator, and, for applications requiring high speed, a key stream can be generated in advance with synchronous stream encryption (see [Brig80]).

With block encryption, transmission errors in one ciphertext block have no affect on other blocks. This is comparable to cipher feedback mode, where a transmission error in one ciphertext character affects only the next n characters, which is equivalent to one block.

Block encryption may be more susceptible to cryptanalysis than either stream mode. Because identical blocks of plaintext yield identical blocks of ciphertext, blocks of blanks or keywords, for example, may be identifiable for use in a known-plaintext attack. This is not a problem with stream encryption because repetitions in the plaintext are enciphered under different parts of the key stream. With block encryption, short blocks at the end of a message must also be padded with blanks or zeros, which may make them vulnerable to cryptanalysis.

In database systems, enciphering each field of a record as a separate block is not usually satisfactory. If the fields are short, padding increases the storage requirements of the database, and may leave the data vulnerable to cryptanalysis. Enciphering the fields with an algorithm that operates on short blocks does not solve the problem, because the algorithm will be weaker.

Even if the fields are full size and cryptanalysis impossible, information can be vulnerable to ciphertext searching. Consider a database containing personnel records. Suppose the *Salary* field of each record is enciphered as a single block, and that all salaries are enciphered under the same key. The *Name* fields are in the clear, so that a particular individual's record can be identified. A user can determine which employees earn salaries equal to Smith's by searching for those records with ciphertext *Salary* fields identical to Smith's. This problem demonstrates the need to protect nonconfidential information as well as confidential information, and the possible pitfalls of enciphering database records by fields, especially when multiple records are enciphered under one key.

Block encryption is more susceptible to replay than stream encryption. If each block is independently enciphered with the same key, one block can be replayed for another. Figure 3.10 shows how a transaction "CREDIT SMITH $10" can be changed to "CREDIT SMITH $5000" by replaying a block containing the ciphertext for $5000 (see [Camp78]). This type of replay is not possible with a stream cipher (assuming the key stream is not repeated). One simple solution is to append checksums to the end of messages.

Replay can also be a problem in databases. Consider again the database of employee records, where each record contains a *Salary* field enciphered as a separate block, and all salaries are enciphered under one key. Suppose a user can

FIGURE 3.10 Replay of ciphertext block.

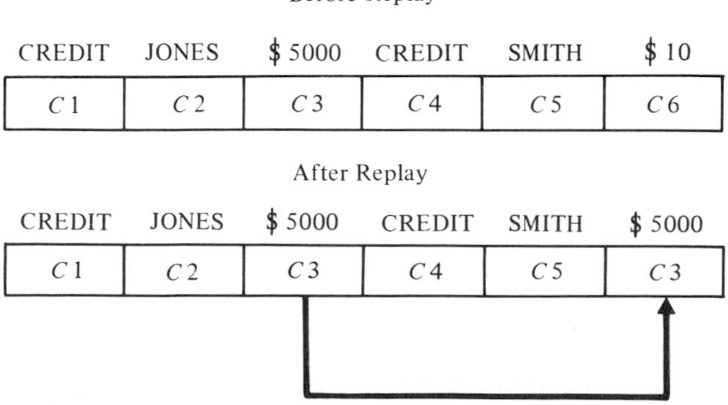

Before Replay

CREDIT	JONES	$ 5000	CREDIT	SMITH	$ 10
$C1$	$C2$	$C3$	$C4$	$C5$	$C6$

After Replay

CREDIT	JONES	$ 5000	CREDIT	SMITH	$ 5000
$C1$	$C2$	$C3$	$C4$	$C5$	$C3$

identify the records in the database belonging to Smith and to Jones, and that Jones's salary is known to be higher than Smith's. By copying Jones's enciphered *Salary* field into Smith's record, Smith's salary is effectively increased. The change will not be detected. Adding a checksum to each record can thwart this type of attack, but cannot protect against attacks based on ciphertext searching as described earlier.

Block encryption is also vulnerable to insertion and deletion of blocks, because these changes to the message stream do not affect surrounding blocks. Although it may be difficult to create false ciphertext for textual data, it may not be for numeric data. If, for example, the objective is simply to make the balance in an account nonzero, any positive integer will do. As noted earlier, applying error detecting codes before encryption protects against this threat. Checksums can also be added.

A database system with secure access controls can prevent unauthorized users from searching or modifying ciphertext (or plaintext) as described in these examples. Access controls are not always foolproof, however, and cannot generally prevent users from browsing through data on removable storage devices such as tapes and disks, or from tapping communications channels.

The following subsections describe two strategies for making block encryption more resistant to attack.

3.4.1 Block Chaining and Cipher Block Chaining

Feistel [Feis73] showed that block ciphers could be made more resistant to cryptanalysis and ciphertext substitution (including replay) using a technique called **block chaining**. Before enciphering each plaintext block M_i, some of the bits of the previous ciphertext block C_i are inserted into unused bit positions of M_i, thereby chaining the blocks together. Kent [Kent76] proposed a similar approach using sequence numbers. Both strategies protect against insertions, deletions, and modi-

FIGURE 3.11 Cipher block chaining (CBC).

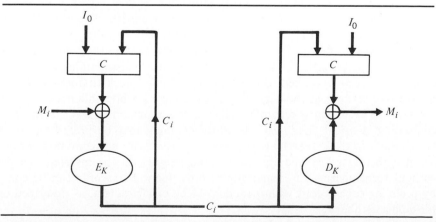

fications in the message stream in much the same way as a stream cipher in cipher feedback mode. But, unlike cipher feedback mode, they reduce the number of available message bits per block.

This is remedied by an approach called **cipher block chaining** (CBC), which has been suggested for use with the DES [GSA77]. CBC is similar to cipher feedback (CFB), except that an entire block of ciphertext is fed back through a register to be exclusive-ored with the next plaintext block. The result is then passed through a block cipher E_K with key K (see Figure 3.11). The ith plaintext block M_i is thus enciphered as

$$C_i = E_K(M_i \oplus C_{i-1}),$$

where $C_0 = I_0$. Deciphering is done by computing

$$
\begin{aligned}
D_K(C_i) \oplus C_{i-1} &= D_K\big(E_K(M_i \oplus C_{i-1})\big) \oplus C_{i-1} \\
&= (M_i \oplus C_{i-1}) \oplus C_{i-1} \\
&= M_i .
\end{aligned}
$$

Because each ciphertext block C_i is computed from M_i and the preceding ciphertext block C_{i-1}, one transmission error affects at most two blocks. At the same time, each C_i is functionally dependent on all preceding ciphertext blocks, so the statistical properties of the plaintext are diffused across the entire ciphertext, making cryptanalysis more difficult. Like cipher feedback mode, the last block serves as a checksum, so the method can also be used to compute checksums for messages encrypted under another scheme or stored as plaintext.

CBC is similar to CFB in its resistance to all forms of attack (including ciphertext searching, replay, insertion, and deletion). It is more efficient than CFB in that it uses a single execution of the block encryption algorithm for each message block. It also protects a block cipher against the time-memory tradeoff attack described in Section 2.6.3. To see why, let C_i be the ciphertext corresponding to the chosen plaintext M_0. Since $D_K(C_i) = M_0 \oplus C_{i-1}$, to determine K a cryptanalyst would have to generate the tables of starting and ending points using $M_0 \oplus C_{i-1}$ rather than M_0. But this would rule out the possibility of precomputing the tables or of using the same tables to break more than one cipher.

CBC is used in the Information Protection System (IPS), a set of cryptographic application programs designed by IBM [Konh80]. The algorithms E and D are implemented with DES. The IPS facilities allow users to encrypt and decrypt entire files, and to call the encryption functions from their programs. Chaining may be applied either to a single record (called block chaining in IPS) or to a collection of records (called record chaining). Under block chaining, the feedback register is reset to I_0 at the beginning of each record, while under record chaining, it retains its value across record boundaries. Record chaining has the advantage of concealing identical lines in a file. Block chaining may be preferable for direct access files and databases, however, because records can be accessed directly without deciphering all preceding records, and records can be inserted and deleted without reenciphering the remaining records. Identical records can be concealed by prefixing each record with a random block of characters, as described earlier for cipher feedback.

The chaining procedure is slightly modified to deal with short blocks. To encipher a trailing short block M_t of j bits, the preceding ciphertext block C_{t-1} is reenciphered, and the first j bits exclusive-ored with M_j; thus $C_t = M_t \oplus E_K(C_{t-1})$. Because C_{t-1} depends on all preceding blocks of the record, the trailing short ciphertext block is as secure as the preceding full ones.

With block chaining, there is a problem securing short records, because there is no feedback from the previous record. To encipher a single short record M_1 of j bits, it is exclusive-ored with the first j bits of I_0; thus, $C_1 = M_1 \oplus I_0$. Although this is not strong, it does superficially conceal the plaintext.

Cipher block chaining is somewhat less efficient for databases than direct block encryption because changing a field requires reenciphering all succeeding fields. Nevertheless, the added protection may offset the performance penalties for many applications. Moreover, if an entire record is fetched during retrieval anyway, encryption and decryption need not degrade performance if implemented in hardware.

3.4.2 Block Ciphers with Subkeys

Davida, Wells, and Kam [Davi81] introduced a new type of block cipher suitable for databases. A database is modeled as a set of records, each with t fields. Each record is enciphered as a unit, so that all fields are diffused over the ciphertext. The individual fields can be separately deciphered, though doing so requires access to an entire ciphertext record. Like cipher block chaining, the scheme protects against all types of attack.

Access to a particular field requires a special **subkey** for the field. There are separate **read subkeys** $d_1, \ldots, d_t$ for deciphering each field, and separate **write subkeys** $e_1, \ldots, e_t$ for enciphering each field. The subkeys are global to the database; that is, all records are enciphered with the same subkeys. Each user is given subkeys only for the fields that user is allowed to read or write.

We shall first describe a simplified, but insecure, version of the scheme, and then discuss the modifications needed for security. The scheme is based on the Chinese Remainder Theorem (see Theorem 1.8 in Section 1.6.2). To construct subkeys, each read subkey d_j is chosen to be a random prime number larger than the maximum possible value for field j. Letting $n = d_1 d_2 \cdots d_t$, the write subkeys are as follows:

$$e_j = \left(\frac{n}{d_j}\right) y_j , \tag{3.3}$$

where y_j is the inverse of $(n/d_j) \bmod d_j$:

$$y_j = inv(n/d_j, d_j) .$$

Let M be a plaintext record with fields $m_1, \ldots, m_t$. The entire record is enciphered as

$$C = \sum_{j=1}^{t} e_j m_j \bmod n . \tag{3.4}$$

FIGURE 3.12 Enciphering and deciphering with subkeys.

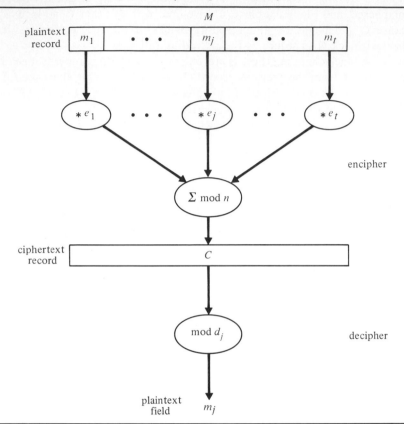

Because C is the solution to the equations

$$C \bmod d_j = m_j \; , \tag{3.5}$$

for $j = 1, \ldots, t$, the jth field is easily deciphered using only the read subkey d_j. Figure 3.12 illustrates the enciphering and deciphering of a record.

The jth field can be updated using only the read and write subkeys d_j and e_j. Letting m_j' denote the new value, the updated ciphertext C' is given by

$$C' = [C - e_j\,(C \bmod d_j) + e_j m_j'] \bmod n \; . \tag{3.6}$$

Example:
Let $t = 3$, $d_1 = 7$, $d_2 = 11$, and $d_3 = 5$. Then $n = 7 * 11 * 5 = 385$ and

$$
\begin{aligned}
y_1 &= inv(385/7, 7) &&= inv(55, 7) &&= 6 \\
y_2 &= inv(385/11, 11) &&= inv(35, 11) &&= 6 \\
y_3 &= inv(385/5, 5) &&= inv(77, 5) &&= 3 \; .
\end{aligned}
$$

The write subkeys are thus:

$$e_1 = 55 * 6 = 330$$
$$e_2 = 35 * 6 = 210$$
$$e_3 = 77 * 3 = 231 \ .$$

Let M be the plaintext record $M = (4, 10, 2)$. Using Eq. (3.4), M is enciphered with the write subkeys as

$$
\begin{aligned}
C &= (e_1 m_1 + e_2 m_2 + e_3 m_3) \bmod n \\
&= (330 * 4 + 210 * 10 + 231 * 2) \bmod 385 \\
&= (1320 + 2100 + 462) \bmod 385 = 3882 \bmod 385 \\
&= 32 \ .
\end{aligned}
$$

Using Eq. (3.5), the fields of M are deciphered with the read subkeys as follows:

$$
\begin{aligned}
m_1 &= C \bmod d_1 = 32 \bmod 7 \ \ = \ \ 4 \\
m_2 &= C \bmod d_2 = 32 \bmod 11 = 10 \\
m_3 &= C \bmod d_3 = 32 \bmod 5 \ \ = \ \ 2 \ .
\end{aligned}
$$

Using Eq. (3.6), the contents of the second field can be changed from 10 to 8 as follows:

$$
\begin{aligned}
C' &= [C - e_2(C \bmod d_2) + e_2 * 8] \bmod n \\
&= [32 - 210 * 10 + 210 * 8] \bmod 385 \\
&= -388 \bmod 385 = -3 \bmod 385 \\
&= 382 \ .
\end{aligned}
$$

The reader should verify that all three fields are still retrievable. ■

There are two weaknesses with the scheme as described thus far. The first lies in the method of enciphering as defined by Eq. (3.4). Let m_{ij} denote the value of the jth field in record i. A user knowing the plaintext values m_{1j} and m_{2j} for two records M_1 and M_2 can determine the read key d_j from the ciphertext C_1 and C_2. Observe that Eq. (3.5) implies

$$
\begin{aligned}
C_1 - m_{1j} &= u_1 d_j \\
C_2 - m_{2j} &= u_2 d_j
\end{aligned}
$$

for some u_1 and u_2. Thus, d_j can be determined with high probability by computing the greatest common divisor of $(C_1 - m_{1j})$ and $(C_2 - m_{2j})$. The solution is to append a random 32-bit (or longer) value x_j to each m_j before enciphering with Eq. (3.4).

The second weakness is that the method of updating fields individually, as defined by Eq. (3.6), can expose the read keys (see exercises at end of chapter). The solution here is to reencipher the entire record, using new random values x_j for all fields.

Because both the read and write subkeys are required to write a field, user A automatically has read access to any field that A can write. This is consistent with most access control policies. But to write a single field, A must also have access to n; this gives A the ability to compute the write subkey for any field for which A has

the read subkey. This is not consistent with most access control policies. To prevent this, n must be hidden in the programs that access the database. To read field
j, A would invoke a read procedure, passing as parameter the read subkey d_j; to
write the field, A would invoke a write procedure, passing as parameters d_j, e_j, and
the new value m_j'.

The write subkey e_j for field j is computed from n and the read subkey d_j.
Therefore, any group of users with access to all the read subkeys can compute n
and determine all the write subkeys. To prevent collusion, dummy fields are added
to each record. The read and write subkeys for these fields are not given to any
user.

3.5 ENDPOINTS OF ENCRYPTION

Data protected with encryption may be transmitted over several links before it
arrives at its final destination. For example, data may be input from a user's
terminal to the user's program, where it is processed and then transmitted to a disk
file for storage. Later, the user may retrieve the data and have it displayed on the
terminal. In computer networks, data may be transmitted from one location on the
network to another for processing or for storage. In the discussion that follows, we
use the terminology **node** for any location (computer, terminal, front-end, or program) where data may be input, stored, encrypted, processed, routed (switched),
or output; and **link** for any communication line or data bus between two nodes.

3.5.1 End-to-End versus Link Encryption

There are many possible choices of endpoints for the encryption. At one extreme,
link encryption enciphers and deciphers a message M at each node between the
source node 0 and the destination node n [Bara64]. The message is processed as
plaintext at the ith node, and transmitted as ciphertext $E_i(M)$ over the ith link (see
Figure 3.13). Each link i has its own pair of transformations E_i and D_i, and different encryption algorithms and message formats may be used on the different links.
This strategy is generally used with physical (hard-wired) connections. At the
other extreme, **end-to-end encryption** enciphers and deciphers a message at the
source and destination only (see Figure 3.14).

There are advantages and disadvantages to both extremes. With link encryp-

FIGURE 3.13 Link encryption.

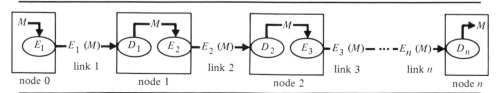

FIGURE 3.14 End-to-end encryption.

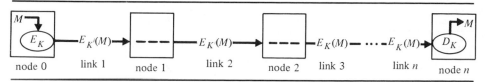

tion users need only one key for communicating with their local systems. With end-to-end encryption, users need separate keys for communicating with each correspondent. In addition, protocols are needed whereby users (or nodes) can exchange keys to establish a secure connection (see Section 3.7).

End-to-end encryption provides a higher level of data security because the data is not deciphered until it reaches its final destination. With link encryption, the data may be exposed to secrecy and authenticity threats when it is in plaintext at the intermediate nodes. Thus, end-to-end encryption is preferable for electronic mail and applications such as electronic-funds transfer requiring a high level of security.

End-to-end encryption, however, is more susceptible to attacks of traffic flow analysis. With link encryption, the final destination addresses of messages can be transmitted as ciphertext along each link. This is not possible with end-to-end encryption, because the intermediate nodes need the addresses for routing (unless there is a single physical connection). The addresses could be used, for example, to learn whether an important business transaction was taking place.

For applications requiring high security, the two approaches can be combined. Figure 3.15 shows how an end-to-end cryptographic system can be interfaced with a communications system using link encryption to encipher addresses. The cryptographic system is on the outside, enciphering messages before they are processed by the communications system, and deciphering messages after they have been processed by the communications system. Each "packet" sent over a link has a header field and a data field. The header field contains the final destination of the message, enciphered using the key for the link, plus other control information used by the communications system. If the channel is used for more than one connection (as in a ring network), the header must also contain the immediate source and destination addresses in plaintext (the source address is needed so the receiver will know which key to use to decipher the final destination address).

Because a packet arriving at a device contains both plaintext and ciphertext, the device must be capable of operating in two modes: normal (plaintext) mode in which arriving control characters are interpreted by the device, and a "transparent" (ciphertext) mode in which arriving characters are not interpreted [Feis75]. With this feature, messages can also be exchanged in either plaintext or ciphertext.

Enciphering the final destinations of messages along the way does not obscure activity on a particular channel. The only solution here is to pad the channel with dummy traffic to make it appear constantly busy.

FIGURE 3.15 End-to-end data encryption with link adress-encryption.

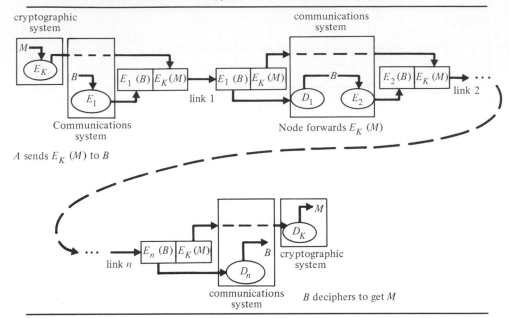

Chaum [Chau81] uses a combination of endpoints to design an electronic mail system based on public-key encryption. His system allows messages to be sent anonymously through a node S (called a "mix"), which collects and shuffles messages to obscure their flow through the network.

Suppose user A (at location A) wishes to send an anonymous message M to user B (at location B). First A enciphers M using B's public transformation E_B (for end-to-end encryption). A then enciphers the destination B plus the enciphered message using S's public transformation E_S, and transmits the result to S:

$$C = E_S(B, E_B(M)) .$$

S deciphers C using its private transformation D_S, and forwards the enciphered message $E_B(M)$ to B, which B deciphers using B's private transformation D_B. The sender A is not revealed to B, and the path from A to B is concealed through encryption of B's address on the path from A to S and shuffling at S.

If A wants to receive a reply from B, A sends along an **untraceable return address** together with a key K that B uses to encipher the reply; the message transmitted through S is thus:

$$C = E_S(B, E_B(M, U, K)) ,$$

where

$$U = E_S(A)$$

is A's untraceable return address. Because A's address is enciphered with S's public key, B cannot decipher it. B can, however, send a reply M' to A through S:

$$C' = E_S(U, E_K(M')) .$$

S deciphers U and forwards the reply $E_K(M')$ to A.

There could be a problem with the scheme as we have described it if there is not enough uncertainty about the message M or the return address (see Section 1.4.1). Because A cannot sign M (doing so would divulge A's identity), someone might be able to determine M by guessing an X and checking whether $E_B(X)$ = $E_B(M)$ using B's public key [this comparison cannot be made if A signs the message, transmitting $D_A(E_B(M))$] . Similarly, B might be able to guess the sender A from the untraceable return address, where the number of candidate addresses may be relatively small. Chaum solves the problem by appending random bit strings to all messages before enciphering.

If the output of one mix is used as the input for a second mix, then both mixes would have to conspire or be compromised for any message to be traced. With a series of mixes, any single mix can ensure the security of the messages. Thus, in the limiting case, each sender or receiver is a mix and need only trust itself.

3.5.2 Privacy Homomorphisms

To process data at a node in the system, it is usually necessary to decipher the data first, and then reencipher it after it has been processed. Consequently, it may be exposed to secrecy or authenticity threats while it is being processed. There are two possible safeguards. The first is to encapsulate the computation in a physically secure area. The second is to process the data in its encrypted state.

Rivest, Adleman, and Dertouzos [Rive78a] describe how the latter might be accomplished with a **privacy homomorphism**. The basic idea is that encrypted data, after processing, should be the same as if the data were first deciphered, processed in plaintext, and finally reenciphered. Suppose the plaintext data is drawn from an algebraic system consisting of

1. Data elements, denoted by a, b, etc.
2. Operations, denoted by f.
3. Predicates, denoted by p.
4. Distinguished constants, denoted by s.

Similarly, suppose the ciphertext is drawn from an algebraic system with corresponding data elements a', b', operations f', predicates p', and distinguished constants s'. Let E_K be the enciphering transformation, and let D_K be the corresponding deciphering transformation. Then D_K is a **homomorphism** from the ciphertext system to the plaintext system if and only if for all cipher elements a', b' the following hold:

1. For all f and corresponding f':

$$f' (a', b', \ldots) = E_K\big(f(D_K(a'), D_K(b'), \ldots)\big) .$$

2. For all p and corresponding p':

FIGURE 3.16 Privacy homomorphism.

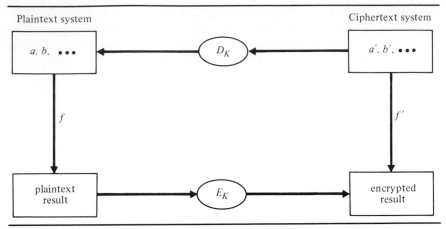

$$p' (a', b', \ldots) \text{ if and only if } p(D_K(a'), D_K(b'), \ldots) \,.$$

3.   For all s and corresponding s':

$$D_K(s') = s \,.$$

Figure 3.16 illustrates the first requirement.

Example:

Consider an exponentiation cipher (see Section 2.7) with enciphering transformation

$$E_K(a) = a^e \bmod n \,,$$

and corresponding deciphering transformation

$$D_K(a') = (a')^d \bmod n \,,$$

where $ed \bmod \phi(n) = 1$. Then D_K is a homomorphism from a ciphertext system consisting of the integers modulo n, with multiplication and test for equality, to an identical plaintext system. Given elements

$$a' = a^e \bmod n, \text{ and}$$
$$b' = b^e \bmod n,$$

we have

$$a' * b' = (a^e \bmod n) * (b^e \bmod n) \bmod n$$
$$= (a * b)^e \bmod n$$

$$a' = b' \text{ if and only if } a = b \,. \quad \blacksquare$$

Privacy homomorphisms have inherent limitations. The most significant of these is described in Theorem 3.1.

Theorem 3.1:

It is not possible to have a secure enciphering function for an algebraic system that includes the ordering predicate "$\leq$" when the encrypted version of the distinguished constants can be determined.

Proof:

Consider the plaintext system over the natural numbers with $+$, $\leq$, and the constants 0 and 1. Let $+'$, $\leq'$, $0'$, and $1'$ denote the corresponding operators and elements in the ciphertext system. Given ciphertext element i', it is possible to determine the corresponding plaintext element i without computing $D_K(i')$ using a simple binary search strategy. First, determine $1'$ (by assumption this is possible). Next, compute

$$2' = 1' +' 1'$$
$$4' = 2' +' 2'$$
$$8' = 4' +' 4'$$
$$\cdot$$
$$\cdot$$
$$\cdot$$
$$(2^j)' = (2^{j-1})' +' (2^{j-1})'$$

until $i' \leq' (2^j)'$ for some j. At this point, it is known that i falls in the interval $[2^{j-1} + 1, 2^j]$. To determine i, apply a similar binary search strategy to search the interval between 2^{j-1} and 2^j (the details of this are left as an exercise for the reader). ■

Privacy homomorphisms are an intuitively attractive method for protecting data. But they are ruled out for many applications because comparisons cannot in general be permitted on the ciphertext. In addition, it is not known whether it is possible to have a secure privacy homomorphism with a large number of operations.

Approximations of the basic principle, however, are used to protect confidential data in statistical databases. A one-way (irreversible) **privacy transformation** $E_K(M)$ transforms ("enciphers") a confidential data value M into a value that can be disclosed without violating the privacy of the individual associated with M [Turn73]. Examples of privacy transformations are "data perturbation", which distorts the value of M (e.g., by rounding), "aggregation", which replaces M with a group average, and "data swapping", which swaps values in one record with those in another (see Chapter 6). A privacy transformation is an approximation of a privacy homomorphism in that statistics computed from the transformed data are estimates of those computed from the original ("deciphered") data. But because it is impossible to restore the data to its original state and the transformation introduces errors, it is not a true privacy homomorphism. (Reed [Reed73] shows how the amount of distortion introduced by a privacy transformation can be measured using information theory, in particular, rate distortion theory.)

The basic principle is also used to protect proprietary software. Many software vendors distribute the source code for their programs so their customers can

FIGURE 3.17 Proprietary software protection.

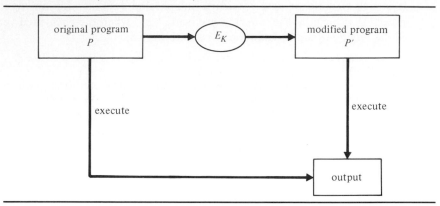

tailor the code to their needs and make corrections. The problem is that a custom-er may illegally sell or give away copies of the program. If the copies have been modified (e.g., by changing the names of variables and rearranging code), it can be difficult to prove an agreement was breached. Indeed, the vendor might not even be aware of the illegal distribution.

One solution is to transform ("encipher") a source program in such a way that the transformed program executes the same as the original but is more diffi-cult to copy [DeMi78]. Let P' be the transformed version of a program P. The transformation should satisfy the following properties:

1. P' should have the same output as P for all valid inputs.
2. P' should have approximately the same performance characteristics as P.
3. P' should have distinguishing features that are difficult to conceal in copies.

Property (1) is similar to the first property of a privacy homomorphism, where the elements a and b are programs and the function f corresponds to program execu-tion (see Figure 3.17); instead of processing data in an encrypted state, we now execute programs in an encrypted state.

One method is to pad a program with code that does not affect the output (at least on valid inputs). Map makers employ a similar technique, introducing minor errors that do not seriously impair navigation, but make copies easily discernible. A second method is to transform the code or constants of the program to obscure the algorithm. A third method is to transform the program so that it will not run on other systems. This could be done by hiding in the code information about the customer; this information would be checked when the program runs. None of these transformations need be cryptographically strong; the objective is only to make it more costly to change a program than to develop it from scratch or obtain it from the vendor.

It is easier to protect proprietary software when the source is not distributed. In a sense, program compilation is a form of encipherment, because the algorithm is obscured in the object code. Object code can be decompiled, however, so the encipherment is cryptographically weak. Still, it is easier to hide customer dependent information in object code than in the source, and many customers will lack the skills needed to decompile and modify the code.

Kent [Kent80] proposes special hardware and cryptographic techniques to protect proprietary software in small computer systems. Externally supplied software would run in tamper-resistant modules that prevent disclosure or modification of the information contained therein. Outside the module, information would be stored and transmitted in encrypted form.

3.6 ONE-WAY CIPHERS

A **one-way cipher** is an irreversible function f from plaintext to ciphertext. It is computationally infeasible to systematically determine a plaintext message M from the ciphertext $C = f(M)$.

One-way ciphers are used in applications that do not require deciphering the data. One such class of applications involves determining whether there is a correspondence between a given message M and a ciphertext C stored in the system. This correspondence is determined by computing $f(M)$, and comparing the result with C. For this to be effective, f should be one-to-one, or at least not too degenerate. Otherwise, a false message M' may pass the test $f(M') = C$.

A one-way cipher can be implemented using a computationally secure block encryption algorithm E by letting

$$f(M) = E_M(M_0) ,$$

where M_0 is any given, fixed message. The message M serves as the key to E. As long as E is secure, it is computationally infeasible to determine the enciphering key M with a known plaintext attack by examining pairs $(M_0, E_M(M_0))$.

Purdy [Purd74] suggests implementing a one-way cipher using a sparse polynomial of the form:

$$f(x) = (x^n + a_{n-1}x^{n-1} + \cdots + a_1 x + a_0) \bmod p ,$$

where p is a large prime and n is also large. Because a polynomial of degree n has at most n roots, there can be at most n messages enciphering to the same ciphertext. The time to invert f (i.e., find its roots) is $O(n^2(\log p)^2)$; for $n \simeq 2^{24}$ and $p \simeq 2^{64}$, this will exceed 10^{16} operations. (See [Evan74] for other methods of implementing one-way ciphers.)

Note that a one-way cipher cannot be implemented using a stream cipher with keystream M and plaintext stream M_0. We would have $C = M_0 \oplus M$, whence M is easily computed by $M = C \oplus M_0$.

3.6.1 Passwords and User Authentication

Password files are protected with one-way ciphers using a scheme developed by Needham [Wilk75]. Rather than storing users' passwords in the clear, they are transformed by a one-way cipher f, and stored as ciphertext in a file which cannot be deciphered even by the systems staff. Each entry in the password file is a pair $(ID, f(P))$, where ID is a user identifier and P is the user's password. To log into the system, a user must supply ID and P. The system computes the enciphered password $f(P)$, and checks this against the password file; the login is permitted only if there is a match.

Because the stored passwords cannot be deciphered, they are completely safe even if the entire password file is (accidentally or maliciously) disclosed. This also implies that a forgotten password P cannot be recovered. A new password P' must be created, and $f(P')$ entered into the password file.

A strong one-way cipher can protect passwords only if users select passwords at random. In practice, users select short, easily remembered passwords. Such passwords are often simple to find by exhaustive search. Sequences of letters are systematically generated, enciphered, and then looked up in the table. In a study of password security on Bell Labs' UNIX, Morris and Thompson [Morr79] discovered that about 86% of all passwords were relatively easy to compromise. The system-supplied passwords were no better; because they were generated by a pseudo-random number generator with only 2^{15} possible outputs, all possible passwords could be tried in about 1 minute on a DEC PDP-11/70.

Two improvements were made to the UNIX password security. First, the password entry program was modified to encourage users to use longer passwords. Second, each password is concatenated with a 12-bit random number (called the **salt**) before encryption, effectively lengthening the password by 12 bits. When a password P is created, a salt X is generated and concatenated to P. Letting PX denote the concatenation, both X and $f(PX)$ are stored in the password file along with the user's ID. When a user logs in, the system gets X from the file, forms the concatenation PX using the password P supplied by the user, and checks $f(PX)$ against the password file.

This does not increase the work factor for finding a particular user's password, because the salt is not protected. But it substantially increases the work factor for generating random passwords and comparing them with the entire password file, since each possible password could be enciphered with each possible salt. If passwords are n bits long, there are 2^{n+12} possibilities for the entries $f(PX)$ in the password table; thus, the effort required to find the password associated with one of these entries is 2^{12} times greater than for a file containing only enciphered passwords.

Suppose a user logs into the system and supplies password P as described earlier. If P is transmitted from the user's terminal to the system in the clear, it could be compromised on the way (e.g., by wiretapping). It may not even make it to the system: a program masquerading as the login procedure might trick the user into typing ID and P.

Feistel, Notz, and Smith [Feis75] describe a login procedure that does not expose the user's password, and allows the user and system to mutually authenticate each other. They assume each user A has a private key on some digital storage medium (e.g., a magnetic-stripe card) which can be inserted into A's terminal, and that a copy of the key is stored on file at the system. To log into the

FIGURE 3.18 Login protocol with passwords.

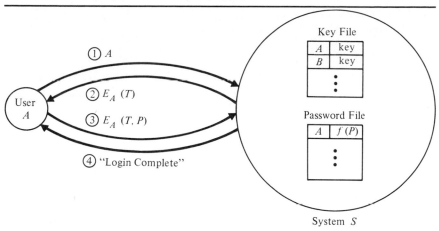

system, A transmits ID in the clear (for simplicity, we assume $ID = A$). The system responds with a "challenge-reply" test that allows A to determine whether the communication is "live" (and not a replay of an earlier login), and allows the system to establish A's authenticity. Letting S denote the system, the protocol is as follows (see also Figure 3.18):

Login protocol using passwords

1. A transmits $ID = A$ to S.
2. S sends to A:

$$X = E_A(T),$$

where T is the current date and time, and E_A is the enciphering transformation derived from A's private key.

3. A deciphers X to get T, and checks that T is current. If it is, A replies to S by sending

$$Y = E_A(T, P)$$

where P is A's password.

4. S deciphers Y to get T and P. It checks T against the time transmitted to A in Step 2, and checks $f(P)$ against the password file. If both check, the login completes successfully.

The protocol is easily modified for a public-key system. In Step 2, the system S uses its private transformation D_S (for sender authenticity) to create $X = D_S(T)$, which A can validate using S's public transformation E_S. In Step 3, A uses the system's public enciphering transformation (for secrecy) to create $Y = E_S(T, P)$. Only S can decipher Y to obtain A's password and complete the login. Note that A's private transformation (i.e., digital signature) can be used for authentication instead of A's password; in this case, the protocol becomes:

Login protocol using digital signatures

1. A transmits $ID = A$ to S.
2. S sends to A:

$$X = D_S(T) ,$$

where T is the current date and time, and D_S is S's private transformation.

3. A computes $E_S(X) = T$ using S's public transformation, and checks that T is current. If it is, A replies to S by sending

$$Y = D_A(T) ,$$

where D_A is A's private transformation.

4. The system validates Y using A's public transformation E_A. If it is valid, the login completes successfully.

One possible weakness with the digital signature protocol is that users can be impersonated if their private keys are stolen. The password protocol has the advantage that memorized passwords are less susceptible to theft than physical keys— provided users do not write them down. The digital signature protocol can be enhanced by combining it with passwords or with a mechanism that uses personal characteristics (e.g., a handprint) for identification. If passwords are used, then A sends to S

$$D_A(T), E_S(T, P)$$

in Step 3 of the protocol.

3.7 KEY MANAGEMENT

A troublesome aspect of designing secure cryptosystems is key management. Unless the keys are given the same level of protection as the data itself, they will be the weak link. Even if the encryption algorithm is computationally infeasible to break, the entire system can be vulnerable if the keys are not adequately protected. In this section we consider various techniques for safeguarding and distributing keys.

3.7.1 Secret Keys

We first consider the management of keys that are used by a single user (or process) to protect data stored in files. The simplest approach is to avoid storing cryptographic keys in the system. In IPS [Konh80], for example, keys do not reside permanently in the system. Users are responsible for managing their own keys and entering them at the time of encipherment or decipherment.

IPS offers users two formats for entering the 56-bit keys needed for DES. The first format is the direct entry of an 8-byte key (56 key bits plus 8 parity bits).

This format should be used only if the 56 key bits are randomly selected; a key formed from English letters only (or even letters and digits) is too easy to find by exhaustive search. Because it is easier for users to remember meaningful strings, IPS provides a second format whereby a key can be entered as a long character string. The string is reduced to a 56-bit key by enciphering it with DES using cipher block chaining, and keeping the rightmost 56 bits (i.e., the checksum). The process is called "key crunching".

Keys could also be recorded in Read Only Memory (ROM) or on magnetic stripe cards [Feis75,Flyn78,Denn79]. The hardware-implemented key could then be entered simply by inserting it into a special reader attached to the user's terminal.

In conventional systems, users may register private keys with the system to establish a secure channel between their terminals and the central computer (master terminal keys are used in some systems for this purpose). These keys must be protected, and the simplest strategy is to store them in a file enciphered under a system master key. Unlike passwords, encryption keys cannot be protected with one-way functions, because it would then be impossible to recover them.

In public-key systems, a user A need not register a private transformation D_A with the system to establish a secure channel. This does not mean D_A requires no security. If it is used for signatures, it must be protected from disclosure to prevent forgery. Indeed, it must be protected from deliberate disclosure by A. If A can give away D_A—or even just claim to have lost D_A—then A has a case for disavowing any message (see [Salt78,Lipt78]). To prevent this, Merkle [Merk80] suggests that A's signature key should not be known to anyone, including A. A single copy of D_A would be kept in a dedicated microcomputer or sealed in a ROM.

Even if D_A is given a high level of protection, some mechanism is needed to handle the case where D_A is compromised. This case can be handled as for lost or stolen credit cards: liability would be limited once the loss or theft is reported to the system. A signature manager S would keep a record of A's past and present public transformations E_A, and the times during which these transformations were valid. To determine whether a message was signed before the loss, messages could be timestamped. A cannot affix the timestamp, however, because A could knowingly affix an incorrect time, and if D_A is compromised, someone else could forge a message and affix a time when D_A was valid. The solution is for S to affix the current time T to a message signed by A, and then add its own signature D_S, thereby playing the role of a notary public [Pope79,Merk80]. A message M would thus be doubly signed as follows:

$$C = D_S(D_A(M), T) \ .$$

Another user receiving C can check (with S) that A's corresponding public transformation E_A was valid at time T before accepting C.

A similar strategy can be used to protect a signature transformation D_A in a conventional system. But because the corresponding enciphering transformations E_A and E_S are secret, the receiver of a signed message $C = D_S(D_A(M), T)$ cannot validate the signature (see Section 1.3.3).

FIGURE 3.19 File encryption with keys record.

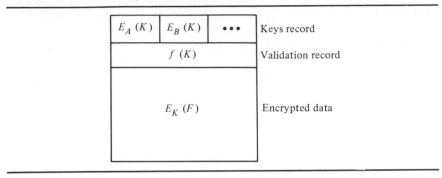

| $E_A(K)$ | $E_B(K)$ | $\bullet\bullet\bullet$ | Keys record |

$f(K)$ — Validation record

$E_K(F)$ — Encrypted data

The keys that unlock a database require special protection. If the database is shared by many users, it is usually better to store the keys in the system under the protection of a key manager than to distribute the keys directly to the users, where they would be vulnerable to loss or compromise. More importantly, it relieves the users of the burden of key management, providing "cryptographic transparency". Database keys could be enciphered under a database master key and stored either in the database or in a separate file.

Gudes [Gude80] has proposed a scheme for protecting file encrypting keys that can be integrated with the access control policies of a system. Let K be the encryption key for a file F. For every user A allowed access to F, the system computes

$$X = E_A(K) \ ,$$

using A's private transformation E_A, and stores X in a **keys record** at the beginning of the encrypted file (see Figure 3.19). When A requests access to F, the system finds A's entry X in the keys record, and computes $D_A(X) = D_A(E_A(K)) = K$; the file is then deciphered using the recovered key. An additional level of protection against unauthorized updates is provided by storing $f(K)$ in a **validation record** of the file, where f is a one-way function. A user is not allowed to update the file unless $f(D_A(X))$ matches the value in the authentication field. If the file is enciphered using a two-key system, with separate read and write keys as described in Section 1.2 (see Figure 1.8), users can be given read access without write access to the file. One drawback with the scheme is that if a user's access rights to a file are revoked, the file must be reenciphered under a new key, and the keys record and validation record recomputed.

Ehrsam, Matyas, Meyer, and Tuchman [Ehrs78,Maty78] describe a complete key management scheme for communication and file security. They assume that each host system has a **master key** $KM0$ with two variants, $KM1$ and $KM2$. The variants can be some simple function of $KM0$. The master keys are used to encipher other encryption keys and to generate new encryption keys. Each terminal also has a **master terminal key** KMT, which provides a secure channel between the terminal and the host system for key exchange. The system stores its copies of these keys in a file enciphered under $KM1$. Other key encrypting keys, such as file master keys (called **secondary file keys**), are stored in files enciphered under $KM2$.

The master key $KM0$ is stored in the nonvolatile storage of a special cryptographic facility or security module. ($KM1$ and $KM2$ are computed from $KM0$ as needed.) The facility is secured so that users cannot access the master key or its derivatives. Data encrypting keys are stored and passed to the cryptographic facility as ciphertext to protect them from exposure.

Special operations are provided by the cryptographic facilities in the host systems and terminals. The following operations are used by the key management scheme in a host:

1. *Set master key (smk)*. A master key $KM0$ is installed with the operation

$$smk(KM0) \ . \tag{3.7}$$

Clearly, this operation requires special protection.

2. *Encipher under master key (emk)*. A key K is protected by encrypting it under $KM0$ with the operation

$$emk(K) = E_{KM0}(K) \ . \tag{3.8}$$

3. *Encipher (ecph)*. To encipher a message M using key K, K is passed to the cryptographic facility enciphered under $KM0$. Letting $X = E_{KM0}(K)$ be the enciphered key, M is enciphered with the operation

$$ecph(X, M) = E_K(M) \ , \tag{3.9}$$

where $K = D_{KM0}(X)$ (see Figure 3.20). This instruction allows keys to be stored and passed to the cryptographic facility as ciphertext.

4. *Decipher (dcph)*. Similarly, a ciphertext message C is deciphered using a key K with the operation

$$dcph(X, C) = D_K(C) \ , \tag{3.10}$$

where $K = D_{KM0}(X)$ (see Figure 3.21).

5. *Reencipher from master key (rfmk)*. A terminal master key KMT is stored under $KM1$ encipherment as $W = E_{KM1}(KMT)$. The reencipher from master key operation allows the key manager to take a key K enciphered under $KM0$ as $X = E_{KM0}(K)$ and put it under KMT encipherment:

FIGURE 3.20 Encipher (*ecph*).

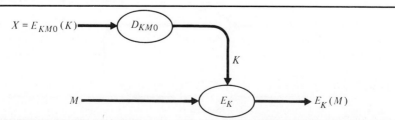

FIGURE 3.21 Decipher (*dcph*).

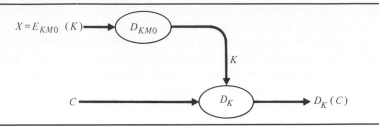

$$rfmk(W, X) = E_{KMT}(K) \; , \tag{3.11}$$

where $KMT = D_{KM1}(W)$, and $K = D_{KM0}(X)$ (see Figure 3.22). This operation is used by the key manager to transmit keys to terminals and other host systems for end-to-end encryption (see Section 3.7.4). As with the preceding operations, none of the keys entering or leaving the cryptographic facility is ever in the clear.

KMT is stored under $KM1$ encipherment to protect K from exposure. If KMT were stored under $KM0$ encipherment as $W' = E_{KM0}(KMT)$, then K could be obtained from $Y = E_{KMT}(K)$ using the *dcph* operation:

$$dcph(W', Y) = D_{KMT}(Y) = K \; .$$

Thus, an eavesdropper obtaining Y, W', and access to the cryptographic facility could decipher messages enciphered under K.

6.   *Reencipher to master key* (*rtmk*). A file encrypting key K is likewise not stored under $KM0$ encipherment; if it were, then any user who obtained access to the encrypted key and the cryptographic facility could decipher the file using the *dcph* operation. Rather, K is stored under the encipherment of a secondary file key KNF as $X = E_{KNF}(K)$; KNF, in turn, is stored under $KM2$ encipherment as $W = E_{KM2}(KNF)$. To use K, it must first be placed under $KM0$ encipherment. This is done with the reencipher to master key operation:

$$rtmk(W, X) = E_{KM0}(K) \tag{3.12}$$

FIGURE 3.22 Reencipher from master key (*rfmk*).

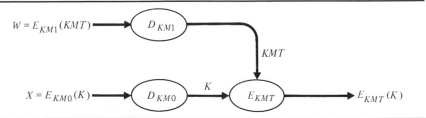

FIGURE 3.23 Reeincipher to master key (*rtmk*).

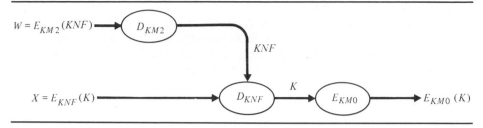

where $K = D_{KNF}(X)$ and $KNF = D_{KM2}(W)$ (see Figure 3.23).

Note that KNF is stored under $KM2$ encipherment rather than under $KM1$ encipherment. This is done to separate the communications and file systems. If the *rtmk* operation used $KM1$ instead of $KM2$, it would be the inverse of *rfmk*. This would allow the key management operations for the file system to be used to obtain keys used by the communications system. In fact, neither *rfmk* nor *rtmk* have inverse operations.

The master key KMT for a terminal is stored in the cryptographic facility of the terminal. The following operations are provided by the facility:

1. *Decipher from master key (dmk)*. This operation takes a key K transmitted to the terminal under KMT encipherment as $E_{KMT}(K)$, deciphers it, and stores it in a special working register of the facility. K remains in the working register until it is changed or the terminal is turned off.
2. *Encipher (ecph)*. This operation enciphers data using the key stored in the working register. The encrypted data is transmitted to its destination, providing end-to-end encryption.
3. *Decipher (dcph)*. This operation deciphers data using the key stored in the working register.

3.7.2 Public Keys

Public keys can be distributed either outside the system or from a public-key directory within the system. In the former case, they could be recorded on some digital medium such as a magnetic stripe card, which can be inserted into a special reader attached to a user's terminal. Users would exchange public keys by giving out copies of their cards.

In the latter case, they could be stored in a file managed by a system directory manager S. It is unnecessary to safeguard the keys from exposure, because their secrecy is not required for secure communication or digital signatures. But it is essential to maintain their integrity so they can be used to transmit messages in secrecy and validate digital signatures. If S (or an imposter) supplies a valid but incorrect public key, a user could unknowingly encipher confidential data that would be decipherable by foe rather than friend, or be tricked into accepting a message with the wrong signature.

Imposters can be thwarted by requiring a signature from S [Rive78b, Need78]. This does not, however, protect against a faulty or untrustworthy system. To deal with both problems, Kohnfelder [Konf78] proposes **certificates**. Upon registering a public transformation E_A with the system, a user A receives a signed certificate from S containing E_A. Using public-key encryption to implement the signature, A's certificate is thus:

$$C_A = D_S(A, E_A, T) \tag{3.13}$$

(strictly speaking, C_A would contain the key to E_A), T is a timestamp giving the current time, and D_S is S's private signature transformation. A can verify that the certificate came from S and contains the correct public key by computing

$$E_S(C_A) = (A, E_A, T) ,$$

using the public transformation E_S of S. Certificates can be distributed either through S or by their owners. The receiver of a certificate C_A can verify its authenticity the same way as the owner. In addition, the receiver can check the timestamp to determine if C_A is current.

There is a problem if the secret signature key used by the system directory manager is compromised. Merkle's [Merk80] **tree authentication** scheme solves this problem by eliminating the secret signature key. All entries in the public file are signed as a unit using a one-way hashing function. Users can authenticate their own keys in a file of n keys knowing $O(\log_2 n)$ intermediate values of the hashing function. These intermediate values form an **authentication path** of a tree, and serve as a form of certificate.

Let $K_1, \ldots, K_n$ denote the file of public enciphering keys. Let $f(x, y)$ be a function that returns a value in the domain of f. The hashing function H is defined recursively by:

$$H(i, j) = \begin{cases} f(H(i, m), H(m + 1, j)) & \text{if } i < j, \text{ where } m = \lfloor (i + j)/2 \rfloor \\ f(K_i, K_i) & \text{if } i = j \end{cases}$$

where $H(1, n)$ is the hash value of the entire public file.

Figure 3.24 illustrates the computation for $n = 8$. Users can compute $H(1, 8)$ by following a path from their key to the root, provided they know the intermediate values of H needed to follow the path. For example, the user with key K_1 can compute $H(1, 8)$ from $H(2, 2)$, $H(3, 4)$, and $H(5, 8)$ by computing the following sequence:

$$H(1, 1) = f(K_1, K_1)$$
$$H(1, 2) = f(H(1, 1), H(2, 2))$$
$$H(1, 4) = f(H(1, 2), H(3, 4))$$
$$H(1, 8) = f(H(1, 4), H(5, 8)) .$$

The values K_1, $H(2, 2)$, $H(3, 4)$, and $H(5, 8)$ form this user's authentication path.

Because the entire file is hashed as a unit, any modification of the file invalidates every certificate. Thus, it is easy for a user to determine whether someone

FIGURE 3.24 Tree authentication.

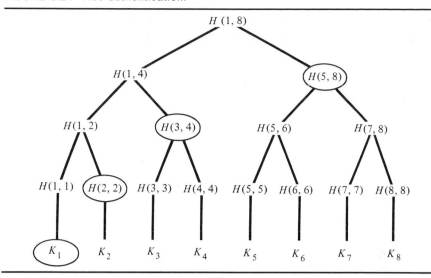

else is attempting to masquerade as the user. There is a drawback, though; the entire file must be rehashed each time an entry is added or changed.

3.7.3 Generating Block Encryption Keys

In Section 3.2 we discussed methods for generating pseudo-random key streams for stream encryption. The streams were generated from a seed I_0 using a block encryption algorithm. We shall now discuss methods for generating single keys. These values should satisfy the same properties of randomness as key streams, and should not be repeated across power failures.

Matyas and Meyer [Maty78] suggest methods for generating keys from the master keys $KM0$, $KM1$, and $KM2$ described in Section 3.7.1. They recommend the master key $KM0$ be generated outside the system by some random process such as tossing coins or throwing dice. The key could be recorded on some digital medium, entered from the medium, and installed with the set master key operation smk.

A set of key-encrypting keys K_i ($i = 1, 2, \ldots$) is derived from a random number R, which is generated outside the system in the same manner as the master key. Each K_i is generated from the operation $rfmk$ [Eq.(3.11)]:

$$K_i = rfmk(R, rfmk(R, T + i)),$$

where T is the current time (the parity bits of K_i are adjusted as needed). Because $rfmk$ is a function of $KM0$, K_i is a function of a random number R, the time, and the master key.

Data encrypting keys are generated inside the system using the operation

FIGURE 3.25 Key generation.

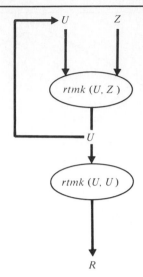

rtmk [Eq. (3.12)]. Consecutive random numbers R_i (i = 1, 2, . . .) are generated from two independent values U_{i-1} and Z_i by

$$R_i = rtmk(U_i, U_i),\qquad\qquad (3.14)$$

where

$$U_i = rtmk(U_{i-1}, Z_i)\quad\text{for }i > 0,$$

and each Z_i is derived from two or more independent clock readings (see Figure 3.25). The initial value U_0 is derived from a combination of user and process dependent information. Each U_i is a function of $KM0$ and all preceding values of U and Z, and each R_i is a function of $KM0$ and U_i; thus, it should be computationally infeasible to determine one R_i from another R_j, and computationally infeasible to determine R_i from U_i or vice versa.

Each random number R_i is defined as the encipherment of a data encrypting key K_i under some other key X; that is,

$$R_i = E_X(K_i).$$

Thus, K_i can be generated without ever being exposed in plaintext. For example, if K is to be used to encipher data stored in a system file, R_i would be defined as

$$R_i = E_{KNF}(K_i),$$

where KNF is a secondary file key.

Keys that are used more than once (e.g., database keys or private keys) can be stored in files, enciphered under some other key. If an application uses a large number of such keys, it is more efficient (in terms of space) to regenerate them when they are needed. This cannot be done using the preceding methods, because the keys are a function of the current state of the system. Bayer and Metzger [Baye76] describe an encipherment scheme for paged file and database structures (including indexed structures) where each page is enciphered under a different page key. The key K for a page P is derived from a file key KF by $K = E_{KF}(P)$. Keys for other objects could be generated by similar means. In capability-based systems (see Chapter 4), each object is identified by a unique name; this name could be used to derive the encryption key for the object. By encrypting each object under a separate key, exposure of a key endangers only one object.

Each record of a database could be enciphered under a different key using a scheme suggested by Flynn and Campasano [Flyn78]. A record key would be a function of a database key and selected plaintext data stored in the record (or supplied by the user), and would be generated at the time the record is accessed. Enciphering each record under a separate key would protect against ciphertext searching and replay as described in Section 3.4. A user authorized to access the encrypted fields of the records either would use a special terminal equipped with the database key, or would be given a copy of the key sealed in a ROM, which could be inserted into any terminal. The scheme could also be used to encipher each field of a record under a separate key, though encrypting the fields of a record separately can introduce security problems as described earlier.

Keys shared by groups of users in a computer network can be generated from information about the group members. Let G be a group of users in a network of N users. Members of G can share a secret **group key** K_G, which allows them to broadcast and receive messages from other members of G, and to access and update files private to G. Users not in G are not allowed access to K_G. There can be at most $2^N - N - 1$ groups of two or more users in the system. Denning and Schneider [Denn81a] and Denning, Meijer, and Schneider [Denn81b] describe schemes for deriving all possible group keys from a list of N user values; thus, the schemes generate an exponential number of keys from a linear number of values. One simple method computes the key K_G for a group G of m users from

$$K_G = 2^{K_1 K_2 \cdots K_m} \bmod p \, ,$$

where $K_1, \ldots, K_m$ are the user's private keys. A user not in G cannot determine K_G or any of the K_i of the members in G without computing a discrete logarithm. In Section 2.7.1, we saw this was infeasible when p was 200 decimal digits long. If a key shorter than 200 digits is needed, K_G can be compressed by enciphering it with a stream cipher in cipher feedback mode or with cipher block chaining, and keeping the rightmost bits.

3.7.4 Distribution of Session Keys

If two users wish to communicate in a network using conventional encryption, they must share a secret **session key** (also called "communication key"). Either a system key manager must supply this key (in which case security of the key distribu-

FIGURE 3.26 Centralized key distribution protocol.

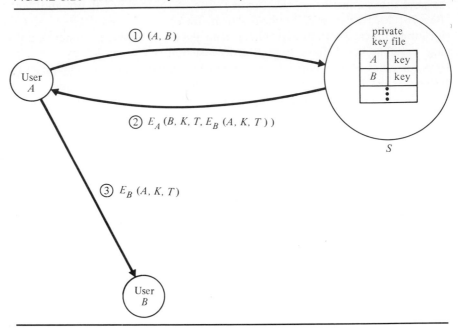

tion facility is required), or else the users must find an independent but secure method for exchanging the key by themselves. We shall show how each of these approaches may be implemented.

We shall first describe a protocol for obtaining session keys from a centralized key distribution facility, sometimes called an "authentication server", S. The protocol is based on one introduced by Needham and Schroeder [Need78] and modified by Denning and Sacco [Denn81c]. We assume each user has a private key, registered with S. If two users wish to communicate, one of them obtains a session key K from S and distributes it to the other. A new key is obtained for each session, so that neither the users nor S need keep lists of session keys. Although S could keep a list of session keys for all possible pairs of users, the storage requirements would be enormous [for n users there are $\binom{n}{2}$ possible pairs], and the keys might be vulnerable to attack. The key distribution facility could be distributed over the network.

User A acquires a key K from S to share with another user B by initiating the following steps (also refer to Figure 3.26):

Centralized key distribution protocol
1. A sends to S the plaintext message

   (A, B)

   stating both A's and B's identity.

2. S sends to A the ciphertext message

$$E_A(B, K, T, C) \ ,$$

where E_A is the enciphering transformation derived from A's private key, K is the session key, T is the current date and time, and

$$C = E_B(A, K, T) \ ,$$

where E_B is the enciphering transformation derived from B's private key.

3. A sends to B the message C from Step 2.

In Step 1, A could conceal B's identity by sending $(A, E_A(B))$ to S. A's identifier cannot be encrypted under E_A, however, because then S would not know with whom to correspond.

In Step 2, S returns the session key K enciphered under B's private key as well as A's so that A can securely send the key to B without knowing B's private key. The timestamp T guards against replays of previous keys.

For added protection, the protocol can be extended to include a "handshake" between B and A [Need78]:

4. B picks a random identifier I and sends to A

$$X = E_K(I) \ .$$

5. A deciphers X to obtain I, modifies it in some predetermined way to get I' (e.g., $I' = I + 1$), and returns to B

$$E_K(I') \ .$$

This confirms receipt of I and the use of K.

With the handshake, A can begin transmitting data to B at Step 5; without the handshake, A can begin at Step 3.

To protect K from exposure between the time it is generated and the time it is enciphered under A's and B's private keys, K should be generated as a random number R in ciphertext as described in the preceding section [see Eq. (3.14)]. Ehrsam, Matyas, Meyer, and Tuchman [Ehrs78] suggest that R be defined as the encipherment of K under the master key $KM0$; that is,

$$R = E_{KM0}(K) \ .$$

If users' private keys are enciphered under a variant master key $KM1$, as described in Section 3.7.1 for terminal master keys, K can be deciphered and reenciphered under A's and B's private keys using the reencipher from master key operation *rfmk* [Eq. (3.11)].

It is desirable to distribute the server S over the network so that all keys do not have to be registered at a single site, and so that no single file contains all private keys. This general approach is used in the protocols given by Ehrsam, Matyas, Meyer, and Tuchman [Ehrs78] for use in the system described in Section 3.7.1. Here the host systems for the users exchange an enciphered session key R.

Each host then uses the *rfmk* instruction to transmit R to its respective user's terminal, enciphered under the terminal master key KMT (users' private keys are used for data encryption only, not for key exchange). The hosts exchange R using the *rfmk* and *rtmk* operations as follows. Let H_A be the host for A and H_B the host for B, and let $KM0_A$ and $KM0_B$ be their respective master keys. H_A and H_B share a **secondary communication key** KNC. KNC is stored as $W_A = E_{KM1_A}(KNC)$ at H_A (for key forwarding) and as $W_B = E_{KM2_B}(KNC)$ at H_B (for key receiving). The encrypted key K is given by $R = E_{KM0_A}(K)$. H_A uses the *rfmk* instruction to forward R to H_B, and H_B uses the *rtmk* instruction to receive R. The complete protocol is as follows:

Key distribution by host systems

1. H_A generates $R = E_{KM0_A}(K)$, and sends to H_B:

    $$rfmk(W_A, R) = E_{KNC}(R) \ .$$

2. H_B obtains R by computing

    $$rtmk(W_B, E_{KNC}(R)) = R \ .$$

3. H_A sends to A:

    $$Z_A = rfmk(Y_A, R) = E_{KMT_A}(K) \ ,$$

    where KMT_A is A's terminal master key, and $Y_A = E_{KM1_A}(KMT_A)$. A obtains K by deciphering Z_A.

4. Similarly, H_B sends to B:

    $$Z_B = rfmk(Y_B, R) = E_{KMT_B}(K) \ ,$$

    where KMT_B is B's terminal master key, and $Y_B = E_{KM1_B}(KMT_B)$. B obtains K by deciphering Z_B.

The scheme is also used to distribute session keys to nodes or processes rather than terminals.

Diffie and Hellman [Diff76] and Merkle [Merk78] have proposed an approach that allows users to exchange session keys directly. Diffie's and Hellman's scheme is based on the computational difficulty of computing discrete logarithms (see Section 2.7.1). The first user, A, picks a random value x_A in the interval [0, $p - 1$], where p is prime (p may be publicly available to all users). The second user, B, also picks a random value x_B in the interval [0, $p - 1$]. Then A sends to B the value

$$y_A = a^{x_A} \bmod p,$$

and B sends to A the value

$$y_B = a^{x_B} \bmod p,$$

for some constant a. For sufficiently large values of x_A and x_B (e.g., 664 bits), the fastest known algorithms for computing the discrete logarithm function are intractable, whence x_A and x_B cannot be practically computed from y_A and y_B (see Section 2.7.1). After the y's are exchanged, A computes the session key

$$K = (y_B)^{x_A} \bmod p$$
$$= (a^{x_B} \bmod p)^{x_A} \bmod p$$
$$= a^{x_A x_B} \bmod p \ ,$$

and similarly for B.

Although an eavesdropper cannot compute K from either y_A or y_B, there is no way A and B can be sure that they are communicating with each other with this mechanism alone. This problem is remedied in the public-key distribution schemes described next.

MITRE is developing a demonstration system that uses public-key distribution for key exchange and the DES for message encryption [Scha79,Scha80]. Each user A obtains a "private key" x_A and registers the "public key" $y_A = a^{x_A}$ mod p with a public-key distribution center (y_A and x_A are not encryption keys in the usual sense since they are not used to encipher and decipher in a public-key cryptosystem). The MITRE system provides three modes of operating the DES for message encryption: standard block mode, cipher feedback mode, and cipher block chaining. For the latter two modes, two users A and B must exchange initialization bit vectors (seeds) I_{AB} and I_{BA} in addition to a session key K; I_{AB} is used for transmission from A to B and I_{BA} for transmissions from B to A. A secure channel is established between A and B as follows:

Exchange of keys using public-key distribution

1. A obtains y_B from the public directory and computes a key $K_{AB} = (y_B)^{x_A}$ mod p as described earlier. A generates random values R and R_{AB} and computes the session key K and initialization vector I_{AB}:

$$K = D_{AB}(R), I_{AB} = D_K(R_{AB}) \ ,$$

where D_{AB} is the DES deciphering transformation with key K_{AB}. A sends to B the plaintext

$$(A, R, R_{AB}) \ .$$

2. B obtains y_A and computes $K_{AB} = (y_B)^{x_A}$ mod p. B computes

$$K = D_{AB}(R), I_{AB} = D_K(R_{AB}) \ .$$

B modifies I_{AB} in a predetermined way to get I'_{AB} and computes

$$X = E_K(I'_{AB}) \ .$$

B generates a random value R_{BA}, computes

$$I_{BA} = D_K(R_{BA}) \ ,$$

and sends (X, R_{BA}) to A.

3. A deciphers X to get $D_K(X) = I'_{AB}$. This confirms receipt of I_{AB} by B. A computes

$$I_{BA} = D_K(R_{BA}) \ .$$

A modifies I_{BA} in a predetermined way to get I'_{BA}, computes

$$Y = E_K(I'_{BA}) \ ,$$

and sends Y to B.

4. B deciphers Y to get $D_K(Y) = I'_{BA}$, confirming receipt of I_{BA} by A.

Note that all ciphertext transmitted between A and B is enciphered under the session key K, which is likely to have a much shorter lifetime than the shared key K_{AB}.

Computation of the public keys y_A and y_B and the private key K_{AB} is implemented in $\mathbf{GF}(2^n)$ using $n = 127$ and irreducible polynomial $p(x) = x^{127} + x + 1$ (see Section 1.6.3). Recall that implementation in $\mathbf{GF}(2^n)$ was also suggested for the Pohlig-Hellman exponentiation cipher, where computation of $y_A = a^{x_A} \bmod p$ corresponds to the encryption of plaintext a using encryption key x_A (see Section 2.7.1).

The MITRE demonstration system provides both central and local public-key distribution modes. With central key distribution, a user acquires public keys directly from the key distribution center each time the user wants to establish a secure connection. With local key distribution, the public key directory is down-loaded to the user's system and stored in local memory. This has the advantage of relieving the central facility of participating in every connection. The demonstration system also provides a non-directory mode corresponding to the original Diffie-Hellman proposal, where the public values are exchanged directly by the users. This mode is suitable when active wiretapping does not pose a serious threat.

A public-key cryptosystem can also be used to exchange session keys [Diff76,Merk80]. Following the timestamp protocol in [Denn81b], let C_A and C_B

FIGURE 3.27 Public-key distribution protocol.

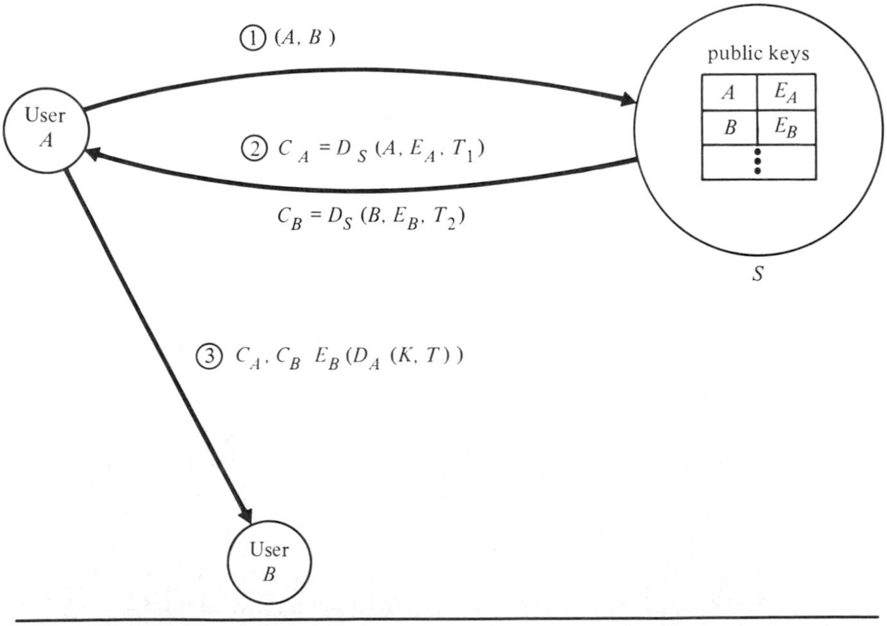

be A's and B's certificates [Eq. (3.13)], signed by S. A and B can exchange a key K with the following protocol (also refer to Figure 3.27):

Public-key distribution protocol

1. A sends the plaintext message (A, B) to S, requesting certificates for A and B.
2. S sends to A the certificates

$$C_A = D_S(A, E_A, T_1)$$
$$C_B = D_S(B, E_B, T_1) \ .$$

3. A checks C_A and gets B's public transformation E_B from C_B. A then generates a random key K, gets the time T, and sends the following to B:

$$(C_A, C_B, X) \ ,$$

where $X = E_B(D_A(K, T))$, and D_A is A's private deciphering transformation.
4. B checks C_B, gets A's public transformation E_A from C_A, and computes

$$E_A(D_B(X)) = (K, T) \ ,$$

where D_B is B's private transformation.

For added protection, the protocol can be extended to include a handshake between B and A, following the approach described for the centralized key distribution protocol. Of course, in a public-key system users can send messages directly using each other's public keys (obtained from certificates). The protocol would be used only if conventional encryption of messages is needed for performance reasons.

If the public keys are distributed among multiple hosts in a network, then the protocol must be extended slightly to allow exchange of certificates among the hosts. In Step 2, if A's host S does not have B's public key, it could dispatch a message to B's host requesting a certificate for B.

For additional reading on protocols for secure communication and key exchange, see Davies and Price [Davs79,Pric81], Kent [Kent78,Kent76], and Popek and Kline [Pope79]. Protocols for secure broadcast scenario are examined in Kent [Kent81].

3.8 THRESHOLD SCHEMES

Ultimately, the safety of all keys stored in the system—and therefore the entire system—may depend on a single master key. This has two serious drawbacks. First, if the master key is accidently or maliciously exposed, the entire system is vulnerable. Second, if the master key is lost or destroyed, all information in the system becomes inaccessible. The latter problem can be solved by giving copies of the key to "trustworthy" users. But in so doing, the system becomes vulnerable to betrayal.

The solution is to break a key K into w **shadows** (pieces) $K_1, \ldots, K_w$ in such a way that:

1. With knowledge of any t of the K_i, computing K is easy; and
2. With knowledge of any $t - 1$ or fewer of the K_i, determining K is impossible because of lack of information.

The w shadows are given to w users. Because t shadows are required to reconstruct the key, exposure of a shadow (or up to $t - 1$ shadows) does not endanger the key, and no group of less than t of the users can conspire to get the key. At the same time, if a shadow is lost or destroyed, key recovery is still possible (as long as there are at least t valid shadows). Such schemes are called (t, w) **threshold schemes** [Sham79], and can be used to protect any type of data. Blakley [Blak79] published the first threshold scheme, which was based on projective geometry. The following subsections describe two other approaches.

3.8.1 Lagrange Interpolating Polynomial Scheme

Shamir [Sham79] has proposed a scheme based on Lagrange interpolating polynomials (e.g., see [Ardi70,Cont72]). The shadows are derived from a random polynomial of degree $t - 1$:

$$h(x) = (a_{t-1}x^{t-1} + \cdots + a_1 x + a_0) \bmod p \qquad (3.15)$$

with constant term $a_0 = K$. All arithmetic is done in the Galois field $\mathbf{GF}(p)$, where p is a prime number larger than both K and w (long keys can be broken into smaller blocks to avoid using a large modulus p). Given $h(x)$, the key K is easily computed by

$$K = h(0) \ .$$

The w shadows are computed by evaluating $h(x)$ at w distinct values $x_1, \ldots, x_w$:

$$K_i = h(x_i) \quad i = 1, \ldots, w \ . \qquad (3.16)$$

Each pair (x_i, K_i) is thus a point on the "curve" $h(x)$. The values $x_1, \ldots, x_w$ need not be secret, and could be user identifiers or simply the numbers 1 through w. Because t points uniquely determine a polynomial of degree $t - 1$, $h(x)$ and, therefore, K can be reconstructed from t shadows. There is not enough information, however, to determine $h(x)$ or K from fewer than t shadows.

Given t shadows $K_{i_1}, K_{i_2}, \ldots, K_{i_t}$, $h(x)$ is reconstructed from the Lagrange polynomial:

$$h(x) = \sum_{s=1}^{t} K_{i_s} \prod_{\substack{j=1 \\ j \neq s}}^{t} \frac{(x - x_{i_j})}{(x_{i_s} - x_{i_j})} \bmod p \ . \qquad (3.17)$$

Because arithmetic is in $\mathbf{GF}(p)$, the divisions in Eq. (3.17) are performed by computing inverses mod p and multiplying.

Example:
Let $t = 3$, $w = 5$, $p = 17$, $K = 13$, and

$$h(x) = (2x^2 + 10x + 13) \bmod 17$$

with random coefficients 2 and 10. Evaluating $h(x)$ at $x = 1, \ldots, 5$, we get five shadows:

$$
\begin{aligned}
K_1 &= h(1) = (2 + 10 + 13) \bmod 17 = 25 \bmod 17 = 8 \\
K_2 &= h(2) = (8 + 20 + 13) \bmod 17 = 41 \bmod 17 = 7 \\
K_3 &= h(3) = (18 + 30 + 13) \bmod 17 = 61 \bmod 17 = 10 \\
K_4 &= h(4) = (32 + 40 + 13) \bmod 17 = 85 \bmod 17 = 0 \\
K_5 &= h(5) = (50 + 50 + 13) \bmod 17 = 113 \bmod 17 = 11 \; .
\end{aligned}
$$

We can reconstruct $h(x)$ from any three of the shadows. Using K_1, K_3, and K_5, we have:

$$h(x) = \left[8\frac{(x-3)(x-5)}{(1-3)(1-5)} + 10\frac{(x-1)(x-5)}{(3-1)(3-5)} + 11\frac{(x-1)(x-3)}{(5-1)(5-3)} \right] \bmod 17$$

$$= \left[8\frac{(x-3)(x-5)}{(-2)(-4)} + 10\frac{(x-1)(x-5)}{(2)(-2)} + 11\frac{(x-1)(x-3)}{(4)(2)} \right] \bmod 17$$

$$
\begin{aligned}
= [&8 * inv(8, 17) * (x-3)(x-5) \\
&+ 10 * inv(-4, 17) * (x-1)(x-5) \\
&+ 11 * inv(8, 17) * (x-1)(x-3)] \bmod 17
\end{aligned}
$$

$$
\begin{aligned}
= [&8 * 15 * (x-3)(x-5) + 10 * 4 * (x-1)(x-5) \\
&+ 11 * 15 * (x-1)(x-3)] \bmod 17
\end{aligned}
$$

$$= [(x-3)(x-5) + 6(x-1)(x-5) + 12(x-1)(x-3)] \bmod 17$$

$$= [19x^2 - 92x + 81] \bmod 17$$

$$= 2x^2 + 10x + 13 \; . \quad \blacksquare$$

Blakley [Blak80] shows the scheme can be more efficiently implemented in $\mathbf{GF}(2^n)$ with modulus $p(x) = x^n + x + 1$ if $p(x)$ is irreducible (which it usually is not—see Section 1.6.3). Here, the coefficients a_i of $h(x)$ are elements of $\mathbf{GF}(2^n)$, and $h(x)$ is reduced mod $p(x)$. Similarly, the coordinates x_i and K_i are elements of $\mathbf{GF}(2^n)$, and Eq. (3.17) is evaluated in $\mathbf{GF}(2^n)$. Note that whereas the "x" in $h(x)$ is a variable or unknown, each "x" in $p(x)$ represents a placeholder for the binary representation of p.

Example:
Consider the field $\mathbf{GF}(2^3)$ with irreducible polynomial

$$p(x) = x^3 + x + 1 = 1011 \text{ (in binary)}$$

The elements of $\mathbf{GF}(2^3)$ are binary strings of length 3. Let $t = 2$, $w = 3$, $K = 011$, and

$$h(x) = (101x + 011) \bmod 1011$$

with random coefficient 101. Evaluating $h(x)$ at $x = 001$, 010, and 011, we get:

$$K_1 = h(001) = (101 * 001 + 011) \bmod 1011$$
$$= 110$$
$$K_2 = h(010) = (101 * 010 + 011) \bmod 1011$$
$$= 001 + 011 = 010$$
$$K_3 = h(011) = (101 * 011 + 011) \bmod 1011$$
$$= 100 + 011 = 111 \ .$$

We can reconstruct $h(x)$ from any two of the shadows. Using K_1 and K_2, we have

$$h(x) = \left[110 \frac{(x - 010)}{(001 - 010)} + 010 \frac{(x - 001)}{(010 - 001)} \right] \bmod 1011$$
$$= \left[110 \frac{(x - 010)}{011} + 010 \frac{(x - 001)}{011} \right] \bmod 1011 \ .$$

Because the inverse of 011 is 110, and subtraction is equivalent to addition, this reduces to:

$$h(x) = [110 * 110 * (x + 010) + 010 * 110 * (x + 001)] \bmod 1011$$
$$= [010 * (x + 010) + 111 * (x + 001)] \bmod 1011$$
$$= 010x + 100 + 111x + 111$$
$$= 101x + 011 \ . \quad \blacksquare$$

Shamir observes that the general approach [implemented in either $\mathbf{GF}(p)$ or $\mathbf{GF}(2^n)$] has several useful properties, namely:

1. The size of each shadow K_i does not substantially exceed the size of the key K [there may be some key expansion in $\mathbf{GF}(p)$, because p must be larger than K].
2. For fixed K, additional shadows can be created without changing existing ones just by evaluating $h(x)$ at more values of x. A shadow can also be destroyed without affecting other shadows.
3. A shadow can be voided without changing K by using a different polynomial $h(x)$ with the same constant term. Voided shadows cannot be used unless there are at least t of them derived from the same polynomial.
4. A hierarchical scheme is possible, where the number of shadows given to each user is proportional to the user's importance. For example, a company president can be given three shadows, each vice-president two, and so forth.
5. Key recovery is efficient, requiring only $O(t^2)$ operations to evaluate Eq. (3.17) using standard algorithms, or $O(t \log^2 t)$ operations using methods discussed in [Knut69,Aho74].

3.8.2 Congruence Class Scheme

Asmuth and Bloom [Asmu80] have proposed a threshold scheme based on the
Chinese Remainder Theorem (see Theorem 1.8 in Section 1.5.2). In their scheme
the shadows are congruence classes of a number associated with K. Let

$$\{p, d_1, d_2, \ldots, d_w\}$$

be a set of integers such that

1. $p > K$
2. $d_1 < d_2 < \cdots < d_w$
3. $gcd(p, d_i) = 1$ for all i
4. $gcd(d_i, d_j) = 1$ for $i \neq j$
5. $d_1 d_2 \cdots d_t > p d_{w-t+2} \, d_{w-t+3} \cdots d_w$.

Requirements (3) and (4) imply the set of integers is pairwise relatively prime.
Requirement (5) implies the product of the t smallest d_i is larger than the product
of p and the $t - 1$ largest d_i. Let $n = d_1 d_2 \cdots d_t$ be the product of the t smallest d_i.
Thus n/p is larger than the product of any $t - 1$ of the d_i. Let r be a random
integer in the range $[0, (n/p) - 1]$. To decompose K into w shadows, $K' = K + rp$
is computed; this puts K' in the range $[0, n - 1]$. The shadows are then as follows:

$$K_i = K' \bmod d_i \quad i = 1, \ldots, w \ . \tag{3.18}$$

To recover K, it suffices to find K'. If t shadows $K_{i_1}, \ldots, K_{i_t}$ are known, then
by the Chinese Remainder Theorem K' is known modulo

$$n_1 = d_{i_1} d_{i_2} \cdots d_{i_t} \ .$$

Because $n_1 \geq n$, this uniquely determines K', which can be computed using algorithm crt in Figure 1.24:

$$K' = crt(n_1, d_{i_1}, \ldots, d_{i_t}, K_{i_1}, \ldots, K_{i_t}) \bmod n \ . \tag{3.19}$$

Finally, K is computed from K', r, and p:

$$K = K' - rp \ . \tag{3.20}$$

If only $t - 1$ shadows $K_{i_1}, \ldots, K_{i_{t-1}}$ are known, K' can only be known
modulo

$$n_2 = d_{i_1} d_{i_2} \cdots d_{i_{t-1}} \ .$$

Because $n/n_2 > p$ and $gcd(n_2, p) = 1$, the numbers x such that $x \leq n$ and $x \equiv_{n_2}$
K' are evenly distributed over all the congruence classes modulo p; thus, there is
not enough information to determine K'.

Example:
Let $K = 3$, $t = 2$, $w = 3$, $p = 5$, $d_1 = 7$, $d_2 = 9$, and $d_3 = 11$. Then

$$n = d_1 d_2 = 7 * 9 = 63 > 5 * 11 = p d_3$$

as required. We need a random number r in the range $[0, (63/5) - 1] =$ $[0, 11]$. Picking $r = 9$, we get

$$K' = K + rp = 3 + 9 * 5 = 48 .$$

The shadows are thus:

$$K_1 = 48 \bmod 7 = 6$$
$$K_2 = 48 \bmod 9 = 3$$
$$K_3 = 48 \bmod 11 = 4 .$$

Given any two of the shadows, we can compute K. Using K_1 and K_3, we have

$$n_1 = d_1 d_3 = 7 * 11 = 77 .$$

Applying algorithm crt, we first compute

$$y_1 = inv(n_1/d_1, d_1) = inv(11, 7) = 2$$
$$y_3 = inv(n_1/d_3, d_3) = inv(7, 11) = 8 .$$

Thus

$$K' = \left[\left(\frac{n_1}{d_1} \right) y_1 K_1 + \left(\frac{n_1}{d_3} \right) y_3 K_3 \right] \bmod n_1$$
$$= [11 * 2 * 6 + 7 * 8 * 4] \bmod 77$$
$$= 356 \bmod 77$$
$$= 48 .$$

Thus,

$$K = K' - rp = 48 - 9 * 5 = 3 . \quad \blacksquare$$

Asmuth and Bloom describe an efficient algorithm for reconstructing K that requires only $O(t)$ time and $O(w)$ space. Thus their scheme is asymptotically more efficient than Shamir's polynomial scheme, which requires $O(t \log^2 t)$ time. For small t, this may not be an important consideration.

Asmuth and Bloom also describe a modification to their scheme for detecting defective shadows before their use. The basic idea is to remove the requirement that the moduli d_i be pairwise relatively prime [requirement (4)]. Then two shadows K_i and K_j will be congruent modulo $gcd(d_i, d_j)$ if both shadows are correct. Because an error in one shadow K_i will change its congruence class modulo $gcd(d_i, d_j)$ for most (if not all) $j \neq i$, defective shadows are easily detected. With this approach, requirement (5) must be changed to require that the least common multiple (lcm) of any t of the d_i is larger than the product of p and the lcm of any $t - 1$ of the d_i. (The general approach can also be incorporated in the polynomial interpolation scheme.)

Other threshold schemes have been proposed. Davida, DeMillo, and Lipton [Davi80] have proposed a scheme based on error correcting codes. Bloom [Bloo81] has outlined a class of schemes approaching optimal speed when the key length is large compared with the threshold value t; his schemes are based on linear maps over finite fields. (See [Blak81] for a study of security proofs for threshold schemes.)

Whereas cryptosystems achieve computational security, threshold schemes achieve unconditional security by not putting enough information into any $t - 1$ shadows to reconstruct the key. Blakley [Blak80] has shown the one-time pad can be characterized as a $t = 2$ threshold scheme protecting a message M. Here, the sender and receiver each has a copy of the pad M_1, which serves as one shadow. The second shadow, constructed by the sender and transmitted to the receiver, is given by the ciphertext $M_2 = M \oplus M_1$. Both M_1 and M_2 are needed to reconstruct M. The interesting point is that classifying the one-time pad as a key threshold scheme explains how it can achieve perfect security when no other cryptosystem can.

EXERCISES

3.1 Suppose the ith ciphertext c_i is deleted from a direct access file enciphered with a synchronous stream cipher, and that the remainder of the file is deciphered and reenciphered using the original key stream, where c_{i+1} is now enciphered under k_i, c_{i+2} under k_{i+1}, and so forth. Show that all key elements k_j and plaintext elements m_j $(j \geq i)$ can be determined from the original and updated ciphertext if m_i is known.

3.2 Let $M = 100011$ and $C = 101101$ be corresponding bit streams in a known plaintext attack, where the key stream was generated with a 3-stage linear feedback register. Using Eq. (3.2) solve for H to get the tap sequence T.

3.3 Describe methods for breaking Vigenère's autokey ciphers.

3.4 Let $d_1 = 3$, $d_2 = 5$, and $d_3 = 7$ be read subkeys in the scheme described in Section 3.4.2. Using Eq. (3.3), find write subkeys e_1, e_2, and e_3. Using Eq. (3.4), encipher a record having fields $m_1 = 2$, $m_2 = 4$, and $m_3 = 3$ (do not bother adding random strings to each field). Show that all three fields can be deciphered using only their read subkeys in Eq. (3.5). Using e_2 and d_2 in Eq. (3.6), modify the ciphertext so that the second field has the value 3 instead of 4. Show that all three fields can be extracted from the modified ciphertext using only their read subkeys.

3.5 Consider the subkey scheme described in Section 3.4.2. Let C_1 and C_2 be two ciphertext records of t fields each, and suppose the first $t - 1$ fields in each record are updated as defined by Eq. (3.6). Letting C'_1 and C'_2 denote the updated ciphertext records, show how the read key d_t can be determined for the tth field from the original and updated ciphertext records.

3.6 Complete the proof of Theorem 3.1 in Section 3.5.2 by showing how the exact value of i can be determined.

3.7 Consider a privacy homomorphism for the system of natural numbers with addition, multiplication, and test for equality. Given a ciphertext element i', show that it is possible to determine whether the corresponding plaintext element i is equal to an arbitrary constant n in $O(n)$ time without using any constants.

3.8   Give the authentication path for the user with key K_6 in Figure 3.24. Show how these values can be used to compute $H(1, 8)$.

3.9   Consider Shamir's key threshold scheme based on Lagrange interpolating polynomials in $\mathbf{GF}(p)$. Let $t = 4$, $p = 11$, $K = 7$, and

$$h(x) = (x^3 + 10x^2 + 3x + 7) \bmod 11 \; .$$

Using Eq. (3.16), compute shadows for $x = 1, 2, 3$, and 4. Using Eq. (3.17), reconstruct $h(x)$ from the shadows.

3.10   Consider Shamir's key threshold scheme based on Lagrange interpolating polynomials in $\mathbf{GF}(2^3)$ with irreducible polynomial $p(x) = x^3 + x + 1 = 1011$. Let $t = 3$, $K = 010$, and

$$h(x) = (001x^2 + 011x + 010) \bmod 1011 \; .$$

Compute shadows for $x = 001, 011$, and 100. Reconstruct $h(x)$ from the shadows.

3.11   Consider Asmuth's and Bloom's key threshold scheme based on the Chinese Remainder Theorem. Let $t = 2$, $w = 4$, $p = 5$, $d_1 = 8$, $d_2 = 9$, $d_3 = 11$, and $d_4 = 13$. Then $n = 8 * 9 = 72$. Let $K = 3$ and $r = 10$, whence $K' = 53$. Using Eq. (3.18), decompose K' into four shadows, K_1, K_2, K_3, and K_4. Using Eq. (3.19) and Eq. (3.20), reconstruct K from K_1 and K_2, and from K_1 and K_4.

3.12   *Class Computer Project:* Implement one of the key threshold schemes.

3.13   Consider a synchronous stream cipher where the ith key element k_i of a stream K is a block given by

$$k_i = (i + 1)^d \bmod n \; ,$$

where d is the private key to an RSA cipher and n is public. Thus,

$$K = k_1, k_2, k_3, k_4, k_5, \ldots$$
$$= 2^d, 3^d, 4^d, 5^d, 6^d, \ldots \;(\bmod n) \; .$$

The ith block m_i of a message stream M is enciphered as $c_i = m_i \oplus k_i$. As shown by Shamir [Sham81], this stream is vulnerable to a known-plaintext attack. Show how a cryptanalyst knowing the plaintext-ciphertext pairs (m_1, c_1) and (m_2, c_2) can determine k_3 and k_5. Given many plaintext-ciphertext pairs, can the cryptanalyst determine d and thereby derive the entire key stream?

3.14   Shamir [Sham81] proposes the following key stream as an alternative to the one given in the preceding exercise:

$$K = k_1, k_2, k_3, \ldots$$
$$= S^{1/d_1}, S^{1/d_2}, S^{1/d_3}, \ldots \;(\bmod n),$$

where $n = pq$ for large primes p and q, the d_i are pairwise relatively prime and relatively prime to $\phi(n)$, S is secret, and $S^{1/d_i} \bmod n$ is the d_ith root of S mod n. An example of a stream is

$$K = S^{1/3}, S^{1/5}, S^{1/7}, \ldots \;(\bmod n).$$

Shamir shows this stream is cryptographically strong; in particular, the difficulty of determining unknown key elements is equivalent to breaking the RSA cipher. Show how the d_ith root of S can be computed to give k_i. [*Hint:* Find the inverse of d_i mod $\phi(n)$.] Show why this technique cannot be used to compute the square root of S.

3.15 Suppose users A and B exchange message M in a public-key system using the following protocol:

1. A encrypts M using B's public transformation, and sends the ciphertext message to B along with plaintext stating both A's and B's identity:

$$(A, B, E_B(M)) .$$

2. B deciphers the ciphertext, and replies to A with

$$(B, A, E_A(M)) .$$

Show how an active wiretapper could break the scheme to determine M. (See Dolev [Dole81] for a study on the security of this and other public key protocols.)

REFERENCES

Aho74. Aho, A., Hopcroft, J., and Ullman, J., *The Design and Analysis of Computer Algorithms,* Addison-Wesley, Reading, Mass. (1974).

Ardi70. Ardin, B. W. and Astill, K. N., *Numerical Algorithms,* Addison-Wesley, Reading, Mass. (1970).

Asmu80. Asmuth, C. and Bloom, J., "A Modular Approach to Key Safeguarding," Math. Dept., Texas A&M Univ., College Station, Tex. (1980).

Bara64. Baran, P., "On Distributed Communications: IX. Security, Secrecy, and Tamper-Free Considerations," RM-3765-PR, The Rand Corp., Santa Monica, Calif. (1964).

Baye76. Bayer, R. and Metzger, J. K., "On the Encipherment of Search Trees and Random Access Files," *ACM Trans. on Database Syst.* Vol. 1(1) pp. 37–52 (Mar. 1976).

Blak79. Blakley, G. R., "Safeguarding Cryptographic Keys," *Proc. NCC,* Vol. 48, AFIPS Press, Montvale, N.J., pp. 313–317 (1979).

Blak80. Blakley, G. R., "One-Time Pads are Key Safeguarding Schemes, Not Cryptosystems," *Proc. 1980 Symp. on Security and Privacy,* IEEE Computer Society, pp. 108–113 (Apr. 1980).

Blak81. Blakley, G. R. and Swanson, L., "Security Proofs for Information Protection Systems," in *Proc. 1981 Symp. on Security and Privacy,* IEEE Computer Society pp. 75–88 (Apr. 1981).

Bloo81. Bloom, J. R., "A Note on Superfast Threshold Schemes," Math. Dept., Texas A&M Univ., College Station, Tex. (1981).

Bran75. Branstad, D. K., "Encryption Protection in Computer Communication Systems," *Proc. 4th Data Communications Symp.,* pp. (8–1)–(8–7) (1975).

Bran78. Branstad, D. K., "Security of Computer Communication," *IEEE Comm. Soc. Mag.* Vol. 16(6) pp. 33–40 (Nov. 1978).

Brig76. Bright, H. S. and Enison, R. L., "Cryptography Using Modular Software Elements," *Proc. NCC,* Vol. 45, AFIPS Press, Montvale, N.J., pp. 113–123 (1976).

Brig80. Bright, H. S., "High-Speed Indirect Cryption," *Cryptologia* Vol. 4(3) pp. 133–139 (July 1980).

Camp78. Campbell, C. M., "Design and Specification of Cryptographic Capabilities," *IEEE Comm. Soc. Mag.* Vol. 16(6) pp. 15–19 (Nov. 1978).

Chai74. Chaitin, G. J., "Information-Theoretic Limitations of Formal Systems," *J. ACM* Vol. 21(3) pp. 403–424 (July 1974).

Chau81. Chaum, D. L., "Untraceable Electronic Mail, Return Addresses, and Digital Pseudonyms," *Comm. ACM* Vol. 24(2) pp. 84–88 (Feb. 1981).

Cont72. Conte, S. D. and deBoor, C., *Elementary Numerical Analysis,* McGraw-Hill, New York (1972).

Davi80. Davida, G. I., DeMillo, R. A., and Lipton, R. J., "Protecting Shared Cryptographic Keys," *Proc. 1980 Symp. on Security and Privacy,* IEEE Computer Society, pp. 100–102 (Apr. 1980).

Davi81. Davida, G. I., Wells, D. L., and Kam, J. B., "A Database Encryption System with Subkeys," *ACM Trans. on Database Syst.,* Vol. 6(2) pp. 312–328 (June 1981).

Davs79. Davies, D. W. and Price, W. L., "A Protocol for Secure Communication," NPL Report NACS 21/79, National Physical Lab., Teddington, Middlesex, England (Nov. 1979).

DeMi78. DeMillo, R., Lipton, R., and McNeil, L., "Proprietary Software Protection," pp. 115–131 in *Foundations of Secure Computation,* Academic Press, New York (1978).

Denn79. Denning, D. E., "Secure Personal Computing in an Insecure Network," *Comm. ACM* Vol. 22(8) pp. 476–482 (Aug. 1979).

Denn81a. Denning, D. E. and Schneider, F. B., "Master Keys for Group Sharing," *Info. Proc. Let.* Vol. 12(1) pp. 23–25 (Feb. 13, 1981).

Denn81b. Denning, D. E., Meijer, H., and Schneider, F. B., "More on Master Keys for Group Sharing," *Info. Proc. Let.* (to appear).

Denn81c. Denning, D. E. and Sacco, G. M., "Timestamps in Key Distribution Protocols," *Comm. ACM* Vol. 24(8) pp. 533–536 (Aug. 1981).

Diff76. Diffie, W. and Hellman, M., "New Directions in Cryptography," *IEEE Trans. on Info. Theory* Vol. IT-22(6) pp. 644–654 (Nov. 1976).

Diff79. Diffie, W. and Hellman, M., "Privacy and Authentication: An Introduction to Cryptography," *Proc. IEEE* Vol. 67(3) pp. 397–427 (Mar. 1979).

Dole81. Dolev, D. and Yao, A. C., "On the Security of Public Key Protocols," *Proc. 22nd Annual Symp. on the Foundations of Computer Science,* (1981).

Ehrs78. Ehrsam, W. F., Matyas, S. M., Meyer, C. H., and Tuchman, W. L., "A Cryptographic Key Management Scheme for Implementing the Data Encryption Standard," *IBM Syst. J.* Vol. 17(2) pp. 106–125 (1978).

Evan74. Evans, A. Jr., Kantrowitz, W., and Weiss, E., "A User Authentication Scheme Not Requiring Secrecy in the Computer," *Comm. ACM* Vol. 17(8) pp. 437–442 (Aug. 1974).

Feis73. Feistel, H., "Cryptography and Computer Privacy," *Sci. Am.* Vol. 228(5) pp. 15–23 (May 1973).

Feis75. Feistel, H., Notz, W. A., and Smith, J. L., "Some Cryptographic Techniques for Machine to Machine Data Communications," *Proc. IEEE* Vol. 63(11) pp. 1545–1554 (Nov. 1975).

Flyn78. Flynn, R. and Campasano, A. S., "Data Dependent Keys for a Selective Encryption Terminal," pp. 1127–1129 in *Proc. NCC,* Vol. 47, AFIPS Press, Montvale, N.J. (1978).

GSA77. "Telecommunications: Compatibility Requirements for Use of the Data Encryption Standard," Proposed Federal Standard 1026, General Services Administration Washington, D.C. (Oct. 1977).

Gait77. Gait, J., "A New Nonlinear Pseudorandom Number Generator," *IEEE Trans. on Software Eng.* Vol. SE-3(5) pp. 359–363 (Sept. 1977).

Golu67. Golumb, S. W., *Shift Register Sequences,* Holden-Day, San Francisco, Calif. (1967).

Gude80. Gudes, E., "The Design of a Cryptography Based Secure File System," *IEEE Trans. on Software Eng.* Vol. SE-6(5) pp. 411–420 (Sept. 1980).

Hell80. Hellman, M. E., "On DES-Based, Synchronous Encryption," Dept. of Electrical Eng., Stanford Univ., Stanford, Calif. (1980).

Kahn67. Kahn, D., *The Codebreakers,* Macmillan Co., New York (1967).

Kent76. Kent, S. T., "Encryption-Based Protection Protocols for Interactive User-Computer Communication," MIT/LCS/TR-162, MIT Lab. for Computer Science, Cambridge, Mass. (May 1976).

Kent78. Kent, S. T., "Protocol Design Considerations for Network Security," *Proc. of the NATO Advanced Studies Inst. on the Interlinking of Computer Networks,* D. Reidel, pp. 239–259 (1978).

Kent80. Kent, S. T., "Protecting Externally Supplied Software in Small Computers," Ph.D. Thesis, Dept. of Electrical Eng. and Computer Science, MIT, Cambridge, Mass. (Sept. 1980).

Kent81. Kent, S. T., "Security Requirements and Protocols for a Broadcast Scenario," *IEEE Trans. on Communications* Vol. COM-29(6) pp. 778–786 (June 1981).

Knut69. Knuth, D., *The Art of Computer Programming;* Vol. 2, *Seminumerical Algorithms,* Addison-Wesley, Reading, Mass. (1969).

Konf78. Kohnfelder, L. M., "A Method for Certification," MIT Lab. for Computer Science, Cambridge, Mass. (May 1978).

Konh80. Konheim, A. G., Mack, M. H., McNeill, R. K., Tuckerman, B., and Waldbaum, G., "The IPS Cryptographic Programs," *IBM Syst. J.* Vol. 19(2) pp. 253–283 (1980).

Lipt78. Lipton, S. M. and Matyas, S. M., "Making the Digital Signature Legal—and Safeguarded," *Data Communications,* pp. 41–52 (Feb. 1978).

Maty78. Matyas, S. M. and Meyer, C. H., "Generation, Distribution, and Installation of Cryptographic Keys," *IBM Syst. J.* Vol. 17(2) pp. 126–137 (1978).

Merk78. Merkle, R. C., "Secure Communication Over an Insecure Channel," *Comm. ACM* Vol. 21(4) pp. 294–299 (Apr. 1978).

Merk80. Merkle, R. C., "Protocols for Public Key Cryptosystems," *Proc. 1980 Symp. on Security and Privacy,* IEEE Computer Society, pp. 122–133 (Apr. 1980).

Meye72. Meyer, C. H. and Tuchman, W. L., "Pseudo-Random Codes Can Be Cracked," *Electronic Design* Vol. 23 (Nov. 1972).

Meye73. Meyer, C. H., "Design Considerations for Cryptography," *Proc. NCC,* Vol. 42 AFIPS Press, Montvale, N.J. pp. 603–606 (1973).

Morr79. Morris, R. and Thompson, K., "Password Security: A Case History," *Comm. ACM* Vol. 22(11) pp. 594–597 (Nov. 1979).

Need78. Needham, R. M. and Schroeder, M., "Using Encryption for Authentication in Large Networks of Computers," *Comm. ACM* Vol. 21(12) pp. 993–999 (Dec. 1978).

Pete72. Peterson, W. W. and Weldon, E. J., *Error Correcting Codes* MIT Press, Cambridge, Mass. (1972).

Pope79. Popek, G. J. and Kline, C. S., "Encryption and Secure Computer Networks," *Computing Surveys* Vol. 11(4) pp. 331–356 (Dec. 1979).

Pric81. Price, W. L. and Davies, D. W., "Issues in the Design of a Key Distribution

Centre," NPL Report DNACS 43/81, National Physical Lab., Teddington, Middlesex, England (Apr. 1981).

Purd74. Purdy, G. P., "A High Security Log-in Procedure," *Comm. ACM* Vol. 17(8) pp. 442–445 (Aug. 1974).

Reed73. Reed, I. S., "Information Theory and Privacy in Data Banks," *Proc. NCC* Vol. 42, AFIPS Press, Montvale, N.J., pp. 581–587 (1973).

Rive78a. Rivest, R. L., Adleman, L., and Dertouzos, M. L., "On Data Banks and Privacy Homomorphisms," pp. 169–179 in *Foundations of Secure Computation*, ed. R. A. DeMillo et al., Academic Press, New York (1978).

Rive78b. Rivest, R. L., Shamir, A., and Adleman, L., "A Method for Obtaining Digital Signatures and Public-Key Cryptosystems," *Comm. ACM* Vol. 21(2) pp. 120–126 (Feb. 1978).

Salt78. Saltzer, J., "On Digital Signatures," *Oper. Syst. Rev.* Vol. 12(2) pp. 12–14 (Apr. 1978).

Sava67. Savage, J. E., "Some Simple Self-Synchronizing Digital Data Scramblers," *Bell System Tech. J.*, pp. 448–487 (Feb. 1967).

Scha79. Schanning, B. P., "Data Encryption with Public Key Distribution," *EASCON '79 Conf. Record*, pp. 653–660 (Oct. 1979).

Scha80. Schanning, B. P., Powers, S. A., and Kowalchuk, J., "Memo: Privacy and Authentication for the Automated Office," *Proc. 5th Conf. on Local Computer Networks*, pp. 21–30 (Oct. 1980).

Sham79. Shamir, A., "How to Share a Secret," *Comm. ACM* Vol. 22(11) pp. 612–613 (Nov. 1979).

Sham81. Shamir, A., "On the Generation of Cryptographically Strong Pseudo-Random Sequences," Dept. of Applied Math., The Weizmann Institute of Science, Rehovot, Israel (1981).

Turn73. Turn, R., "Privacy Transformations for Databank Systems," *Proc. NCC,* Vol. 42, AFIPS Press, Montvale, N.J., pp. 589–600 (1973).

Wilk75. Wilkes, M. V., *Time-Sharing Computing Systems,* Elsevier/MacDonald, New York (1968; 3rd ed., 1975).

Zier68. Zierler, N. and Brillhart, J., "On Primitive Trinomials (Mod 2)," *Info. and Control* Vol. 13 pp. 541–554 (1968).

Zier69. Zierler, N. and Brillhart, J., "On Primitive Trinomials (Mod 2)," *Info. and Control* Vol. 14 pp. 566–569 (1969).

4

Access Controls

Access controls ensure that all direct accesses to objects are authorized. By regulating the reading, changing, and deletion of data and programs, access controls protect against accidental and malicious threats to secrecy, authenticity, and system availability (see Chapter 1).

Many access controls incorporate a concept of **ownership**—that is, users may dispense and revoke privileges for objects they own. This is common in file systems intended for the long-term storage of user data sets and programs. Not all applications include this concept; for example, patients do not own their records in a medical information system.

The effectiveness of access controls rests on two premises. The first is proper user identification: no one should be able to acquire the access rights of another. This premise is met through authentication procedures at login as described in Chapter 3. The second premise is that information specifying the access rights of each user or program is protected from unauthorized modification. This premise is met by controlling access to system objects as well as to user objects.

In studying access controls, it is useful to separate policy and mechanism. An access control **policy** specifies the authorized accesses of a system; an access control **mechanism** implements or enforces the policy. This separation is useful for three reasons. First, it allows us to discuss the access requirements of systems independent of how these requirements may be implemented. Second, it allows us to compare and contrast different access control policies as well as different mechanisms that enforce the same policies. Third, it allows us to design mechanisms capable of enforcing a wide range of policies. These mechanisms can be integrated into the hardware features of the system without impinging on the flexibility of the system to adapt to different or changing policies.

4.1 ACCESS-MATRIX MODEL

The access-matrix model provides a framework for describing protection systems. The model was independently developed by researchers in both the operating systems area and the database area. The operating systems version of the model was formulated by Lampson [Lamp71] in conjunction with the COSINE Task Force on Operating Systems [DenP71a]. The model was subsequently refined by Graham and Denning [GrDe72,DenP71b]. Harrison, Ruzzo, and Ullman [Harr76] later developed a more formal version of the model as a framework for proving properties about protection systems. At about the same time the access matrix was introduced as a model of protection in operating systems, Conway, Maxwell, and Morgan [Conw72] of the ASAP project at Cornell University independently modeled protection in database systems with a security matrix.

  The model is defined in terms of states and state transitions, where the state of a protection system is represented by a matrix, and the state transitions are described by commands.

4.1.1 The Protection State

The state of a system is defined by a triple (S, O, A), where:

1. S is a set of **subjects**, which are the active entities of the model. We will assume that subjects are also considered to be objects; thus $S \subseteq O$.
2. O is a set of **objects**, which are the protected entities of the system. Each object is uniquely identified by a name.
3. A is an **access matrix**, with rows corresponding to subjects and columns to objects. An entry $A[s, o]$ lists the access **rights** (or privileges) of subject s for object o.

  In operating systems, the objects typically include files, segments of memory, and processes (i.e., activations of programs). The subjects may be users, processes, or domains; a **domain** is a protection environment in which a process executes. A process may change domains during its execution.

  The access rights specify the kinds of accesses that may be performed on different types of objects. The rights for segments and files usually include R (read), W (write), and E (execute). (Some systems have an append right, which allows subjects to add data to the end of an object but not overwrite existing data.) Some rights may be **generic**, applying to more than one type of object; R, W, E, and Own (ownership) are examples. The number of generic rights is finite.

Example:
Figure 4.1 illustrates the state of a simple system having two processes (subjects), two memory segments, and two files. Each process has its own private segment and owns one file. Neither process can control the other process. ■

FIGURE 4.1 Access matrix.

		Objects					
		M1	M2	F1	F2	P1	P2
Subjects	P1	R W E		Own R W			
	P2		R W E		Own R E		

Graham and Denning associate with each type of object a **monitor** that controls access to the object. The monitor for an object *o* prevents a subject *s* from accessing *o* when $A[s, o]$ does not contain the requisite right. A monitor can be implemented in hardware, software, or some combination of hardware and software. An example of a monitor is the hardware that checks an address to determine if it is within the memory bounds associated with a process. Another example is the file system monitor that validates requests for file accesses.

Protection within a program is modeled with a more refined matrix in which the subjects are procedures (or activations of procedures), and the objects are data structures and procedures. The access rights for a data object are determined by the operations and procedures that may be applied to objects of that type. For example, the access rights for an **integer** variable consist of the arithmetic and relational operators (+, *, <, etc.) and assignment (:=); the rights for an **integer** constant (or variable passed by value) exclude assignment. Note that the right to apply the assignment operator is granted by *W*-access to an object, whereas the right to apply the remaining operators is granted by *R*-access to the object.

The access rights for a programmer-defined object of type stack may be restricted to *push* and *pop* procedures, so the program cannot manipulate the underlying representation of the stack (e.g., to delete an element from the middle of the stack). The *pop* and *push* procedures, however, have access to the representation of stacks.

The protection provided by language structures must be enforced by both the language processor and the run-time system. The language processor is responsible for screening out **specification errors** (e.g., violations of syntax, type, and scope rules). The run-time system is responsible for screening out **execution errors** (e.g., linkage errors, binding errors, addressing errors, or I/O errors). The system also provides protection in case of changes to compiled programs. If access checking is implemented in hardware, it can be performed in parallel with program execution, and need not degrade the performance of the system. The strongest protection comes from a combination of compiler and system support: the compiler prevents programs with detectable specification errors from executing; the system ensures that programs execute according to their specifications and to the current protection state.

In database systems, the subjects correspond to users and the objects to files, relations, records, or fields within records. Each entry $A[s, o]$ is a **decision rule**, specifying the conditions under which user s may access data object o, and the operations that s is permitted to perform on o.

The decision rules are a generalization of the concept of access rights. The rules may specify both **data-independent** conditions, which are analogous to the rights in operating systems, and **data-dependent** conditions, which are a function of the current values of the data being accessed. For example, permitting a user to alter the contents of only those student records for which the *Department* field is *Physics* is an example of a data-dependent condition. The concept of dependency may be extended to include **time-dependent** conditions, which are functions of the clock (e.g., a user may be permitted to access the payroll records between 9 and 5 only), **context-dependent** conditions, which are functions of combinations of data (e.g., a user may be permitted to see student grades or student names, but not pairs of names and grades), and **history-dependent** conditions, which are functions of previous states of the system (e.g., a process may not be allowed to write into an unclassified file if it previously processed classified data) [Hart76]. In general, a decision may depend on any available information describing the present or past state of the system.

The decision rules are similar to the control procedures described in Hoffman's [Hoff71] **formulary model**. In Hoffman's system, all security is enforced by a set of database access procedures called **formularies**. A formulary consists of control procedures that determine whether to grant an access request, addressing procedures that map logical names into virtual addresses, and encryption and decryption procedures. Hoffman's formularies are like the object monitors described by Graham and Denning.

4.1.2 State Transitions

Changes to the state of a system are modeled by a set of **commands**. Commands are specified by a sequence of primitive operations that change the access matrix. These operations are conditioned on the presence of certain rights in the access matrix and are controlled by a monitor responsible for managing the protection state. Harrison, Ruzzo, and Ullman identified six **primitive operations**:

> **enter** r into $A[s, o]$
> **delete** r from $A[s, o]$
> **create subject** s
> **create object** o
> **destroy subject** s
> **destroy object** o .

Their effect on the access matrix is formally defined in Table 4.1. Let *op* be a primitive operator, and let $Q = (S, O, A)$ be a system state. Then execution of *op* in state Q causes a **transition** from Q to the state $Q' = (S', O', A')$ under the conditions defined in Table 4.1. This is written as

TABLE 4.1 Primitive operations.

op	conditions	new state
enter r into $A[s, o]$	$s \in S$ $o \in O$	$S' = S$ $O' = O$ $A'[s, o] = A[s, o] \cup \{r\}$ $A'[s_1, o_1] = A[s_1, o_1] \ (s_1, o_1) \neq (s, o)$
delete r from $A[s, o]$	$s \in S$ $o \in O$	$S' = S$ $O' = O$ $A'[s, o] = A[s, o] - \{r\}$ $A'[s_1, o_1] = A[s_1, o_1] \ (s_1, o_1) \neq (s, o)$
create subject s'	$s' \notin O$	$S' = S \cup \{s'\}$ $O' = O \cup \{s'\}$ $A'[s, o] = A[s, o] \ s \in S, o \in O$ $A'[s', o] = \varnothing , o \in O'$ $A'[s, s'] = \varnothing , s \in S'$
create object o'	$o' \notin O$	$S' = S$ $O' = O \cup \{o'\}$ $A'[s, o] = A[s, o] \ s \in S, o \in O$ $A'[s, o'] = \varnothing , s \in S'$
destroy subject s'	$s' \in S$	$S' = S - \{s'\}$ $O' = O - \{s'\}$ $A'[s, o] = A[s, o] \ s \in S', o \in O'$
destroy object o'	$o' \in O$ $o' \notin S$	$S' = S$ $O' = O - \{o'\}$ $A'[s, o] = A[s, o] \ s \in S', o \in O'$

$$Q \vdash_{op} Q'$$

(read "Q derives Q' under op") .

Harrison, Ruzzo, and Ullman consider commands of the following form:

> **command** $c(x_1, \ldots, x_k)$
> **if** r_1 in $A[x_{s1}, x_{o1}]$ and
> r_2 in $A[x_{s2}, x_{o2}]$ and
>
> .
> .
> .
>
> r_m in $A[x_{sm}, x_{om}]$
> **then**
> op_1;
> op_2;

$$\vdots$$

$$op_n$$
   end ,

where $r_1, \ldots, r_m$ are rights, and $s1, \ldots, sm$ and $o1, \ldots, om$ are integers between 1 and k. A command may have an empty set of conditions (i.e., $m = 0$). We assume, however, that each command performs at least one operation.

   The effect of a command on the state of a protection system is as follows. Let $c(a_1, \ldots, a_k)$ be a command with actual parameters $a_1, \ldots, a_k$, and let $Q = (S, O, A)$ be a state of a protection system. Then Q yields state Q' under c, written

$$Q \vdash_{c(a_1, \ldots, a_k)} Q' ,$$

provided

1. $Q' = Q$ if one of the conditions of c is not satisfied, and
2. $Q' = Q_n$ otherwise, where there exist states $Q_0, Q_1, \ldots, Q_n$ such that

$$Q = Q_0 \vdash_{op_1^*} Q_1 \vdash_{op_2^*} \ldots \vdash_{op_n^*} Q_n ,$$

where op_i^* denotes the primitive operation op_i, substituting the actual parameters a_i for the formal parameters x_i.

   We shall write $Q \vdash_c Q'$ if there exist actual parameters $a_1, \ldots, a_k$ such that $Q \vdash_{c(a_1, \ldots, a_k)} Q'$; and $Q \vdash Q'$ if there exists a command c such that $Q \vdash_c Q'$. Finally, we shall write $Q \vdash^* Q'$ if there exists a sequence of length $n \geq 0$: $Q = Q_0 \vdash Q_1 \vdash \ldots \vdash Q_n = Q'$.

   The access-matrix model is an abstract representation of the protection policies and mechanisms found in real systems. As such, it provides a conceptual aid to understanding and describing protection systems, a common framework for comparing different protection systems, and a formal model for studying the inherent properties of protection systems. Some mechanisms are more easily described by other models, however. We shall later use graphs to describe mechanisms that involve the transfer of rights.

   Protection systems should not be implemented using the matrix and associated commands. One reason is there are much better ways of representing the access state of a system than with a matrix that is likely to be large and sparse. Another is that the commands are too primitive for most applications.

Example:
We shall show how the model can be used to describe the transfer of rights in operating systems with processes, segments, and owned files, as illustrated by Figure 4.1. Our example is similar to the one given by Harrison, Ruzzo, and Ullman.

   Any process may create a new file. The process creating a file is automatically given ownership of the file and RW-access to the file. This is represented by the command:

```
command create.file(p, f)
    create object f;
    enter Own into A[p, f];
    enter R into A[p, f];
    enter W into A[p, f]
end .
```

The process owning a file may change its rights to the file. For example, a process p owning a file f can protect f from inadvertent modification by removing its W-access to f. It may also confer any right to the file (except ownership) on other processes. For example, R-access may be conferred by process p on process q with the command:

```
command confer.read(p, q, f)
    if Own in A[p, f]
    then enter R into A[q, f]
end .
```

(Similar commands confer W- and E-access.)

The preceding command states that the owner of an object can grant a right to the object it does not have. In particular, it can grant this right to itself. This allows it to revoke its W-access to an object, and later restore the right to modify the object. This violates the principle of **attenuation of privilege**, which states that a process can never increase its rights, or transfer rights it does not have. We shall apply this principle only to nonowners, as is done in most systems.

Removal of access rights is a subject of much controversy. Here we shall assume that the owner of an object may revoke access rights to the object at any time. Commands for removing access rights from the access matrix are similar to those for conferring rights; for example, process p may revoke R-access from process q with the command:

```
command revoke.read(p, q, f)
    if Own in A[p, f]
    then delete R from A[q, f]
end .
```

Some systems permit subjects to transfer an access right r to an unowned object. This is modeled with a **copy flag** (denoted by an asterisk placed after r). Following the principle of attenuation of privilege, a process may transfer any access right it holds for an object provided the copy flag of the attribute is set. The following command transfers R-access from process p to q, but does not give q the ability to transfer the right further:

```
command transfer.read(p, q, f)
    if R* in A[p, f]
    then enter R into A[q, f]
end .
```

Alternatively, a process may be able to transfer an access right, but forfeit the right in so doing. This is modeled with a **transfer-only flag** (denoted by +). The following command transfers R-access under these conditions:

> **command** *transfer-only.read* (p, q, f)
>   **if** $R+$ in $A[p, f]$
>   **then delete** $R+$ from $A[p, f]$;
>   **enter** $R+$ into $A[q, f]$
> **end** .

The owner of an object would be able to confer rights with or without either of the flags.

Some systems permit a process to spawn subordinate processes and control the access rights of its subordinates. A process p can create a subordinate process q having memory segment m with the command:

> **command** *create.subordinate*(p, q, m)
>   **create subject** q;
>   **create object** m;
>   **enter** $Ctrl$ into $A[p, q]$
>   **enter** R into $A[q, m]$
>   **enter** W into $A[q, m]$
>   **enter** E into $A[q, m]$
> **end** .

Process p is given the $Ctrl$ right to q, allowing it to take or revoke any of q's rights, including those conferred on q by other processes. The following command gives p R-access to q's memory segment:

> **command** *take.subordinate.read*(p, q, m)
>   **if** $Ctrl$ in $A[p, q]$ and
> R in $A[q, m]$
>   **then enter** R in $A[p, m]$
> **end** .

The following command revokes q's R-access to file f:

> **command** *revoke.subordinate.read*(p, q, f)
>   **if** $Ctrl$ in $A[p, q]$
>   **then delete** R from $A[q, f]$
> **end** .

If our command format permitted disjunctions, we could combine *revoke.subordinate.read* with *revoke.read:*

> **command** *revoke.read*(p, q, f)
>   **if** Own in $A[p, f]$ or
> $Ctrl$ in $A[p, q]$
>   **then delete** R from $A[q, f]$
> **end** .

FIGURE 4.2 Access matrix after command sequence.

				Objects				
	M1	M2	M3	F1	F2	P1	P2	P3
P1	R W E			Own R W				
Subjects P2		R W E	R W		Own R W			Ctrl
P3			R W E		R			

Because any command with disjunctions is equivalent to a list of separate commands, we have restricted commands to the simpler format.

Figure 4.2 shows the effect of executing the following commands on the initial state shown in Figure 4.1:

> *create.subordinate(P2, P3, M3)*
> *take.subordinate.read(P2, P3, M3)*
> *take.subordinate.write(P2, P3, M3)*
> *confer.read(P2, P3, F2) .* ∎

4.1.3. Protection Policies

A configuration of the access matrix describes what subjects can do—not necessarily what they are authorized to do. A **protection policy** (or **security policy**) partitions the set of all possible states into authorized versus unauthorized states. The next example shows how a simple policy regulating message buffers shared by two communicating processes can be formally described in terms of authorized states.

Example:
The following specifies that for every message buffer *b*, there exists exactly one process *p* that can write into the buffer and one process *q* that can read from the buffer (see Figure 4.3).

FIGURE 4.3 Shared message buffer.

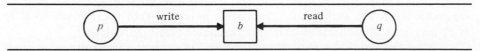

A state $Q = (S, O, A)$ is authorized if and only if for every buffer $b \in O$, there exists exactly one process $p \in S$ such that $W \in A[p, b]$ and exactly one process $q \neq p$ such that $R \in A[q, b)$. ■

Whether a state is authorized can depend on the previous state and the command causing the state transition:

Example:
Consider the system described in the previous section. The following specifies that no subject can acquire access to a file unless that right has been explicitly granted by the file's owner:
Let $Q = (S, O, A)$ be an authorized state such that $Own \in A[p, f]$ for subject p and file f, but $r \notin A[q, f]$ for subject q and right r. Let $Q' = (S', O', A')$ be a state such that $r \in A'[q, f]$ and $Q \vdash_c Q'$. Then Q' is authorized if and only if

$$c = confer.read(p, q, f) . \quad ■$$

(See also [Krei80] for descriptions of protection policies).

4.2 ACCESS CONTROL MECHANISMS

4.2.1 Security and Precision

The access control mechanisms of a system enforce the system's security policies by ensuring that the physical states of the system correspond to authorized states of the abstract model. These mechanisms must monitor all accesses to objects as well as commands that explicitly transfer or revoke rights. Otherwise, the system could enter a physical state that does not correspond to an authorized state of the model. For example, a subject could bypass a file system and issue a read request directly to the physical location of a file on disk. The security mechanisms must also ensure that the physical resource states correspond to logical object states of the model. Systems that do not clear memory between use, for example, may expose data to unauthorized subjects.

The security mechanisms of a system may be overprotective in the sense of preventing entry to an authorized state or of denying an authorized access. For example, a system might never allow a subject access to a file unless the subject owns the file. Systems that are overprotective are secure, but may not satisfy other requirements of the system.

The preceding requirements are summarized with the aid of Figure 4.4. Let S be the set of all possible states, and let P be the subset of S authorized by the protection policies of the system. Let R be the subset of S that is reachable with the security mechanisms in operation. The system is **secure** if $R \subseteq P$; that is, if all reachable states are authorized. The system is **precise** (not overprotective) if $R = P$; that is, if all authorized states are reachable (see Figure 4.4).

After discussing the general requirements of security mechanisms, we shall describe particular mechanisms. We shall then turn to the problem of designing

FIGURE 4.4 Security and precision.

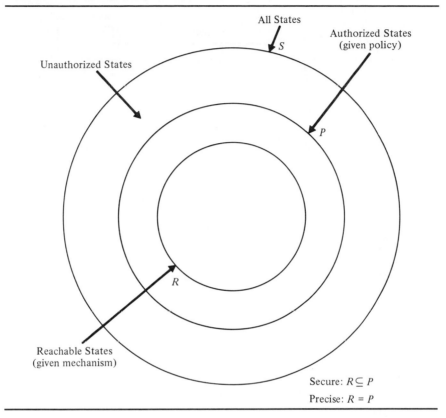

All States

Authorized States
(given policy)

Unauthorized States

S

P

R

Reachable States
(given mechanism)

Secure: $R \subseteq P$

Precise: $R = P$

systems whose security can be verified. Finally, we shall examine theoretical questions related to proving properties about the transfer of rights in abstract models.

4.2.2 Reliability and Sharing

Protection mechanisms enforce policies of controlled sharing and reliability. Several levels of sharing are possible:

1.   No sharing at all (complete isolation).
2.   Sharing copies of data objects.
3.   Sharing originals of data objects.
4.   Sharing untrusted programs.

Each level of sharing imposes additional requirements on the security
mechanisms of a system. The sharing of data introduces a problem of **suspicion**,
where the owner s of a data object x may not trust another subject s_1 with whom s
shares access. For example, s may fear that s_1 will grant its access rights to x to

FIGURE 4.5 Suspicion.

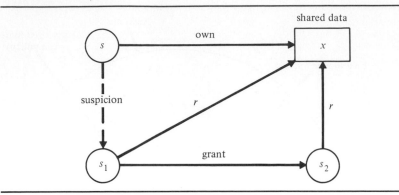

another subject s_2 (see Figure 4.5). Alternatively, s may fear that s_1 will simply misuse its privileges—for example, s_1 could read x and broadcast its contents to other subjects (see Figure 4.6). The second problem does not fall under the scope of an access control policy, however, because it involves the transfer of information rather than the transfer of rights; controls for information flow are studied in the next chapter.

Most systems have facilities for sharing originals of programs or data. On-line database systems often allow multiple users simultaneous access to a common database. Most operating systems allow concurrent processes to execute the same code and access global system tables or file directories.

There are several reasons for sharing originals of data (or programs) rather than just copies. A principal reason is to save space. Another is to save time that

FIGURE 4.6 Misuse of privilege.

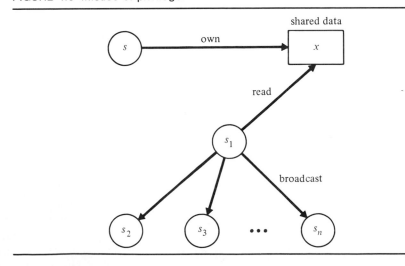

FIGURE 4.7 Trojan Horse.

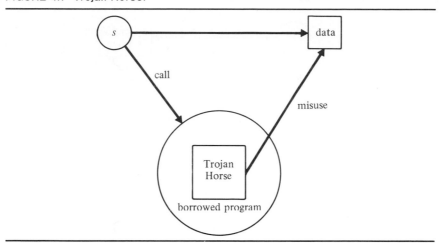

would otherwise be needed to make duplicates or transfer updates to a master copy. A third reason is to ensure each subject has a consistent, up-to-date view of the data.

Protecting originals of data imposes additional requirements on the security mechanisms, however, because a subject with write-access to the original might destroy the data. Concurrent accesses to the data must be controlled to prevent writing subjects from interfering with other subjects.

If programs are shared, the protection problem is considerably more complex than if only data is shared. One reason is a **Trojan Horse** may be lurking inside a borrowed program. A Trojan Horse performs functions not described in the program specifications, taking advantage of rights belonging to the calling environment to copy, misuse, or destroy data not relevant to its stated purpose (see Figure 4.7). A Trojan Horse in a text editor, for example, might copy confidential information in a file being edited to a file accessible to another user. The attack was first identified by D. Edwards and described in the Anderson report [Ande72]. The term Trojan Horse is often used to refer to an entry point or "trapdoor" planted in a system program for gaining unauthorized access to the system, or to any unexpected and malicious side effect [Lind75]. Protection from Trojan Horses requires encapsulating programs in small domains with only the rights needed for the task, and no more.

Even if encapsulated, a borrowed program may have access to confidential parameters passed by the calling subject s. The program could transmit the data to the program's owner s', or retain it in objects owned by s' for later use (see Figure 4.8). For example, a compiler might make a copy of a proprietary software program. A program that cannot retain or leak its parameters is said to be **memoryless** or **confined**.

Lampson [Lamp73] was the first to discuss the many subtleties of the confinement problem. As long as a borrowed program does not have to retain any

FIGURE 4.8 The confinement problem.

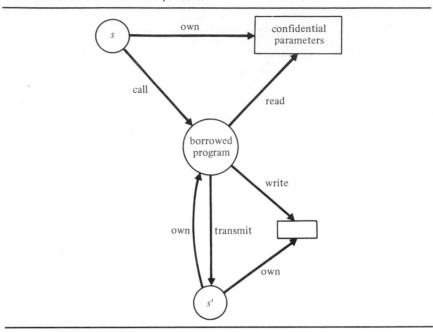

information, confinement can be implemented by restricting the access rights of the program (and programs called by it). But as soon as the program must retain nonconfidential information, access controls alone are insufficient, because there is no way of ensuring the program does not also retain confidential information. This is called the **selective confinement** problem, and is treated in the next chapter.

Protecting proprietary programs is also difficult. The owner needs assurances that borrowers can execute the programs, but cannot read or copy them. We saw in Chapter 3 how a form of encryption can be used to protect proprietary programs run on the customer's system. Access controls can be used to protect programs run on the owner's system, because the borrower cannot copy a program if it is only given access rights to execute (but not read) the program.

The sharing of software, therefore, introduces a problem of **mutual suspicion** between the owner and the borrower: the owner of a program p may be concerned the borrower will steal p; the borrower may be concerned the owner will steal confidential input to p (see Figure 4.9).

Protection mechanisms are needed for reliability as much as sharing. They prevent malfunctioning programs from writing into segments of memory belonging to the supervisor or to other programs. They prevent undebugged software from disrupting the system. They prevent user programs from writing directly on a disk, destroying files and directories. They provide backup copies of files in case of hardware error or inadvertent destruction. By limiting the damage caused by mal-

FIGURE 4.9 Mutual suspicion.

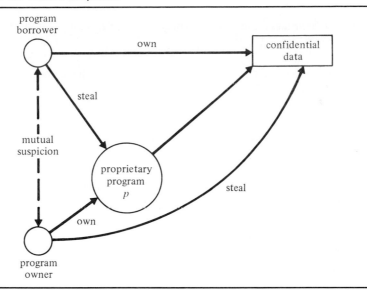

functioning programs, they provide error confinement and an environment for recovery.

Protection was originally motivated by time-sharing systems serving multiple users simultaneously and providing long-term storage for their programs and data. Protection was essential both for reliability and controlled sharing.

The recent trend toward distributed computing through networks of personal computers mitigates the need for special mechanisms to isolate users and programs—each user has a private machine. It is often unnecessary for users to share originals of programs in this environment, because it is more economical to run a separate copy on each user's machine. Controlled sharing is still essential, however; the difference is that it must now be provided by the network rather than by the users' personal computers. Users may wish to exchange data and programs on the network, store large files in central storage facilities, access database systems, or run programs on computers having resources not provided by their own computers.

Network security requires a combination of encryption and other security controls. Encryption is needed to protect data whose transmission over the network is authorized. Information flow controls are needed to prevent the unauthorized dissemination of confidential data, classified military data, and proprietary software over the network. Access controls are needed to prevent unauthorized access to the key management facilities, to shared databases, and to computing facilities. They are needed for reliability; loss of a single node on the network should not bring down the entire network, or even make it impossible to transmit messages that would have been routed through that node.

4.2.3 Design Principles

Saltzer and Schroeder identified several design principles for protection mechanisms [Salt75]:

1.   **Least privilege:** Every user and process should have the least set of access rights necessary. This principle limits the damage that can result from error or malicious attack. It implies processes should execute in **small protection domains**, consisting of only those rights needed to complete their tasks. When the access needs of a process change, the process should switch domains. Furthermore, access rights should be acquired by explicit permission only; the default should be lack of access (Saltzer and Schroeder called this a "fail-safe" default). This principle is fundamental in containing Trojan Horses and implementing reliable programs; a program cannot damage an object it cannot access.

2.   **Economy of mechanism:** The design should be sufficiently small and simple that it can be verified and correctly implemented. Implementing security mechanisms in the lowest levels of the system (hardware and software) goes a long way toward achieving this objective, because the higher levels are then supported by a secure base. This means, however, security must be an integral part of the design. Attempting to augment an existing system with security mechanisms usually results in a proliferation of complex mechanisms that never quite work. Although the system must be sufficiently flexible to handle a variety of protection policies, it is better to implement a simple mechanism that meets the requirements of the system than it is to implement one with complicated features that are seldom used.

3.   **Complete mediation:** Every access should be checked for authorization. The mechanism must be efficient, or users will find means of circumventing it.

4.   **Open design:** Security should not depend on the design being secret or on the ignorance of the attackers [Bara64]. This principle underlies cryptographic systems, where the enciphering and deciphering algorithms are assumed known.

5.   **Separation of privilege:** Where possible, access to objects should depend on more than one condition being satisfied. The key threshold schemes discussed in Section 3.8 illustrate this principle; here more than one shadow is needed to restore a key.

6.   **Least common mechanism:** Mechanisms shared by multiple users provide potential information channels and, therefore, should be minimized. This principle leads to mechanisms that provide user isolation through physically separate hardware (distributed systems) or through logically separate virtual machines [Pope74,Rush81].

7.   **Psychological acceptability:** The mechanisms must be easy to use so that they will be applied correctly and not bypassed. In particular, it must not be substantially more difficult for users to restrict access to their objects than it is to leave access to them unrestricted.

Access control mechanisms are based on three general concepts:

1. **Access Hierarchies**, which automatically give privileged subjects a superset of the rights of less privileged subjects.
2. **Authorization Lists**, which are lists of subjects having access rights to some particular object.
3. **Capabilities**, which are like "tickets" for objects; possession of a capability unconditionally authorizes the holder access to the object.

Examples of mechanisms based on one or more of these concepts are discussed in Sections 4.3–4.5.

4.3 ACCESS HIERARCHIES

We shall describe two kinds of mechanisms based on access hierarchies: privileged modes and nested program units.

4.3.1 Privileged Modes

Most existing systems implement some form of **privileged mode** (also called **supervisor state**) that gives supervisor programs an access domain consisting of every object in the system. The state word of a process has a 1-bit flag indicating whether the process is running in privileged mode or in nonprivileged (user) mode. A process running in privileged mode can create and destroy objects, initiate and terminate processes, access restricted regions of memory containing system tables, and execute privileged instructions that are not available to user programs (e.g., execute certain I/O operations and change process statewords). This concept of privileged mode is extended to users in UNIX, where a "super user" is allowed access to any object in the system.

The **protection rings** in MULTICS are a generalization of the concept of supervisor state [Grah68,Schr72,Orga72]. The state word of a process p specifies an integer ring number in the range $[0, r - 1]$. Each ring defines a domain of access, where the access privileges of ring j are a subset of those for ring i, for all $0 \leq i < j \leq r - 1$ (see Figure 4.10). The supervisor state has $r = 2$.

Supervisor states and ring structures are contrary to the principle of least privilege. Systems programs typically run with considerably more privilege than they require for their tasks, and ring 0 programs have full access to the whole system. A single bug or Trojan Horse in one of these programs could do considerable damage to data in main memory or on disk.

There are numerous examples of users who have exploited a design flaw that enabled them to run their programs in supervisor state or plant a Trojan Horse in some system module. For example, Popek and Farber [Pope78] describe an "ad-

FIGURE 4.10 MULTICS rings.

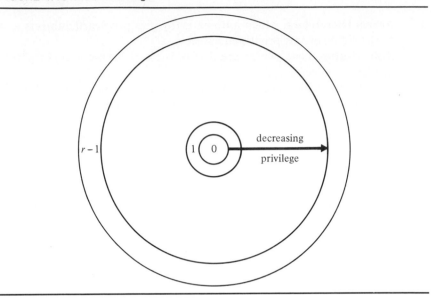

dress wraparound" problem in the PDP-10 TENEX system: under certain conditions, a user could force the program counter to overflow while executing a
supervisor call, causing the privileged-mode bit in the process state word to be
turned on, and control to return to the user's program in privileged mode.

    This does not mean supervisor states are inherently bad. They have strength-
ened the security of many systems at low cost. But systems requiring a high level
of security need additional mechanisms to limit the access rights of programs
running in supervisor state. Moreover, these systems require verifying that there
are no trapdoors whereby a user can run programs in supervisor state.

4.3.2 Nested Program Units

The scope rules of languages such as ALGOL, PL/I, and Pascal automatically
give inner program units (e.g., procedures and blocks) access to objects declared in
enclosing units—even if they do not require access to these objects. The inner
program units are, therefore, much like the inner rings of MULTICS. Whereas
objects declared in the inner units are hidden from the rest of the program, objects
declared in the outer units may be accessible to most of the program.

    Example:
Consider the program structure shown in Figure 4.11. The inner program
unit $S1$ has access to its own local objects as well as global objects declared
in the enclosing units $R1$, $Q1$, and $P1$ (as long as there are no name con-
flicts). No other unit can access objects local to $S1$ unless they are explicitly
passed as parameters by $S1$. The outermost unit $P1$ has access only to the

FIGURE 4.11 Block structured program.

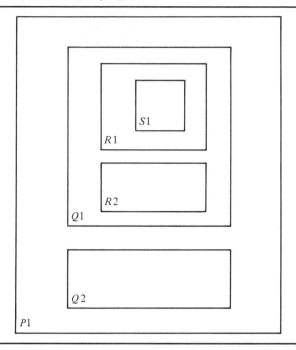

objects declared in $P1$, though these objects are global to the entire program. ■

Programs that exploit the full capabilities of nested scopes are often difficult to maintain. An inner unit that modifies a global data object has side effects that can spread into other units sharing the same global objects. Changes to the code in the innermost units can affect code in the other units. Changes to the structure of a global object can affect code in the innermost units of the program.

Some recent languages have facilities for restricting access to objects in enclosing program units. In Euclid [Lamp76a], for example, a program unit can access only those objects that are accessible in the immediately enclosing unit and either explicitly **imported** into the unit (through an **imports list**) or declared **pervasive** (global) in some enclosing block. Ada† has a similar facility, where a **restricted** program unit can access only those objects declared in an enclosing unit and included in the **visibility list** for the unit.

4.4 AUTHORIZATION LISTS

An **authorization list** (also called an **access-control list**) is a list of $n \geq 0$ subjects who are authorized to access some particular object x. The ith entry in the list gives the name of a subect s_i and the rights r_i in $A[s_i, x]$ of the access matrix:

†Ada is a trademark of the Department of Defense.

Authorization List

$$s_1, r_1$$
$$s_2, r_2$$

.

.

.

$$s_n, r_n \;.$$

An authorization list, therefore, represents the nonempty entries in column x of the access matrix.

4.4.1 Owned Objects

Authorization lists are typically used to protect owned objects such as files. Each file has an authorization list specifying the names (or IDs) of users or user groups, and the access rights permitted each. Figure 4.12 illustrates.

The owner of a file has the sole authority to grant access rights to the file to other users; no other user with access to the file can confer these rights on another user (in terms of the abstract model, the copy flag is off). The owner can revoke (or decrease) the access rights of any user simply by deleting (or modifying) the user's entry in the authorization list.

MULTICS uses authorization lists to protect segments in long-term storage [Dale65,Bens72,Orga72]. Each segment has an access-control list with an entry for each user permitted access to the segment. Each entry in the list indicates the

FIGURE 4.12 Authorization list for file.

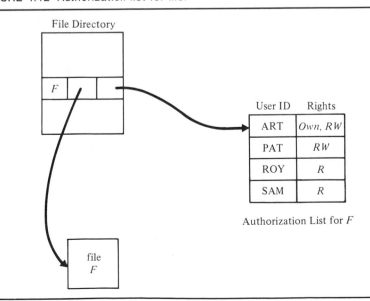

type of access (read, write, or execute) permitted, together with the range of rings (bracket) over which this permission is granted:

(r_1, r_2)—the read bracket, $r_1 \leq r_2$
(w_1, w_2)—the write bracket, $w_1 \leq w_2$
(e_1, e_2)—the execute bracket, $e_1 \leq e_2$.

A process executing in ring i (see previous section) is not allowed access to a segment unless the user associated with the process is listed in the access-control list, and i falls within the range corresponding to the type of access desired.

In the SWARD system, authorization lists are associated with **access sets** for objects [Buck80]. Users can group objects together into object sets, and then define access sets over objects, object sets, and other access sets.

Example:
Figure 4.13 illustrates an access set for the object sets X, Y, and Z. The access set $A1$ is defined by the expression $X + Y - Z$, which evaluates left-to-right to the set of objects $\{a_2, c\}$ (duplicate names in Y are removed; thus a_1, the first version of a, is not included). Because the set $A1$ is defined by an expression, its constituency can change as objects are added to or deleted from the object sets X, Y, and Z. ■

To access an object, a user must specify the name of the object and an access

FIGURE 4.13 Access sets in SWARD.

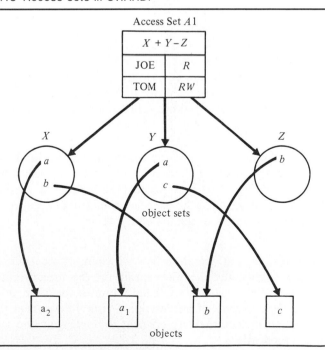

FIGURE 4.14 UNIX file directory tree.

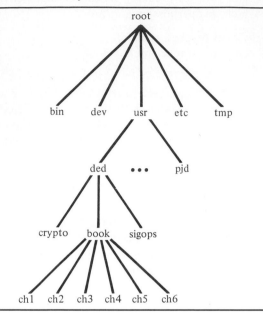

set. The user is granted access to the object only if it is included in the access set; in addition, the authorization list for the set must have an entry for the user with the appropriate access rights.

In UNIX, each file has an authorization list with three entries: one specifying the owner's access rights; a second specifying the access rights of all users in the owner's group (e.g., faculty, students, etc.), and a third specifying the access rights of all others [Ritc74]. The access rights for each entry include R, W, and E, (E is interpreted as "directory search" for directory files). The UNIX file system has a tree-structured directory, and files are named by paths in the tree.

Example:
Figure 4.14 shows a portion of the tree structure for the UNIX file system that contains the working version of this book. A user (other than ded) wishing to read Chapter 4 must specify the path name /usr/ded/book/ch4. Access is granted provided the user has E-access to the directories usr, ded, and book, and R-access to the file ch4. ■

Many systems use authorization lists with only two entries: one specifying the owner's access rights, and the other specifying the access rights of all others. The access rights in these systems are usually limited to R and W.

These degenerate forms of authorization lists do not meet the objective of least privilege. Nevertheless, they are efficient to implement and search, and adequate for many applications.

Because an authorization list can be expensive to search, many systems do not check the authorization list for every access. A file system monitor, for example, might check a file's authorization list when the file is opened, but not for each read or write operation. Consequently, if a right is revoked after a file is opened, the revocation does not take effect until the file is closed. Because of their inefficiencies, authorization lists are not suitable for protecting segments of memory, where address bounds must be checked for every reference.

We saw in Section 3.7.1 (see Figure 3.19) how access to a file F encrypted under a key K (or keys if separate read and write keys are used) could be controlled by a "keys record", where every user allowed access to F has an entry in the record containing a copy of K enciphered under the user's private transformation. The keys record is like an authorization list, and is impossible to forge or bypass (the key is needed to access the file). Standard authorization lists for encrypted or unencrypted files could also be protected from unauthorized modification by encrypting them under a file monitor key.

4.4.2 Revocation

The authorization lists we have described so far have the advantage of giving the owner of an object complete control over who has access to the object; the owner can revoke any other user's access to the object by deleting the user's entry in the list (though the revocation might not take effect immediately as noted earlier). This advantage is partially lost in systems that use authorization lists to support nonowned objects, and allow any user to grant and revoke access rights to an object.

An example of such a system is System R [Grif76], a relational database system [Codd70,Codd79] developed at the IBM Research Laboratory in San Jose. The protected data objects of System R consist of **relations**, which are sets (tables) of n-tuples (rows or records), where each n-tuple has n attributes (columns). A relation can be either a **base relation**, which is a physical table stored in memory, or a **view**, which is a logical subset, summary, or join of other relations.

Example:
An example of a relation is

  Student (Name, Sex, Major, Class, SAT, GP).

Each tuple in the *Student* relation gives the name, sex, major, class, SAT score, and grade-point of some student in the database (see Table 6.1 in Chapter 6). ∎

The access rights for a relation (table) include:

Read: for reading rows of the table, using the relation in queries, or defining views based on the relation.
Insert: for adding new rows to a table.

Delete: for deleting rows in a table.
Update: for modifying data in a table or in certain columns of a table.
Drop: for deleting a table.

Any user *A* with access rights to a table can grant these rights to another user *B* (provided the copy flag is set). *A* can later revoke these rights, and the state of the system following a revocation should be as if the rights had never been granted. This means that if *B* has subsequently granted these rights to another user *C*, then *C*'s rights must also be lost. In general, any user who could not have obtained the rights without the grant from *A* to *B* must lose these rights.

To implement this, each access right granted to a user is recorded in an access list called *Sysauth*. *Sysauth* is a relation, where each tuple specifies the user receiving the right, the name of the table the user is authorized to access, the type of table (view or base relation), the grantor making the authorization, the access rights granted to the user, and a copy flag (called a *Grant* option). Each access right (except for *Update*) is represented by a column of *Sysauth* and indicates the time of the grant (a time of 0 means the right was not granted). The timestamps are used by the revocation mechanism to determine the path along which a right has been disseminated.

The column for *Update* specifies *All*, *None*, or *Some*. If *Some* is specified, then for each updatable column, a tuple is placed in a second authorization table called *Syscolauth*. It is unnecessary to provide a similar feature for *Read*, because any subset of columns can be restricted through the view mechanism. For example, access only to *Name*, *Sex*, *Major*, and *Class* for the *Student* relation can be granted by defining a view over these attributes only (i.e., excluding *SAT* and *GP*).

Note that the authorization list for a particular relation *X* can be obtained from *Sysauth* by selecting all tuples such that *Table* = *X*.

Example:
The following shows the tuples in *Sysauth* that result from a sequence of grants for a relation *X* created by user *A*. (Columns for table type and the rights *Delete*, *Update*, and *Drop* are not shown.)

User	Table	Grantor	Read	Insert	... Copy
B	*X*	*A*	10	10	yes
D	*X*	*A*	15	0	no
C	*X*	*B*	20	20	yes
D	*X*	*C*	30	30	yes .

User *B* obtained both *Read* and *Insert* access to *X* from *A* at time $t = 10$, and passed both rights to *C* at time $t = 20$. User *D* obtained *Read* access to *X* from *A* at time $t = 15$, and both *Read* and *Insert* access to *X* from *C* at time $t = 30$. Whereas *D* can grant the rights received from *C*, *D* cannot grant the *Read* right received from *A*. ■

FIGURE 4.15 Transfer of rights for relation X.

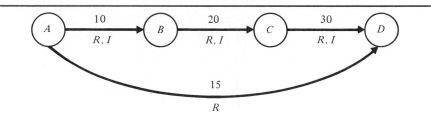

Griffiths and Wade [Grif76] use directed graphs to illustrate the transfer and revocation of rights for a particular relation. Each node of a graph represents a user with access to the relation. Each edge represents a grant and is labeled with the time of the grant; we shall also label an edge with the rights transferred.

Example:
Figure 4.15 shows a graph for the relation X of the previous example. Suppose that at time $t = 40$, A revokes the rights granted to B. Then the entries in *Sysauth* for both B and C must be removed because C received these rights from B. Although D is allowed to keep rights received directly from A, D must forfeit other rights received from C. The final state of *Sysauth* is thus:

User	Table	Grantor	Read	Insert . . . Copy		
D	X	A	15	0	no . ■

Example:
Figure 4.16 illustrates a more complicated situation, where B first grants rights to C received from A ($t = 15$), and then later grants rights to C received from D ($t = 25$). The state of *Sysauth* is thus:

FIGURE 4.16 Transfer of rights for relation Y.

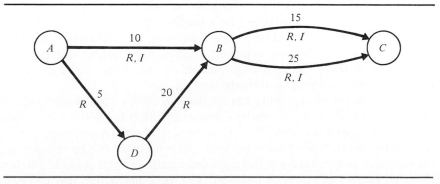

User	Table	Grantor	Read	Insert	... Copy
D	Y	A	5	0	yes
B	Y	A	10	10	yes
C	Y	B	15	15	yes
B	Y	D	20	0	yes
C	Y	B	25	25	yes . ∎

In the preceding example, we recorded in *Sysauth* the duplicate grants from *B* to *C* (at $t = 15$ and $t = 25$). This differs from the procedure given by Griffiths and Wade, which records only the earliest instance of a grant and, therefore, would not have recorded the one at $t = 25$. Fagin [Fagi78] observed that unless all grants are recorded, the revocation procedure may remove more rights than necessary.

> ### Example:
> Suppose *A* revokes the *Read* and *Insert* rights given to *B*. *B* should be allowed to keep the *Read* right received from *D*, and *C* should be allowed to keep the *Read* right received from *B* at time $t = 25$ that was passed along the path (A, D, B, C). Both *B* and *C*, however, must forfeit their *Insert* rights. The final state of *Sysauth* should therefore be:

User	Table	Grantor	Read	Insert	... Copy
D	Y	A	5	0	yes
B	Y	D	20	0	yes
C	Y	B	25	0	yes .

If the duplicate entry at time $t = 25$ had not been recorded in *Sysauth*, *C*'s *Read* right for *Y* would have been lost. ∎

4.5 CAPABILITIES

A **capability** is a pair (x, r) specifying the unique name (logical address) of an object x and a set of access rights r for x (some capabilities also specify an object's type). The capability is a ticket in that possession unconditionally authorizes the holder r-access to x. Once the capability is granted, no further validation of access is required. Without the capability mechanism, validation would be required on each access by searching an authorization list.

The concept of capability has its roots in Iliffe's "codewords", which were implemented in the Rice University Computer [Ilif62] in 1958, and generalized in the Basic Language Machine [Ilif72] in the early 1960s. A codeword is a descriptor specifying the type of an object and either its value (if the object is a single element such as an integer) or its length and location (if the object is a structure of elements such as an array). A codeword also has a special tag that allows it to be recognized and interpreted by the hardware. A similar concept was embodied in the "descriptors" of the Burroughs B5000 computer in 1961.

Dennis and VanHorn [DeVH66] introduced the term "capability" in 1966. They proposed a model of a multiprogramming system that used capabilities to control access to objects that could either be in main memory or in secondary (long-term) storage. In their model, each process executes in a domain called a "sphere of protection", which is defined by a **capability list**, or **C-list** for short. The C-list for a domain s is a list of $n \geq 0$ capabilities for the objects permitted to s:

C-List

x_1, r_1

x_2, r_2

   .

   .

   .

x_n, r_n

where r_i gives the rights in $A[s, x_i]$ of the access matrix. The C-list for s, therefore, represents the nonempty entries in row s of the access matrix.

Example:
Figure 4.17 illustrates a C-list that provides read/execute-access (RE) to the code for procedure A, read-only-access (R) to data objects B and C, and read/write-access (RW) to data object D. The diagram shows each capability pointing directly to an object; the mapping from capabilities to object locations is described in Section 4.5.3. ■

FIGURE 4.17 Capability list.

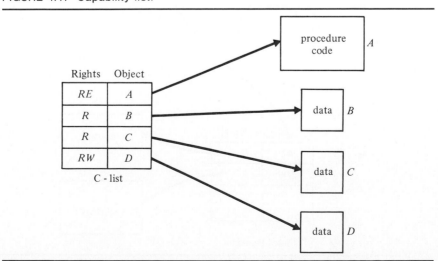

Capabilities have been the underlying protection mechanism in several systems, including the Chicago Magic Number Computer [Fabr71a], the BCC model I system [Lamp69], the SUE system [Sevc74], the Cal system [Lamp76b], the Plessey System 250 [Engl74], HYDRA [Wulf74,Cohe75], the CAP system [Need77], StarOS for CM∗ [Jone79], UCLA Secure UNIX [Pope79], iMAX for the INTEL iAPX 432 [Kahn81], the SWARD system [Myer80,Myer78], and PSOS [Feie79,Neum80].

4.5.1 Domain Switching with Protected Entry Points

Dennis and VanHorn envisaged a mechanism for supporting small protection domains and abstract data types. A principal feature of their mechanism was an enter capability (denoted by the access right *Ent*). An enter capability points to a C-list and gives the right to transfer into the domain defined by the C-list. Enter capabilities provide a mechanism for implementing **protected entry points** into

FIGURE 4.18 Domain switch with protected entry points.

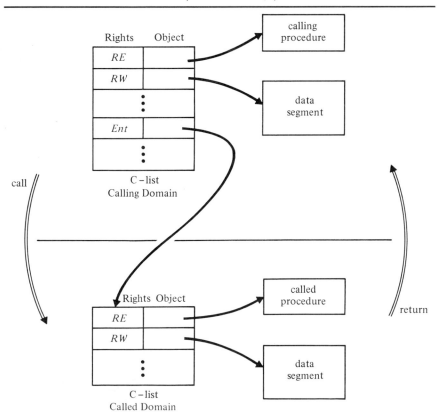

procedures, or **protected subsystems**. When a process calls a protected procedure, its C-list (and therefore domain) is changed. When the procedure returns, the former C-list is restored (see Figure 4.18).

This concept of giving each procedure its own set of capabilities supports the principle of least privilege. Each capability list need contain entries only for the objects required to carry out its task. Damage is confined in case the program contains an error. An untrusted program can be encapsulated in an **inferior sphere of protection** where it cannot endanger unrelated programs. Data can be hidden away in a domain accessible only to the programs allowed to manipulate it. This provides a natural environment for implementing abstract data types (see also [Linn76]).

4.5.2 Abstract Data Types

An **abstract data type** is a collection of objects and operations that manipulate the objects. Programming languages that support abstract data types have facilities for defining a **type module** that specifies:

1.   The **name** t of an object type.
2.   The **operations** (procedures, functions) that may be performed on objects of type t. There are two categories of operations: external operations, which provide an interface to the module from the outside, and internal operations, which are available within the module only. The semantics of the operations may be defined by a set of axioms.
3.   The **representation** or implementation of objects of type t in terms of more primitive objects. This representation is hidden; it is not available to procedures outside the module.

Abstract data types are also called **extended-type objects**, because they extend the basic built-in types of a programming language. Languages that support abstract data types include Simula 67 [Dahl72], CLU [Lisk77], Alphard [Wulf76], MODEL [Morr78], and Ada. These languages are sometimes called "object-oriented" languages.

Example:
Figure 4.19 shows the principal components of a type module for a stack of integer elements, implemented as a sequential vector; all procedures are available outside the module. ■

A type module encapsulates objects in a small protection domain. These objects can be accessed only through external procedures that serve as protected entry points into the module. The module provides an environment for **information hiding**, where the low-level representation of an object is hidden from outside procedures that perform high-level operations on the data.

The principal motivation for abstract data types is program reliability and

FIGURE 4.19 Type module for stacks.

```
module stack
    constant size = 100;
    type stack =
      record of
          top: integer, init 0;
          data: array[1 .. size] of integer;
      end;
    procedure push(var s: stack; x: integer);
      begin
          s.top := s.top + 1;
          if s.top > size
             then "stack overflow"
             else s.data[s.top] := x
      end;
    procedure pop(var s: stack): integer;
      begin
          if s.top = 0
             then "stack underflow"
             else begin
                pop := s.data[s.top];
                s.top := s.top − 1;
             end
      end;
    procedure empty(var s: stack): boolean;
      begin
          if s.top = 0
             then empty := true
             else empty := false
      end
end stack
```

maintenance. Because the representation of an object is confined to a single module, changes to the representation should have little effect outside the module.

Capability-based systems provide an attractive environment for implementing abstract data types because the objects required by a program can be linked to the program by capabilities, and capabilities provide a uniform mechanism for accessing all types of objects. Iliffe's codewords, in fact, were devised to support data abstraction.

In HYDRA, for example, each procedure in a type module is represented by a C-list that includes capabilities for the procedure's code and local objects, and templates for the parameters passed to the procedure. If a process creates an instance x of the object type defined by the module, it is given a capability C for x with rights to pass x to the procedures of the module (or a subset of the procedures), but it is not given RW rights to the representation of x. Because the procedures of the type module require RW rights to the internal representation of x, they are permitted to **amplify** the rights in C to those specified in an "amplification template".

FIGURE 4.20 Abstract data type and rights amplification.

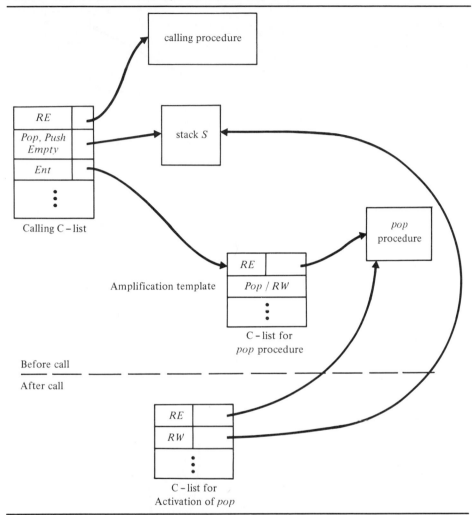

Example:
Let *S* be an instance of type *stack* as defined in Figure 4.19. Figure 4.20 shows a calling C-list with *Pop, Push,* and *Empty* rights to *S,* and an *Ent* right for the *pop* procedure. The C-list for the *pop* procedure has an amplification template that allows it to amplify the *pop* right in a capability for a stack to *RW.* When the *pop* procedure is called with parameter *S,* a C-list for the activation of *pop* is created with *RW* rights for *S* (activation C-lists are analogous to procedure activation records). ∎

FIGURE 4.21 Object encapsulated in private domain.

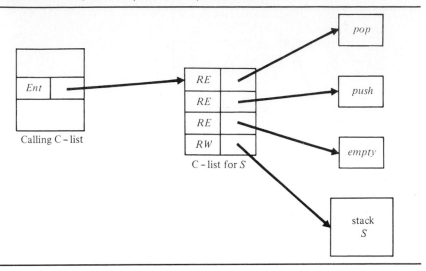

FIGURE 4.22 Sealed objects.

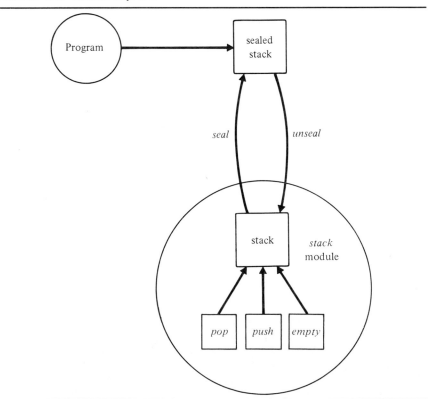

The capability mechanisms of HYDRA are implemented completely in software. Many of the features in HYDRA have been implemented in hardware in the INTEL iAPX 432. Its operating system, iMAX, is implemented in Ada. An Ada type module (called a "package") is represented by a capability list for the procedures and data objects of the module. If objects are passed to the module as parameters, their capabilities are represented by templates (called descriptor-control objects), and rights amplification is used as in HYDRA.

Objects can also be encapsulated in private domains, in which case rights amplification is not needed (see Figure 4.21). The private domain contains capabilities for the object plus the procedures for manipulating it. This strategy is also used in CAP.

Rights amplification is one way of implementing the *unseal* operation described by Morris [Mors73]. Morris suggested that an object of type *t* be *sealed* by the type manager for *t* such that only the type manager can *seal* and *unseal* it, and operations applied to the sealed object cause an error. The seal, therefore, serves to authenticate the internal structure of the object to the type manager, while hiding the structure from the remainder of the program. Figure 4.22 shows a sealed stack.

Seal and *unseal* could also be implemented with encryption. The type manager would encrypt an object before releasing it to the program, and only the type manager would be able to decrypt it for processing. This could degrade performance if the time required to encrypt and decrypt the object exceeds the processing time. When abstract data types are used primarily for program reliability and maintenance rather than for protection against malicious attacks, more efficient mechanisms are preferable. (A more general form of cryptographic sealing is described in Section 4.5.5.)

The SWARD machine designed by Myers effectively seals objects through its tagged memory. Every object in memory is tagged with a descriptor that identifies its type and size. If an object is a nonhomogeneous structure (e.g., a record structure), its elements are also tagged. A program must know the internal structure of an object to access it in memory. This means a program can hold a capability with *RW*-access to an object without being able to exercise these rights—only the type module will know the representation of the object and, therefore, be able to access it. This does not guarantee that a program cannot guess the internal representation of its objects and thereby access them, but it does prevent programs from accidentally modifying their objects. Myers calls this a "second level of protection"—the capabilities providing the "first level".

Although object-oriented languages have facilities for specifying access constraints on object types, they do not have facilities for specifying additional constraints on instances of a type. For example, it is not possible in these languages to specify that a procedure is to have access only to the *push* procedure for a stack S_1 and the *pop* and *empty* procedures for another stack S_2. Jones and Liskov [Jone76a] proposed a language extension that permits the specification of **qualified types** that constrain an object type to a subset of the operations defined on that type. The constraints imposed by qualified types can be enforced by the compiler or by the underlying capability mechanism.

Minsky [MinN78] has extended the concept of capability to distinguish between **tickets** for operands (data objects) and **activators** for operators (functions or procedures). A ticket is like a capability. An activator A has the following structure:

$$A = (o, p_1, \ldots, p_k \,|\, G) \rightarrow p_o$$

where o is an operator-identifier, p_i is an access constraint on the ith operand of $o (1 \leq i \leq k)$, G is a global constraint defined on all operands, and p_o is a constraint on the result of the operator. The constraints p_i may be data-dependent or state-dependent; the global constraint G allows for the specification of context dependent conditions. A subject can apply the operator o of an activator A only if the operands satisfy the constraints of A.

The scheme could be implemented using a capability-based system that supports enter capabilities for protected modules. An activator A for operator o would be implemented as a capability to enter a protected module. The module would check the operands to determine if they satisfy the constraints of A; if so, it would execute the operator o.

Minsky believes, however, that an underlying mechanism that implements both tickets and activators is preferable. He shows that such a scheme could support abstract data types without using rights amplification.

> ### *Example:*
> A process owning a stack S would be given a ticket for S and activators for popping and pushing arbitrary stacks. The type module, on the other hand, would be given activators for reading and writing the representation of stacks; these activators can be applied to the stack S if the process owning S passes the ticket for S to the type module. The activators within the type module serve the same purpose as the templates used in HYDRA. ■

4.5.3 Capability-Based Addressing

Capabilities provide an efficient protection mechanism that can be integrated with a computer's addressing mechanism. This is called **capability-based addressing**. Figure 4.23 illustrates how the ith word of memory in a segment X is addressed with a capability. The instruction address specifies a capability C for X and the offset i (the capability may be loaded on a hardware stack or in a register). The logical address of X is mapped to a physical address through a **descriptor** in a mapping table: the descriptor gives the base B and length L of the memory segment containing the object. The base address B could be an address in either primary or secondary memory (a flag, called the presence bit, indicates which); if the object is in secondary memory, it is moved to primary memory and B updated. The process is given access to the memory address $B + i$ only if the offset is in range; that is, if $0 \leq i < L$. With the descriptor table, an object can be relocated without changing the capability; only the entry in the descriptor table requires updating.

FIGURE 4.23 Capability-based addressing.

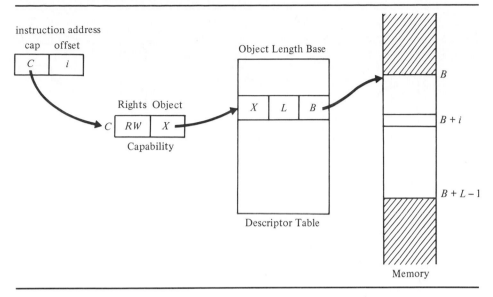

A capability does not usually index the mapping table directly. Instead it gives the unique name of the object, and this name is hashed to a slot in the table. This has special advantages when programs are shared or saved in long-term storage. Because the capabilities are invariant, the program can run in any domain at any time without modification. All variant information describing the location of the program and the objects referenced by it is kept in a central descriptor table under system control.

This property of invariance distinguishes capability systems from segmented virtual memory systems based on codewords and descriptors. In a descriptor-addressed system, a program accesses an object through a local address that points directly to an entry in the descriptor table. (Access rights are stored directly in the descriptors.) If local addresses refer to fixed positions in the descriptor table, sharing requires the participants to prearrange definitions (bindings) of local addresses. (See [Fabr71b,Fabr74] for a detailed discussion of capability-based addressing.)

The capabilities and hashed descriptor table need not significantly degrade addressing speed. Information in the descriptor table can be stored in high-speed associative registers, as is done for virtual memories. Table lookup time can be reduced by picking object names that hash to unique slots in the table (in SWARD, this is done by incrementing a counter until the value hashes to an empty slot).

With capability-based addressing, subjects sharing an object need only store a capability to an entry point in the structure, and different subjects can have different entry points and different access rights.

FIGURE 4.24 Shared subdirectory.

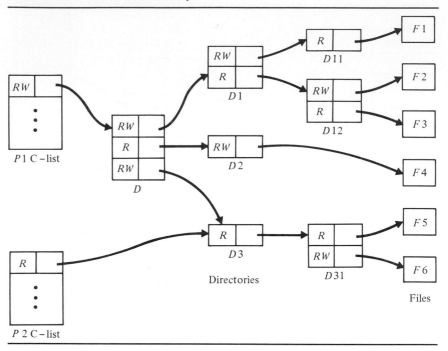

Example:
Figure 4.24 shows a process $P1$ with an RW-capability for the root D of a file directory. To read file $F1$, $P1$ would first get the RW-capability for directory $D1$ from D; it would then get the RW-capability for $D11$ from $D1$, and finally get an R-capability for $F1$ from $D11$. Similarly, $P1$ can acquire capabilities to access other files in the directory or to modify directories addressed by RW-capabilities (namely, D, $D1$, $D11$, and $D3$). Process $P1$ can share the subdirectory $D3$ with a process $P2$ by giving it an R-capability for the subdirectory $D3$; thus $P2$ can only access files $F5$ and $F6$; it cannot modify any of the directories. ■

With capability-based addressing, the protection state of a system is more naturally described with a directed graph such as shown in Figure 4.24 than with a matrix. The nodes of a graph correspond to the subjects and objects of the matrix; the edges to rights.

If the memory of the machine is not tagged, then the capabilities associated with a process or object must be stored in capability lists that are managed separately from other types of data. This means any object that has both capabilities and other types of data must be partitioned into two parts: a capability part and a data part. The system must keep these parts separate to protect the capabilities from unauthorized modification. This approach is used in most capability systems.

If the memory is tagged, capabilities can be stored anywhere in an object and used like addresses. Because their tags identify them as capabilities, the system can protect them from unauthorized modification. To address an object with a capability, the capability could be loaded either onto a hardware stack (in a stack architecture) or into a register (in a register architecture). The tagged memory approach simplifies addressing, domain switching, and storage management relative to partitioning (e.g., see [Dens80,Myer78]). Tagged memory, like capabilities, has its origins in the Rice Computer, the Basic Language Machine, and the Burroughs B5000 [Ilif72]. The SWARD machine and PSOS operating systems use tagged memories, as well as the capability-based machine designs of Dennis [Dens80] and Gehringer [Gehr79]. In SWARD, for example, a program can address local objects directly; capabilities are only used to address nonlocal objects. A capability can refer either to an entire object or to an element within an object. Indirect capabilities can be created to set up indirect address chains.

A system can use both capabilities and authorization lists—capabilities for currently active objects and authorization lists for inactive ones. Both MULTICS and SWARD, for example, provide a segmented name space through a single-level logical store. To access a segment in MULTICS, a process requests a descriptor (capability in SWARD) for it; this is granted provided the user associated with the process is listed in the authorization list for the target segment (access set in SWARD). Thereafter, the process can access the segment directly through the capability.

4.5.4 Revocation

Capabilities are easy to copy and disseminate, especially when they are stored in a tagged memory rather than in C-lists. This facilitates sharing among procedures or processes. There is, however, a drawback to this if objects are owned, and the owners can revoke privileges. If all access rights to an object are stored in a single

FIGURE 4.25 Revocation of rights with indirection.

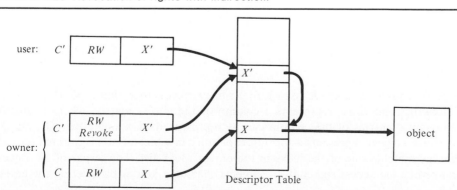

FIGURE 4.26 Revocation of rights with indirect capability in SWARD.

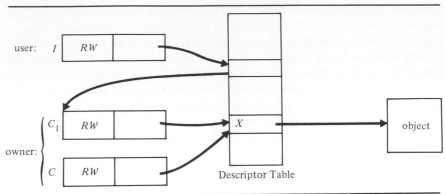

authorization list, it is relatively simple to purge them. But if they are scattered throughout the system, revocation could be more difficult.

Redell [Rede74] proposed a simple solution to this problem based on indirect addressing. The owner of an object X with capability C creates a capability C' with name X'. Rather than pointing to the object directly, the entry for X' in the descriptor table points to the entry for X. The owner grants access to X by giving out copies of the capability C' (see Figure 4.25). If the owner later revokes C', the entry for X' is removed from the descriptor table, breaking the link to X. The indirect capabilities of SWARD can also be used for revocation. Here the user is given an indirect capability I that points to a copy C_1 of the owner's capability for X. The owner revokes access to X by changing C_1 (see Figure 4.26).

4.5.5 Locks and Keys

Locks and keys combine aspects of list-oriented and ticket-oriented mechanisms. Associated with each object x is a list of locks and access rights:

L_1, r_1
L_2, r_2

$\cdot$

$\cdot$

$\cdot$

L_n, r_n .

A subject s is given a key K_i to lock L_i if s has r_i-access to x; that is, if $A[s, x] = r_i$. A lock list, therefore, represents a column of the access matrix, where identical (nonempty) entries of the column can be represented by a single pair (L_i, r_i). A key for an object represents a form of capability in which access is granted only if the key matches one of the locks in the object's lock list. The owner of an object can revoke the access rights of all subjects sharing a key K_i by deleting the entry for L_i in the lock list. Typically $n = 1$; that is, an object contains a single lock. In this case, a key is like an indirect capability, because the owner can revoke the key by changing the lock.

This method of protection resembles the "storage keys" used in IBM System/360 [IBM68]; the program status word of a process specifies a 4-bit key that must match a lock on the region of memory addressed by the process.

The ASAP file maintenance system designed at Cornell uses locks and keys [Conw72]. Each field in a record has associated with it one of eight possible classes (locks). Users are assigned to one or more of the classes (keys), and can only access those fields for which they have a key. There is also associated with each user a list of operations (e.g., *Update, Print*) the user is allowed to perform, and a set of data-dependent access restrictions. Whereas the data-independent restrictions are enforced at compile-time, the data-dependent restrictions are enforced at run-time.

Encryption is another example of a lock and key mechanism. Encrypting data places a lock on it, which can be unlocked only with the decryption key. Gifford [Giff82] has devised a scheme for protecting objects with encryption, which he calls **cryptographic sealing**. Let X be an object encrypted with a key K; access to X, therefore, requires K. Access to K can be controlled by associating an **opener** R with X. Openers provide different kinds of sharing, three of which are as follows:

1. **OR-Access,** where K can be recovered with any D_i in a list of n deciphering transformations $D_1, \ldots, D_n$. Here the opener R is defined by the list

$$R = (E_1(K), E_2(K), \ldots, E_n(K)),$$

where E_i is the enciphering transformation corresponding to D_i. Because K is separately enciphered under each of the E_i, a process with access to any one of the D_i can present D_i to obtain K. The opener is thus like the "keys record" in Gudes's scheme described in Section 3.7.1 (see Figure 3.19).

2. **AND-Access,** where every D_i in a list of deciphering transformations $D_1, \ldots, D_n$ must be present to recover K. Here the opener R is defined by

$$R = E_n\big(E_{n-1}(\ldots E_2(E_1(K))\ldots)\big).$$

Clearly, every D_i must be present to obtain K from the inverse function

$$D_1\big(D_2(\ldots D_{n-1}(D_n(R))\ldots)\big) = K.$$

3. **Quorum-Access,** where K can be recovered from any subset of t of the D_i in a list $D_1, \ldots, D_n$. Here R is defined by the list

$$R = (E_1(K_1), E_2(K_2), \ldots, E_n(K_n)),$$

where each K_i is a shadow of K in a (t, n) threshold scheme (see Section 3.8).

The different types of access can be combined to give even more flexible forms of sharing. The scheme also provides mechanisms for constructing submaster keys and indirect keys (that allow keys to be changed), and providing check-sums in encrypted objects (for authentication—see Section 3.4). It can be used with both single-key and public-key encryption.

4.5.6 Query Modification

A high-level approach to security may be taken in **query-processing systems** (also called transaction-processing systems). The commands (queries) issued by a user are calls on a small library of transaction programs that perform specific oper-ations, such as retrieving and updating, on a database. The user is not allowed to write, compile, and run arbitrary programs. In such systems, the only programs allowed to run are the certified transaction programs.

A user accesses a set of records with a **query** of the form (f, T, E), where f is an operation, T is the name of a table, and E is a logical expression identifying a group of records in T.

> *Example:*
> An example of an expression is $E = $ "*Sex = Female*". A request to retrieve this group of records from a table *Student* is specified by the query:
>
> > *Retrieve, Student, (Sex = Female) .* ■

Stonebraker and Wong [Ston74] proposed an access control mechanism based on **query modification**. Associated with each user is a list with entries of the form (T, R), where T is the name of a table and R is a set of access restrictions on T. The list is similar to a capability list in that it defines a user's access rights to the database. Each access restriction is of the form (f, S), where S is an expression identifying a subset of T; it authorizes the user to perform operation f on the subset defined by S. If the user poses the query (f, T, E), the transaction program modifies E according to the expression S; it then proceeds as if the user had actually presented a formula $(E \cdot S)$, where "$\cdot$" denotes logical and (see Figure 4.27).

> *Example:*
> If a user is permitted to retrieve only the records of students in the depart-ment of computer science, then $S = $ "*Dept = CS*", and the preceding request would be transformed to:
>
> > *Retrieve, Student, (Sex = Female) $\cdot$ (Dept = CS) .* ■

Query modification may be used in systems with different underlying struc-tures. Stonebraker and Wong developed it for the INGRES system, a relational database management system; it is also used in the GPLAN system [Cash76], a network-based database system designed around the CODASYL Data Base Task Group report.

FIGURE 4.27 Query modification.

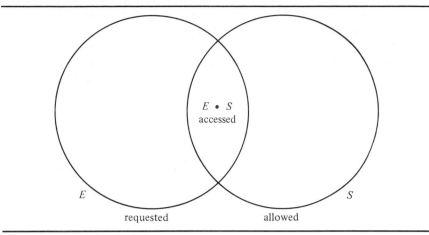

The technique has the advantage of being conceptually simple and easy to implement, yet powerful enough to handle complex access constraints. It is, however, a high-level mechanism applicable only at the user interface. Lower-level mechanisms are needed to ensure the transaction programs do not violate their constraints, and to ensure users cannot circumvent the query processor.

4.6 VERIFIABLY SECURE SYSTEMS

The presence of protection mechanisms does not guarantee security. If there are errors or design flaws in the operating system, processes may still be able to acquire unauthorized access to objects or bypass the protection mechanisms. For example, a user may be able to bypass an authorization list for a file stored on disk by issuing I/O requests directly to the disk.

In the 1960s, the Systems Development Corporation (SDC) developed an approach for locating security flaws in operating systems [Lind75]. The methodology involves generating an inventory of suspected flaws called "flaw hypotheses", testing the hypotheses, and generalizing the findings to locate similar flaws. SDC applied the technique to locate and repair flaws in several major systems (see also [Hebb80] for a more recent application).

Most flaws satisfy certain general patterns; for example, a global variable used by the supervisor is tampered with between calls, and the supervisor does not check the variable before use. The University of Southern California Information Sciences Institute (ISI) has developed tools (some automatic) for finding these error patterns in operating systems [Carl75].

Penetration analysis (sometimes called a "tiger team" approach) has helped locate security weaknesses. But like program testing, it does not prove the absence of flaws.

In general, it is not possible to prove an arbitrary system is secure. The reason is similar to the reason we cannot prove programs halt, and is addressed in Section 4.7. But just as it is possible to write verifiably correct programs (e.g., the program "$i := 7 + 10$" always halts and satisfies the post-condition "$i = 17$"), it is possible to build provably secure systems. The key is to integrate the verification of a system into its specification, design, and implementation; that is described in the subsections that follow. Neumann [Neum78] believes the approach has led to systems with fewer flaws, but suggests combining it with penetration analysis to further strengthen the security of a system. Again, an analogy with program development holds; we would not put into production a verified but untested air traffic control program.

Even with advanced technology for developing and verifying systems, it is unlikely systems will be absolutely secure. Computer systems are extremely complex and vulnerable to many subtle forms of attack.

We shall first examine two techniques for structuring systems that aid verification, and then examine the verification process itself.

4.6.1 Security Kernels

The objective is to isolate the access checking mechanisms in a small system nucleus responsible for enforcing security. The nucleus, called a **security kernel**, mediates all access requests to ensure they are permitted by the system's security policies. The security of the system is established by proving the protection policies meet the requirements of the system, and that the kernel correctly enforces the policies. If the kernel is small, the verification effort is considerably less than that required for a complete operating system.

The concept of security kernel evolved from the **reference monitor** concept described in the Anderson report [Ande72], and was suggested by Roger Schell. A reference monitor is an abstraction of the access checking function of object monitors [GrDe72] (see Section 4.1.1).

Several kernel-based systems have been designed or developed, including the MITRE security kernel for the DEC PDP-11/45 [Schi75,Mill76]; MULTICS with AIM [Schr77]; the MULTICS-based system designed at Case Western Reserve [Walt75]; the UCLA Data Secure UNIX system (DSU) for the PDP-11/45 and PDP-11/70 [Pope79]; the UNIX-based Kernelized Secure Operating System (KSOS) developed at Ford Aerospace for the PDP-11/70 (KSOS-11) [McCa79,Bers79] and at Honeywell for a Honeywell Level 6 machine (KSOS-6 or SCOMP) [Broa76]; and Kernelized VM/370 (KVM/370) developed at the System Development Corporation [Gold79].

With the exception of UCLA Secure UNIX, these systems were all developed to support the Department of Defense **multilevel security** policy described in the next chapter. Informally, this policy states that classified information must not be accessible to subjects with a lower security clearance. This means, for example, a user having a *Secret* clearance must not be able to read from *Top Secret* files

FIGURE 4.28 UCLA secure UNIX architecture.

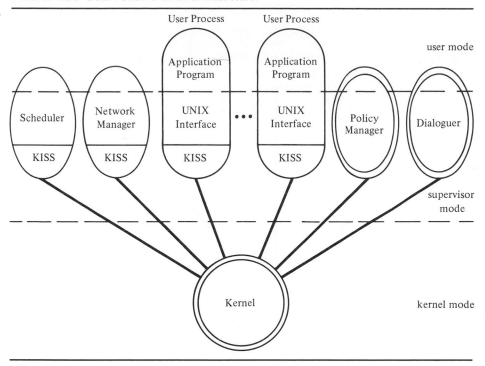

(i.e., "read up") or write *Secret* information in *Confidential* or *Unclassified* files (i.e., "write down").

We shall briefly describe UCLA Secure UNIX and KSOS-11. Both systems support a UNIX interface and run on PDP-11 hardware; both exploit the three execution modes of the PDP-11: kernel (highest privilege), supervisor, and user (least privilege). But different strategies have been used to structure and develop the two systems.

Figure 4.28 shows the architecture of the UCLA Secure UNIX system. Each user process runs in a separate protection domain, and is partitioned into two virtual address spaces. One address space contains the user (application) program and runs in user mode; the other contains a UNIX interface and runs in supervisor mode. The UNIX interface consists of a scaled down version of the standard UNIX operating system and a Kernel Interface SubSystem (KISS) that interfaces with the kernel.

The protection domain of a process is represented by a capability list managed by the kernel. The kernel enforces the protection policy represented by the capabilities, but does not alter the protection data. The power to grant and revoke capabilities is invested in a separate policy manager that manages the protection policies for shared files and kernel objects (processes, pages, and devices). Pro-

FIGURE 4.29 KSOS-11 architecture.

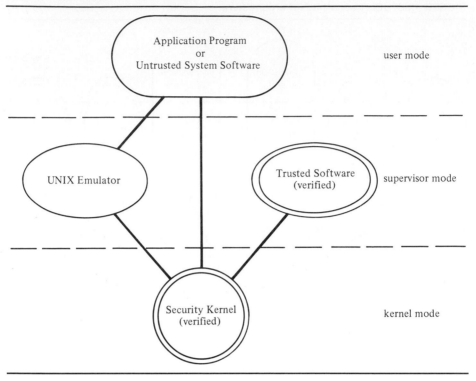

cesses cannot directly pass capabilities. The policy manager relies on a separate process (called a "dialoguer") to establish a secure connection between a user and terminal. The security policies and mechanisms of the system, therefore, are invested in the kernel, the policy manager, and the dialoguer (shown highlighted in Figure 4.28).

The kernel supports four types of objects: capabilities, processes, pages, and devices. It does not support type extensibility through abstract data types. Capabilities are implemented in software. The kernel is small (compared with other kernels), consisting of less than 2000 lines of code. The system architecture also includes a resource scheduler and network manager for the ARPANET.

Figure 4.29 shows the architecture of KSOS. Like the UCLA kernel, the KSOS kernel is at the lowest level and runs in kernel mode. But the KSOS kernel is substantially larger than the UCLA kernel, providing more operating system functions, file handling, and a form of type extension (the kernel is closer to a complete operating system than a simple reference monitor). The kernel enforces both an access control policy and the multilevel security policy.

A UNIX emulator and a "trusted" portion of nonkernel system software run in supervisor mode and interface directly with the kernel. The emulator translates system calls at the UNIX interface into kernel calls. Untrusted (nonverified) system software and application programs run in user mode and interface with the UNIX emulator or directly with the kernel. They can communicate with trusted processes through interprocess communication messages provided by the kernel. The trusted software consists of support services such as login, the terminal interface, and the telecommunications interface; and security mechanisms for applications with policies that conflict with the multilevel security policies of the kernel (see Section 5.6.3 for an example). Trusted processes are at least partially verified or audited.

Security kernels have also been used to structure database systems. Downs and Popek [Down77] describe a database system that uses two security kernels: a "kernel input controller", which processes user requests at the logical level, and a "base kernel", which accesses the physical representation of the data. All security related operations are confined to the kernels. Separate (nonverified) data management modules handle the usual data management functions, such as selecting access methods, following access paths, controlling concurrent accesses, and formatting data. The base kernel is the only module allowed to access the database.

4.6.2 Levels of Abstraction

The basic idea is to decompose a system (or security kernel) into a linear hierarchy of abstract machines, $M_0, \ldots, M_n$. Each abstract machine M_i $(0 < i \leq n)$ is implemented by a set of abstract programs P_{i-1} running on the next lower level machine M_{i-1}. Thus the programs at level i depend only on the programs at levels $0, \ldots, i - 1$. They are accessible at level $i + 1$, but may be invisible at levels above that. The system is verified one level at a time, starting with level 0; thus verification of each level can proceed under the assumption that all lower levels are correct. The general approach originated with Dijkstra [Dijk68], who used it to structure the "THE" (Technische Hoogeschule Eindhoven) multiprogramming system.

The Provably Secure Operating System (PSOS), designed at SRI under the direction of Peter Neumann, has a design hierarchy with 17 levels of abstraction (see Figure 4.30) [Feie79,Neum80]. PSOS is a capability-based system supporting abstract data types. Because capabilities provide the basic addressing and protection mechanisms of the system, they are at the lowest level of abstraction. All levels below virtual memory (level 8) are invisible at the user interface, except for capabilities and basic operations (level 4). In the first implementation, levels 0 through 8 are expected to be implemented in hardware (or microcode) along with a few operations at the higher levels.

Imposing a loop-free dependency structure on a system design is not always straightforward (see [Schr77]). Some abstractions—for example, processes and memory—are seemingly interdependent. For example, the process manager depends on memory for the storage of process state information; the virtual memory manager depends on processes for page swaps. Because neither processes nor memory can be entirely below the other, these abstractions are split into "real"

FIGURE 4.30 PSOS design hierarchy.

Level	Abstractions
16	Command interpreter
15	User environments and name space
14	User input/output
13	Procedure records
12	User processes and visible input/output
11	Creation and deletion of user objects
10	Directories
9	Abstract data types
8	Virtual memory (segmentation)
7	Paging
6	System processes and system input/output
5	Primitive input/output
4	Basic arithmetic and logical operations
3	Clocks
2	Interrupts
1	Real memory (registers and storage)
0	Capabilities

and "virtual" components. In PSOS, real memory is below processes, but a few fixed (real) system processes with real memory are below virtual memory. User (virtual) processes are above virtual memory. (In PSOS, the design hierarchy is also separated from the implementation hierarchy.)

4.6.3 Verification

Verification involves developing formal specifications for a system, proving the specifications satisfy the security policies of the system, and proving the implementation satisfies the specifications.

SRI researchers have developed a Hierarchical Design Methodology (HDM) to support the development of verifiable systems [Neum80,Robi79]. HDM has been used in the design of PSOS and the development of KSOS.

HDM decomposes a system into a hierarchy of abstract machines as described in the preceding section. Each abstract machine is specified as a module in the language SPECIAL (SPECIfication and Assertion Language). A module is defined in terms of an internal state space (abstract data structures) and state transitions, using a specification technique introduced by Parnas [Parn72,Pric73]. The states and state transitions are specified by two types of functions:

1. **V-functions**, that give the value of a state variable (**primitive** V-function) or a value computed from the values of state variables (**derived** V-function). The initial value of a primitive V-function is specified in the module definition.

FIGURE 4.31 Specification of *stack* module.

---

module *stack*;
  Vfun *top*() : **integer**;
        "primitive *V*-function giving the index
          of the top of the stack"
      hidden;
      initially: *top* = 0;
      exceptions: none;
    Vfun *data*(*i*: **integer**) : **integer**;
        "primitive *V*-function giving the value
          of the *i*th element of the stack"
      hidden;
      initially: $\forall i \, (data(i) = \textbf{undefined})$;
      exceptions: ($i < 0$) or ($i > size$);
    Vfun *empty*() : **boolean**;
        "derived *V*-function giving status of stack"
      derived: **if** *top* = 0 **then** true **else** false;
    Ofun *push*(*x*: **integer**);
        "push element *x* onto top of stack"
      exceptions: *top* $\geq$ *size*;
      effects: '*top* = *top* + 1;
              '*data*('*top*) = *x*;
              $\forall j \neq$ '*top*, '*data*(*j*) = *data*(*j*)
  end *stack*

---

2.   ***O*-functions**, that perform an operation changing the state. State transitions
      (called **effects**) are described by assertions relating new values of primitive
      V-functions to their prior values. A state variable cannot be modified unless
      its corresponding primitive *V*-function appears in the effects of an *O*-
      function.

A function can both perform an operation and return a value, in which case it is
called an ***OV*-function**. Functions may be either **visible** or **invisible** (**hidden**) outside
the module. Primitive *V*-functions are always hidden.
     The specification of a function lists **exceptions** which state abnormal condi-
tions under which the function is not defined. The implementation must ensure the
code for the function is not executed when these conditions are satisfied (e.g., by
making appropriate tests).

Example:
Figure 4.31 shows a specification of a module for a subset of the *stack*
module shown in Figure 4.19. A *V*-function name preceded by a prime (')
refers to the value of the *V*-function after the transition caused by the effects
of an *O*-function; the unprimed name refers to its original value. Specification of the *pop* operation is left as an exercise. ∎

HDM structures the development of a system into five stages:

S0. **Interface Definition.** The system interface is defined and decomposed into a set of modules. Each module manages some type of system object (e.g., segments, directories, processes), and consists of a collection of V-, and O- functions. (Formal specifications for the functions are deferred to Stage S2.) The security requirements of the system are formulated. For PSOS, these requirements are described by two general principles:

    a. **Detection Principle:** There shall be no unauthorized acquisition of information.

    b. **Alteration Principle:** There shall be no unauthorized alteration of information.

These are low-level principles of the capability mechanism; each type manager uses capabilities to enforce its own high-level policy.

S1. **Hierarchical Decomposition.** The modules are arranged into a linear hierarchy of abstract machines $M_0, \ldots, M_n$ as described in Section 4.6.1. The consistency of the structure and of the function names is verified.

S2. **Module Specification.** Formal specifications for each module are developed as described. Each module is verified to determine if it is self-consistent and satisfies certain global assertions. The basic security requirements of the system are represented as global assertions and verified at this stage. For PSOS, the alteration and detection principles are specified in terms of capabilities providing read and write access.

S3. **Mapping Functions.** A mapping function is defined to describe the state space at level i in terms of the state space at level $i - 1$ ($0 < i \leq n$). This is written as a set of expressions relating the V-functions at level i to those at level $i - 1$. Consistency of the mapping function with the specifications and the hierarchical decomposition is verified.

S4. **Implementation.** Each module is implemented in hardware, microcode, or a high-level language, and the consistency of the implementation with the specifications and mapping function is verified. Implementation proceeds one level at a time, from the lowest level to the highest. Each function at level i is implemented as an abstract program which runs on machine M_{i-1}.

    Each abstract program is verified using Floyd's [Floy67] inductive-assertion method, which is extended to handle V- and O-function calls. Entry and exit assertions are constructed for each program from the specifications. A program is proved correct by showing that if the entry assertions hold when the program begins execution, then the exit assertions will hold when the program terminates, regardless of the execution path through the program. The proof is constructed by inserting intermediate assertions into the program; these define entry and exit conditions for simple paths of the program. A simple path is a sequence of statements with a single entry and a single exit. For each simple path S with entry assertion P and exit assertion Q, a verification condition (VC) in the form of an implication $P' \supset Q'$ is derived by transforming P and Q to reflect the effects of executing S. The program is proved (or disproved) correct by proving (or disproving) the VCs are theorems. The proof techniques are described in [Robi77]. Program proving is studied in Section 5.5.

Researchers at SRI have developed several tools [Silv79] to support HDM and its specification language SPECIAL. These include tools to check the consistency of specifications and mappings, the Boyer-Moore theorem-prover [Boye79], and verification condition generators for several programming languages including FORTRAN [Boye80] and Pascal [Levi81].

At UCLA, Popek and others have adopted a two-part strategy to develop and verify the UCLA security kernel [Pope78,Walk80]. The first part involves developing successively more detailed specifications of the kernel until an implementation is reached:

1. **Top-Level Specifications**, which give a high-level, intuitive description of the security requirements of the system.
2. **Abstract-Level Specifications**, which give a more refined description.
3. **Low-Level Specifications**, which give a detailed description.
4. Pascal **Code** satisfying the specifications.

The specifications at each level are formulated in terms of an abstract machine with states and state transitions satisfying the following general requirements:

1. Protected objects may be modified only by explicit request.
2. Protected objects may be read only by explicit request.
3. Specific access to protected objects is permitted only when the recorded protection data allows it; i.e., all accesses must be authorized.

These requirements are essentially the same as the Detection and Alteration principles of PSOS.

The second part involves verifying that the Pascal implementation satisfies the low-level specifications, and verifying that the specifications at each level are consistent with each other. Note that whereas for PSOS the implementation is constructed from the hierarchy of specifications and mapping functions, for UCLA Secure UNIX it represents a refinement of the bottom-level specifications. Verification of UCLA Secure UNIX was assisted by the AFFIRM verification system and its predecessor XIVUS, developed at ISI.

For further reading on specification and verification systems, see Cheheyl, Gasser, Huff, and Millen [Cheh81]. This paper surveys four systems, including HDM and AFFIRM. The other two systems are Gypsy, developed at the University of Texas at Austin, and the Formal Development Methodology (FDM) and its specification language Ina Jo, developed at SDC.

Rushby [Rush81] has proposed a new approach to the design and verification of secure systems. His approach is based on a distributed system architecture that provides security through physical separation of subjects where possible, trusted modules that control the communication channels among subjects, and a security kernel that enforces the logical separation of subjects sharing the same physical resources. Verification involves showing that the communication channels are used in accordance with the security policies of the system, and that the subjects become completely isolated when these channels are cut. The latter part, called "proof of separability," involves showing that a subject cannot distinguish its actual environment on a shared machine from its abstract environment on a private virtual machine. The approach is particularly suited for the development of secure networks that use encryption to protect data transmitted over the channels.

4.7 THEORY OF SAFE SYSTEMS

Harrison, Ruzzo, and Ullman [Harr76] studied the feasibility of proving properties about a high-level abstract model of a protection system. They used as their model the access-matrix model described in Section 4.1; thus, the state of a system is described by an access matrix A, and state transitions by commands that create and destroy subjects and objects, and enter and delete rights in A. They defined an unauthorized state Q to be one in which a generic right r could be **leaked** into A; the right would be leaked by a command c that, when run in state Q, would execute a primitive operation entering r into some cell of A not previously containing r. An initial state Q_0 of the system is defined to be **safe** for r if it cannot derive a state Q in which r could be leaked.

Leaks are not necessarily bad, as any system that allows sharing will have many leaks. Indeed, many subjects will intentionally transfer (leak) their rights to other "trustworthy" subjects. The interesting question is whether transfer of a right r violates the security policies of the system. To answer this question, safety for r is considered by deleting all trustworthy subjects from the access matrix.

Proving a system is safe does not mean it is secure—safety applies only to the abstract model. To prove security, it is also necessary to show the system correctly implements the model; that is, security requires both safety and correctness. Thus, safety relates to only part of the verification effort described in the preceding section.

Harrison, Ruzzo, and Ullman showed safety is undecidable in a given arbitrary protection system. Safety is decidable, however, if no new subjects or objects can be created. They also showed safety is decidable in a highly constrained class of systems permitting only "mono-operational" commands, which perform at most one elementary operation. We first review their results for mono-operational systems, and then review their results for general systems.

We then consider the prospects for developing a comprehensive theory of protection (or even a finite number of such theories) sufficiently general to enable proofs or disproofs of safety. Not surprisingly, we can show there is no decidable theory adequate for proving all propositions about safety.

These results must be interpreted carefully. They are about the fundamental limits of our abilities to prove properties about an abstract model of a protection system. They do not rule out constructing individual protection systems and proving they are secure, or finding practical restrictions on the model that make safety questions tractable. Yet, these results do suggest that systems without severe restrictions on their operation will have security questions too expensive to answer. Thus we are forced to shift our concern from proving arbitrary systems secure to designing systems that are provably secure. PSOS, KSOS, UCLA Unix, and the other systems described in the last section are provably secure only because they were designed to satisfy specified security requirements. Their security was continually verified at each stage in the development of the system.

We conclude this chapter with a discussion of safety in systems constrained by the "take-grant" graph rules. For such systems, safety is not only decidable, but decidable in time linear in the size of the protection graph.

4.7.1 Mono-Operational Systems

A protection system is **mono-operational** if each command performs a single primitive operation. Harrison, Ruzzo, and Ullman prove the following theorem:

Theorem 4.1:
There is an algorithm that decides whether a given mono-operational system and initial state Q_0 is safe for a given generic right r.

> *Proof:*
> We will show that only a finite number of command sequences need be checked for the presence of a leak. Observe first that we can ignore command sequences containing **delete** and **destroy** operators, since commands only check for the presence of rights, not their absence. Thus, if a leak occurs in a sequence containing these commands, then the leak would occur in one without them.
>
> Observe next that we can ignore command sequences containing more than one **create** operator. The reason is that all commands that enter or check for rights in new positions of the access matrix can be replaced with commands which enter or check for rights in existing positions of the matrix; this is done simply by changing the actual parameters from the new subjects and objects to existing subjects and objects. It is necessary, however, to retain one **create subject** command in case the initial state has no subjects (to ensure that the matrix has at least one position in which to enter rights).
>
> This means the only command sequences we need consider are those consisting of **enter** operations and at most one **create subject** operation.
>
> Now, the number of distinct **enter** operations is bounded by gn_sn_o, where g is the number of generic rights, $n_s = |S_0| + 1$ is the number of subjects, and $n_o = |O_0| + 1$ is the number of objects. Because the order of **enter** operations in a command sequence is not important, the number of command sequences that must be inspected is, therefore, bounded by:
>
> $$2^{gn_sn_o+1} . \quad \blacksquare$$

Although it is possible to construct a general decision procedure to determine the decidability of arbitrary mono-operational systems, Harrison, Ruzzo, and Ullman show the problem to be **NP**-complete and thus intractable. They note, however, that by using the technique of "dynamic programming" (e.g., see [Aho74]), an algorithm polynomial in the size of the initial matrix can be devised for any given system.

Most systems are not mono-operational, as illustrated by the examples of Section 4.1.2. Nevertheless, the results are enlightening in that they show the safety question for general systems will, at best, be extremely difficult.

4.7.2 General Systems

Harrison, Ruzzo, and Ullman show that the general safety problem is undecidable. To prove this result, they show how the behavior of an arbitrary Turing machine (e.g., see [Aho74,Mins67]) can be encoded in a protection system such that leakage of a right corresponds to the Turing machine entering a final state. Therefore, if safety is decidable, then so is the halting problem. Because the halting problem is undecidable, the safety problem must also be undecidable.

A **Turing machine** T consists of a finite set of **states** K and a finite set of **tape symbols** Γ, which includes a **blank** b. The **tape** consists of an infinite number of cells numbered 1, 2, . . . , where each cell is initially blank. A **tape head** is always positioned at some cell of the tape.

The **moves** of T are specified by a function $\delta\colon K \times \Gamma \rightarrow K \times \Gamma \times \{L, R\}$. If $\delta(q, X) = (p, Y, R)$ and T is in state q scanning symbol X with its tape head at cell i, then T enters state p, overwrites X with Y, and moves its tape head right one cell (i.e., to cell $i + 1$). If $\delta(q, X) = (p, Y, L)$ the same thing happens, but the tape head is moved left one cell (unless $i = 1$).

T begins in an initial state q_0, with its head at cell 1. There is also a final state q_f such that if T enters q_f it halts. The "halting problem" is to determine whether an arbitrary Turing machine ever enters its final state. It is well-known that this problem is undecidable. We shall now show the safety problem is also undecidable.

Theorem 4.2:
It is undecidable whether a given state of a given protection system is safe for a given generic right.

> *Proof:*
> Let T be an arbitrary Turing machine. We shall first show how to encode the state of T as an access matrix in a protection system, and then show how to encode the moves of T as commands of the system. The tape symbols will be represented as generic access rights, and the tape cells as subjects of the matrix.
> Suppose that T is in state q. At that time, T will have scanned a

FIGURE 4.32 Encoding of Turing machine.

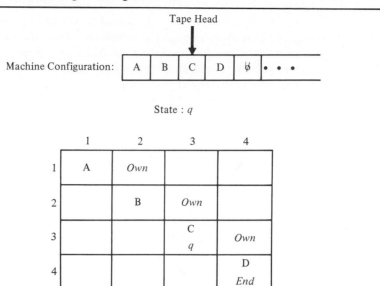

finite number k of cells, and cells $k + 1, k + 2, \ldots$ will be blank. State q is represented as an access matrix A with k subjects and k objects (all subjects) such that:

1. If cell s of the tape contains the symbol X, then $A[s, s]$ contains the right X.
2. $A[s, s + 1]$ contains the right *Own* ($s = 1, \ldots, k - 1$) (this induces an ordering on the subjects according to the sequence of symbols on the tape).
3. $A[k, k]$ contains the right *End* (this signals the current end of the tape).
4. If the tape head is positioned at cell s, then $A[s, s]$ contains the right q.

Figure 4.32 shows the access matrix corresponding to a Turing machine in state q whose first four cells hold ABCD, with the tape head at cell 3.

Note that the machine's tape is encoded along the diagonal of the matrix. It cannot be encoded along a row (or column) of the matrix because for a given subject s, there is no concept of a predecessor or successor of s. The only way of ordering the subjects is by giving each subject s a right (such as *Own*) for another subject (denoted $s + 1$).

The initial state q_0 is represented as an access matrix with one subject s_0, corresponding to the first tape cell. The rights in $A[s_0, s_0]$ include q_0, b (since all cells are blank), and *End*.

The moves of T are represented as commands. A move $\delta(q, X)$ = (p, Y, L) is represented by a command that revokes the right q from subject s' and grants the right p to subject s, where s' represents the current position of the tape head, and s represents the cell to the left of s'. The command, shown next, also substitutes the right Y for the right X in the cell represented by s'.

> **command** $C_{qX}(s, s')$
>   **if**
>   *Own* in $A[s, s']$ and
> q in $A[s', s']$ and
> X in $A[s', s']$
>   **then**
>   **delete** q from $A[s', s']$
>   **delete** X from $A[s', s']$
>   **enter** Y into $A[s', s']$
>   **enter** p into $A[s, s]$
>   **end** .

A move $\delta(q, X) = (p, Y, R)$ is represented by two commands to handle the possibility that the tape head could move past the current end of the tape (in which case a new subject must be created). The specification of these commands is left as an exercise for the reader.

Now, if the Turing machine reaches its final state q_f, then the right q_f will be entered into some position of the corresponding access matrix. Equivalently, if the Turing machine halts, then the right q_f is leaked by the protection system. Because the halting problem is undecidable, the safety problem must, therefore, also be undecidable. ∎

Theorem 4.2 means that the set of safe protection systems is not **recursive**; that is, it is not possible to construct an algorithm that decides safety for all systems. Any procedure alleged to decide safety must either make mistakes or get hung in a loop trying to decide the safety of some systems.

We can, however, generate a list of all unsafe systems; this could be done by systematically enumerating all protection systems and all sequences of commands in each system, and outputting the description of any system for which there is a sequence of commands causing a leak. This is stated formally by Theorem 4.3:

Theorem 4.3:
The set of unsafe systems is **recursively enumerable**. ∎

We cannot, however, enumerate all safe systems, for a set is recursive if and only if both it and its complement are recursively enumerable.

Whereas the safety problem is in general undecidable, it is decidable for finite systems (i.e., systems that have a finite number of subjects and objects).

Harrison, Ruzzo, and Ullman prove, however, the following theorem, which implies that any decision procedure is intractable:

Theorem 4.4:
The question of safety for protection systems without **create** commands is **PSPACE**-complete (complete in polynomial space). ∎

This means that safety for these systems can be solved in polynomial time (time proportional to a polynomial function of the length of the description of the system) if and only if **PSPACE** = **P**; that is, if and only if any problem solvable in polynomial space is also solvable in polynomial time. Although the relationship between time and space is not well understood, many believe **PSPACE** ≠ **P** and exponential time is required for such problems (see Section 1.5.2). The proof of Theorem 4.4 involves showing any polynomial-space bounded Turing machine can be reduced in polynomial time to an initial access matrix whose size is polynomial in the length of the Turing machine input.

Harrison and Ruzzo [Harr78] considered **monotonic** systems, which are restricted to the elementary operations **create** and **enter** (i.e., there are no **destroy** or **delete** operators). Even for this highly restricted class of systems, the safety problem is undecidable.

4.7.3 Theories for General Systems

Denning, Denning, Garland, Harrison, and Ruzzo [Denn78] studied the implications of the decidability results for developing a theory of protection powerful enough to resolve safety questions. Before presenting these results, we shall first review the basic concepts of theorem-proving systems. Readers can skip this section without loss of continuity.

A **formal language** L is a recursive subset of the set of all possible strings over a given finite alphabet; the members of L are called **sentences**.

A **deductive theory** T over a formal language L consists of a set A of **axioms**, where $A \subseteq L$, and a finite set of **rules of inference**, which are recursive relations over L. The set of **theorems** of T is defined inductively as follows:

1.   If t is an axiom (i.e., $t \in A$), then t is a theorem of T; and
2.   If $t_1, \ldots, t_k$ are theorems of T and $<t_1, \ldots, t_k, t> \in R$ for some rule of inference R, then t is a theorem of T.

Thus, every theorem t of T has a **proof**, which is a finite sequence $<t_1, \ldots, t_n>$ of sentences such that $t = t_n$ and each t_i is either an axiom or follows from some subset of $t_1, \ldots, t_{i-1}$ by a rule of inference. We write $T \vdash t$ to denote t is a theorem of T (is provable in T).

Two theories T and T' are said to be **equivalent** if they have the same set of theorems. Equivalent theories need not have the same axioms or rules of inference.

A theory T is **recursively axiomatizable** if it has (or is equivalent to a theory with) a recursive set of axioms. The set of theorems of any recursively axiomatizable theory is recursively enumerable: we can effectively generate all finite sequences of sentences, check each to see if it is a proof, and enter in the enumeration the final sentence of any sequence that is a proof.

A theory is **decidable** if its theorems form a recursive set.

Because the set of safe protection systems is not recursively enumerable, it cannot be the set of theorems of a recursively axiomatizable theory. This means the set of all safe protection systems cannot be effectively generated by rules of inference from a finite (or even recursive) set of safe systems. (Note this does not rule out the possibility of effectively generating smaller, but still interesting classes of safe systems.) This observation can be refined, as we shall do, to establish further limitations on any recursively axiomatizable theory of protection.

A **representation of safety** over a formal language L is an effective map $p \longrightarrow t_p$ from protection systems to sentences of L. We interpret t_p as a statement of the safety of protection system p.

A theory T is **adequate for proving safety** if and only if there is a representation $p \longrightarrow t_p$ of safety such that

$$T \vdash t_p \text{ if and only if } p \text{ is safe.}$$

Analogs of the classical Church and Gödel theorems for the undecidability and incompleteness of formal theories of arithmetic follow for formal theories of protection systems.

Theorem 4.5:
Any theory T adequate for proving safety must be undecidable. ■

This theorem follows from Theorem 4.2 by noting that, were there an adequate decidable T, we could decide whether a protection system p were safe by checking whether $T \vdash t_p$.

Theorem 4.6:
There is no recursively axiomatizable theory T adequate for proving safety. ■

This theorem follows from Theorems 4.2 and 4.3. If T were adequate and recursively axiomatizable, we could decide the safety of p by enumerating simultaneously the theorems of T and the set of unsafe systems; eventually, either t_p will appear in the list of theorems or p will appear in the list of unsafe systems, enabling us to decide the safety of p.

Theorem 4.6 shows that, given any recursively axiomatizable theory T and any representation $p \longrightarrow t_p$ of safety, there is some system whose safety either is established incorrectly by T or is not established when it should be. This result in itself is of limited interest for two reasons: it is not constructive (i.e., it does not show us how to find such a p); and, in practice, we may be willing to settle for inadequate theories as long as they are sound, that is, as long as they do not err by falsely establishing the safety of unsafe systems. Formally, a theory T is **sound** if and only if p is safe whenever $T \vdash t_p$. The next theorem overcomes the first limitation, showing how to construct a protection system p that is unsafe if and only if $T \vdash t_p$; the idea is to design the commands of p so that they can simulate a Turing machine that "hunts" for a proof of the safety of p; if and when a sequence of commands finds such a proof, it generates a leak. If the theory T is sound, then such a protection system p must be safe but its safety cannot be provable in T.

Theorem 4.7:

Given any recursively axiomatizable theory T and any representation of safety in T, one can construct a protection system p for which $T \vdash t_p$ if and only if p is unsafe. Furthermore, if T is sound, then p must be safe, but its safety is not provable in T.

Proof:

Given an indexing $\{M_i\}$ of Turing machines and an indexing $\{p_i\}$ of protection systems, the proof of Theorem 4.2 shows how to define a recursive function f such that

(a) M_i halts iff $p_{f(i)}$ is unsafe.

Since T is recursively axiomatizable and the map $p \rightarrow t_p$ is computable, there is a recursive function g such that

(b) $T \vdash t_{p_i}$ iff $M_{g(i)}$ halts;

the Turing machine $M_{g(i)}$ simply enumerates all theorems of T, halting if t_{p_i} is found. By the Recursion Theorem [Roge67], one can find effectively an index j such that

(c) M_j halts iff $M_{g(f(j))}$ halts.

Combining (a), (b), and (c), and letting $p = p_{f(j)}$, we get

(d) $T \vdash t_p$ iff $M_{g(f(j))}$ halts
   iff M_j halts
   iff $p_{f(j)} = p$ is unsafe ,

as was to be shown.

Now, suppose T is sound. Then t_p cannot be a theorem of T lest p be simultaneously safe by soundness and unsafe by (d). Hence, $T \nvdash t_p$, and p is safe by (d) . ■

The unprovability of the safety of a protection system p in a given sound theory T does not imply p's safety is unprovable in every theory. We can, for example, augment T by adding t_p to its axioms. But no matter how much we augment T, there will always exist another safe p' whose safety is unprovable in the new theory T'. In other words, this abstract view shows that systems for proving safety are necessarily **incomplete**: no single effective deduction system can be used to settle all questions of safety.

We also considered theories for protection systems of bounded size. Although the safety question becomes decidable (Theorem 4.4), any decision procedure is likely to require enormous amounts of time. This rules out practical mechanical safety tests, but not the possibility that ingenious or lucky people might always be able to find proofs faster than any mechanical method. Unfortunately, we found even this hope ill-founded. If we consider reasonable proof systems in which we can decide whether a given string of symbols constitutes a proof in time polynomial in the string's length, then we have the following:

Theorem 4.8:
For the class of protection systems in which the number of objects and domains of access is bounded, safety (or unsafety) is polynomial verifiable by some reasonable logical system if and only if **PSPACE = NP**; that is, if and only if any problem solvable in polynomial space is solvable in nor_deterministic polynomial time. ∎

Many believe **PSPACE ≠ NP** (see Section 1.5.2).

4.7.4 Take-Grant Systems

Jones, Lipton, and Snyder [Jone76b] introduced the **Take-Grant** graph model to describe a restricted class of protection systems. They showed that for such systems, safety is decidable even if the number of subjects and objects that can be created is unbounded. Furthermore, it is decidable in time linear in the size of the initial state. We shall describe these results, following their treatment in a survey paper by Snyder [Snyd81a].

As in the access-matrix model, a protection system is described in terms of states and state transitions. A protection state is described by a directed graph G, where the nodes of the graph represent the subjects and objects of the system (subjects are not objects in the take-grant model), and the edges represent rights. We shall let (x, y) denote the set of access rights on an edge from x to y, where $r \epsilon (x, y)$ means that x has right r for y. If x is a subject, then (x, y) in G is like $A[x, y]$ in the access matrix.

There are two special rights: **take** (abbreviated t), and **grant** (abbreviated g). If a subject s has the right t for an object x, then it can take any of x's rights; if it has the right g for x, then it can share any of its rights with x. These rights describe certain aspects of capability systems. If a subject has a capability to read from an object x containing other capabilities, then it can take capabili·ies (rights) from x; similarly, if it has a capability to w_ite into x, it can grant capabilities to x.

Example:
Figure 4.33 shows the graph representation of the directory structure shown in Figure 4.24. We have used "●" to represent subject nodes, and "o" to represent object nodes. Note that R and W capabilities for a directory be-

FIGURE 4.33 Take-grant representation of directory structure.

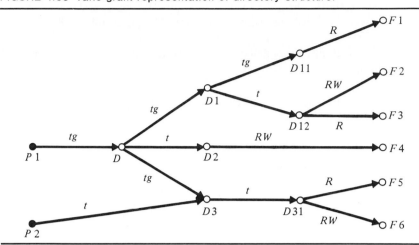

come take and grant rights, respectively, in the take-grant model, whereas R and W capabilities for files remain as R and W rights. ■

The take-grant model describes the **transfer of authority** (rights) in systems. It does not describe the protection state with respect to rights that cannot be transferred. Thus, it abstracts from the complete state only information needed to answer questions related to safety.

Example:
Figure 4.34 shows only part of the protection state of Figure 4.2. A process can grant rights for any of its owned files to any other process, so there is an edge labeled g connecting each pair of processes. But only process $P2$ is allowed to take rights from another process, namely its subordinate $P3$, so there is only one edge labeled t. Because rights for memory segments cannot

FIGURE 4.34 Take-grant graph for system shown in Figure 4.2.

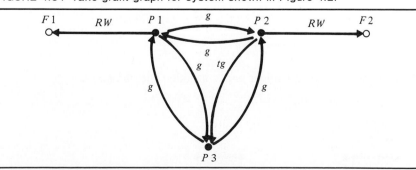

be granted along the g-edges (memory is not owned and the copy flag is not set), these rights are not shown. Consequently, the graph does not show $P2$ can take $P3$'s rights for memory segment $M3$ (as it did). ■

State transitions are modeled as graph rewriting rules for commands. There are four rules:

1. **Take:** Let s be a subject such that $t \epsilon (s, x)$, and $r \epsilon (x, y)$ for some right r and nodes x and y. The command

    s **take** r for y from x

    adds r to (s, y). Graphically,

    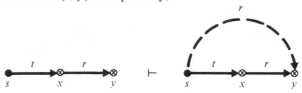

    where the symbol "⊗" denotes vertices that may be either subjects or objects.
2. **Grant:** Let s be a subject such that $g \epsilon (s, x)$ and $r \epsilon (s, y)$ for some right r and nodes x and y. The command

    s **grant** r for y to x

    adds r to (x, y). Graphically,

3. **Create:** Let s be a subject and ρ a set of rights. The command

    $$s \text{ create } \rho \text{ for new} \begin{Bmatrix} \textbf{subject} \\ \textbf{object} \end{Bmatrix} x$$

    adds a new node x and sets $(s, x) = \rho$. Graphically,

    ●   ⊢   ●-- -▶⊗
    s s x

4. **Remove:** Let s be a subject and x a node. The command

    s **remove** r for x

    deletes r from (s, x). Graphically,

    ρ $\rho - r$
    ●───▶⊗   ⊢   ●───▶⊗
    s x s x

We have stated the commands **take**, **grant**, and **remove** as operations on a single right *r*. These commands can also be applied to subsets of rights, as is done in [Jone76b,Snyd81a].

Example:
The following commands show how process *P*1 can create a new file *F*7 and add it to the directory *D*11 shown in Figure 4.33.

1.   *P*1 **create** *RW* for **new object** *F*7
2.   *P*1 **take** *t* for *D*1 from *D*
3.   *P*1 **take** *g* for *D*11 from *D*1
4.   *P*1 **grant** *RW* for *F*7 to *D*11

The effect of these commands is shown in Figure 4.35. ■

Let *G* be a protection graph. We shall write $G \vdash_c G'$ if command *c* transforms *G* into graph *G'*, $G \vdash G'$ if there exists some command *c* such that $G \vdash_c G'$, and $G \vdash^* G'$ if there exists a (possibility null) sequence of commands that transforms *G* into *G'*.

We are now ready to consider safety in the context of protection graphs. Suppose there exists a node *s* with right *r* for node *x*; thus $r \in (s, x)$. Recall that the safety question is to determine whether another subject can acquire the right *r* (not necessarily for *x*). Rather than considering whether an arbitrary subject can acquire the right *r* for an arbitrary node, we shall consider whether a particular node *p* (subject or object) can acquire the particular right *r* for *x*. We are interested in knowing whether this question is decidable, and, if so, the computational

FIGURE 4.35 Adding a new file *F*7 to directory *D*11.

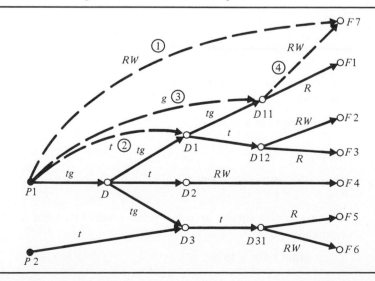

complexity of the decision procedure. Note that if this question is decidable with a decision procedure having linear time complexity $T = O(n)$ for an initial graph with n nodes, then the more general question is decidable within time $T = O(n^3)$ [only nodes (p and x) existing in the initial graph need be considered].

The safety question is formalized as follows. Given an initial graph G_0 with nodes s, x, and p such that $r \epsilon (s, x)$ and $r \notin (p, x)$, G_0 is **safe** for the right r for x if and only if $r \notin (p, x)$ in every graph G derivable from G_0 (i.e., $G_0 \vdash^* G$). We shall consider the question in two contexts: first, where s can "share" its right with other nodes (but not necessarily p), and second, where the right must be "stolen" from s.

Given an initial graph G_0 with nodes p and x such that $r \notin (p, x)$ in G_0, the predicate $can.share(r, x, p, G_0)$ is true if and only if there exists a node s in G_0 such that $r \epsilon (s, x)$ and G_0 is unsafe for the right r for x; that is, p can acquire the right r for x. To determine the conditions under which the predicate $can.share$ is true, we first observe that rights can only be transferred along edges labeled with either t or g. Two nodes x and y are **tg-connected** if there is a path between them such that each edge on the path is labeled with either t or g (the direction of the edge is not important); they are **directly tg-connected** if the path is the single edge (x, y) or (y, x). Jones, Lipton, and Snyder prove the following sufficient condition for $can.share$:

Theorem 4.9:
$can.share(r, x, p, G_0)$ is true if p is a subject and

1.   There exists a subject s in G_0 such that $r \epsilon (s, x)$ in G_0, and
2. s and p are directly tg-connected.

Proof:
There are four cases to consider:

Case 1.

The first case is simple, as p can simply take the right r from s with the command:

p **take** r for x from s

Case 2.

This case is also simple, as s can grant (share) its right to p with the command:

s **grant** r for x to p

Case 3.

This case is less obvious, as *p* cannot acquire the right with a single command. Nevertheless, with the cooperation of *s*, *p* can acquire the right with four commands:

p **create** *tg* for **new object** *y*

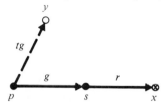

p **grant** *g* for *y* to *s*

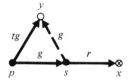

s **grant** *r* for *x* to *y*

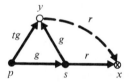

p **take** *r* for *x* from *y*

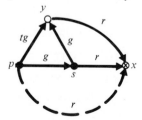

Case 4.

This case also requires four commands; we leave it as an exercise for the reader. ■

This result is easily extended to handle the case where subjects s and p are tg-connected by a path of length ≥ 1 consisting of subjects only. Letting $p = p_0, p_1,$ $\ldots, p_n = s$ denote the path between p and s, each p_i (for $i = n - 1, n - 2, \ldots, 0$) can acquire the right from p_{i+1} as described in Theorem 4.9. It turns out that tg-connectivity is also a necessary condition for *can.share* in graphs containing only subjects; this is summarized in the following theorem:

Theorem 4.10:
If G_0 is a subject-only graph, then *can.share*(r, x, p, G_0) is true if and only if:

1.   There exists a subject s in G_0 such that $r \in (s, x)$, and
2. s is tg-connected to p. ∎

If the graph can contain both subjects and objects, the situation is more complicated. Before we can state results for this case, we must first introduce some new concepts.

An **island** is any maximal subject-only tg-connected subgraph. Clearly, once a right reaches an island, it can be shared with any of the subjects on the island. We must also describe how rights are transferred between two islands.

A **tg-path** is a path $s_1, o_2, \ldots, o_{n-1}, s_n$ of $n \geq 3$ tg-connected nodes, where s_1 and s_n are subjects, and $o_2, \ldots, o_{n-1}$ are objects. A **tg-semipath** is a path $s_1, o_2,$ $\ldots, o_n$ of $n \geq 2$ tg-connected nodes, where s_1 is a subject, and $o_2, \ldots, o_n$ are objects. Each tg-path or semipath may be described by a word over the alphabet $\{\vec{t}, \vec{g}, \overleftarrow{t}, \overleftarrow{g}\}$.

Example:
The tg-path connecting p and s in the following graph

is described by the word $\vec{t}\ \vec{t}\ \overleftarrow{g}\ \overleftarrow{t}$. ∎

A **bridge** is a tg-path with an associated word in the regular expression:

$$(\vec{t})* \cup (\overleftarrow{t})* \cup (\vec{t})*\ \vec{g}\ (\overleftarrow{t})* \cup (\vec{t})*\ \overleftarrow{g}\ (\overleftarrow{t})* \ .$$

Bridges are used to transfer rights between two islands. The path $\vec{t}\ \vec{t}\ \overleftarrow{g}\ \overleftarrow{t}$ in the preceding example is a bridge; as an exercise, the reader should show how s can share its right r for x with p.

An **initial span** is a tg-semipath with associated words in

$$(\vec{t})*\ \vec{g}$$

and a **terminal span** is a tg-semipath with associated word in

$$(\vec{t})* \ .$$

The arrows emanate from the subject s_1 in the semipaths. Note that a bridge is a composition of initial and terminal spans. The idea is that a subject on one island is responsible for transferring a right over the initial span of a bridge, and a subject on the other island is responsible for transferring the right over the terminal span; the middle of the bridge represents a node across which neither subject alone can transfer rights.

We now have the following theorem:

Theorem 4.11:
The predicate *can.share*(r, x, p, G_0) is true if and only if:

1. There exists a node s such that $r \epsilon (s, x)$ in G_0; and
2. There exist subjects p' and s' such that
   a. $p' = p$ (if p is a subject) or p' is *tg*-connected to p by an initial span (if p is an object), and
   b. $s' = s$ (if s is a subject) or s' is *tg*-connected to s by a terminal span (if s is an object); and
   c. There exist islands $I_1, \ldots, I_u$ ($u \geq 1$) such that $p' \epsilon I_1$, $s' \epsilon I_u$, and there is a bridge from I_j to I_{j+1} ($1 \leq j < u$). ■

An initial span is used only when p is an object; it allows the transfer of a right

FIGURE 4.36 Path over which *r* for *x* may be transferred from *s* to *p*.

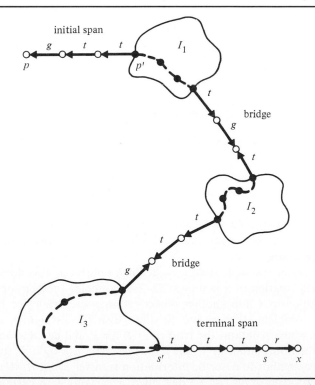

from an island to p (p is like the middle node of a bridge). A terminal span is similarly used only when s is an object; it allows the transfer of the right r from s to an island (s is like the middle node of a bridge). Figure 4.36 illustrates the path along which the right r for x is transferred from s to p.

Jones, Lipton, and Snyder proved the following theorem:

Theorem 4.12:
There is an algorithm for testing *can.share* that operates in linear time in the size of the initial graph. ■

The algorithm performs a depth first search of the protection graph (e.g., see [Aho74]).

We now turn to the question of stealing. Intuitively, a node p steals a right r for x from an owner s if it acquires r for x without the explicit cooperation of s. Formally, the predicate *can.steal*(r, x, p, G_0) is true if and only if p does not have r for x in G_0 and there exist graphs $G_1, \ldots, G_n$ such that:

1. $G_0 \vdash_{c_1} G_1 \vdash_{c_2} \ldots \vdash_{c_n} G_n$;
2. $r \epsilon (p, x)$ in G_n; and
3. For any subject s such that $r \epsilon (s, x)$ in G_0, no command c_i is of the form

    s **grant** r for x to y

    for any node y in G_{i-1}.

Note, however, that condition (3) does not rule out an owner s from transferring other rights. Snyder [Snyd81b] proved the following theorem, which states that a right must be stolen (taken) directly from its owner:

Theorem 4.13:
can.steal(r, x, p, G_0) is true if and only if:

1. There is a subject p' such that $p' = p$ (if p is a subject) or p' initially spans to p (if p is an object), and
2. There is a node s such that $r \epsilon (s, x)$ in G_0 and *can.share*(t, s, p', G_0) is true; i.e., p' can acquire the right to take from s. ■

This means if a subject cannot acquire the right to take from s, then it cannot steal a right from s by some other means. Subjects that participate in the stealing are called **conspirators**.

If a subject p cannot steal a right for an object x, this does not necessarily mean the information in x is protected. For example, another subject s may copy the information in x into another object y that p can read (see Figure 4.37). To handle this problem, Bishop and Snyder [Bish79] distinguish between **de jure** acquisition, where p obtains the read right R for x, and **de facto** acquisition, where p obtains the information in x, but not necessarily the right R for x. They introduce four commands to describe information transfer using R, W rights, and show that de facto acquisition can be described by graphs with certain kinds of RW-

FIGURE 4.37 De facto acquisition.

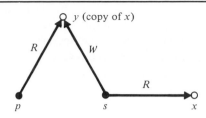

paths (analogous to the *tg*-paths). They also show de facto acquisition can be decided in time linear in the size of the initial graph. The problem of securing information flow is discussed in the next chapter.

The take-grant model is not intended to model any particular system or classes of systems, although it does describe many aspects of existing systems, especially capability systems. Nevertheless, the results are significant because they show that in properly constrained systems, safety decisions are not only possible but relatively simple. Safety is undecidable in the Harrison, Ruzzo, Ullman model because the commands of a system were unconstrained; a command could, if desired, grant some right *r* for *x* to every subject in the system. The take-grant model, on the other hand, constrains commands to pass rights only along *tg*-paths.

Snyder [Snyd77] investigated the problem of designing systems based on the take-grant model. He showed it is possible to design systems powerful enough to solve certain protection problems. One of his designs is outlined in the exercises at the end of this chapter.

Jones suggested an extension to the take-grant model for handling procedure calls and parameter passing [Jone78]. Her extension associates "property sets" with subjects and with passive procedure objects that serve as templates for subject creation. Execution of a procedure call causes a new subject to be created with rights defined by the templates.

EXERCISES

4.1 Consider the revocation scheme used by System R (see Section 4.4.2), and suppose *Sysauth* contains the following tuples for a relation *Z* created by user *A*:

User	Table	Grantor	Read	Insert	...	Copy
D	Z	A	5	5		yes
B	Z	A	10	0		yes
C	Z	B	15	0		yes
C	Z	D	20	20		yes
B	Z	C	30	30		yes
E	Z	B	40	40		no

Draw a graph showing the transfer of rights. Suppose that at time $t = 50$, A revokes all rights granted to D. Show the resulting state of *Sysauth*.

4.2 Write an algorithm for implementing the revocation procedure of System R.

4.3 Specify a policy for confinement (see Section 4.2.2), and design a capability-based mechanism for enforcing the policy.

4.4 Complete the specifications of the module shown in Figure 4.31 by writing an *OV*-function for *pop*.

4.5 Consider the representation of a Turing machine as a protection system as described in Section 4.7.2. Complete the proof of Theorem 4.2 by showing how the move $\delta(q, X) = (p, Y, R)$ can be represented with two commands. Given the access matrix shown in Figure 4.32, show the matrix that results after the following two moves:

$$\delta(q, C) = (p, D, R)$$
$$\delta(p, D) = (s, E, R) \ .$$

4.6 Complete the proof of Theorem 4.9 by giving the command sequence for Case 4.

4.7 Give a sequence of commands showing how the right r for x can be transferred over the bridge $\overrightarrow{t}\ \overrightarrow{t}\ \overleftarrow{g}\ \overleftarrow{t}$ connecting p and s in the following graph:

4.8 Let G_0 be the protection graph:

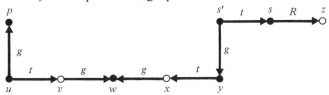

a. Give a sequence of rule applications showing *can.share*(R, z, p, G_0) is true.

b. Is *can.share*(t, s', p, G_0) true? Why or why not?

c. Show *can.steal*(R, z, p, G_0) is true, and list the conspirators.

4.9 Consider a system in which processes p and q communicate information stored in their private files through a shared message buffer b provided by a trusted supervisor process s. Show that this system can be modeled as a take-grant system with subjects s, p, and q. Show an initial state in which process p owns a file x, process q owns a file y, and the supervisor s has whatever rights it needs to establish the buffer (do not give the supervisor any more rights than it needs to do this). Construct a command sequence whereby the buffer is established, and show the graph produced by the command sequence.

REFERENCES

Aho74. Aho, A., Hopcroft, J., and Ullman, J., *The Design and Analysis of Computer Algorithms,* Addison-Wesley, Reading, Mass. (1974).

Ande72. Anderson, J. P., "Computer Security Technology Planning Study," ESD-TR-73-51, Vols. I and II, USAF Electronic Systems Div., Bedford, Mass. (Oct. 1972).

Bara64. Baran, P., "On Distributed Communications: IX. Security, Secrecy, and Tamper-Free Considerations," RM-3765-PR, The Rand Corp., Santa Monica, Calif. (1964).

Bens72. Bensoussan, A., Clingen, C. T., and Daley, R. C., "The MULTICS Virtual Memory: Concepts and Design," *Comm. ACM* Vol. 15(5) pp. 308–318 (May 1972).

Bers79. Berson, T. A. and Barksdale, G. L., "KSOS—Development Methodology for a Secure Operating System," pp. 365–371 in *Proc. NCC,* Vol. 48, AFIPS Press, Montvale, N.J. (1979).

Bish79. Bishop, M. and Snyder, L., "The Transfer of Information and Authority in a Protection System," *Proc. 7th Symp. on Oper. Syst. Princ., ACM Oper. Syst. Rev.,* pp. 45–54 (Dec. 1979).

Boye79. Boyer, R. and Moore, J. S., *A Computational Logic,* Academic Press, New York (1979).

Boye80. Boyer, R. and Moore, J. S., "A Verification Condition Generator for Fortran," Computer Science Lab. Report CSL-103, SRI International, Menlo Park, Calif. (June 1980).

Broa76. Broadbridge, R. and Mekota, J., "Secure Communications Processor Specification," ESD-TR-76-351, AD-A055164, Honeywell Information Systems, McLean, Va. (June 1976).

Buck80. Buckingham, B. R. S., "CL/SWARD Command Language," SRI-CSL-79-013c, IBM Systems Research Institute, New York (Sept. 1980).

Carl75. Carlstedt, J., Bisbey, R. II, and Popek, G., "Pattern-Directed Protection Evaluation," NTIS AD-A012-474, Information Sciences Inst., Univ. of Southern Calif., Marina del Rey, Calif. (June 1975).

Cash76. Cash, J., Haseman, W. D., and Whinston, A. B., "Security for the GPLAN System," *Info. Systems* Vol. 2 pp. 41–48 (1976).

Cheh81. Cheheyl, M. H., Gasser, M., Huff, G. A., and Millen, J. K. "Verifying Security," *ACM Computing Surveys* Vol. 13(3) pp. 279–339 (Sept. 1981).

Codd70. Codd, E. F., "A Relational Model for Large Shared Data Banks," *Comm. ACM* Vol. 13(6) pp. 377–387 (1970).

Codd79. Codd, E. F., "Extending the Database Relational Model to Capture More Meaning," *ACM Trans. on Database Syst.* Vol. 4(4) pp. 397–434 (Dec. 1979).

Cohe75. Cohen, E. and Jefferson, D., "Protection in the HYDRA Operating System," *Proc. 5th Symp. on Oper. Syst. Princ., ACM Oper. Syst. Rev.* Vol. 9(5) pp. 141–160 (Nov. 1975).

Conw72. Conway, R. W., Maxwell, W. L., and Morgan, H. L., "On the Implementation of Security Measures in Information Systems," *Comm. ACM* Vol. 15(4) pp. 211–220 (Apr. 1972).

Dahl72. Dahl, O. J. and Hoare, C. A. R., "Hierarchical Program Structures," in *Structured Programming,* ed. Dahl, Dijkstra, Hoare, Academic Press, New York (1972).

Dale65. Daley, R. C. and Neumann, P. G., "A General-Purpose File System for Secondary Storage," pp. 213–229 in *Proc. Fall Jt. Computer Conf.,* Vol. 27, AFIPS Press, Montvale, N.J. (1965).

Denn78. Denning, D. E., Denning, P. J., Garland, S. J., Harrison, M. A., and Ruzzo, W. L.,

"Proving Protection Systems Safe," Computer Sciences Dept., Purdue Univ., W. Lafayette, Ind. (Feb. 1978).

DenP71a. Denning, P. J., "An Undergraduate Course on Operating Systems Principles," Report of the Cosine Comm. of the Commission on Education, National Academy of Engineering, Washington, D.C. (June 1971).

DenP71b. Denning, P. J., "Third Generation Computer Systems," *Computing Surveys* Vol. 3(4) pp. 175–216 (Dec. 1971).

DeVH66. Dennis, J. B. and VanHorn, E. C., "Programming Semantics for Multipro-grammed Computations," *Comm. ACM* Vol. 9(3) pp. 143–155 (Mar. 1966).

Dens80. Dennis, T. D., "A Capability Architecture," Ph.D. Thesis, Computer Sciences Dept., Purdue Univ., W. Lafayette, Ind. (1980).

Dijk68. Dijkstra, E. W., "The Structure of the 'THE'—Multiprogramming System," *Comm. ACM* Vol. 11(5) pp. 341–346 (May 1968).

Down77. Downs, D. and Popek, G. J., "A Kernel Design for a Secure Data Base Manage-ment System," pp. 507–514 in *Proc. 3rd Conf. Very Large Data Bases,* IEEE and ACM, New York (1977).

Engl74. England, D. M., "Capability Concept Mechanism and Structure in System 250," pp. 63–82 in *Proc. Int. Workshop on Protection in Operating Systems,* Inst. Re-cherche d'Informatique, Rocquencourt, Le Chesnay, France (Aug. 1974).

Fabr71a. Fabry, R. S., "Preliminary Description of a Supervisor for a Machine Oriented Around Capabilities," ICR Quarterly Report 18, Univ. of Chicago, Chicago, Ill. (Mar. 1971).

Fabr71b. Fabry, R. S., "List Structured Addressing," Ph.D. Thesis, Univ. of Chicago, Chicago, Ill. (Mar. 1971).

Fabr74. Fabry, R. S. "Capability-Based Addressing," *Comm. ACM* Vol. 17(7) pp. 403–412 (July 1974).

Fagi78. Fagin, R., "On an Authorization Mechanism," *ACM Trans. on Database Syst.* Vol. 3(3) pp. 310–319 (Sept. 1978).

Feie79. Feiertag, R. J. and Neumann, P. G., "The Foundations of a Provably Secure Operating System (PSOS)," pp. 329–334 in *Proc. NCC,* Vol. 48, AFIPS Press, Montvale, N.J. (1979).

Floy67. Floyd, R. W., "Assigning Meaning to Programs," pp. 19–32 in *Math. Aspects of Computer Science,* ed. J. T. Schwartz, Amer. Math. Soc. (1967).

Gehr79. Gehringer, E., "Variable-Length Capabilities as a Solution to the Small-Object Problem," *Proc. 7th Symp. on Oper. Syst. Princ., ACM Oper. Syst. Rev.,* pp. 131–142 (Dec. 1979).

Giff82. Gifford, D. K., "Cryptographic Sealing for Information Security and Authentica-tion," *Comm. ACM* (Apr. 1982).

Gold79. Gold, B. D., Linde, R. R., Peeler, R. J., Schaefer, M., Scheid, J. F., and Ward, P. D., "A Security Retrofit of VM/370," pp. 335–344 in *Proc. NCC,* Vol. 48, AFIPS Press, Montvale, N.J. (1979).

GrDe72. Graham, G. S. and Denning, P. J., "Protection—Principles and Practice," pp. 417–429 in *Proc. Spring Jt. Computer Conf.,* Vol. 40, AFIPS Press, Montvale, N. J. (1972).

Grah68. Graham, R. M., "Protection in an Information Processing Utility," *Comm. ACM* Vol. 11(5) pp. 365–369 (May 1968).

Grif76. Griffiths, P. P. and Wade, B. W., "An Authorization Mechanism for a Relational Database System," *ACM Trans. on Database Syst.* Vol. 1(3) pp. 242–255 (Sept. 1976).

Harr76. Harrison, M. A., Ruzzo, W. L., and Ullman, J. D., "Protection in Operating Systems," *Comm. ACM* Vol. 19(8) pp. 461–471 (Aug. 1976).

Harr78. Harrison, M. A. and Ruzzo, W. L., "Monotonic Protection Systems," pp. 337–365 in *Foundations of Secure Computation,* ed. R. A. DeMillo et al., Academic Press, New York (1978).

Hart76. Hartson, H. R. and Hsiao, D. K., "Full Protection Specifications in the Semantic Model for Database Protection Languages," *Proc. 1976 ACM Annual Conf.,* pp. 90–95 (Oct. 1976).

Hebb80. Hebbard, B. et al., "A Penetration Analysis of the Michigan Terminal System," *ACM Oper. Syst. Rev.* Vol. 14(1) pp. 7–20 (Jan. 1980).

Hoff71. Hoffman, L. J., "The Formulary Model for Flexible Privacy and Access Control," pp. 587–601 in *Proc. Fall Jt. Computer Conf.,* Vol. 39, AFIPS Press, Montvale, N.J. (1971).

IBM68. IBM, "IBM System/360 Principles of Operation," IBM Report No. GA22-6821 (Sept. 1968).

Ilif62. Iliffe, J. K. and Jodeit, J. G., "A Dynamic Storage Allocation System," *Computer J.* Vol. 5 pp. 200–209 (1962).

Ilif72. Iliffe, J. K., *Basic Machine Principles,* Elsevier/MacDonald, New York (1st ed. 1968, 2nd ed. 1972).

Jone76a. Jones, A. K. and Liskov, B. H., "A Language Extension Mechanism for Controlling Access to Shared Data," *Proc. 2nd Int. Conf. Software Eng.,* pp. 62–68 (1976).

Jone76b. Jones, A. K., Lipton, R. J., and Snyder, L., "A Linear Time Algorithm for Deciding Security," *Proc. 17th Annual Symp. on Found. of Comp. Sci.* (1976).

Jone78. Jones, A. K., "Protection Mechanism Models: Their Usefulness," pp. 237–254 in *Foundations of Secure Computation,* ed. R. A. DeMillo et al., Academic Press, New York (1978).

Jone79. Jones, A. K., Chansler, R. J., Durham, I., Schwans, K., and Vegdahl, S. R., "StarOS, a Multiprocessor Operating System for the Support of Task Forces," *Proc. 7th Symp. on Oper. Syst. Princ., ACM Oper. Sys. Rev.,* pp. 117–121 (Dec. 1979).

Kahn81. Kahn, K. C., Corwin, W. M., Dennis, T. D., D'Hooge, H., Hubka, D. E., Hutchins, L. A., Montague, J. T., Pollack, F. J., Gifkins, M. R., "iMAX: A Multiprocessor Operating System for an Object-Based Computer," *Proc. 8th Symp. on Oper. Syst. Princ., ACM Oper. Syst. Rev.,* Vol. 15(5), pp. 127–136 (Dec. 1981).

Krci80. Kreissig, G., "A Model to Describe Protection Problems," pp. 9–17 in *Proc. 1980 Symp. on Security and Privacy,* IEEE Computer Society (Apr. 1980).

Lamp69. Lampson, B. W., "Dynamic Protection Structures," pp. 27–38 in *Proc. Fall Jt. Computer Conf.,* Vol. 35, AFIPS Press, Montvale, N.J. (1969).

Lamp71. Lampson, B. W., "Protection," *Proc. 5th Princeton Symp. of Info. Sci. and Syst.,* pp. 437–443 Princeton Univ., (Mar. 1971). Reprinted in *ACM Oper. Syst. Rev.,* Vol. 8(1) pp. 18–24 (Jan. 1974).

Lamp73. Lampson, B. W., "A Note on the Confinement Problem," *Comm. ACM* Vol. 16(10) pp. 613–615 (Oct. 1973).

Lamp76a. Lampson, B. W., Horning, J. J., London, R. L., Mitchell, J. G., and Popek, G. J., "Report on the Programming Language Euclid" (Aug. 1976).

Lamp76b. Lampson, B. W. and Sturgis, H. E., "Reflections on an Operating System Design," *Comm. ACM* Vol. 19(5) pp. 251–265 (May 1976).

Levi81. Levitt, K. N. and Neumann, P. G., "Recent SRI Work in Verification," *ACM SIGSOFT Software Engineering Notes* Vol. 6(3) pp. 33–47. (July 1981).

Lind75. Linde, R. R., "Operating System Penetration," pp. 361–368 in *Proc. NCC,* Vol. 44,

AFIPS Press, Montvale, N.J. (1975).

Linn76. Linden, T. A., "Operating System Structures to Support Security and Reliable Software," *Computing Surveys* Vol. 8(4) pp. 409–445 (Dec. 1976).

Lisk77. Liskov, B. H., Snyder, A., Atkinson, R., and Schaffert, C., "Abstraction Mechanisms in CLU," *Comm. ACM* Vol. 20(8) pp. 564–576 (Aug. 1977).

McCa79. McCauley, E. J. and Drongowski, P. J., "KSOS—The Design of a Secure Operating System," pp. 345–353 in *Proc. NCC,* Vol. 48, AFIPS Press, Montvale, N.J. (1979).

Mill76. Millen, J. K., "Security Kernel Validation in Practice," *Comm. ACM* Vol. 19(5) pp. 243–250 (May 1976).

Mins67. Minsky, M., *Computation: Finite and Infinite Machines,* Prentice-Hall, Englewood Cliffs, N.J. (1967).

MinN78. Minsky, N., "The Principle of Attenuation of Privileges and its Ramifications," pp. 255–276 in *Foundations of Secure Computation,* ed. R. A. DeMillo et al., Academic Press, New York (1978).

Morr78. Morris, J. B., "Programming by Successive Refinement," Dept. of Computer Sciences, Purdue Univ., W. Lafayette, Ind. (1978).

Mors73. Morris, J. H., "Protection in Programming Languages," *Comm. ACM* Vol. 16(1) pp. 15–21 (Jan. 1973).

Myer78. Myers, G., *Advances in Computer Architecture,* John Wiley & Sons, New York (1978).

Myer80. Myers, G. and Buckingham, B. R. S., "A Hardware Implementation of Capability-Based Addressing," *ACM Oper. Syst. Rev.* Vol. 14(4) pp. 13–25 (Oct. 1980).

Need77. Needham, R. M. and Walker, R. D. H., "The Cambridge CAP Computer and Its Protection System," *Proc. 6th Symp. on Oper. Syst. Princ., ACM Oper. Syst. Rev.* Vol. 11(5) pp. 1–10 (Nov. 1977).

Neum78. Neumann, P. G., "Computer Security Evaluation," pp. 1087–1095 in *Proc. NCC,* Vol. 47, AFIPS Press, Montvale, N.J. (1978).

Neum80. Neumann, P. G., Boyer, R. S., Feiertag, R. J., Levitt, K. N., and Robinson, L., "A Provably Secure Operating System: The System, Its Applications, and Proofs," Computer Science Lab. Report CSL-116, SRI International, Menlo Park, Calif. (May 1980).

Orga72. Organick, E. I., *The Multics System: An Examination of Its Structure,* MIT Press, Cambridge, Mass. (1972).

Parn72. Parnas, D. L., "A Technique for Module Specification with Examples," *Comm. ACM* Vol. 15(5) pp. 330–336 (May 1972).

Pope74. Popek, G. J. and Kline, C. S., "Verifiable Secure Operating System Software," pp. 145–151 in *Proc. NCC,* Vol. 43, AFIPS Press, Montvale, N.J. (1974).

Pope78. Popek, G. J. and Farber, D. A., "A Model for Verification of Data Security in Operating Systems," *Comm. ACM* Vol. 21(9) pp. 737–749 (Sept. 1978).

Pope79. Popek, G. J., Kampe, M., Kline, C. S., Stoughton, A., Urban, M., and Walton, E., "UCLA Secure Unix," pp. 355–364 in *Proc. NCC,* Vol. 48, AFIPS Press, Montvale, N.J. (1979).

Pric73. Price, W. R., "Implications of a Vertical Memory Mechanism for Implementing Protection in a Family of Operating Systems," Ph.D. Thesis, Comp. Sci. Dept., Carnegie-Mellon Univ., Pittsburgh, Pa. (1973).

Rede74. Redell, D. R. and Fabry, R. S., "Selective Revocation and Capabilities," pp. 197–209 in *Proc. Int. Workshop on Protection in Operating Systems,* Inst. de Recherche d'Informatique, Rocquencourt, Le Chesnay, France (Aug. 1974).

Ritc74. Ritchie, D. M. and Thompson, K., "The UNIX Time-Sharing System," *Comm. ACM* Vol. 17(7) pp. 365–375 (July 1974).

Robi77. Robinson, L. and Levitt, K. N., "Proof Techniques for Hierarchically Structured Programs," *Comm. ACM* Vol. 20(4) pp. 271–283 (Apr. 1977).

Robi79. Robinson, L.,"The HDM Handbook, Volume I: The Foundations of HDM," SRI Project 4828, SRI International, Menlo Park, Calif. (June 1979).

Roge67. Rogers, H., *Theory of Recursive Functions and Effective Computability,* McGraw-Hill, New York (1967). Section 11.2

Rush81. Rushby, J. M., "Design and Verification of Secure Systems," *Proc. 8th Symp. on Oper. Syst. Princ., ACM Oper. Syst. Rev.,* Vol. 15(5), pp. 12–21 (Dec. 1981).

Salt75. Saltzer, J. H. and Schroeder, M. D., "The Protection of Information in Computer Systems," *Proc. IEEE* Vol. 63(9) pp. 1278–1308 (Sept. 1975).

Schi75. Schiller, W. L., "The Design and Specification of a Security Kernel for the PDP 11/45," ESD-TR-75-69, The MITRE Corp., Bedford, Mass. (Mar. 1975).

Schr72. Schroeder, M. D. and Saltzer, J. H., "A Hardware Architecture for Implementing Protection Rings," *Comm. ACM* Vol. 15(3) pp. 157–170 (Mar. 1972).

Schr77. Schroeder, M. D., Clark, D. D., and Saltzer, J. H., "The MULTICS Kernel Design Project," *Proc. 6th Symp. on Oper. Syst. Princ., ACM Oper. Syst. Rev.* Vol. 11(5) pp. 43–56 (Nov. 1977).

Sevc74. Sevcik, K. C. and Tsichritzis, D. C., "Authorization and Access Control Within Overall System Design," pp. 211–224 in *Proc. Int. Workshop on Protection in Operating Systems,* IRIA, Rocquencourt, Le Chesnay, France (1974).

Silv79. Silverberg, B., Robinson, L., and Levitt, K., "The HDM Handbook, Volume II: The Languages and Tools of HDM," SRI Project 4828, SRI International, Menlo Park, Calif. (June 1979).

Snyd77. Snyder, L., "On the Synthesis and Analysis of Protection Systems," *Proc. 6th Symp. on Oper. Syst. Princ., ACM Oper. Syst. Rev.* Vol. 11(5) pp. 141–150 (Nov. 1977).

Snyd81a. Snyder, L., "Formal Models of Capability-Based Protection Systems," *IEEE Trans. on Computers* Vol. C-30(3) pp. 172–181 (Mar. 1981).

Snyd81b. Snyder, L., "Theft and Conspiracy in the Take-Grant Model," *JCSS* Vol. 23(3), pp. 333–347 (Dec. 1981).

Ston74. Stonebraker, M. and Wong, E., "Access Control in a Relational Data Base Management System by Query Modification," *Proc. 1974 ACM Annual Conf.,* pp. 180–186 (Nov. 1974).

Walk80. Walker, B. J., Kemmerer, R. A., and Popek, G. J., "Specification and Verification of the UCLA Unix Security Kernel," *Comm. ACM* Vol. 23(2) pp. 118–131 (Feb. 1980).

Walt75. Walter, K. G. et al., "Structured Specification of a Security Kernel," *Proc. Int. Conf. Reliable Software, ACM SIGPLAN Notices* Vol. 10(6) pp. 285–293 (June 1975).

Wulf74. Wulf, W. A., Cohen, E., Corwin, W., Jones, A., Levin, R., Pierson, C., and Pollack, F., "HYDRA: The Kernel of a Multiprocessor System," *Comm. ACM* Vol. 17(6) pp. 337–345 (June 1974).

Wulf76. Wulf, W. A., London, R. L., and Shaw, M., "An Introduction to the Construction and Verification of Alphard Programs," *IEEE Trans. on Software Eng.* Vol. SE-2(4) pp. 253–265 (Dec. 1976).

5

Information Flow Controls

Access controls regulate the accessing of objects, but not what subjects might do with the information contained in them. Many difficulties with information "leakage" arise not from defective access control, but from the lack of any policy about information flow. Flow controls are concerned with the right of **dissemination of information,** irrespective of what object holds the information; they specify valid channels along which information may flow.

5.1 LATTICE MODEL OF INFORMATION FLOW

We shall describe flow controls using the lattice model introduced by Denning [Denn75,Denn76a]. The lattice model is an extension of the Bell and LaPadula [Bell73] model, which describes the security policies of military systems (see Section 5.6).

The lattice model was introduced to describe policies and channels of information flow, but not what it means for information to flow from one object to another. We shall extend the model to give a precise definition of information flow in terms of classical information theory.

An **information flow system** is modeled by a lattice-structured flow policy, states, and state transitions.

5.1.1 Information Flow Policy

An information flow policy is defined by a lattice $(SC, \leq)$, where SC is a finite set of **security classes,** and $\leq$ is a binary relation† partially ordering the classes of

---

† In [Denn76a], the notation "$\rightarrow$" is used to denote the relation "$\leq$".

SC. The security classes correspond to disjoint classes of information; they are intended to encompass, but are not limited to, the familiar concepts of "security classifications" and "security categories" [Weis69,Gain72].

For security classes *A* and *B*, the relation $A \leq B$ means class *A* information is lower than or equal to class *B* information. Information is permitted to flow within a class or upward, but not downward or to unrelated classes; thus, class *A* information is permitted to flow into class *B* if and only if $A \leq B$. There is a lowest class, denoted *Low*, such that $Low \leq A$ for all classes *A* in *SC*. *Low* security information is permitted to flow anywhere. Similarly, there is a highest class, denoted *High*, such that $A \leq High$ for all *A*. *High* security information cannot leave the class *High*. The lattice properties of $(SC, \leq)$ are discussed in Sections 5.1.4 and 5.1.5.

Example:

The simplest flow policy specifies just two classes of information: confidential (*High*) and nonconfidential (*Low*); thus, all flows except those from confidential to nonconfidential objects are allowed. This policy specifies the requirements for a **selectively confined** service program that handles both confidential and nonconfidential data [Denn74,Fent74]. The service program is allowed to retain the customer's nonconfidential data, but it is not allowed to retain or leak any confidential data. An income tax computing service, for example, might be allowed to retain a customer's address and the bill for services rendered, but not the customer's income or deductions. This policy is enforced with flow controls that assign all outputs of the service program to class *Low,* except for the results returned to the customer. ■

Example:

The **multilevel security** policy for government and military systems represents each security class by a pair (*A, C*), where *A* denotes an **authority level** and *C* a **category**. There are four authority levels:

  0—*Unclassified*
  1—*Confidential*
  2—*Secret*
  3—*Top Secret* .

There are 2^m categories, comprising all possible combinations of *m* compartments for some *m*; examples of compartments might be *Atomic* and *Nuclear*. Given classes (*A, C*) and (*A', C'*), $(A, C) \leq (A', C')$ if and only if $A \leq A'$ and $C \subseteq C'$. Transmissions from (2, {*Atomic*}) to (2, {*Atomic, Nuclear*}) or to (3, {*Atomic*}) are permitted, for example, but those from (2, {*Atomic*}) to (1, {*Atomic*}) or to (3, {*Nuclear*}) are not. ■

5.1.2 Information State

The **information state** of a system is described by the value and security class of each object in the system. An object may be a logical structure such as a file, record, field within a record, or program variable; or it may be a physical structure such as a memory location, register (including an address or instruction register), or a user. For an object x, we shall write "x" for both the name and value of x (the correct interpretation should be clear from context), and $\underline{x}$ (x with an underbar) for its security class. When we want to specify the value and class of x in some particular state s, we shall write x_s and $\underline{x}_s$, respectively. We shall write simply x and $\underline{x}$ when the state is clear from context or unimportant to the discussion.

The class of an object may be either constant or varying. With **fixed** or **constant** classes (also called "static binding"), the class of an object x is constant over the lifetime of x; that is, $\underline{x}_s = \underline{x}_{s'}$ for all states s and s' that include x. With **variable** classes (also called "dynamic binding"), the class of an object x varies with its contents; that is, $\underline{x}_s$ depends on x_s. A flow control mechanism could support both fixed and variable classes—for example, fixed classes for permanent or global objects, and variable ones for temporary or local ones. Users are assigned fixed classes called "security clearances". Unless explicitly stated otherwise, all objects have fixed security classes.

Given objects x and y, a flow from x to y is **authorized** (permitted) by a flow policy if and only if $\underline{x} \leq \underline{y}$; if y has a variable class, then $\underline{y}$ is its class after the flow.

5.1.3 State Transitions and Information Flow

State transitions are modeled by operations that create and delete objects, and operations that change the value or security class of an object. Information flows are always associated with operations that change the value of an object. For example, execution of the file copy operation "$copy(F1, F2)$" causes information to flow from file $F1$ to file $F2$. Execution of the assignment statement "$y := x/1000$" causes some information to flow from x to y, but less than the assignment "$y := x$".

To determine which operations cause information flow, and the amount of information they transfer, we turn to information theory [see Section 1.4.1; in particular, Eq. (1.1) and (1.2)]. Let s' be the state that results from execution of a command sequence α in state s, written

$$s \vdash_\alpha s'$$

(read "s derives s' under α"). Given an object x in s and an object y in s', let $H_y(x)$ be the equivocation (conditional entropy) of x_s given $y_{s'}$, and let $H_y(x)$ be the equivocation of x_s given the value y_s of y in state s; if y does not exist in state s, then $H_y(x) = H(x)$, where $H(x)$ is the entropy (uncertainty) of x. Execution of α in state s causes **information flow** from x to y, denoted

$$x_s \rightarrow_\alpha y_{s'} \; ,$$

if new information about x_s can be determined from $y_{s'}$; that is, if

$$H_{y'}(x) < H_y(x) \; .$$

We shall write $x \rightarrow_\alpha y$, or simply $x \rightarrow y$, if there exist states s and s' such that execution of command sequence α causes a flow $x \to y$. Cohen's [Cohe77,Cohe78] definition of "strong dependency" and Millen's [Mill78] and Furtek's [Furt78] deductive formulations of information flow are similar to this definition, but they do not account for the probability distribution of the values of variables as provided by Shannon's information theory.

A flow $x_s \to_\alpha y_{s'}$ is authorized if and only if $\underline{x}_s \leq \underline{y}_{s'}$; that is, the final class of y is at least as great as the initial class of x.

The **amount of information** (in bits) transferred by a flow $x_s \to_\alpha y_{s'}$ is measured by the reduction in the uncertainty about x:

$$I(\alpha, x, y, s, s') = H_y(x) - H_{y'}(x) .$$

Letting $P_s(x)$ denote the probability distribution of x in state s, the **channel capacity** of $x \to_\alpha y$ is defined by the maximum amount of information transferred over all possible probability distributions of x:

$$C(\alpha, x, y) = \max_{P_s(x)} I(\alpha, x, y, s, s')$$

Note that if y can be represented with n bits, the channel capacity of any command sequence transferring information to y can be at most n bits. This means that if the value of y is derived from m inputs $x_1, \ldots, x_m$, on the average only m/n bits can be transferred from each input.

The following examples illustrate how the previous definitions are applied.

Example:
Consider the assignment

$$y := x .$$

Suppose x is an integer variable in the range $[0, 15]$, with all values equally likely. Letting p_i denote the probability that $x = i$, we have

$$p_i = \begin{cases} \dfrac{1}{16} & 0 \leq i \leq 15 \\ 0 & \text{otherwise} . \end{cases}$$

If y is initially null, then

$$H_y(x) = H(x) = \sum_i p_i \log_2\left(\frac{1}{p_i}\right) = 16\left(\frac{1}{16}\right) \log_2 16 = 4 .$$

Because the exact value of x can be determined from y after the statement is executed, $H_{y'}(x) = 0$. Thus, 4 bits of information are transferred to y.

The capacity of an assignment "$y := x$" is usually much greater than 4 bits. If x and y are represented as 32-bit words, for example, the capacity is 32 bits. Or, if x and y are vectors of length n, where each vector element is a 32-bit word, the capacity is $32n$. In both cases, the capacity is achieved when all possible words are equally likely.

Note that the statement "$y := x$" does not cause a flow $x \to y$ if the value of x is known. This is because $H_{y'}(x) = H_y(x) = H(x) = 0$. ∎

Example:
Consider the sequence of statements

$z := x;$
$y := z .$

Execution of this sequence can cause an "indirect flow" $x \rightarrow y$ through the intermediate variable z, as well as a direct flow $x \rightarrow z$. Note, however, that the sequence does not cause a flow $z \rightarrow y$, because the final value of y does not reveal any information about the initial value of z. ■

Example:
Consider the statement

$z := x + y .$

Let x and y be in the range [0, 15] with all values equally likely; thus $H(x)$ $= H(y) = 4$ bits. Given z, the values of x and y are no longer equally likely (e.g., $z = 0$ implies both x and y must be 0, $z = 1$ implies either $x = 0$ and y $= 1$ or $x = 1$ and $y = 0$). Thus, both $H_z(x)$ and $H_z(y)$ are less than 4 bits, and execution of the statement reduces the uncertainty about both x and y.

Now, little can be deduced about the values of x and y from their sum when both values are unknown. Yet if one of the elements is known, the other element can be determined exactly. In general, the sum $z = x_1 + \dots$ $+ x_n$ of n elements contains some information about the individual elements. Given additional information about some of the elements, it is often possible to deduce the unknown elements (e.g., given the sum $z1$ of $n - 1$ elements, the nth element can be determined exactly from the difference $z - z1$). The problem of hiding confidential information in sums (and other statistics) is studied in the next chapter. ■

Example:
It may seem surprising that the syntactically similar statement

$z := x \oplus y ,$

where x and y are as described in the previous example and "$\oplus$" denotes the exclusive-or operator, does not cause information to flow to z. This is because the value of z does not reduce the uncertainty about either x or y (all values of x and y are equally likely for any given z). This is a Vernam cipher, where x is the plaintext, y is the key, and z is the ciphertext. This example shows it is not enough for an object y to be functionally dependent on an object x for there to be a flow $x \rightarrow y$. It must be possible to learn something new about x from y.

We saw in Chapter 1 that most ciphers are theoretically breakable given enough ciphertext; thus, encryption generally causes information to flow from a plaintext message M to a ciphertext message $C = E_K(M)$. Determining M from C may be computationally infeasible, however, whence the information in C is not practically useful. Thus, in practice high security information can be encrypted and transmitted over a low security channel without violating a flow policy. ■

Example:

Consider the **if** statement

if $x = 1$ then $y := 1$,

where y is initially 0. Suppose x is 0 or 1, with both values equally likely; thus $H(x) = 1$. After this statement is executed, y contains the exact value of x, giving $H_y(x) = 0$. Thus, 1 bit of information is transferred from x to y. Even if x is not restricted to the range [0, 1], the value of y reduces the uncertainty about x ($y = 1$ implies $x = 1$ and $y = 0$ implies $x \neq 1$).

The flow $x \longrightarrow y$ caused by executing the **if** statement is called an **implicit flow** to distinguish it from an **explicit flow** caused by an assignment. The interesting aspect of an implicit flow $x \longrightarrow y$ is that it can occur even in the absence of any explicit assignment to y. For the preceding **if** statement, the flow occurs even when $x \neq 1$ and the assignment to y is skipped. There must be a possibility of executing an assignment to y, however, and this assignment must be conditioned on the value of x; otherwise, the value of y cannot reduce the uncertainty about x.

The information in an implicit flow is encoded in the program counter (instruction register) of a process when it executes a conditional branch instruction. This information remains in the program counter as long as the execution path of the program depends on the outcome of the test, but is lost thereafter. ■

Example:

Consider the statement

if $(x = 1)$ and $(y = 1)$ then $z := 1$,

where z is initially 0. Suppose x and y are both 0 or 1, with both values equally likely; thus $H(x) = H(y) = 1$. Execution of this statement transfers information about both x and y to z ($z = 1$ implies $x = y = 1$, and $z = 0$ implies $x = 0$ with probability 2/3 and $x = 1$ with probability 1/3; similarly for y). The equivocations $H_z(x)$ and $H_z(y)$ are both approximately .7 (derivation of this is left as an exercise). Thus, the amount of information transferred about each of x and y is approximately .3 bit, and the total amount of information transferred is about .6 bit.

Rewriting the statement as a nested conditional structure

if $x = 1$
    then if $y = 1$ then $z := 1$

shows that implicit flows can be transferred through several layers of nesting. ■

Example:

Consider the **if** statement

$$\text{if } x \geq 8 \text{ then } y := 1 \ ,$$

where y is initially 0. Again suppose x is an integer variable in the range [0, 15], with all values equally likely, so $H(x) = 4$. To derive the equivocation $H_y(x)$ from executing this statement, let q_j be the probability $y' = j$ ($j = 0$ or 1), and let $q_j(i)$ be the probability $x = i$ given $y' = j$. Then

$$q_0 = q_1 = \frac{1}{2}$$

$$q_0(i) = \begin{cases} \frac{1}{8} & 0 \leq i \leq 7 \\ 0 & \text{otherwise} \end{cases}$$

$$q_1(i) = \begin{cases} \frac{1}{8} & 8 \leq i \leq 15 \\ 0 & \text{otherwise} \end{cases}$$

and

$$H_y(x) = \sum_{j=0}^{1} q_j \sum_{i=0}^{15} q_j(i) \log_2 \left(\frac{1}{q_j(i)} \right)$$

$$= \left(\frac{1}{2} \right) [8 \left(\frac{1}{8} \right) \log_2 8] + \left(\frac{1}{2} \right) [8 \left(\frac{1}{8} \right) \log_2 8]$$

$$= \left(\frac{1}{2} \right) 3 + \left(\frac{1}{2} \right) 3 = 3 \ .$$

Execution of this statement, therefore, transfers 1 bit of information about x to y (namely, the high-order bit).

Suppose instead x has the following distribution:

$$p_i = \begin{cases} \frac{1}{16} & 0 \leq i \leq 7 \\ \frac{1}{2} & i = 8 \\ 0 & \text{otherwise} \ . \end{cases}$$

The uncertainty of x is:

$$H(x) = 8 \left(\frac{1}{16} \right) \log_2 16 + \left(\frac{1}{2} \right) \log_2 2 = 2.0 + 0.5 = 2.5 \ .$$

The probability distributions of y and of x given y are:

$$q_0 = q_1 = \frac{1}{2}$$

$$q_0(i) = \begin{cases} \dfrac{1}{8} & 0 \le i \le 7 \\ 0 & \text{otherwise} \end{cases}$$

$$q_1(i) = \begin{cases} 1 & i = 8 \\ 0 & \text{otherwise} \end{cases} .$$

Therefore,

$$H_{y'}(x) = \left(\frac{1}{2}\right) 8 \left(\frac{1}{8}\right) \log_2 8 + \left(\frac{1}{2}\right) \log_2 1 = \left(\frac{1}{2}\right) 3 + \left(\frac{1}{2}\right) 0 = 1.5 .$$

Again, 1 bit of information is transferred. This is because y is assigned the value 1 with probability $1/2$. It may seem that more than 1 bit of information can be transferred by this statement, because when y is assigned the value 1, there is no uncertainty about x—it must be 8. On the other hand, when y is assigned the value 0, there is still uncertainty about the exact value of x—it could be anything between 0 and 7. The equivocation $H_{y'}(x)$ measures the expected uncertainty of x over all possible assignments to y. ∎

In general, an **if** statement of the form

if $f(x)$ **then** $y := 1$

for some function f transfers 1 bit when the probability $f(x)$ is true is $1/2$. Let p_i be the probability $x = i$ for all possible values i of x. Assuming y is initially 0 and $H_y(x) = H(x)$, we have

$$q_0 = q_1 = \frac{1}{2}$$

$$q_0(i) = \begin{cases} 2p_i & \text{if } f(i) \text{ is false} \\ 0 & \text{otherwise} \end{cases}$$

$$q_1(i) = \begin{cases} 2p_i & \text{if } f(i) \text{ is true} \\ 0 & \text{otherwise} \end{cases}$$

whence:

$$H_{y'}(x) = \left(\frac{1}{2}\right) \sum_i q_0(i) \log_2 \left(\frac{1}{q_0(i)}\right) + \left(\frac{1}{2}\right) \sum_i q_1(i) \log_2 \left(\frac{1}{q_1(i)}\right)$$

$$= \left(\frac{1}{2}\right) \sum_i 2p_i \log_2 \left(\frac{1}{2p_i}\right) = \sum_i p_i \log_2 \left(\frac{1}{2p_i}\right)$$

$$= \sum_i p_i \log_2 \left(\frac{1}{p_i}\right) - \sum_i p_i \log_2 2$$

$$= H(x) - 1 .$$

If the probability $f(x)$ is true is not $1/2$, less than 1 bit of information will be transferred (see exercises at end of chapter).

It should now come as no surprise that the channel capacity of the statement

if $f(x)$ **then** $y := 1$

is at most 1 bit. The reason is simple: because y can be represented by 1 bit (0 or 1), it cannot contain more than 1 bit of information about x.

5.1.4 Lattice Structure

A flow policy $(SC, \leq)$ is a **lattice** if it is a partially ordered set (poset) and there exist least upper and greatest lower bound operators, denoted $\oplus$ and $\otimes$ respectively†, on SC (e.g., see [Birk67]). That $(SC, \leq)$ is a **poset** implies the relation $\leq$ is reflexive, transitive, and antisymmetric; that is, for all A, B, and C in SC:

1. Reflexive: $A \leq A$
2. Transitive: $A \leq B$ and $B \leq C$ implies $A \leq C$
3. Antisymmetric: $A \leq B$ and $B \leq A$ implies $A = B$.

That $\oplus$ is a **least upper bound** operator on SC implies for each pair of classes A and B in SC, there exists a unique class $C = A \oplus B$ in SC such that:

1. $A \leq C$ and $B \leq C$, and
2. $A \leq D$ and $B \leq D$ implies $C \leq D$ for all D in SC .

By extension, corresponding to any nonempty subset of classes $S = \{A_1, \ldots, A_n\}$ of SC, there is a unique element $\oplus S = A_1 \oplus A_2 \oplus \ldots \oplus A_n$ which is the least upper bound for the subset. The highest security class, $High$, is thus $High = \oplus SC$.

That $\otimes$ is a **greatest lower bound** operator on SC implies for each pair of classes A and B in SC, there exists a unique class $E = A \otimes B$ such that:

1. $E \leq A$ and $E \leq B$, and
2. $D \leq A$ and $D \leq B$ implies $D \leq E$ for all D in SC .

By extension, corresponding to any subset $S = \{A_1, \ldots, A_n\}$ of SC, there is a unique element $\otimes S = A_1 \otimes A_2 \otimes \ldots \otimes A_n$ which is the greatest lower bound for the subset. The lowest security class, Low, is thus $Low = \otimes SC$. Low is an identity element on $\oplus$; that is, $A \oplus Low = A$ for all $A \in SC$. Similarly, $High$ is an identity element on $\otimes$.

Example:
Figure 5.1 illustrates a lattice with 11 classes, where an arrow from a class X to a class Y means $X \leq Y$. The graphical representation is a standard precedence graph showing only the nonreflexive, immediate relations. We have, for example,

---

† In the remainder of this chapter, "$\oplus$" denotes least upper bound rather than exclusive-or.

FIGURE 5.1 Lattice.

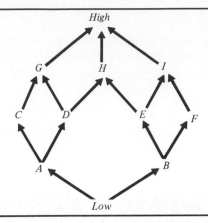

High

$A \oplus C = C, A \otimes C = A$
$C \oplus D = G, C \otimes D = A$
$C \oplus D \oplus E = High, C \otimes D \otimes E = Low.$ ■

A **linear lattice** is simply a linear ordering on a set of n classes $SC = \{0, 1, \dots, n - 1\}$ such that for all $i, j \in [0, n - 1]$:

a. $i \oplus j = \max(i, j)$
b. $i \otimes j = \min(i, j)$
c. $Low = 0; High = n - 1$.

FIGURE 5.2 Subset lattice.

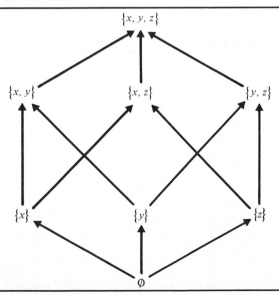

For $n = 2$, this lattice describes systems that distinguish confidential data in class 1 (*High*) from nonconfidential data in class 0 (*Low*). For $n = 4$, it describes the authority levels in military systems.

Given a set X, a **subset lattice** is derived from a nonlinear ordering on the set of all subsets of X. The ordering relation $\leq$ corresponds to set inclusion $\subseteq$, the least upper bound $\oplus$ to set union $\cup$, and the greatest lower bound $\otimes$ to set intersection $\cap$. The lowest class corresponds to the empty set and the highest class to X. Figure 5.2 illustrates for $X = \{x, y, z\}$.

A subset lattice is particularly useful for specifying arbitrary **input-output relations**. Suppose a program has m input parameters $x_1, \ldots, x_m$ and n output parameters $y_1, \ldots, y_n$ such that each output parameter is allowed to depend on only certain inputs [Jone75]. A subset lattice can be constructed from the subsets of $X = \{x_1, \ldots, x_m\}$. The class associated with each input x_i is the singleton set $\underline{x}_i = \{x_i\}$, and the class associated with each output y_j is the set $\underline{y}_j = \{x_i \mid x_i \rightarrow y_j$ is allowed$\}$.

Example:
Suppose a program has three input parameters x_1, x_2, and x_3, and two output parameters y_1 and y_2 subject to the constraint that y_1 may depend only on x_1 and x_2, and y_2 may depend only on x_1 and x_3. Then $\underline{y}_1 = \{x_1, x_2\}$ and $\underline{y}_2 = \{x_1, x_3\}$. ■

A subset lattice also describes policies for which X is a set of categories or properties, and classes are combinations of categories; information in an object a is allowed to flow into an object b if and only if b has at least the properties of a.

Example:
Consider a database containing medical, financial, and criminal records on individuals, and let $X = \{Medical, Financial, Criminal\}$. Medical information is permitted to flow into an object b if and only if *Medical* ϵ $\underline{b}$, and a combination of medical and financial information is permitted to flow into b if and only if both *Medical* ϵ $\underline{b}$ and *Financial* ϵ $\underline{b}$. ■

Another example is the set of security categories in military systems. Karger [Karg78] discusses the application of such lattices to the private sector and decentralized computer networks, where the security lattices may be large.

Still richer structures can be constructed from combinations of linear and subset lattices.

Example: Multilevel security.
The security classes of the military multilevel security policy (see Section 5.1.1) form a lattice determined by the (Cartesian) product of the linear lattice of authority levels and the subset lattice of categories. Let (A, C) and (A', C') be security classes, where A and A' are authority levels and C and C' are categories. Then

a. $(A, C) \leq (A', C')$ iff $A \leq A', C \subseteq C'$
b. $(A, C) \oplus (A', C') = (\max(A, A'), C \cup C')$
c. $(A, C) \otimes (A', C') = (\min(A, A'), C \cap C')$
d. $Low = (0, \{\}) = (Unclassified, \{\})$
e. $High = (3, X) = (Top\ Secret, X)$,

where X is the set of all compartments.   ■

Because any arbitrary set of allowable input/output relations can be described by a subset lattice, we lose no generality or flexibility by restricting attention to lattice-structured flow policies.

It is also possible to take an arbitrary flow policy $P = (SC, \leq)$ and transform it into a lattice $P' = (SC', \leq')$; classes A and B in SC have corresponding classes A' and B' in SC' such that $A \leq B$ in P if and only if $A' \leq B'$ in P' [Denn76b]. This means that a flow is authorized under P if and only if it is authorized under P', where objects bound to class A in P are bound to class A' in P'. The transformation requires only that the relation $\leq$ be reflexive and transitive. To derive a relation $\leq'$ that is also antisymmetric, classes forming cycles (e.g., $A \leq B \leq C \leq A$) are compressed into single classes. To provide least upper and greatest lower bound operators, new classes are added. Figure 5.3 illustrates. The class AB is added to give A and B a least upper bound; the classes Low and $High$ are added to give bounds on the complete structure. The classes D and E forming a cycle in the original structure are compressed into the single class DE in the lattice.

5.1.5 Flow Properties of Lattices

The lattice properties can be exploited in the construction of enforcement mechanisms. Transitivity of the relation $\leq$ implies any indirect flow $x \rightarrow y$ resulting from a sequence of flows

$$x = z_0 \rightarrow z_1 \rightarrow \ldots \rightarrow z_{n-1} \rightarrow z_n = y$$

is permitted if each flow $z_{i-1} \rightarrow z_i$ $(1 \leq i \leq n)$ is permitted, because

$$\underline{x} = \underline{z_0} \leq \underline{z_1} \leq \ldots \leq \underline{z_{n-1}} \leq \underline{z_n} = \underline{y}$$

implies $\underline{x} \leq \underline{y}$. Therefore, an enforcement mechanism need only verify direct flows.

Example:
The security of the indirect flow $x \rightarrow y$ caused by executing the sequence of statements

    $z := x;$
    $y := z$

FIGURE 5.3 Transformation of nonlattice policy into a lattice.

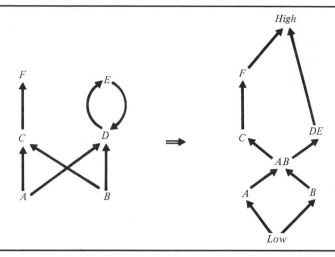

automatically follows from the security of the individual statements; that is, $\underline{x} \leq \underline{z}$ and $\underline{z} \leq \underline{y}$ implies $\underline{x} \leq \underline{y}$. ■

In general, transitivity of the relation $\leq$ implies that if executing each of the statements $S_1, \ldots, S_n$ is authorized, then executing the statements in sequence is authorized.

Transitivity greatly simplifies verifying implicit flows. To see why, suppose the value of a variable x is tested, and the program follows one of two execution paths depending on the outcome of the test. At some point, the execution paths join. Before the paths join, implicit flows from x (encoded in the program counter) must be verified. But after the paths join, information can only flow indirectly from x, and transitivity automatically ensures the security of these flows.

Example:
Consider the sequence

        $z := 0;$
        if $x = 1$ **then** $z := 1;$
        $y := z,$

where x is initially 0 or 1. Execution of this sequence implicitly transfers information from x to z, and then explicitly from z to y. Because of transitivity, the security of the indirect flow $x \rightarrow y$ automatically follows from the security of the flows $x \rightarrow z$ and $z \rightarrow y$. ■

The existence of a least upper bound operator $\oplus$ implies that if $\underline{x}_1 \leq \underline{y}, \ldots,$ $\underline{x}_n \leq \underline{y}$ for objects $x_1, \ldots, x_n$ and y, then there is a unique class $\underline{x} = \underline{x}_1 \oplus \ldots \oplus$

x_n such that $x \leq y$. This means that a set of flows $x_1 \rightarrow y, \ldots, x_n \rightarrow y$ is authorized if the single relation $x \leq y$ holds. This simplifies the design of verification mechanisms.

Example:

To verify the security of an assignment statement:

$$y := x_1 + x_2 * x_3 ,$$

a compiler can form the class $x = x_1 \oplus x_2 \oplus x_3$ as the expression on the right is parsed, and then verify the relation $x \leq y$ when the complete statement is recognized. Similarly, a run-time enforcement mechanism can form the class x as the expression is evaluated, and verify the relation $x \leq y$ when the assignment to y is performed. ▪

The least upper bound operator $\oplus$ can be interpreted as a "class combining operator" specifying the class of a result $y = f(x_1, \ldots, x_n)$. With variable security classes, $x = x_1 \oplus \ldots \oplus x_n$ is the minimal class that can be assigned to y such that the flows $x_i \rightarrow y$ are secure.

The existence of a greatest lower bound operator $\otimes$ implies that if $x \leq y_1$, $\ldots, x \leq y_n$ for objects x and $y_1, \ldots, y_n$, then there is a unique class $y = y_1 \otimes \ldots \otimes y_n$ such that $x \leq y$. This means a set of flows $x \rightarrow y_1, \ldots, x \rightarrow y_n$ is authorized if the single relation $x \leq y$ holds. This also simplifies the design of verification mechanisms.

Example:

To verify the security of an **if** statement

```
if x then
   begin
      y₁ := 0;
      y₂ := 0;
      y₃ := 0
   end ,
```

a compiler can form the class $y = y_1 \otimes y_2 \otimes y_3$ as the statements are parsed, and then verify the implicit flows $x \rightarrow y_i$ ($i = 1, 2, 3$) by checking that $x \leq y$. ▪

The least security class *Low* consists of all information that is unrestricted. This includes all data values that can be expressed in the language (e.g., integers and characters), and implies that execution of statements such as

```
x := 1
x := x + 1
x := 'On a clear disk you can seek forever'
```

is always authorized. Because *Low* is an identity on $\oplus$, the class of the expression "$x + 1$" is simply $x \oplus Low = x$.

5.2 FLOW CONTROL MECHANISMS

5.2.1 Security and Precision

Let F be the set of all possible flows in an information flow system, let P be the subset of F authorized by a given flow policy, and let E be the subset of F "executable" given the flow control mechanisms in operation. The system is **secure** if $E \subseteq P$; that is, all executable flows are authorized. A secure system is **precise** if $E = P$; that is, all authorized flows are executable. Figure 5.4 illustrates.

Note the similarity of Figure 5.4 with Figure 4.4, where a secure system is defined to be one that never enters an unauthorized state. We can also define a secure information flow system in terms of authorized states. Let s_0 be an initial state; s_0 is authorized, because flows are associated with state transitions. Let s be a state derived from s_0 by executing a command sequence α; then s is authorized if and only if all flows $x_{s_0} \rightarrow_\alpha y_s$ are authorized (i.e., $\underline{x}_{s_0} \leq \underline{y}_s$). By transitivity of the relation $\leq$, the state of the system remains authorized if the flows caused by each state transition are authorized. Defining secure information flow in terms of authorized states allows us to use a single definition of security for a system that supports both an access control policy and an information flow policy, as do most systems.

Although it is simple to construct a mechanism that provides security (by

FIGURE 5.4 Security and precision.

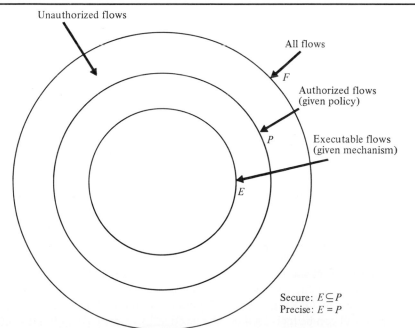

Unauthorized flows

All flows

F

Authorized flows
(given policy)

P

Executable flows
(given mechanism)

E

Secure: $E \subseteq P$
Precise: $E = P$

inhibiting all operations) it is considerably more difficult to construct a mechanism that provides precision as well.

Example:

Consider the assignment

$$y := k * x \ ,$$

and a policy in which $k \leq y$ but $x \npreceq y$; that is, information may flow from k to y but not from x to y. A mechanism that always prohibits execution of this statement will provide security. It may not be precise, however, because execution of the statement does not cause a flow $x \rightarrow y$ if either $k = 0$ or $H(x) = 0$ (i.e., there is no uncertainty about x). To design a mechanism that verifies the relation $x \leq y$ only for actual flows $x \rightarrow y$ is considerably more difficult than designing one that verifies the relation $x \leq y$ for any operation that can potentially cause a flow $x \rightarrow y$. ∎

To further complicate the problem, it is generally undecidable whether a given system is secure or precise.

Example:

Consider the statement

if $f(n)$ *halts* **then** $y := x$ **else** $y := 0$,

where f is an arbitrary function and $x \npreceq y$. Consider two systems: one that always allows execution of this statement, and another that always prohibits its execution. Clearly, it is undecidable whether the first system is secure or the second precise without solving the halting problem. To make matters worse, it is theoretically impossible to construct a mechanism that is both secure and precise [Jone75]. ∎

In a secure system, the security class y of any object y will be at least as high as the class of the information stored in y. This does not imply, however, that a variable class y must monotonically increase over time. If information is removed from y, then y may decrease.

Example:

Consider the following sequence of statements:

$$y := x;$$
$$z := y;$$
$$y := 0 \ .$$

After the first statement is executed, y must satisfy $x \leq y$ to reflect the flow $x \rightarrow y$. After the last statement is executed, however, y can be lower than x, because y no longer contains information about x. Thus, the security class of an object can be increased or decreased at any time as long it does not violate security. ∎

In some systems, trusted processes are permitted to violate the flow requirements—for example, to lower the security class of an object. These processes, however, must meet the security policies of the system as a whole (see Section 5.6.3 for an example).

5.2.2 Channels of Flow

Lampson [Lamp73] observed that information flows along three types of channels:

* **Legitimate Channels,** which are intended for information transfer between processes or programs—e.g., the parameters of a procedure.
* **Storage Channels,** which are objects shared by more than one process or program—e.g., a shared file or global variable.
* **Covert Channels,** which are not intended for information transfer at all—e.g., a process's effect on the system load.

Legitimate channels are the simplest to secure. Securing storage channels is considerably more difficult, because every object—file, variable, and status bit—must be protected.

Example:
To illustrate the subtlety of this point, consider the following scheme by which a process p can transfer a value x to a process q through the lock bit of a shared file f: p arranges regular intervals of use and nonuse of the file according to the binary representation of x; q requests use of the file each interval, and determines the corresponding bit of x according to whether the request is granted. ∎

Although it is possible in principle to enforce security for all flows along legitimate and storage channels, covert channels are another matter (see also [Lipn75]). The problem is that information can be encoded in some physical phenomenon detectable by an external observer. For example, a process may cause its running time to be proportional to the value of some confidential value x which it reads. By measuring the running time on a clock that operates independently of the system, a user can determine the value of x. This type of covert channel is called a "timing channel"; other resource usage patterns may be exploited, such as the electric power consumed while running a program, or system throughput.

The only known technical solution to the problem of covert channels requires that jobs specify in advance their resource requirements. Requested resources are dedicated to a job, and the results, even if incomplete, are returned at precisely the time specified. With this strategy, nothing can be deduced from running time or resource usage that was not known beforehand; but even then, users can deduce something from whether their programs successfully complete. This scheme can be prohibitively expensive. Cost effective methods of closing all covert channels probably do not exist.

5.3 EXECUTION-BASED MECHANISMS

Security can be enforced either at execution time by validating flows as they are about to occur (prohibiting unauthorized ones), or at compile time by verifying the flows caused by a program before the program executes. This section studies the first approach; Sections 5.4–5.6 study the second approach. Before describing specific execution-based mechanisms, we discuss the general problem of dynamically enforcing security for implicit flows.

5.3.1 Dynamically Enforcing Security for Implicit Flow

Initially we assume objects have fixed security classes. We then consider the problems introduced by variable classes.

Dynamically enforcing security for explicit flows is straightforward, because an explicit flow always occurs as the result of executing an assignment of the form

$$y := f(x_1, \ldots, x_n) \ .$$

A mechanism can enforce the security of the explicit flows $x_i \rightarrow y$ $(1 \leq i \leq n)$ by verifying the relation $\underline{x_1} \oplus \ldots \oplus \underline{x_n} \leq \underline{y}$ at the time of the assignment to y. If the relation is not true, it can generate an error message, and the assignment can be skipped or the program aborted.

Dynamically enforcing security for implicit flows would appear to be more difficult, because an implicit flow can occur in the absence of any explicit assignment. This was illustrated earlier by the statement

if $x = 1$ **then** $y := 1$.

This seems to suggest that verifying implicit flows to an object only at the time of an explicit assignment to the object is insecure. For example, verifying the relation $\underline{x} \leq \underline{y}$ only when the assignment "$y := 1$" is performed in the preceding statement would be insecure.

The interesting result, proved by Fenton [Fent74], is that security can be enforced by verifying flows to an object only at the time of explicit assignments to the object. But there is one catch: attempted security violations cannot generally be reported. This means if an unauthorized implicit flow is detected at the time of an assignment, not only must that assignment be skipped, but the error must not be reported to the user, and the program must keep running as though nothing has happened. The program cannot abort or even generate an error message to the user unless the user's clearance is at least that of the information causing the flow violation. It would otherwise be possible to use the error message or abnormal termination to leak high security data to a user with a low security clearance. Moreover, the program must terminate in a low security state; that is, any information encoded in the program counter from tests must belong to the class *Low*. Details are given in Sections 5.3.3 and 5.3.4.

Example:

Secure execution of the **if** statement

> **if** $x = 1$ **then** $y := 1$

is described by

> **if** $x = 1$
>   **then if** $\underline{x} \le \underline{y}$ **then** $y := 1$ **else skip**
>   **else skip** .

Suppose x is 0 or 1, y is initially 0, $\underline{x} = High$, and $\underline{y} = Low$; thus, the flow $x \rightarrow y$ is not secure. Because the assignment to y is skipped both when $x = 1$ (because the security check fails) and when $x = 0$ (because the test "$x = 1$" fails), y is always 0 when the statement terminates, thereby giving no information about x. Note that if an error flag E is set to 1 when the security check fails, then the value of x is encoded in the flag ($E = 1$ implies $x = 1$, $E = 0$ implies $x = 0$). ■

In general, suppose an assignment

$$y := f(x_1, \ldots, x_m)$$

is directly conditioned on variables $x_{m+1}, \ldots, x_n$. Then the explicit and implicit flow to y can be validated by checking that the relation

$$\underline{x_1} \oplus \ldots \oplus \underline{x_m} \oplus \underline{x_{m+1}} \oplus \ldots \oplus \underline{x_n} \le \underline{y}$$

holds, skipping the assignment if it does not. This is secure, because the value of y is not changed when the security check fails; it is as though the program never even made the test that would have led to the assignment and, therefore, the implicit flow.

Fenton's result is significant for two reasons. First, it is much simpler to construct a run-time enforcement mechanism if all implicit and explicit flows can be validated only at the time of actual assignments. Second, such a mechanism is likely to be more precise than one that checks implicit flows that occur in the absence of explicit assignments.

Example:

Consider the statement

> **if** $x = 1$ **then** $y := 1$ **else** $z := 1$

where $\underline{x} = High$. Suppose that when $x = 1$, $\underline{y} = High$ and $\underline{z} = Low$, but when $x \ne 1$, $\underline{y} = Low$ and $\underline{z} = High$. If both relations $\underline{x} \le \underline{y}$ and $\underline{x} \le \underline{z}$ are tested on both branches, the program will be rejected, even though it can be securely executed using Fenton's approach. (Verification of this is left to the reader.) ■

Now, an error flag can be securely logged in a record having a security class at least that of the information. Although it is insecure to report it to a user in a lower class, the capacity of the leakage channel is at most 1 bit (because at most 1 bit can be encoded in a 1-bit flag). The error message can, however, potentially disclose the exact values of all variables in the system. To see why, suppose all information in the system is encoded in variables $x_1, \ldots, x_n$, and there exists a variable y known to be 0 such that $\underline{x_i} \preceq \underline{y}$ ($i = 1, \ldots, n$). Then execution of the statement

    if $(x_1 = val_1)$ and $(x_2 = val_2)$ and ... and $(x_n = val_n)$
       then $y := 1$

generates an error message when $x_1 = val_1, \ldots, x_n = val_n$, disclosing the exact values of $x_1, \ldots, x_n$. But if a single $x_i \neq val_i$, an error message is not generated, and little can be deduced from the value of y. Thus, an intruder could not expect to learn much from the statement. Similarly, execution of the statement

    if $\sim \left((x_1 = val_1) \text{ and } (x_2 = val_2) \text{ and } \ldots \text{ and } (x_n = val_n) \right)$
       then $y := 1$

terminates successfully (without causing a security error) when $x_1 = val_1, \ldots, x_n = val_n$, leaking the exact values of $x_1, \ldots, x_n$. Note, however, that the values of $x_1, \ldots, x_n$ are not encoded in y, because y will be 0 even when the test succeeds. The values are encoded in the termination status of the program, which is why only 1 bit of information can be leaked.

    It is clearly unsatisfactory not to report errors, but errors can be logged, and offending programs removed from the system. This solution may be satisfactory in most cases. It is not satisfactory, however, if the 1 bit of information is sufficiently valuable (e.g., a signal to attack). There is a solution—we can verify the security of all flows caused by a program before the program executes. This approach is studied in Sections 5.4 and 5.5.

    Suppose now that objects have variable security classes. If an object y is the target of an assignment "$y := f(x_1, \ldots, x_m)$" conditioned on objects $x_{m+1}, \ldots, x_n$, changing y's class to

$$\underline{y} := \underline{x_1} \oplus \ldots \oplus \underline{x_m} \oplus \underline{x_{m+1}} \oplus \ldots \oplus \underline{x_n}$$

at the time of the assignment might seem sufficient for security. Although it is secure for the explicit flows, it is not secure for the implicit flows, because the execution path of the program will be different for different values of $x_{m+1}, \ldots, x_n$. This is illustrated by the following example.

Example:
Consider the execution of the procedure *copy1* shown in Figure 5.5. Suppose the local variable z has a variable class (initially *Low*), z is changed whenever z is assigned a value, and flows into y are verified whenever y is assigned a value. Now, if the procedure is executed with $x = 0$, the test "$x = 0$" succeeds and $(z, \underline{z})$ becomes $(1, \underline{x})$; hence the test "$z = 0$" fails, and y remains 0. If it is executed with $x = 1$, the test "$x = 0$" fails, so $(z, \underline{z})$ remains $(0, Low)$; hence the test "$z = 0$" succeeds, y is assigned the value 1,

FIGURE 5.5 Procedure *copy1*.

```
procedure copy1(x: integer; var y: integer);
  "copy x to y"
  var z: integer;
  begin
    y := 0;
    z := 0;
    if x = 0 then z := 1;
    if z = 0 then y := 1
  end
end copy1
```

and the relation $Low \leq y$ is verified. In either case, execution terminates with $y = x$, but without verifying the relation $\underline{x} \leq \underline{y}$. The system, therefore, is insecure when $\underline{x} \not\leq \underline{y}$. ∎

To construct a secure mechanism for variable classes, several approaches are possible. Denning [Denn75] developed an approach that accounts for all implicit flows, including those occurring in the absence of explicit ones. In the *copy1* program, for example, z would be increased to $\underline{x}$ even when the test "$x = 0$" fails, and the relation $\underline{z} \leq \underline{y}$ would be verified regardless of whether the test "$z = 0$" succeeds. The disadvantage of this approach is that a compiler must analyze the flows of a program to determine what objects could receive an implicit flow, and insert additional instructions into the compiled code to increase a class if necessary.

Fenton [Fent73] and Gat and Saal [Gat75] proposed a different solution. Their solution involves restoring the class and value of any object whose class was increased during execution of a conditional structure to the class and value it had just before entering the structure. Hence, the objects whose class and value are restored behave as "local objects" within the conditional structure. This ensures the security of all implicit flows by nullifying those that caused a class increase. The disadvantage of this approach is the added complexity to the run-time enforcement mechanism.

Lampson suggested another approach that is much simpler to implement than either of the preceding. The class of an object would be changed only to reflect explicit flows into the object; implicit flows would be verified at the time of explicit ones, as for fixed classes. For example, execution of the statement "**if** $x = 1$ **then** $y := z$" would set $\underline{y}$ to $\underline{z}$, and then verify the relation $\underline{x} \leq \underline{y}$.

5.3.2 Flow-Secure Access Controls

Simple flow controls can be integrated into the access control mechanisms of operating systems. Each process p is assigned a security clearance $\underline{p}$ specifying the highest class p may read from and the lowest class p may write into. Security is

FIGURE 5.6 Access control mechanism.

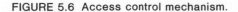

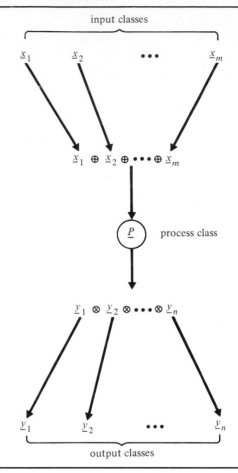

enforced by access controls that permit p to acquire read access to an object x only if $\underline{x} \le \underline{p}$, and write access to an object y only if $\underline{p} \le \underline{y}$. Hence, p can read from x_1, ..., x_m and write into y_1, ..., y_n only if

$$\underline{x}_1 \oplus \ldots \oplus \underline{x}_m \le \underline{p} \le \underline{y}_1 \otimes \ldots \otimes \underline{y}_n$$

(see Figure 5.6). This automatically guarantees the security of all flows, explicit or implicit, internal to the process.

In military systems, access controls enforce both a **nondiscretionary** policy of information flow based on the military classification scheme (the multilevel security policy), and a **discretionary** policy of access control based on "need-to-know" (that is, on the principle of least privilege). A process running with a *Secret* clearance, for example, is permitted to read only from *Unclassified, Confidential,* and *Secret* objects; and to write only to *Secret* and *Top Secret* objects (although integrity constraints may prevent it from writing into *Top Secret* objects). All the kernel-based systems discussed in Section 4.6.1 use access controls to enforce multilevel security for user and untrusted system processes.

One of the first systems to use access controls to enforce multilevel security was the ADEPT-50 time-sharing system developed at SDC in the late 1960s [Weis69]. In ADEPT, the security clearance p of a process p, called its "high water mark", is dynamically determined by the least upper bound of the classes of all files opened for read or write operations; thus p is monotonically nondecreasing. When the process closes a newly created file f, the class f is set to p. Rotenberg's [Rote74] Privacy Restriction Processor is similar, except that p is determined by the $\oplus$ of the classes opened for read, and whenever the process writes into a file f, the file's class is changed to $f := f \oplus p$.

This approach of dynamically assigning processes and objects to variable security classes can lead to leaks, as illustrated by the following example.

Example:
Suppose the procedure *copy1* (see Figure 5.5) is split between processes $p1$ and $p2$, where $p1$ and $p2$ communicate through a global variable z dynamically bound to its security class:

> $p1$: **if** $x = 0$ **then** $z := 1$
> $p2$: **if** $z = 0$ **then** $y := 1$.

Now suppose $p1$ and $p2$ are set to the $\oplus$ of the classes of all objects opened for read or write operations, y and z are initially 0 and in class *Low*, z is changed only when z is opened for writing, and flows to y are verified only when y is opened for writing. When $x = 0$, $p1$ terminates with $z = 1$ and $z = p1 = x$; thus, $p2$ is set to x. But the test "$z = 0$" in $p2$ fails, so y is never opened for writing, and the relation $p2 \leq y$ is never verified. When $x = 1$, $p1$ terminates with $p1 = x$; however, because z is never opened for writing, (z, z) remains $(0, Low)$; thus, $p2 = Low$, y becomes 1, and the relation $Low \leq y$ is verified. In both cases, $p2$ terminates with $y = x$, even though the relation $x \leq y$ is never verified. Thus, a leak occurs if $x \nleq y$.

This problem does not arise when objects and processes have fixed security classes. To see why, suppose $p1$ runs in the minimal class needed to read x; i.e., $p1 = x$. Then $p1$ will never be allowed to write into z unless $x \leq z$. Similarly, $p2$ will not be allowed to read z unless $z \leq p2$, and it will never be allowed to write into y unless $p2 \leq y$. Hence, no information can flow from x to y unless $x \leq z \leq y$. ∎

Because of the problems caused by variable classes, most access-control-based mechanisms bind objects and processes to fixed security classes. The class of a process p is determined when p is initiated.

Flow-secure access controls provide a simple and efficient mechanism for enforcing information flow within user processes. But they are limited, because they do not distinguish different classes of information within a process. For example, if a process reads both confidential (*High*) and nonconfidential (*Low*) data, then p must be *High*, and any objects written by p must be in class *High*. The process cannot be given write access to objects in class *Low*, because there would be no way of knowing whether the information transferred to these objects was confidential or nonconfidential. The process cannot, therefore, transfer information derived only from the nonconfidential inputs to objects in class *Low*.

In general, it is not possible with access controls alone to enforce security in processes that handle different classes of information simultaneously. This rules out using access controls to enforce the security of certain operating system processes that must access information in different classes and communicate with processes at different levels. Yet the flows within system processes must be secure, lest other processes exploit this to establish leakage channels through system state variables. For example, a Trojan Horse in a file editor could use such a channel to leak *Top Secret* information in a file being edited to a user with a lower clearance.

To enforce security within processes that handle different classes of information, the information flow internal to a process must be examined. The remainder of this chapter describes hardware and software mechanisms to do this.

5.3.3 Data Mark Machine

Fenton [Fent74,Fent73] studied a run-time validation mechanism in the context of an abstract machine called a **Data Mark Machine** (DMM). The Data Mark Machine is a Minsky machine [Mins67] extended to include tags (**data marks**) for marking the security class of each register (memory location).

A Minsky machine has three instructions:

$x := x + 1$ "increment"
if $x = 0$ **then goto** n **else** $x := x - 1$ "branch on zero or decrement"
halt ,

where x is a register and n is a statement label. Despite its simplicity, the machine can compute all computable functions as long as there are at least two (infinite) registers and a register containing zero.

Fenton's important observation was that a **program counter class**, $\underline{pc}$, could be associated with a process to validate all implicit flows caused by the process. This class is determined as follows: whenever a process executes a conditional branch

if $x = 0$ **then goto** n ,

the current value and class of pc is pushed onto a stack, and $(pc, \underline{pc})$ is replaced with $(n, \underline{pc} \oplus \underline{x})$. The class $\underline{pc}$ is increased by $\underline{x}$ because information about x is encoded in the execution path of the program. The only way $\underline{pc}$ can be decreased is by executing a **return** instruction, which restores $(pc, \underline{pc})$ to its earlier value. This forces the program to return to the instruction following the conditional branch, whence the execution path is no longer directly conditioned on the value of x.

Initially $\underline{pc}$ = *Low*, so that immediately before executing an instruction on a path directly conditioned on the values of $x_1, \ldots, x_m$, $\underline{pc} = \underline{x}_1 \oplus \ldots \oplus \underline{x}_m$. If the

TABLE 5.1 Data Mark Machine (DMM).

Instruction	Execution
$x := x + 1$	if $pc \leq x$ then $x := x + 1$ else skip
if $x = 0$	if $x = 0$
then goto n	then $\{push(pc, pc); pc := pc \oplus x; pc := n\}$
else $x := x - 1$	else $\{$if $pc \leq x$ then $x := x - 1$ else skip$\}$
if' $x = 0$	if $x = 0$
then goto n	then $\{$if $x \leq pc$ then $pc := n$ else skip$\}$
else $x := x - 1$	else $\{$if $pc \leq x$ then $x := x - 1$ else skip$\}$
return	$pop(pc, pc)$
halt	if empty stack then Halt

instruction is an assignment "$y := y + 1$" or "$y := y - 1$" then the hardware validates the relation $pc \leq y$, inhibiting the assignment if the condition is not satisfied; this ensures the security of the implicit flows $x_i \rightarrow y$ ($i = 1, \ldots, m$). The **halt** instruction requires the stack be empty, so the program cannot terminate without returning from each branch. This ensures the final state of the program contains only *Low* security information. If security violations are not reported, the mechanism is completely secure as discussed earlier. If violations are reported and insecure programs aborted, an insecure program can leak at most 1 bit.

The complete semantics of the Data Mark Machine are summarized in Table 5.1. The second **if** statement, denoted **if'**, allows a program to branch without stacking the program counter (stacking is unnecessary for security because $x \leq pc$ implies $pc = pc \oplus x$) .

Example:

Figure 5.7 shows how the *copy1* program of Figure 5.5 can be translated into instructions for the DMM. For simplicity, we assume y and z are initially 0. Note that the translated program modifies the value of x; this does not affect its flow from x to y.

The following execution trace shows the effect of executing each instruction when $x = 0$ and $x \leq z$:

Instruction	x	y	z	pc	Security Check
initial	0	0	0	*Low*	
1				x	
4		1			$x \leq z$
5				*Low*	
2		0			*Low* $\leq z$
3					

The reader should verify that the program causes information to flow from x to y only when $x \leq z \leq y$. ∎

FIGURE 5.7 Translation of *copy1* for DMM.

```
1   if x = 0 then goto 4 else x := x − 1
2   if z = 0 then goto 6 else z := z − 1
3   halt
4   z := z + 1
5   return
6   y := y + 1
7   return
```

5.3.4 Single Accumulator Machine

The protection features of the Data Mark Machine can be implemented in actual systems. We shall outline how this could be done on a single accumulator machine (SAM) with a tagged memory. Our approach is similar to the one proposed in [Denn75].

The security class of each data object is stored in the tag field of the corresponding memory location. A variable tag acc represents the class of the information in the accumulator. As in the Data Mark Machine, there is a program counter stack, and a class pc associated with the current program counter. The semantics of typical instructions are shown in Table 5.2. (The semantics for operations to subtract, multiply, etc. would be similar to those for ADD.)

Example:
Execution of the statement "$y := x1 * x2 + x3$" is shown next:

Operation	Execution Trace
LOAD $x1$	$acc := x1$; $\underline{acc} := \underline{x1} \oplus \underline{pc}$
MULT $x2$	$acc := acc * x2$; $\underline{acc} := \underline{acc} \oplus \underline{x2} \oplus \underline{pc}$
ADD $x3$	$acc := acc + x3$; $\underline{acc} := \underline{acc} \oplus \underline{x3} \oplus \underline{pc}$
STORE y	if $\underline{acc} \oplus \underline{pc} \le \underline{y}$ then $y := acc$

TABLE 5.2 Single accumulator machine (SAM) .

Operation	Execution
LOAD x	$acc := x$; $\underline{acc} := \underline{x} \oplus \underline{pc}$
STORE y	if $\underline{acc} \oplus \underline{pc} \le \underline{y}$ then $y := acc$ else skip
ADD x	$acc := acc + x$; $\underline{acc} := \underline{acc} \oplus \underline{x} \oplus \underline{pc}$
B n	$pc := n$
BZ n	if $(acc = 0)$ then $\{push(pc, \underline{pc})$; $\underline{pc} := \underline{pc} \oplus \underline{acc}$; $pc := n\}$
BZ' n	if $(acc = 0)$ and $(\underline{acc} \le \underline{pc})$ then $pc := n$ else skip
RETURN	$pop(pc, \underline{pc})$
STOP	if empty stack then stop

FIGURE 5.8 Translation of procedure *copy1* on SAM.

$y := 0;$	1	LOAD 0	
	2	STORE y	
$z := 0;$	3	LOAD 0	
	4	STORE z	
if $x = 0$	5	LOAD x	
	6	BZ 8	"*push* (7, *pc*)"
	7	B 11	
then $z := 1;$	8	LOAD 1	
	9	STORE z	
	10	RETURN	"*pop* − goto 7"
if $z = 0$	11	LOAD z	
	12	BZ 14	"*push* (13, *pc*)"
	13	B 17	
then $y := 1$	14	LOAD 1	
	15	STORE y	
	16	RETURN	"*pop* − goto 13"
	17	STOP	

TABLE 5.3 Semantics for STORE on variable class machine.

Operation	Execution
STORE y	if $\underline{pc} \leq \underline{acc}$ then $\{y := acc; \underline{y} := \underline{acc}\}$

Note the check associated with the STORE verifies $\underline{x1} \oplus \underline{x2} \oplus \underline{x3} \oplus \underline{pc} \leq \underline{y}$. ■

Figure 5.8 shows how the procedure *copy1* in Figure 5.5 can be translated into instructions on the single accumulator machine. Execution of the program is left as an exercise.

If the memory tags are variable, security cannot be guaranteed by changing the semantics of the STORE operation to:

$$y := acc; \underline{y} := \underline{acc} \oplus \underline{pc} \ .$$

(See the discussion of the procedure *copy1*.) Security can be guaranteed, however, by changing an object's class to reflect explicit flows to the object, as long as implicit flows are verified as for fixed classes. This approach is taken in Table 5.3.

5.4 COMPILER-BASED MECHANISM

We first consider a simple program certification mechanism that is easily integrated into any compiler. The mechanism guarantees the secure execution of each statement in a program—even those that are not executed, or, if executed, do not cause an information flow violation. The mechanism is not precise, however, as it will reject secure programs. For example, consider the following program segment

> **if** $x = 1$ **then** $y := a$ **else** $y := b$.

Execution of this segment causes either a flow $a \rightarrow y$ or a flow $b \rightarrow y$, but not both. The simple certification mechanism, however, requires that both $\underline{a} \leq \underline{y}$ and $\underline{b} \leq \underline{y}$. This is not a problem if both relations hold; but if $\underline{a} \leq \underline{y}$ holds only when $x = 1$, and $\underline{b} \leq \underline{y}$ holds only when $x \neq 1$, we would like a more precise mechanism. To achieve this, in Section 5.5 we combine flow proofs with correctness proofs, so that the actual execution path of a program can be taken into account.

The mechanism described here is based on [Denn75,Denn77]. It was developed for verifying the internal flows of applications programs running in an otherwise secure system, and not for security kernel verification.

5.4.1 Flow Specifications

We first consider the certification of procedures having the following structure:

> **procedure** $pname(x_1, \ldots, x_m; \textbf{var } y_1, \ldots, y_n)$;
>   **var** $z_1, \ldots, z_p$; "local variables"
> S "statement body"
> **end** $pname$,

where $x_1, \ldots, x_m$ are input parameters, and $y_1, \ldots, y_n$ are output parameters or input/output parameters. Let u denote an input parameter x or input/output parameter y, and let v denote either a parameter or local variable. The declaration of v has the form

> v: type **class** $\{u \mid u \rightarrow v \text{ is allowed}\}$,

where the **class** declaration specifies the set of all parameters permitted to flow into v. Note that the class of an input parameter x will be specified as the singleton set $\underline{x} = \{x\}$. The class of an input/output parameter y will be of the form $\{y, u_1, \ldots, u_k\}$, where $u_1, \ldots, u_k$ are other inputs to y. If y is an output only, the class of y will be of the form $\{u_1, \ldots, u_k\}$ (i.e., $y \notin \underline{y}$); hence, its value must be cleared on entry to the procedure to ensure its old value cannot flow into the procedure. References to global variables are not permitted; thus, each nonlocal object referenced by a procedure must be explicitly passed as a parameter.

The class declarations are used to form a subset lattice of allowable input-output relations as described in Section 5.1.4. Specifying the security classes of the parameters and local variables as a subset lattice simplifies verification. Because each object has a fixed security class during program verification, the problems caused by variable classes are avoided. At the same time, the procedure is not restricted to parameters having specific security classes; the classes of the actual parameters need only satisfy the relations defined for the formal parameters. We could instead declare specific security classes for the objects of a program; the mechanism described here works for both cases.

Example:

The following gives the flow specifications of a procedure that computes the maximum of its inputs:

> **procedure** *max*(*x*: **integer class** {*x*};
>   *y*: **integer class** {*y*};
>   **var** *m*: **integer class** {*x*, *y*});
>   **begin**
>   **if** *x* > *y* **then** *m* := *x* **else** *m* := *y*
>   **end**
>   **end** *max* .

The security class specified for the output *m* implies that $\underline{x} \leq \underline{m}$ and $\underline{y} \leq \underline{m}$. ∎

Example:

The following gives the input-output specifications of a procedure that swaps two variables *x* and *y*, and increments a counter *i* (recording the number of swaps):

> **procedure** *swap*(**var** *x*, *y*: **integer class** {*x*, *y*};
>   **var** *i*: **integer class** {*i*});
>   **var** *t*: **integer class** {*x*, *y*};
>   **begin**
>   *t* := *x*;
>   *x* := *y*;
>   *y* := *t*;
>   *i* := *i* + 1
>   **end**
>   **end** *swap* .

Because both $\underline{x} \leq \underline{y}$ and $\underline{y} \leq \underline{x}$ are required for security, the specifications state that $\underline{x} = \underline{y}$; this class is also assigned to the local variable *t*. Note that *i* is in a class by itself because it does not receive information from either *x* or *y*. ∎

5.4.2 Security Requirements

A procedure is **secure** if it satisfies its specifications; that is, for each input *u* and output *y*, execution of the procedure can cause a flow *u* → *y* only if the classes specified for *u* and *y* satisfy the relation $\underline{u} \leq \underline{y}$. The procedures in the preceding examples are secure.

    We shall define the security requirements for the statement (body) *S* of a procedure recursively, giving sufficient conditions for security for each statement type. These conditions are expressed as constraints on the classes of the parameters and local variables. A procedure is then secure if its flow specifications (i.e., class declarations) imply these constraints are satisfied. The conditions are not necessary for security, however, and some secure programs will be rejected. Initially, we assume S is one of the following:

1. Assignment: $b := e$
2. Compound: **begin** $S_1; \ldots ; S_n$ **end**
3. Alternation: **if** e **then** S_1 [**else** S_2]
4. Iteration: **while** e **do** S_1
5. Call: $q(a_1, \ldots , a_m, b_1, \ldots , b_n)$

where the S_i are statements, and e is an expression with operands $a_1, \ldots , a_n$, which we write as

$$e = f(a_1, \ldots , a_n) \, ,$$

where the function f has no side effects. The class of e is given by

$$\underline{e} = \underline{a_1} \oplus \ldots \oplus \underline{a_n} \, .$$

We assume all data objects are simple scalar types or files, and all statements terminate and execute as specified; there are no abnormal terminations due to exceptional conditions or program traps. Structured types and abnormal program terminations are considered later.

The security conditions for the explicit flow caused by an assignment are as follows:

Security conditions for assignment:
Execution of an assignment

$$b := e$$

is secure if $\underline{e} \leq \underline{b}$. ∎

Because input and output operations can be modeled as assignments in which the source or target object is a file, they are not considered separately here.

Because the relation $\leq$ is transitive, the security conditions for a compound statement are as follows:

Security conditions for compound:
Execution of the statement

begin $S_1; \ldots ; S_n$ **end**

is secure if execution of each of $S_1, \ldots , S_n$ is secure. ∎

Consider next the alternation statement

if e **then** S_1 [**else** S_2] .

If objects $b_1, \ldots , b_m$ are targets of assignments in S_1 [or S_2], then execution of the

if statement can cause implicit flows from e to each b_j. We therefore have the following:

> ### Security conditions for alternation:
> Execution of the statement
>
> > **if** e **then** S_1 [**else** S_2]
>
> is secure if
> (i) Execution of S_1 [and S_2] is secure, and
> (ii) $\underline{e} \leq \underline{S}$, where $\underline{S} = \underline{S_1}$ [$\otimes$ $\underline{S_2}$] and
> $\underline{S_1} = \otimes\{\underline{b} \mid b$ is a target of an assignment in $S_1\}$,
> $\underline{S_2} = \otimes\{\underline{b} \mid b$ is a target of an assignment in $S_2\}$ ■

Condition (ii) implies $\underline{e} \leq \underline{b_1} \otimes \ldots \otimes \underline{b_m}$, and, therefore, $\underline{e} \leq \underline{b_j}$ $(1 \leq j \leq m)$.

> ### Example:
> For the following statement
>
> > **if** $x > y$ **then**
> > > **begin**
> > > > $z := w;$
> > > > $i := k + 1$
> > > **end** ,
>
> condition (ii) is given by $\underline{x} \oplus \underline{y} \leq \underline{z} \otimes \underline{i}$. ■

Consider an iteration statement

> **while** e **do** S_1 .

If $b_1, \ldots, b_m$ are the targets of flows in S_1, then execution of the statement can cause implicit flows from e to each b_j. Security is guaranteed by the same condition as for the **if** statement:

> ### Security conditions for iteration:
> Execution of the statement
>
> > **while** e **do** S_1
>
> is secure if
> (i) S terminates,
> (ii) Execution of S_1 is secure, and
> (iii) $\underline{e} \leq \underline{S}$, where $\underline{S} = \underline{S_1}$ and
> $\underline{S_1} = \otimes \{\underline{b} \mid b$ is a target of a possible flow in $S_1\}$. ■

Because other iterative structures (e.g., **for** and **repeat-until**) can be described in terms of the **while**, we shall not consider them separately here.

Nonterminating loops can cause additional implicit flows, because execution of the remaining statements is conditioned on the loop terminating—this is discussed later. Even terminating loops can cause covert flows, because the execution time of a procedure depends on the number of iterations performed. There appears to be no good solution to this problem.

Finally, consider a call

$$q(a_1, \ldots, a_m, b_1, \ldots, b_n) \ ,$$

where $a_1, \ldots, a_m$ are the actual input arguments and $b_1, \ldots, b_n$ the actual input/output arguments corresponding to formal parameters $x_1, \ldots, x_m$ and $y_1, \ldots, y_n$, respectively. Assuming q is secure, execution of q can cause a flow $a_i \rightarrow b_j$ only if $\underline{x_i} \leq \underline{y_j}$; similarly, it can cause a flow $b_i \rightarrow b_j$ only if $\underline{y_i} \leq \underline{y_j}$. We therefore have the following:

Security conditions for procedure call:
Execution of the call

$$q(a_1, \ldots, a_m, b_1, \ldots, b_n)$$

is secure if

(i) q is secure, and
(ii) $\underline{a_i} \leq \underline{b_j}$ if $\underline{x_i} \leq \underline{y_j}$ $(1 \leq i \leq m, 1 \leq j \leq n)$ and
      $\underline{b_i} \leq \underline{b_j}$ if $\underline{y_i} \leq \underline{y_j}$ $(1 \leq i \leq n, 1 \leq j \leq n)$ ■

If q is a main program, the arguments correspond to actual system objects. The system must ensure the classes of these objects satisfy the flow requirements before executing the program. This is easily done if the certification mechanism stores the flow requirements of the parameters with the object code of the program.

Example:
Consider the procedure $max(x, y, m)$ of the preceding section, which assigns the maximum of x and y to m. Because the procedure specifies that $\underline{x} \leq \underline{m}$ and $\underline{y} \leq \underline{m}$ for output m, execution of a call "$max(a, b, c)$" is secure if $\underline{a} \leq \underline{c}$ and $\underline{b} \leq \underline{c}$.   ■

Example:
The security requirements of different statements are illustrated by the procedure shown in Figure 5.9, which copies x into y using a subtle combination of implicit and explicit flows (the security conditions are shown to the right of each statement). Initially x is 0 or 1. When $x = 0$, the first test "$z = 1$" succeeds, and the first iteration sets $y = 0$ and $z = x = 0$; the second test "$z = 1$" then fails, and the program terminates. When $x = 1$, the first test "$z = 1$" succeeds, and the first iteration sets $y = 0$ and $z = x = 1$; the second test "$z = 1$" also succeeds, and the second iteration sets $y = 1$ and $z = 0$; the third test "$z = 1$" then fails, and the program terminates. In both cases, the program terminates with $y = x$. The flow $x \rightarrow y$ is indirect: an explicit flow x

FIGURE 5.9 Procedure *copy2*.

---

procedure *copy2*(*x*: **integer class** {*x*};
                          var *y*: **integer class** {*x*});
  "copy *x* to *y*"
  var *z*: **integer class** {*x*};
  begin
      z := 1; $Low \leq \underline{z}$
      y := −1; $Low \leq \underline{y}$
      while *z* = 1 **do** $\underline{z} \leq \underline{y} \otimes \underline{z}$
          begin
              y := *y* + 1; $\underline{y} \leq \underline{y}$
              if *y* = 0 $\underline{y} \leq \underline{z}$
                 then *z* := *x* $\underline{x} \leq \underline{z}$
                 else *z* := 0 $Low \leq \underline{z}$
          end
    end
end *copy2*

→ *z* occurs during the first iteration; this is followed by an implicit flow *z* →
y during the second iteration due to the iteration being conditioned on *z*.

    The security requirements for the body of the procedure imply the
relations $\underline{x} \leq \underline{z} \leq \underline{y} \leq \underline{z}$ must hold. Because the flow specifications state $\underline{y}$
$= \underline{z} = \underline{x} = \{x\}$, the security requirements are met, and the procedure is
secure. If the specifications did not state the dependency of either *y* or *z* on *x*,
the security requirements would not be satisfied.

    Now, consider a call "*copy2*(*a*, *b*)", for actual arguments *a* and *b*.
Because *y* is the only formal output parameter in *copy2* and *x* satisfies the
relation $\underline{x} \leq \underline{y}$, the call is secure provided $\underline{a} \leq \underline{b}$. Although the stronger
relation $\underline{x} = \underline{y}$ holds in *copy2*, it is unnecessary that $\underline{a} = \underline{b}$ because the
argument *a* is not an output of *copy2* (hence the relation $\underline{b} \leq \underline{a}$ need not
hold). Thus, a call "*copy2*(*a*, *b*)" is secure if *b* is in a higher class than *a*, but
not vice versa. ■

5.4.3 Certification Semantics

The certification mechanism is sufficiently simple that it can be easily integrated
into the analysis phase of a compiler. Semantic actions are associated with the
syntactic types of the language as shown in Table 5.4 (see [Denn75,Denn77] for
details). As an expression $e = f(a_1, \ldots, a_n)$ is parsed, the class $\underline{e} = \underline{a}_1 \oplus \ldots \oplus \underline{a}_n$ is
computed and associated with the expression. This facilitates verification of explic-
it and implicit flows from $a_1, \ldots, a_n$.

    Example:
As the expression $e =$ "*a* + *b*∗*c*" is parsed, the classes of the variables are
associated with the nodes of the syntax tree and propagated up the tree,
giving $\underline{e} = \underline{a} \oplus \underline{b} \oplus \underline{c}$. ■

TABLE 5.4 Certification semantics.

Expression e	Semantic Actions
$f(a_1, \ldots, a_n)$	$\underline{e} := \underline{a_1} \oplus \ldots \oplus \underline{a_n}$
Statement S	

$b := e$	$\underline{S} := \underline{b};$ verify $\underline{e} \leq \underline{S}$
begin $S_1; \ldots; S_n$ end	$\underline{S} := \underline{S_1} \otimes \ldots \otimes \underline{S_n}$
if e then S_1 [else S_2]	$\underline{S} := \underline{S_1} \,[\otimes \underline{S_2}]\,;$ verify $\underline{e} \leq \underline{S}$
while e do S_1	$\underline{S} := \underline{S_1};$ verify $\underline{e} \leq \underline{S}$
$q(a_1, \ldots, a_m; b_1, \ldots, b_n)$	verify $\underline{a_i} \leq \underline{b_j}$ if $x_i \leq y_j$ verify $\underline{b_i} \leq \underline{b_j}$ if $y_i \leq y_j$ $\underline{S} := \underline{b_1} \otimes \ldots \otimes \underline{b_n}$

Similarly, as each statement S is recognized, a class $\underline{S} = \otimes\{\underline{b} \mid b$ is the target of an assignment in $S\}$ is computed and associated with the statement. This facilitates verification of implicit flows into S.

Example:
Figure 5.10 illustrates the certification of the statement

```
if a = b then
   begin
      c := 0;
      d := d + 1
   end
   else d := c * e .
```

The overall parse is represented as a syntax tree for the statement. The security classes (in parentheses) and verification checks (circled) are shown opposite each subtree. The semantic actions propagate the classes of expressions and statements up the tree. ■

We shall now consider extensions to the flow semantics and certification mechanisms to handle structured data types, arbitrary control structures for sequential programs, concurrent programs, and abnormal terminations.

5.4.4 General Data and Control Structures

The mechanism can be extended to handle complex data structures. We shall outline the security requirements for 1-dimensional arrays here. Consider a vector

FIGURE 5.10 Certification of a statement.

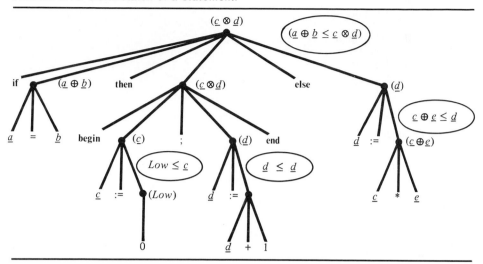

$a[1:n]$. We first observe that if an array reference "$a[e]$" occurs within an expression, where e is a subscript expression, then the array reference can contain information about $a[e]$ or e.

Example:
Consider the statement

$$b := a[e] \ .$$

If e is known but $a[e]$ is not, then execution of this statement causes a flow $a[e] \rightarrow b$. If $a[i]$ is known for $i = 1, \ldots, n$ but e is not, it can cause a flow $e \rightarrow b$ (e.g., if $a[i] = i$ for $i = 1, \ldots, n$, then $b = e$). ■

We next observe that an assignment of the form "$a[e] := b$" can cause information about e to flow into $a[e]$.

Example:
If an assignment "$a[e] := 1$" is made on an all-zero array, the value of e can be obtained from the index of the only nonzero element in a. ■

If all elements $a[i]$ belong to the same class $\underline{a}$, the certification mechanism is easily extended to verify flows to and from arrays. For an array reference "$a[e]$", the class $\underline{a} \oplus \underline{e}$ can be associated with the reference to verify flows from a and e. For an array assignment "$a[e] := b$", the relation $\underline{e} \leq \underline{a}$ can be verified along with the relation $\underline{b} \leq \underline{a}$.

If the elements belong to different classes, it is necessary to check only the classes $a[i]$ for those i in the range of e. This is because there can be no flow to or from $a[j]$ if e never evaluates to j (there must be a possibility of accessing an object for information to flow).

Example:

Given $a[1:4]$ and $b[1:4]$, the statement

> **if** $x \le 2$ **then** $b[x] := a[x]$

requires only that

$$\underline{x} \oplus \underline{a[i]} \le \underline{b[i]}, i = 1, 2. \quad \blacksquare$$

Performing such a flow analysis is beyond the scope of the present mechanism.

As a general rule, a mechanism is needed to ensure addresses refer to the objects assumed during certification. Otherwise, a statement like "$a[e] := b$" might cause an invalid flow $b \rightarrow c$, where c is an object addressed by $a[e]$ when e is out of range. There are several possible approaches to constructing such a mechanism. One method is for the compiler to generate code to check the bounds of array subscripts and pointer variables. The disadvantage of this approach is that it can substantially increase the size of a program as well as its running time. A more efficient method is possible if each array object in memory has a descriptor giving its bounds; the hardware can then check the validity of addresses in parallel with instruction execution. A third method is to prove that all subscripts and pointer variables are within their bounds; program proving is discussed in the next section.

The certification mechanism can be extended to control structures arising from arbitrary **goto** statements. Certifying a program with unrestricted **goto**s, however, requires a control flow analysis of the program to determine the objects receiving implicit flows. (This analysis is unnecessary if **goto**s are restricted—for example, to loop exits—so that the scope of conditional expressions can be determined during syntax analysis.) Following is an outline of the analysis required to do the certification. All **basic blocks** (single-entry, single-exit substructures) are

FIGURE 5.11 Procedure *copy2* with goto.

---

procedure *copy2*(x: **integer class** $\{x\}$;
                       var y: **integer class** $\{x\}$) ;
    "copy x to y"
var z: **integer class** $\{x\}$;
begin

1:	$z := 1;$ $y := -1;$	b_1
2:	**if** $z \ne 1$ **then goto** 6	b_2
3:	$y := y + 1;$ **if** $y \ne 0$ **then goto** 5;	b_3
4:	$z := x;$ **goto** 2;	b_4
5:	$z := 0;$ **goto** 2;	b_5
6:	**end**	b_6

end *copy2*

---

identified. A **control flow graph** is constructed, showing transitions among basic blocks; associated with block b_i is an expression e_i that selects the successor of b_i in the graph (e.g., see [Alle70]). The security class of block b_i is the $\otimes$ of the classes of all objects that are the targets of flows in b_i (if there are no such objects, this class is *High*). The **immediate forward dominator** $IFD(b_i)$ is computed for each block b_i. It is the closest block to b_i among the set of blocks that lie on all paths from b_i to the program exit and, therefore, is the point where the divergent execution paths conditioned on e_i converge. Define B_i as the set of blocks on some path from b_i to $IFD(b_i)$ excluding b_i and $IFD(b_i)$. The security class of B_i is $\underline{B_i} = \otimes \{\underline{b_j} \mid b_j \epsilon B_i\}$. Because the only blocks directly conditioned on the selector expression e_i of b_i are those in B_i, the program is secure if each block b_i is independently secure and $\underline{e_i} \leq \underline{B_i}$ for all i.

Example:

Figure 5.11 shows how the *copy2* procedure of Figure 5.9 can be written with **goto**s and partitioned into blocks. The control flow graph of the program is shown in Figure 5.12. Proof that the program is secure is left as an exercise. ■

FIGURE 5.12 Control flow graph of *copy2*.

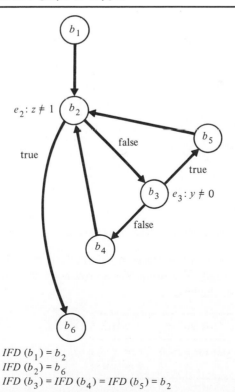

$$IFD\,(b_1) = b_2$$
$$IFD\,(b_2) = b_6$$
$$IFD\,(b_3) = IFD\,(b_4) = IFD\,(b_5) = b_2$$

5.4.5 Concurrency and Synchronization

Reitman [Reit79] and Andrews and Reitman [Andr80] show that information can
flow among concurrent programs over synchronization channels.

> *Example:*
> Suppose procedures p and q synchronize through a shared semaphore s as
> follows:
>
> > **procedure** $p(x$: **integer class** $\{x\}$;
> >   **var** s: **semaphore class** $\{s, x\}$);
> >   **begin**
> >   **if** $x = 1$ **then signal**(s)
> >   **end**
> > **end** p
> > **procedure** $q($**var** y: **integer class** $\{s, y\}$;
> >   **var** s: **semaphore class** $\{s, y\}$);
> >   **begin**
> > $y := 0$;
> >   **wait**(s);
> > $y := 1$
> >   **end**
> > **end** q
>
> where **wait**(s) delays q until p issues a **signal**(s) operation. Concurrent execu-
> tion of these procedures causes an implicit flow of information from param-
> eter x of p to parameter y of q over the synchronization channel associated
> with the semaphore s: if $x = 0$, y is set to 0, and q is delayed indefinitely on s;
> if $x = 1$, q is signaled, and y is set to 1. Thus, if p and q are invoked
> concurrently as follows:
>
> > **cobegin**
> > $p(a, s)$
> > $\|$
> > $q(b, s)$
> > **coend**
>
> the value of argument a flows into argument b.   ■

The flow $x \longrightarrow y$ in the preceding example is caused by **wait**(s) and **signal**(s),
which read and modify the value of s as follows (the complete semantics of these
operations are not shown):

	Read	Write
wait(s)	wait for $s > 0$	$s := s - 1$
signal(s)		$s := s + 1$

FIGURE 5.13 Synchronization flows.

```
procedure copy3(x: integer class {x};
                var y: integer class {x});
    "copy x to y"
    var s0: semaphore class {x};
        s1: semaphore class {x});
    cobegin
        "Process 1"
        if x = 0 then signal(s0) else signal(s1)
    ||
        "Process 2"
        wait(s0); y := 1; signal(s1);
    ||
        "Process 3"
        wait(s1); y := 0; signal(s0);
    coend
end copy3
```

Therefore, execution of the **if** statement in p causes an implicit flow from x to s, causing the value of x to flow into q.

When $x = 0$, q is left waiting on semaphore s. Because this is similar to a nonterminating **while** loop, we might wonder if all synchronization channels are associated with abnormal terminations from timeouts. If so, they would have a channel capacity of at most 1 bit, and could be handled as described in the next section. Reitman and Andrews show, however, that information can flow along synchronization channels even when the procedures terminate normally.

Example:
Consider the program *copy3* shown in Figure 5.13. When $x = 0$, process 2 executes before process 3, so the final value of y is 0; when $x \neq 0$, process 3 executes before process 2, so the final value of y is 1. Hence, if x is initially 0 or 1, execution of *copy3* sets y to the value of x. ∎

Because each statement logically following a **wait**(s) operation is conditioned on a **signal**(s) operation, there is an implicit flow from s to every variable that is the target of an assignment in a statement logically following the **wait**. To ensure the security of these flows, Reitman and Andrews require the class of every such variable y satisfy the relation $\underline{s} \leq \underline{y}$.

With parallel programs, information can also flow over global channels associated with loops.

Example:
Consider the program *copy4* shown in Figure 5.14. Execution of *copy4* trans-

FIGURE 5.14 Global flows in concurrent programs.

```
procedure copy4(x: integer class {x};
                  var y: integer class {x});
  "copy x to y"
  var e0, e1: boolean class {x};
  begin
    e0 := e1 := true ;
    cobegin
      if x = 0 then e0 := false else e1 := false
      ||
        begin
          while e0 do ;
          y := 1;
          e1 := false
        end
      ||
        begin
          while e1 do ;
          y := 0;
          e0 := false
        end
    coend
  end
end copy4
```

fers information from x to y, with variables $e0$ and $e1$ playing the role of semaphores $s0$ and $s1$. ∎

Our present certification mechanism would not verify the relations $e0 \leq y$ and $e1 \leq y$ in the preceding example, because the assignments to y are outside the loop bodies. To verify these "global flows", Reitman and Andrews consider the expression e of a statement "**while** e **do** S_1," to have a global scope that includes any statement logically following the **while**; the relation $e \leq y$ is verified for every object y that is the target of an assignment in the global scope. A "**while** e", therefore, is treated like a "**wait**(e)". Extending the certification semantics of Table 5.4 to verify synchronization and global flows in parallel programs is left as an exercise.

Rccd and Kanodia [Rccd79] observed that synchronization flows can also emanate from a waiting process; because **wait**(s) modifies the value of s, another waiting process can be blocked or delayed as a result. They show that by using **eventcounts** for process synchronization, information flows are restricted to signalers.

A signaling process can covertly leak a value by making the length of delay proportional to the value. The problem is the same as with loops, and there does not appear to be a satisfactory solution to either.

5.4.6 Abnormal Terminations

Information can flow along covert channels associated with abnormal program terminations.

Example:
Consider the following copy procedure:

```
procedure copy5(x: integer class {x};
                      var y: integer class {});
      "insecure procedure that leaks x to y"
      begin
         y := 0;
         while x = 0 do ;
         y := 1
      end
   end copy5 .
```

If $x = 0$, then y becomes 0, and the procedure hangs in the loop; if $x = 1$, then y becomes 1, and the procedure terminates. ■

The flow $x \rightarrow y$ in the *copy5* procedure occurs because the statement "$y := 1$" is conditioned on the value of x; thus there is an implicit flow $x \rightarrow y$, even though y is not the target of a flow in the statements local to the loop.

Such covert flows are not confined to nonterminating loops.

Example:
If the **while** statement in *copy5* is replaced by the statement:

if $x = 0$ then $x := 1/x$;

the value of x can still be deduced from y; if $x = 0$, the procedure abnormally terminates with a divide-by-zero exception and $y = 0$; if $x = 1$, the procedure terminates normally with $y = 1$. ■

Indeed, the nonterminating **while** statement could be replaced by any action that causes abnormal program termination: end-of-file, subscript-out-of-range, etc. Furthermore, the leak occurs even without the assignments to y, because the value of x can be determined by whether the procedure terminates normally.

Example:
Consider this copy procedure:

```
procedure copy6(x: integer class {x};
                 var y: integer class {}) ;
  "insecure procedure that leaks x to y"
  var sum: integer class {x};
      z: integer class {};
  begin
    z := 0;
    sum := 0;
    y := 0;
    while z = 0 do
       begin
         sum := sum + x;
         y := y + 1;
       end
  end
end copy6 .
```

This procedure loops until the variable *sum* overflows; the procedure then terminates, and x can be approximated by MAX/y, where MAX is the largest possible integer. The program trap causes an implicit flow $x \rightarrow y$ because execution of the assignment to y is conditioned on the value of *sum*, and thus x, but we do not require that $\underline{x \leq y}$. ∎

The problem of abnormal termination can be handled by inhibiting all traps except those for which actions have been explicitly defined in the program [Denn77]. Such definitions could be made with a statement similar to the **on** statement of PL/I:

   on condition **do** statement ,

where "condition" names a trap condition (overflow, underflow, end-of-file, divide-by-zero, etc.) for some variable, and "statement" specifies the action to be taken. When the trap occurs, the statement is executed, and control then returns to the point of the trap. The security requirements for programs can then be extended to ensure the secure execution of all programmer defined traps.

Example:
If the statement

   on overflow *sum* **do** $z := 1$

were added to the *copy6* procedure, the security check $\underline{sum \leq z}$ would be made, and the procedure would be declared insecure. ∎

This still leaves the problem of undefined traps and abnormal terminations from timeouts and similar events (overflowing a page limit or punched card limit, or running out of memory or file space). Many such problems can be eliminated by proving properties about the security and correctness of procedures; this is discussed in the next section. A mechanism that detects and logs abnormal termination of certified procedures is also essential.

5.5 PROGRAM VERIFICATION

Andrews and Reitman [Andr80] developed a deductive system for information flow based on the lattice model and on Hoare's [Hoar69] deductive system for functional correctness. The flow requirements of a procedure q are expressed as **assertions** about the values and classes of objects before and after q executes. Given an assertion P (precondition) about the initial state of q, and an assertion Q (postcondition) about the final state of q, q's security is proved (or disproved) by showing that Q satisfies the security requirements, and that if P is true on entry to q, Q will be true on exit. The proof is constructed by inserting intermediate assertions into the program, and applying **axioms** and **proof rules** defined over the statements of the language.

The approach has two advantages over the simple certification mechanism. First, it provides a single system for proving both security and correctness. Second, it gives a more precise enforcement mechanism for security.

Example:
Consider this procedure:

> **procedure** $copy7(x, a, b$: **integer**; **var** y: **integer**);
>   **if** $x = 1$ **then** $y := a$ **else** $y := b$
> **end** $copy7$.

Because of the implicit flow from x to y and the explicit flows from a and b to y, the certification mechanism requires the following relations hold for any execution of $copy7$:

> $\underline{x} \leq \underline{y}, \underline{a} \leq \underline{y}$, and $\underline{b} \leq \underline{y}$.

This is stronger than necessary, because any particular execution will transfer information from either a into y or from b into y but not both. ∎

To achieve a more precise enforcement mechanism, the flow logic assigns a variable v to a variable class $\underline{v}$ representing the **information state** of v at any given point in the program. An assertion about the information state of v is of the form

$$\underline{v} \leq C,$$

where C is a security class. The assertion states the information in v is no more sensitive than C. The bound C may be expressed as a specific class, as in $\underline{v} \leq Low$, which states v contains information belonging to the lowest security class only. This assertion would hold, for example, after the unconditional execution of the assignment "$v := 0$". The bound may be expressed as the fixed class of v, as in $\underline{v} \leq \underline{v}$, which states that v contains information no more sensitive than its class $\underline{v}$

permits. The bound may also be expressed as a join of the information states of other variables, as in $v \leq u_1 \oplus \ldots \oplus u_n$, which states v contains information no more sensitive than that in $u_1, \ldots, u_n$.

A special class pc represents the information state of the program counter (Andrews and Reitman call this class *local*); pc simulates the program counter class pc in Fenton's Data Mark Machine (see Section 5.3.3), and is used to prove properties about implicit flows.

Assertions about the classes of variables can be combined with assertions about their values. An assertion about the final state of the *copy7* procedure is given by:

$$\{pc \leq PC_{c7},$$
$$(x = 1) \supset (y \leq x \oplus a \oplus PC_{c7}), (x \neq 1) \supset (y \leq x \oplus b \oplus PC_{c7})\},$$

where PC_{c7} represents a bound on pc upon entering *copy7*. This says when $x = 1$, the information in y is no more sensitive than that in x, a, and the program counter pc; when $x \neq 1$, the information in y is no more sensitive than that in x, b, and pc.

In the flow logic, execution of an assignment statement

$$v := f(u_1, \ldots, u_n)$$

is described by the assertion

$$v \leq u_1 \oplus \ldots \oplus u_n,$$

relating the information state of v to that of $u_1, \ldots, u_n$. Note that this differs from the certification mechanism of the previous section, where the assignment statement imposes the security condition

$$u_1 \oplus \ldots \oplus u_n \leq v,$$

relating the fixed security class of v to that of $u_1, \ldots, u_n$. Section 5.5.6 shows how security conditions relate to assertions in the flow logic.

An assertion P will be expressed as a predicate in first-order calculus using "," for conjunction, "$\supset$" for implication, "$\sim$" for negation, and "$\forall$" for universal quantification (we shall not use disjunction or existential quantification in our examples).

Let P and Q be assertions about the information state of a program. For a given statement S,

$$\{P\} S \{Q\}$$

means if the **precondition** P is true before execution of S, then the **postcondition** Q is true after execution of S, assuming S terminates. The notation

$$P[x \leftarrow y]$$

means the assertion P with every free occurrence of x replaced with y.

The simplest proof rule is the rule of consequence:

Rule of consequence:

Given: $P \supset P', \{P'\} S \{Q'\}, Q' \supset Q$
Conclusion: $\{P\} S \{Q\}$ ■

The axioms and proof rules for each statement type are now given in Sections 5.5.1–5.5.5.

5.5.1 Assignment

Let S be the statement

$b := e$,

and let P be an assertion about the information state after S is executed. The axiom for correctness is simply

$\{P[b \leftarrow e]\} \; b := e \; \{P\}$,

because any assertion about b that is true after the assignment must be true of the value of e before the assignment. Note, however, the change in b is reflected in the postcondition P, and not the precondition.

Example:
Consider the statement

$y := x + 1$.

The axiom can be used to prove that the precondition $\{0 \leq x \leq 4\}$ implies the postcondition $\{1 \leq y \leq 5\}$:

$\{0 \leq x \leq 4\}$
$\{1 \leq (x + 1) \leq 5\}$
$y := x + 1$
$\{1 \leq y \leq 5\}$.

The second assertion follows from the first by simple implication. The third follows from the second (and the effect of executing the assigment statement) by the axiom for assignment. ■

The precondition $\{P[b \leftarrow e]\}$ of the assignment axiom is called a **weakest precondition** because it is the weakest condition needed to establish the postcondition. Of course, the rule of consequence always allows us to substitute stronger conditions.

Example:
The following is also true:

$\{x = 3, z = 0\}$

$$y := x + 1$$
$$\{1 \leq y \leq 5\}. \quad \blacksquare$$

In general, we would like to establish the minimal precondition needed to prove security and correctness.

Extending the assignment axiom to include information flow, we must account for both the explicit flow from e and the implicit flow from pc. We get

Assignment axiom:

$$\{P[b \leftarrow e; \underline{b} \leftarrow \underline{e} \oplus \underline{pc}]\}\, b := e\, \{P\} \quad \blacksquare$$

This states the sensitivity of b after the assignment will be no greater than that of e and pc before the assignment.

Example:

Suppose execution of the statement "$y := x + 1$" is conditioned on the value of variable z. Given the precondition $\{0 \leq x \leq 4, \underline{pc} \leq \underline{z}\}$, we can prove:

$$\{0 \leq x \leq 4, \underline{pc} \leq \underline{z}\}$$
$$\{0 \leq x \leq 4, \underline{x} \oplus \underline{pc} \leq \underline{x} \oplus \underline{z}, \underline{pc} \leq \underline{z}\}$$
$$y := x + 1$$
$$\{1 \leq y \leq 5, \underline{y} \leq \underline{x} \oplus \underline{z}, \underline{pc} \leq \underline{z}\}$$

The postcondition $\{\underline{y} \leq \underline{x} \oplus \underline{z}\}$ states that the information in y after the statement is executed is no more sensitive than that in x and z. $\quad \blacksquare$

5.5.2 Compound

Let S be the statement

begin $S_1; \ldots; S_n$ **end** .

The proof rule for correctness is

Compound rule:

Given: $\{P_i\}\, S_i\, \{P_{i+1}\}$ for $i = 1, \ldots, n$

Conclusion: $\{P_1\}$ **begin** $S_1; \ldots; S_n$ **end** $\{P_{n+1}\}$ $\quad \blacksquare$

No extensions are needed to handle information flow security.

Example:

Consider the statement

```
begin "compute y = x mod n for x ≥ 0"
    i := x div n;
    y := x − i * n
end
```

The following proves $y = x \bmod n$ when $x \geq 0$ and $n > 0$, and $\underline{y} \leq \underline{x} \oplus \underline{n}$ when $\underline{pc} \leq Low$:

$\{x \geq 0, n > 0, \underline{pc} \leq Low\}$
   begin
      $\{0 \leq x - (x \text{ div } n)*n < n, \underline{x} \oplus \underline{n} \leq \underline{x} \oplus \underline{n}, \underline{pc} \leq Low\}$
      $i := x \text{ div } n;$
      $\{0 \leq x - i*n < n, \underline{i} \leq \underline{x} \oplus \underline{n}, \underline{pc} \leq Low\}$
      $\{0 \leq x - i*n < n, (x - i*n - x) \bmod n = 0,$
        $\underline{x} \oplus \underline{i} \oplus \underline{n} \leq \underline{x} \oplus \underline{n}, \underline{pc} \leq Low\}$
      $y := x - i*n$
   end
$\{0 \leq y < n, (y - x) \bmod n = 0, \underline{y} \leq \underline{x} \oplus \underline{n}, \underline{pc} \leq Low\}$.

Because the initial value of i does not flow into y, its class does not appear in the postcondition. The proof consists of a sequence of statements and assertions. Each assertion follows from its preceding assertion either by simple implication (e.g., the second and fourth assertions), or by the axioms and proof rules (e.g., the third and fifth assertions). ■

5.5.3 Alternation

Let S be the statement

   if e **then** S_1 **else** S_2 ,

where S_2 is the null statement when there is no **else** part. The proof rule for correctness follows:

   Given: $\{P, e\} S_1 \{Q\}$
                 $\{P, \sim e\} S_2 \{Q\}$
   Conclusion: $\{P\}$ **if** e **then** S_1 **else** $S_2 \{Q\}$ ■

Example:
Consider the statement

   if $x \geq 0$ **then** $y := x$ **else** $y := -x$.

We can prove that execution of this statement sets $y = |x|$ for any initial value of x:

   $\{\}$
   if $x \geq 0$
      $\{x \geq 0\}$
      $\{x \geq 0, x = |x|\}$
      then $y := x$
      $\{y = |x|\}$
   $- - - - - - - -$
      $\{x < 0\}$

$$\{x < 0, -x = |x|\}$$
$$\textbf{else } y := -x$$
$$\{y = |x|\}$$
$$\{y = |x|\}. \quad \blacksquare$$

To extend the proof rule to secure information flow, we must account for the implicit flow from e into S_1 and S_2 via the program counter. To do this, the precondition P is written as a conjunction $P = \{V, L\}$, where L is an assertion about $\underline{pc}$ and V is an assertion about the remaining information state. Similarly, the postcondition Q is written as a conjunction $Q = \{V', L\}$. On entry to (and exit from) S_1 and S_2, L is replaced with an assertion L' such that $\{V, L\}$ implies the assertion $L'[\underline{pc} \leftarrow \underline{pc} \oplus \underline{e}]$. This allows the class $\underline{pc}$ to be temporarily increased by $\underline{e}$ on entry to S_1 or S_2, and then restored on exit. Because $\underline{pc}$ is restored after execution of the **if** statement, the assertion L is invariant (i.e., it is the same in P and Q); however, the assertion V may be changed by S_1 or S_2. We thus have the following rule:

Alternation rule:

Given: $P = \{V, L\}, Q = \{V', L\}$
             $\{V, e, L'\} S_1 \{V', L'\}$
             $\{V, \sim e, L'\} S_2 \{V', L'\}$
             $P \supset L' [\underline{pc} \leftarrow \underline{pc} \oplus \underline{e}]$
Conclusion: $\{P\}$ **if** e **then** S_1 **else** $\bar{S}_2 \{Q\}$ $\blacksquare$

Example:

Consider the statement

   if $x = 1$ **then** $y := a$ **else** $y := b$

of the procedure *copy7*. We can prove for all x, a, and b,

$$\{\underline{pc} \leq Low\}$$
$$\textbf{if } x = 1$$
$$\quad \{x = 1, \underline{pc} \leq \underline{x}\}$$
$$\quad \{x = 1, \underline{pc} \oplus \underline{a} \leq \underline{x} \oplus \underline{a}, \underline{pc} \leq \underline{x}\}$$
$$\quad \textbf{then } y := a$$
$$\quad \{x = 1, \underline{y} \leq \underline{x} \oplus \underline{a}, \underline{pc} \leq \underline{x}\}$$
$$\text{-----------------------}$$
$$\quad \{x \neq 1, \underline{pc} \leq \underline{x}\}$$
$$\quad \{x \neq 1, \underline{pc} \oplus \underline{b} \leq \underline{x} \oplus \underline{b}, \underline{pc} \leq \underline{x}\}$$
$$\quad \textbf{else } y := b$$
$$\quad \{x \neq 1, \underline{y} \leq \underline{x} \oplus \underline{b}, \underline{pc} \leq \underline{x}\}$$
$$\{\underline{pc} \leq Low,$$
$$\quad (x = 1) \supset (\underline{y} \leq \underline{x} \oplus \underline{a}), (x \neq 1) \supset (\underline{y} \leq \underline{x} \oplus \underline{b})\}. \quad \blacksquare$$

5.5.4 Iteration

Let S be the statement

while e **do** S_1 .

The proof rule for correctness is

> Given: $\{P, e\}\ S_1\ \{P\}$
> Conclusion: $\{P\}$ **while** e **do** S_1 $\{P, \sim e\}$ ∎

where P is the loop invariant. This is extended to security as for alternation:

Iteration rule:
Given: $P = \{V, L\}$
$\qquad\quad \{V, L', e\}\ S_1\ \{V, L'\}$
$\qquad\quad P \supset L'\ [\underline{pc} \leftarrow \underline{pc} \oplus \underline{e}]$
Conclusion: $\{P\}$ **while** e **do** S_1 $\{P, \sim e\}$ ∎

To handle parallel programs, a slightly more complicated rule is needed. To certify "global flows" from the loop condition e to statements outside S_1 that logically follow the **while** statement, the assertions P and Q are expressed as the conjunctions

$$P = \{V, L, G\}$$
$$Q = \{V, \sim e, L, G'\}\ ,$$

where G is an assertion about a special class *global*, and

$$P \supset G'[\underline{global} \leftarrow \underline{global} \oplus \underline{pc} \oplus \underline{e}]\ .$$

Unlike *pc*, *global* is never restored; instead it continually increases, because all subsequent statements of the program are conditioned on loop terminations.

The class *global* is also used to certify synchronization flows (see exercises at end of chapter).

5.5.5 Procedure Call

Let q be a procedure of the form:

> **procedure** $q(x;$ **var** $y)$;
> local variable declarations;
> $\{P, \underline{pc} \leq PC_q\}$
> S
> $\{Q\}$
> **end** q ,

where x is a vector of input parameters, and y is a vector of output parameters (or input/output parameters). The body S may reference global variables z and global constants. We assume all variables in x, y, and z are disjoint (see [Grie80] for proof rules for overlapping variables).

We assume the security proof of q is of the form

$$\{P, \underline{pc} \le PC_q\}\ S\ \{Q\}\ ,$$

where P is a precondition that must hold at the time of the call, PC_q is a place-holder for a bound on $\underline{pc}$ at the time of the call, and Q is a postcondition that holds when q terminates. We assume Q does not reference the local variables of q. Q may reference the value parameters x; we assume all such references are to the initial values and classes passed to q (assignments to x in q do not affect the actual parameters anyway). Q may reference the variable parameters y and global varia-bles z; the initial values and classes of these variables at the time of call are referenced by y', $\underline{y'}$ and z', $\underline{z'}$.

Consider a call of the form

$$q(a;\ b)\ ,$$

where a is a vector of arguments corresponding to the parameters x, and b is a vector of arguments corresponding to the parameters y.

Reitman and Andrews give a proof rule for verifying the security of proce-dure calls, but not their correctness. We shall instead use the following proof rule, which is an extension of correctness proof rules (e.g., see [Grie80,Lond78]), allow-ing for the substitution of classes as well as values:

Procedure call rule:
Given: $\{P, \underline{pc} \le PC_q\}\ S\ \{Q\}$
Conclusion: $\{P[(x, \underline{x}) \leftarrow (a, \underline{a});\ (y, \underline{y}) \leftarrow (b, \underline{b});\ PC_q \leftarrow PC],$
$\forall u, v:$
$Q[(x, \underline{x}) \leftarrow (a, \underline{a});$
$(y, \underline{y}) \leftarrow (u, \underline{u});\ (y', \underline{y'}) \leftarrow (b, \underline{b});$
$(z, \underline{z}) \leftarrow (v, \underline{v});\ (z', \underline{z'}) \leftarrow (z, \underline{z});\ PC_q \leftarrow PC] \supset$
$R[(b, \underline{b}) \leftarrow (u, \underline{u});\ (z, \underline{z}) \leftarrow (v, \underline{v})]\}$
$q(a, b)$
$\{R\}$ ■

where PC is a bound on $\underline{pc}$ at the time of the call; that is, $\underline{pc} \le PC$ is implied by the precondition of the call. The assertion $\{\forall u, v:Q[]\supset R[]\}$ says R can be true after the call if and only if for all possible values u assigned to the variable parameters y, and all possible values v assigned to the global variables z, the postcondition Q implies R before the call when a is substituted for x, b for y', z for z', and the current bound PC for PC_q.

Example:
Consider the following procedure, with precondition and postcondition as shown:

```
procedure f(var y1, y2: integer);
  {pc ≤ PC_f}
  begin
      y2 := y1;
      y1 := 0
  end
```

$$\{\underline{y1} \leq PC_f, \underline{y2} \leq \underline{y1}' \oplus PC_f, \underline{pc} \leq PC_f\}$$
end f .

Note the precondition of f consists only of an assertion about $\underline{pc}$ (i.e., the condition P in the proof rule is "true"). The postcondition states the final value of $y1$ is no more sensitive than the program counter, and that of $y2$ is no more sensitive than the initial value of $y1$ and the program counter. Consider a call "$f(b1, b2)$". Given the precondition $\{\underline{pc} \leq Low, \underline{b1} \leq High, \underline{b2} \leq Low\}$, we can prove execution of f lowers $\underline{b1}$ but raises $\underline{b2}$ as follows:

$$\{\underline{b1} \leq High, \underline{b2} \leq Low, \underline{pc} \leq Low\}$$
$$\{\underline{pc} \leq Low,$$
$$\forall u1, u2: (\underline{u1} \leq Low, \underline{u2} \leq High, \underline{pc} \leq Low) \supset,$$
$$(\underline{u1} \leq Low, \underline{u2} \leq High, \underline{pc} \leq Low)\}$$
$$f(b1, b2)$$
$$\{\underline{b1} \leq Low, \underline{b2} \leq High, \underline{pc} \leq Low\} \ . \quad \blacksquare$$

Example:
Consider the following procedure, which deciphers a string x (we shall assume the key is part of the decipher function):

procedure *decipher*(x: **string** "ciphertext";
               var y: **string** "plaintext");
  "decipher x into y"
  $\{\underline{pc} \leq PC_d\}$
  "decipher transformation"
  $\{\underline{y} \leq \underline{x} \oplus PC_d, \underline{pc} \leq PC_d\}$
end *decipher* .

The postcondition states the final state of y is no more sensitive than the state of x and the program counter.

Now, consider the procedure shown in Figure 5.15, which calls *deci-*

FIGURE 5.15 Procedure *getmsg*.

---

procedure *getmsg*(c: **string**; **var** p: **string**);
  "get message: decipher c and return the
  corresponding plaintext p if the authority
  of the calling program is at least level 2
  (*Secret*); the authority is represented by
  the global constant a"
  $\{\underline{a} \leq Low, \underline{pc} \leq PC_g\}$
  if $a \geq 2$
    then *decipher* (c, p)
    else $p :=$ null
  $\{\underline{a} \leq Low, \underline{pc} \leq PC_g,$
  $(a \geq 2) \supset (\underline{p} \leq \underline{c} \oplus PC_g), \quad (a < 2) \supset (\underline{p} \leq PC_g)\}$
  end *getmsg*

---

pher. The postcondition states the final class of p is bounded by $\underline{c} \oplus PC_g$ when $a \geq 2$, and by PC_g when $a < 2$, where PC_g is a placeholder for a bound on $\underline{\underline{pc}}$ at the time of the call. Because the initial value of p is lost, its initial sensitivity does not affect its final sensitivity. The authority level a is in the lowest class. We shall now prove that the precondition of *getmsg* implies the postcondition.

$$\{\underline{\underline{a}} \leq Low, \underline{\underline{pc}} \leq PC_g\}$$
$\quad$ **if** $a \geq 2$
$$\{\underline{a} \geq 2, \underline{\underline{a}} \leq Low, \underline{\underline{pc}} \leq PC_g\}$$
$$\{\underline{\underline{pc}} \leq P\bar{C}_g,$$
$$\forall u{:}(\underline{u} \leq \underline{c} \oplus PC_g, \underline{\underline{pc}} \leq PC_g) \supset$$
$$(\underline{a} \geq \bar{2}, \underline{\underline{a}} \leq Low, \underline{u} \leq \underline{c} \oplus PC_g, \underline{\underline{pc}} \leq PC_g)\}$$
$\quad$ **then** *decipher*(c, p)
$$\{\underline{a} \geq 2, \underline{\underline{a}} \leq Low, \underline{p} \leq \underline{c} \oplus PC_g, \underline{\underline{pc}} \leq PC_g\}$$
$\quad$ -
$$\{\underline{a} < 2, \underline{\underline{a}} \leq Low, \underline{\underline{pc}} \leq PC_g\}$$
$\quad$ **else** $p :=$ null
$$\{\underline{a} < 2, \underline{\underline{a}} \leq Low, \underline{p} \leq PC_g, \underline{\underline{pc}} \leq PC_g\}$$
$$\{\underline{\underline{a}} \leq Low, \underline{\underline{pc}} \leq PC_g,$$
$$(\underline{a} \geq 2) \supset (\underline{p} \leq \underline{c} \oplus PC_g), (\underline{a} < 2) \supset (\underline{p} \leq PC_g)\} \; . \quad \blacksquare$$

5.5.6 Security

Proving a program satisfies its assertions does not automatically imply the program is secure. The assertions must also satisfy the security requirements imposed by the flow policy.

$\quad$ Given a statement S and a proof $\{P\}\ S\ \{Q\}$, execution of S is secure if and only if:

1. P is initially true,
2. For every object v assigned to a fixed security class $\underline{v}$, $Q \supset \{\underline{v} \leq \underline{v}\}$

The second requirement states that the information represented in the final value of v (represented by $\underline{v}$) must be no more sensitive than that permitted by the class $\underline{v}$.

Example:
Earlier we proved:

$$\{\underline{\underline{pc}} \leq Low\}$$
$\quad$ **if** $x = 1$ **then** $y := a$ **else** $y := b$
$$\{\underline{\underline{pc}} \leq Low,$$
$$(x = 1) \supset (\underline{y} \leq \underline{x} \oplus \underline{a}), \quad (x \neq 1) \supset (\underline{y} \leq \underline{x} \oplus \underline{b})\} \; .$$

Let $x = 1$, $\underline{x} = Low$, $\underline{a} = Low$, $\underline{b} = High$, $\underline{y} = Low$, and $\underline{\underline{pc}} = Low$. Since the postcondition does not contain any assertions about the sensitivity of information in x, a, or b, it does not imply that $x \leq Low$, $\underline{a} \leq Low$, $\underline{b} \leq High$, and $\underline{y} \leq Low$. To show execution of this statement is secure, we instead prove:

$\{x = 1, x \leq Low, \underline{a} \leq Low, \underline{b} \leq High, \underline{pc} \leq Low\}$
if $x = 1$ **then** $y := a$ **else** $y := b$
$\{x = 1, x \leq Low, \underline{a} \leq Low, \underline{b} \leq High, \underline{y} \leq x \oplus \underline{a}, \underline{pc} \leq Low\}$
$\{x = 1, \underline{x} \leq Low, \underline{a} \leq Low, \underline{b} \leq High, \underline{y} \leq Low, \underline{pc} \leq Low\}$. ∎

Example:

Consider the following statement, which passes objects c and p to the procedure *getmsg* of Figure 5.15 (we have chosen the same names for our actual arguments as for the formal parameters of g)

$getmsg(c, p)$.

Let $a = 3$ (*Top Secret*), $\underline{a} = 0$ (*Unclassified* or *Low*), $c = 2$ (*Secret*), $p = 3$, and $PC = 3$. Because $a \geq 2$, the ciphertext c will be deciphered, and the result assigned to p. We can prove:

$\{a = 3, \underline{a} \leq Low, \underline{c} \leq 2, \underline{pc} \leq 3\}$
$\{\underline{a} \leq Low, \underline{pc} \leq 3,$
$\quad \forall u:(\underline{a} \leq Low, u \leq 3, \underline{pc} \leq 3) \supset$
$\quad\quad (a = 3, \underline{a} \leq Low, \underline{c} \leq 2, u \leq 3, \underline{pc} \leq 3)\}$
$getmsg(c, p)$
$\{a = 3, \underline{a} \leq Low, \underline{c} \leq 2, \underline{p} \leq 3, \underline{pc} \leq 3\}$.

Because the postcondition implies the contents of each object is no more sensitive than its fixed class, the preceding call is secure.

Next let $a = 1$ (*Confidential*), $\underline{a} = 0$, $c = 2$, $p = 1$, and $PC = 1$. Here $a < 2$, so c will not be deciphered, and p will be assigned the null value. We can prove:

$\{a = 1, \underline{a} \leq Low, \underline{c} \leq 2, \underline{pc} \leq 1\}$
$\{\underline{a} \leq Low, \underline{pc} \leq 1,$
$\quad \forall u:(\underline{a} \leq Low, u \leq 1, \underline{pc} \leq 1) \supset$
$\quad\quad (a = 1, \underline{a} \leq Low, \underline{c} \leq 2, u \leq 1, \underline{pc} \leq 1)\}$
$getmsg(c, p)$
$\{a = 1, \underline{a} \leq Low, \underline{c} \leq 2, \underline{p} \leq 1, \underline{pc} \leq 1\}$.

Again the postcondition implies execution of the call is secure.

If $a \geq 2$ and $\underline{p} < c$, we cannot prove execution of the call is secure (because it is not secure!—see exercises at the end of Chapter). Assuming only verified programs are allowed to execute, this means a top secret process, for example, cannot cause secret ciphertext to be deciphered into a lower classified variable. ∎

Once a procedure has been formally verified, we would like assurances it has not been tampered with or replaced by a Trojan Horse. This is a good application for digital signatures (see Section 1.3.1). The verification mechanism would sign the code for a procedure after its security had been proved, and the operating system would not load and execute any code without a valid signature.

5.6 FLOW CONTROLS IN PRACTICE

5.6.1 System Verification

Efforts to build verifiably secure systems have been motivated largely by the security requirements of the Department of Defense. Prior to the 1970s, no commercially available system had withstood penetration, and no existing system could adequately enforce multilevel security. To deal with this problem, classified information was processed one level at a time, and the system was shut down and cleared before processing information at another level. This was a costly and cumbersome mode of operation.

In the early 1970s, the Air Force Electronic Systems Division sponsored several studies aimed at developing techniques to support the design and verification of multilevel security systems. The methodology that emerged from these studies was founded on the concept of security kernel (see Section 4.6.1), and was reported in papers by Anderson [Ande72], Schell, Downey, and Popek [Sche72], Bell and Burke [Bell74], and Bell and LaPadula [Bell73]. By the late 1970s, the methodology had been applied (to various degrees) to the design and verification of several security kernels including those listed in Section 4.6.1.

A security kernel is specified in terms of states and state transitions, and verified following the general approach described in Section 4.6.3. The multilevel security requirements of the kernel are based on a model introduced by Bell and LaPadula at MITRE [Bell73]. The model assumes objects have fixed security classes; this assumption is formalized by an axiom called the **tranquility principle**. Multilevel security is given in terms of two axioms called the simple security condition and the *-property (pronounced "star-property"). The **simple security condition** states that a process p may not have read access to an object x unless $x \leq p$. The ***-property** states that a process may not have read access to an object x and write access to an object y unless $x \leq y$. This is stronger than necessary, because p may not cause any information flow from x to y; applications of the model to security kernel verification have relaxed this to require $x \leq y$ only when y is functionally dependent on x.

Researchers at MITRE [Mill76,Mill81] and at SRI [Feie77,Feie80] have developed techniques for verifying multilevel security in formal program specifications expressed as V- and O-functions (see Section 4.6.3). Flows from state variables are specified by references to primitive V-functions, and flows into state variables by changes to primitive V-functions (specified by the effects of O-functions). Security is verified by proving the security classes of the state variables and of the process executing the specified function satisfy the conditions for simple security and the *-property. The principal difference between security proofs for specifications and those for programs (such as described in the preceding sections) is that specifications are nondeterministic; that is, the statements in the effects of an *O*-function are unordered.

Feiertag [Feie80] developed a model and tool for verifying multilevel security for *V*- and *O*-function specifications written in SPECIAL. The tool is part of SRI's Hierarchical Design Methodology HDM (see Section 4.6.3). A formula generator constructs formulas from the specifications that either prove or disprove a module is multilevel secure. Nontrivial formulas are passed to the Boyer-Moore theorem prover, where they are proved (or disproved) to be theorems. The user specifies the security classes of the state variables and the partial ordering relation ≤, so the tool is not limited to the military classification scheme. The Feiertag model is the basis for the PSOS secure object manager [Feie77,Neum80]. The tool has been used to verify the specifications of both the KSOS-11 and KSOS-6 (SCOMP) kernels. Verification of the KSOS kernel revealed several insecure channels in the design, some of which will remain as known potential low-bandwidth signaling paths [Neum80].

MITRE [Mill81] has also developed an automated tool for analyzing flows in modules written in a specification language. The flow analyzer associates semantic attributes with the syntactic types of the specification language in much the same way as in the compiler-based mechanism described in Section 5.4.3. This information is then used to produce tables of formulas which, if true, give sufficient conditions for security (as in Feiertag's tool). The analyzer is generated using the YACC parser generator on UNIX, so it can be easily adapted to different specification languages; analyzers for subsets of SPECIAL and Ina Jo (the specification language developed at SDC) have been implemented.

The MITRE flow analyzer is based in part on the deductive formulation of information flow developed jointly by Millen [Mill78] and Furtek [Furt78]. The deductive formulation describes information flow in a module by transition **constraints** on the values of the state variables on entry to and exit from the module. Such a constraint is of the form

$$x1_{u1} \ldots xk_{uk} \times y_v ,$$

where $x1, \ldots, xk$, and y are state variables; and $u1, \ldots, uk$, and v represent their respective values. The constraint states that if xi has the value ui $(i = 1, \ldots, k)$ on entry to the module, then y cannot have the value v on exit from the module. Thus, the condition on the right of the "×" represents an impossible exit condition given the entry condition on the left. The constraint thus limits the possible values of the variables, making it possible to deduce something about the value of one variable from the values of other variables.

Example:
Consider the statement (formal specification)

$$'y = x ,$$

relating the new (primed) value of y to the old (unprimed) value of x. This statement is described by the set of constraints

$$\{x_u \times y_v \mid v \neq u\} \, ,$$

which states that if x initially has the value u, then the new value of y cannot be v for any $v \neq u$. Thus the initial value of x can be deduced from the new value of y, and the security requirements of the statement are given by the condition

$$\underline{x} \leq \underline{y} \, . \quad \blacksquare$$

Example:
The specification statement

> **if** $x = 0$ **then** $'y = 0$ **else** $'y = 1$

is described by the set of constraints

$$\{x_0 \times y_v \mid v \neq 0\} \cup \{x_u \times y_v \mid u \neq 0, v \neq 1\} \, ,$$

which shows that access to the new value of y can be used to deduce something about the initial value of x. The security requirements of this statement are given by the same condition as the previous statement. $\blacksquare$

The MITRE flow analyzer can handle arrays of elements belonging to different classes.

Example:
Consider the specification statement

> **if** $x < 2$ **then** $'y = a[x]$.

This statement is described by the set of constraints

$$\{x_i \, a[i]_u \times y_v \mid v \neq u, i < 2\} \, .$$

The security requirements of the statement are thus given by

$$\underline{x} \leq \underline{y}$$
$$\underline{a[i]} \leq \underline{y} \text{ for } i < 2 \, . \quad \blacksquare$$

Rushby's [Rush81] approach to the design and verification of secure systems (see Section 4.6.3) seems to obviate the need to prove multilevel flow security for a security kernel. Since the kernel serves to isolate processes sharing the same machine, it suffices to prove such an isolation is achieved. Proofs of multilevel security are needed only for the explicit communication channels connecting processes.

5.6.2 Extensions

Practical systems often have information flow requirements that extend or conflict with the information flow models we have described thus far; for example,

1. **Integrity.** Information flow models describe the dissemination of information, but not its alteration. Thus an *Unclassified* process, for example, can write nonsense into a *Top Secret* file without violating the multilevel security policy. Although this problem is remedied by access controls, efforts to develop a multilevel integrity model have been pursued. Biba [Biba77] proposed a model where each object and process is assigned an integrity level, and a process cannot write into an object unless its integrity level is at least that of the object (in contrast, its security level must be no greater than that of the object).

2. **Sanitization and Downgrading.** Written documents routinely have their security classifications lowered ("downgraded"), and sensitive information is edited ("sanitized") for release at a lower level. Because these operations violate the multilevel security policy, they cannot be handled by the basic flow control mechanisms in a security kernel. The current practice is to place them in trusted processes that are permitted to violate the policies of the kernel. The trusted processes are verified (or at least audited) to show they meet the security requirements of the system as a whole. An example of such a trusted process is described in the next section.

3. **Aggregation.** An aggregate of data might require a higher classification than the individual items. This is because the aggregate might give an overall picture that cannot be deduced (or easily deduced) from an individual item. For example, the aggregate of all combat unit locations might reveal a plan of attack. This is the opposite of the inference problem discussed in the next chapter, where the problem is to provide a means of releasing statistics that give an overall picture, while protecting the individual values used to compute the statistics.

5.6.3 A Guard Application

The ACCAT Guard [Wood79] is an interesting blend of flow controls and cryptography. Developed by Logicon at the Advanced Command and Control Architectural Testbed (ACCAT), the Guard is a minicomputer interface between two computers (or networks of computers) of different classifications (called *Low* and *High*).

The Guard supports two types of communication: network mail and database transactions. The Guard allows information to flow without human intervention from *Low* to *High* computers, but approval by a Security Watch Officer is required for flows from *High* to *Low*. Figure 5.16 shows the role of the Security Watch Officer for both types of communication. For mail, information flows in one direction only, so human intervention is required only for mail transmitted from *High* to *Low* computers (Figure 5.16b). Database transactions always require human intervention, however, because information flows in one direction with the query and the reverse direction with the response. Queries from a *High* computer to a *Low* computer must pass through the Security Watch Officer,

FIGURE 5.16 Information flow through the Guard and Security Watch Officer.

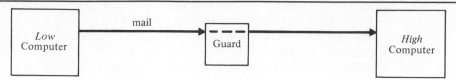

a) Mail transmitted from *Low* to *High* computer.

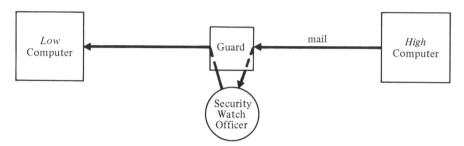

b) Mail transmitted from *High* to *Low* computer.

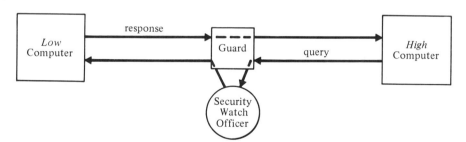

c) Database query from *High* to *Low* computer.

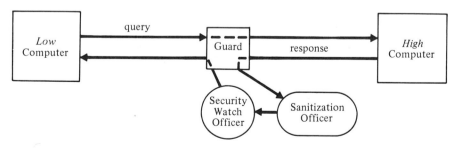

d) Database query from *Low* to *High* computer.

though the response can be returned without human intervention (Figure 5.16c). Queries from a *Low* to *High* computer can pass through the Guard without human intervention, but here the response must be reviewed. The Guard passes the response first through a Sanitization Officer, who edits the response as needed to

FIGURE 5.17 The ACCAT Guard.

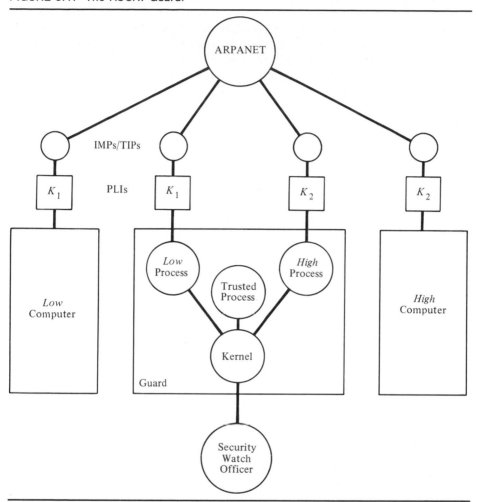

remove *High* security information, and then through the Security Watch Officer (Figure 5.16d).

Figure 5.17 shows the structure of the Guard system. The computers are connected to encryption devices called Private Line Interfaces (PLIs). The PLIs in turn are connected to the ARPANET (Advance Research Projects Agency NETwork) through Interface Message Processors (IMPs) or Terminal Interface Processors (TIPs). Separate encryption keys logically connect the *Low* computers to a *Low* process in the Guard and the *High* computers to a *High* process in the Guard. Because the keys are different, the *Low* and *High* computers cannot communicate directly.

The *Low* and *High* processes run in a secure UNIX environment (such as provided by KSOS). Flows from *Low* to *High* processes in the Guard are handled by the security mechanisms provided by the kernel. Because flows from *High* to *Low* processes violate the multilevel security policy, they are controlled by a trusted process that interfaces with the Security Watch Officer and downgrades information. Verification of the downgrade trusted process requires showing that all flows from *High* to *Low* are approved by the Security Watch Officer (see [Ames80]). The *Low* and *High* processes communicate with the trusted processes through inter-process communication messages provided by the kernel. The Security Watch Officer's terminal is directly connected to the kernel to prevent spoofing.

The multilevel security problem can be solved in part by running each classification level on a separate machine, and using encryption to enforce the flow requirements between machines [Davi80]. But this is only a partial solution. As illustrated by the Guard, some applications must process multiple classification levels and even violate the general flow policy. These applications must be supported by a secure system so they cannot be misused. The design and verification of specialized systems (such as the Guard), however, should be simpler than for general-purpose systems.

EXERCISES

5.1 Consider the following statement

   if $x > k$ **then** $y := 1$,

   where x is an integer variable in the range $[1, 2m]$, with all values equally likely, y is initially 0, and k is an integer constant. Give a formula for $H_y(x)$, the equivocation of x given the value of y after the statement is executed. Show that the amount of information transferred by this statement is maximal when $k = m$ by showing this problem is equivalent to showing that the entropy of a variable with two possible values is maximal when both values are equally likely (see Exercise 1.4).

5.2 Consider the statement

   if $x > k$ **then** $y := 1$,

   where x has the probability distribution

$$
p_i = \begin{cases}
\dfrac{1}{2} & x = 0 \\[6pt]
\dfrac{1}{4} & x = 1 \\[6pt]
\dfrac{1}{4} & x = 2 ,
\end{cases}
$$

   and y is initially 0. Compute the entropy $H(x)$. Compute the equivocation $H_y(x)$ both for $k = 0$ and $k = 1$.

5.3 Consider the statement

   if $(x = 1)$ **and** $(y = 1)$ **then** $z := 1$,

where x and y can each be 0 or 1, with both values equally likely, and z is initially 0. Compute the equivocations $H_{z'}(x)$ and $H_{z'}(y)$.

5.4 Consider the statement

$$z := x + y,$$

where x and y can each be 0 or 1, with both values equally likely. Compute the equivocations $H_{z'}(x)$ and $H_{z'}(y)$.

5.5 Let x be an integer variable in the range $[0, 2^{32} - 1]$, with all values equally likely. Write a program that transfers x to y using implicit flows. Compare the running time of your program with the trivial program "$y := x$".

5.6 Consider the lattice in Figure 5.1. What class corresponds to each of the following?

   a. $A \oplus B, A \otimes B$
   b. $B \oplus I, B \otimes I$
   c. $B \oplus C, B \otimes C$
   d. $A \oplus C \oplus D, A \otimes C \otimes D$
   e. $A \oplus B \oplus D, A \otimes B \otimes D$.

5.7 Trace the execution of the procedure *copy1* on the Data Mark Machine (see Figure 5.7 and Table 5.1) for $x = 1$ when $z \leq y$. Show that execution of *copy1* is secure when $x \nleq y$ both for $x = 0$ and $x = 1$. Note that if $x \nleq y$, then either $x \nleq z$ or $z \nleq y$.

5.8 Trace the execution of the procedure *copy1* on the single accumulator machine (see Figure 5.8 and Table 5.2) for both $x = 0$ and $x = 1$ when $x = High$, $y = Low$, $z = High$, and $\underline{pc}$ is initially Low, showing that execution of this procedure is secure.

5.9 Draw a syntax tree showing how the certification mechanism of Section 5.4.3 verifies the flows in the following statement:

    while $a > 0$ **do**
        begin
            $a := a - x;$
            $b := a * y$
        end .

5.10 Following the approach in Section 5.4.2, give security conditions for a **case** statement:

    case a **of**
        $v_1: S_1;$
        $v_2: S_2;$
           .
           .
           .
        $v_n: S_n;$
    end ,

where a is a variable and $v_1, \ldots, v_n$ are values.

5.11 For each Boolean expression in the *copy2* procedure shown in Figures 5.11 and 5.12, identify the set of blocks directly conditioned on the expression.

Assume the value of x can be any integer (i.e., is not restricted to the values 0 and 1). Use your results to identify all implicit flows in the procedure, showing that the procedure is secure.

5.12 Extend the certification semantics of Table 5.6 to include the following statements for concurrent programs:

signal(s) ;
wait(s) ;
cobegin $S_1; \ldots; S_n$ **end** .

Your semantics should provide an efficient method of verifying the relations $\underline{s} \le \underline{y}$ for every object y that is the target of an assignment in a statement logically following an operation **wait**(s). Note that you will have to extend the semantics of other statements to do this. In particular, you will have to extend the semantics of the **while** statement to certify global flows from the loop condition. Show how the extended mechanism certifies the procedures *copy3* (Figure 5.13) and *copy4* (Figure 5.14).

5.13 Given the statement

if $x = 0$
    then begin
        $t := a$;
        $y := t$
    end ,

prove the precondition $\{\underline{x} \le Low, \underline{pc} \le Low\}$ implies the postcondition $\{\underline{x} \le Low, (x = 0) \supset (\underline{y} \le \underline{a}), \underline{pc} \le Low\}$.

5.14 Prove the precondition implies the postcondition in the following procedure:

procedure *mod*(x, n: **integer**; **var** y: **integer**); **var** i: **integer**;
    $\{n > 0, \underline{pc} \le PC_m\}$
    begin "compute $y = x \bmod n$"
        $i := x$ **div** n;
        $y := x - i * n$;
        if $y < 0$ **then** $y := y + n$
    end .
    $\{0 \le y < n, (y - x) \bmod n = 0, \underline{y} \le \underline{x} \oplus \underline{n} \oplus PC_m, \underline{pc} \le PC_m\}$
    end *mod* .

5.15 Using the procedure *mod* in the preceding exercise, prove the following:

$\{a = 12, n = 5, \underline{pc} \le Low, \underline{n} \le Low\}$
mod(a, n, b)
$\{b = 2, \underline{b} \le \underline{a}, \underline{pc} \le Low, \underline{n} \le Low\}$.

5.16 Give a proof rule for an array assignment of the form

$a[i_1, \ldots, i_n] := b$.

Prove the following:

$$\{n \le Low, pc \le Low\}$$
begin
    $i := 1;$
    while $i \le n$ **do**
        begin
            $a[i] := 0;$
            $i := i + 1$
        end
end
$$\{\forall j: (1 \le j \le n) \supset \underline{a[j]} \le Low, \underline{n} \le Low, \underline{pc} \le Low\} .$$

5.17 Consider a call $getmsg(c, p)$ to the $getmsg$ procedure of Figure 5.15, where a = 2, a = Low, PC = 2, $\underline{c}$ = 2, and $\underline{p}$ = 1. Show it is not possible to prove execution of the call is secure.

5.18 Develop axioms and proof rules for the following statements for concurrent programs:

signals$(s);$
wait$(s);$
cobegin $S_1; \ldots ; S_n$ **end** .

You will have to introduce a class *global* to verify global flows and flows caused by synchronization. The class *global* should increase by both $\underline{s}$ and $\underline{pc}$ after execution of **wait**(s) [note that to do this, you must make your syntactic substitution in the precondition of **wait**(s)]. You should assume the flow proofs

$$\{P_1\} S_1 \{Q_1\}, \ldots , \{P_n\} S_n \{Q_n\}$$

are "interference free" in the sense that executing some S_i does not invalidate the proof of $S_j (1 \le j \le n)$. Unlike $\underline{pc}$, the class *global* is never restored. Show how *global* can be included in the proof rules for procedure calls. Consider the procedure *copy3* of Figure 5.13. Prove that the postcondition $\{y \le X, \underline{pc} \le PC\}$ follows from the precondition $\{x \le X, \underline{pc} \le PC\}$ and the body of the procedure. Do the same for the procedure *copy4* of Figure 5.14.

5.19 Following Millen's and Furtek's deductive formulation of information flow as described in Section 5.6.1, give constraints for the following specification statements, where x, y, and z are variables:

a. $'y = x + 1$.
b. $'z = x + y$.
c.   **if** $x = 1$ **then** $'y = a$ **else** $'y = b$, for variables a and b.
d.   **if** $x < 2$ **then** $'b[x] = a[x]$, for arrays $a[1:n]$ and $b[1:n]$.

REFERENCES

Alle70. Allen, F. E., "Control Flow Analysis," *Proc. Symp. Compiler Optimization, ACM SIGPLAN Notices* Vol. 5(7) pp. 1–19 (July 1970).

Ames80. Ames, S. R. and Keeton-Williams, J. G., "Demonstrating Security for Trusted Applications on a Security Kernel Base," pp. 145–156 in *Proc. 1980 Symp. on Security and Privacy*, IEEE Computer Society (April 1980).

Ande72. Anderson, J. P., "Computer Security Technology Planning Study," ESD-TR-73-51, Vols. I and II, USAF Electronic Systems Div., Bedford, Mass. (Oct. 1972).

Andr80. Andrews, G. R. and Reitman, R. P., "An Axiomatic Approach to Information Flow in Parallel Programs," *ACM Trans. on Prog. Languages and Systems* Vol. 2(1) pp. 56–76 (Jan. 1980).

Bell73. Bell, D. E. and LaPadula, L. J., "Secure Computer Systems: Mathematical Foundations and Model," M74-244, The MITRE Corp., Bedford, Mass. (May 1973).

Bell74. Bell, D. E. and Burke, E. L., "A Software Validation Technique for Certification: The Methodology," ESD-TR-75-54, Vol. I, The MITRE Corp., Bedford, Mass. (Nov. 1974).

Biba77. Biba, K. J., "Integrity Considerations for Secure Computer Systems," ESD-TR-76-372, USAF Electronic Systems Division, Bedford, Mass. (Apr. 1977).

Birk67. Birkhoff, G., *Lattice Theory*, Amer. Math. Soc. Col. Pub., XXV, 3rd ed. (1967).

Cohe77. Cohen, E., "Information Transmission in Computational Systems," *Proc. 6th Symp. on Oper. Syst. Princ., ACM Oper. Syst. Rev.* Vol. 11(5) pp. 133–139 (Nov. 1977).

Cohe78. Cohen, E., "Information Transmission in Sequential Programs," pp. 297–335 in *Foundations of Secure Computation*, ed. R. A. DeMillo et al., Academic Press, New York (1978).

Davi80. Davida, G. I., DeMillo, R. A., and Lipton, R. J., "A System Architecture to Support a Verifiably Secure Multilevel Security System," pp. 137–145 in *Proc. 1980 Symp. on Security and Privacy*, IEEE Computer Society (Apr. 1980).

Denn74. Denning, D. E., Denning, P. J., and Graham, G. S., "Selectively Confined Subsystems," in *Proc. Int. Workshop on Protection in Operating Systems*, IRIA, Rocquencourt, LeChesnay, France, pp. 55–61 (Aug. 1974).

Denn75. Denning, D. E., "Secure Information Flow in Computer Systems," Ph.D. Thesis, Purdue Univ., W. Lafayette, Ind. (May 1975).

Denn76a. Denning, D. E., "A Lattice Model of Secure Information Flow," *Comm. ACM* Vol. 19(5) pp. 236–243 (May 1976).

Denn76b. Denning, D. E., "On the Derivation of Lattice Structured Information Flow Policies," CSD TR 180, Computer Sciences Dept., Purdue Univ., W. Lafayette, Ind. (Mar. 1976).

Denn77. Denning, D. E. and Denning, P. J., "Certification of Programs for Secure Information Flow," *Comm. ACM* Vol. 20(7) pp. 504–513 (July 1977).

Feie77. Feiertag, R. J., Levitt, K. N., and Robinson, L., "Proving Multilevel Security of a System Design," *Proc. 6th Symp. on Oper. Syst. Princ., ACM Oper. Syst. Rev.* Vol. 11(5) pp. 57–66 (Nov. 1977).

Feie80. Feiertag, R. J., "A Technique for Proving Specifications are Multilevel Secure," Computer Science Lab. Report CSL-109, SRI International, Menlo Park, Calif. (Jan. 1980).

Fent73. Fenton, J. S., "Information Protection Systems," Ph.D. Dissertation, Univ. of Cambridge, Cambridge, England (1973).

Fent74. Fenton, J. S., "Memoryless Subsystems," *Comput. J.* Vol. 17(2) pp. 143–147 (May 1974).

Furt78. Furtek, F., "Constraints and Compromise," pp. 189–204 in *Foundations of Secure Computation*, ed. R. A. DeMillo et al., Academic Press, New York (1978).

Gain72. Gaines, R. S., "An Operating System Based on the Concept of a Supervisory Computer," *Comm. ACM* Vol. 15(3) pp. 150–156 (Mar. 1972).

Gat75. Gat, I. and Saal, H. J., "Memoryless Execution: A Programmer's Viewpoint," IBM Tech. Rep. 025, IBM Israeli Scientific Center, Haifa, Israel (Mar. 1975).

Grie80. Gries, D. and Levin, G., "Assignment and Procedure Call Proof Rules," *ACM Trans. on Programming Languages and Systems* Vol. 2(4) pp. 564–579 (Oct. 1980).

Hoar69. Hoare, C. A. R., "An Axiomatic Basis for Computer Programming," *Comm. ACM* Vol. 12(10) pp. 576–581 (Oct. 1969).

Jone75. Jones, A. K. and Lipton, R. J., "The Enforcement of Security Policies for Computation," *Proc. 5th Symp. on Oper. Syst. Princ., ACM Oper. Syst. Rev.* Vol. 9(5), pp. 197–206 (Nov. 1975).

Karg78. Karger, P. A., "The Lattice Model in a Public Computing Network," *Proc. ACM Annual Conf.* Vol. 1 pp. 453–459 (Dec. 1978).

Lamp73. Lampson, B. W., "A Note on the Confinement Problem," *Comm. ACM* Vol. 16(10) pp. 613–615 (Oct. 1973).

Lipn75. Lipner, S. B., "A Comment on the Confinement Problem," *Proc. 5th Symp. on Oper. Syst. Princ., ACM Oper. Syst. Rev.* Vol 9(5) pp. 192–196 (Nov. 1975).

Lond78. London, R. L., Guttag, J. V., Horning, J. J., Lampson, B. W., Mitchell, J. G., and Popek, G. J., "Proof Rules for the Programming Language Euclid," *Acta Informatica* Vol. 10 pp. 1–26 (1978).

Mill76. Millen, J. K., "Security Kernel Validation in Practice," *Comm. ACM* Vol. 19(5) pp. 243–250 (May 1976).

Mill78. Millen, J. K., "Constraints and Multilevel Security," pp. 205–222 in *Foundations of Secure Computation*, ed. R. A. DeMillo et al., Academic Press, New York (1978).

Mill81. Millen, J. K., "Information Flow Analysis of Formal Specifications," in *Proc. 1981 Symp. on Security and Privacy*, IEEE Computer Society, pp. 3–8 (Apr. 1981).

Mins67. Minsky, M., *Computation: Finite and Infinite Machines*, Prentice-Hall, Englewood Cliffs, N.J. (1967).

Neum80. Neumann, P. G., Boyer, R. S., Feiertag, R. J., Levitt, K. N., and Robinson, L., "A Provably Secure Operating System: The System, Its Applications, and Proofs," Computer Science Lab. Report CSL-116, SRI International, Menlo Park, Calif. (May 1980).

Reed79. Reed, D. P. and Kanodia, R. K., "Synchronization with Eventcounts and Sequencers," *Comm. ACM* Vol. 22(2) pp. 115–123 (Feb. 1979).

Reit79. Reitman, R. P., "A Mechanism for Information Control in Parallel Programs," *Proc. 7th Symp. on Oper. Syst. Princ., ACM Oper. Syst. Rev.*, pp. 55–62 (Dec. 1979).

Rote74. Rotenberg, L. J., "Making Computers Keep Secrets," Ph.D. Thesis, TR-115, MIT (Feb. 1974).

Rush81. Rushby, J. M., "Design and Verification of Secure Systems," *Proc. 8th Symp. on Oper. Syst. Princ., ACM Oper. Syst. Rev.*, Vol. 15(5), pp. 12–21 (Dec. 1981).

Sche72. Schell, R., Downey, P., and Popek, G., "Preliminary Notes on the Design of a Secure Military Computer System," MCI-73-1, USAF Electronic Systems Div., Bedford, Mass. (Oct. 1972).

Weis69. Weissman, C., "Security Controls in the ADEPT-50 Time-Sharing System," pp. 119–133 in *Proc. Fall Jt. Computer Conf.*, Vol. 35, AFIPS Press, Montvale, N.J. (1969).

Wood79. Woodward, J. P. L., "Applications for Multilevel Secure Operating Systems," pp. 319–328 in *Proc. NCC*, Vol. 48. AFIPS Press, Montvale, N.J. (1979).

6

Inference Controls

When information derived from confidential data must be declassified for wider distribution, simple flow controls as described in the previous chapter are inadequate. This is true of statistical databases, which can contain sensitive information about individuals or companies. The objective is to provide access to statistics about groups of individuals, while restricting access to information about any particular individual. Census bureaus, for example, are responsible for collecting information about all citizens and reporting this information in a way that does not jeopardize individual privacy.

The problem is that statistics contain vestiges of the original information. By correlating different statistics, a clever user may be able to deduce confidential information about some individual. For example, by comparing the total salaries of two groups differing only by a single record, the user can deduce the salary of the individual whose record is in one group but not in the other. The objective of inference controls is to ensure that the statistics released by the database do not lead to the disclosure of confidential data.

Although many databases are used for statistics only (e.g., census data), general-purpose database systems may provide both statistical and nonstatistical access. In a hospital database, for example, doctors may be given direct access to patients' medical records, while researchers are only permitted access to statistical summaries of the records. Although we are primarily interested in protection mechanisms for general-purpose systems, we shall also describe mechanisms for statistics-only databases.

6.1 STATISTICAL DATABASE MODEL

We shall describe a statistical database in terms of an abstract model.† Although
the model does not accurately describe either the logical or physical organization
of most database systems, its simplicity allows us to focus on the disclosure problem and compare different controls.

6.1.1 Information State

The **information state** of a statistical database system has two components: the
data stored in the database and external knowledge. The database contains information about the attributes of N individuals (organizations, companies, etc.).
There are M **attributes** (also called **variables**), where each attribute A_j ($1 \leq j$
$\leq M$) has $|A_j|$ possible values. An example of an attribute is *Sex*, whose two
possible values are *Male* and *Female*. We let x_{ij} denote the value of attribute j for
individual i. When the subscript j is not important to the discussion, we shall write
simply x_i to denote the value of an attribute A for individual i.

It is convenient to view a statistical database as a collection of N records,
where each record contains M fields, and x_{ij} is stored in record i, field j (see Figure
6.1). Note that this is equivalent to a relation (table) in a relational database
[Codd70,Codd79], where the records are M-tuples of the relation. If the information stored in the database is scattered throughout several relations, then the relation depicted in Figure 6.1 corresponds to the "natural join" of these relations. We
shall assume that each field is defined for all individuals, and that each individual
has a single record.

> *Example:*
> Table 6.1 shows a (sub) database containing $N = 13$ confidential student
> records for a hypothetical university having 50 departments. Each record has
> $M = 5$ fields (excluding the identifier), whose possible values are shown in
> Table 6.2. The attribute *SAT* specifies a student's average on the *SAT*
> (Scholastic Aptitude Test) and *GP* specifies a student's current grade-point.
> Unless otherwise stated, all examples refer to this database. ■

External knowledge refers to the information users have about the database.
There are two broad classes of external knowledge: working knowledge and supplementary knowledge. **Working knowledge** is knowledge about the attributes represented in the database (e.g., the information in Table 6.2) and the types of

---

† Jan Schlörer, Elisabeth Wehrle, and myself [Denn82] have extended the model described
here, showing how a statistical database can be viewed as a lattice of tables, and how different controls
can be interpreted in terms of the lattice structure. Because this work was done after the book had gone
into production, it was not possible to integrate it into this chapter.

FIGURE 6.1 Abstract view of a statistical database.

Record	A_1 ... A_j ... A_M
1	x_{11} ... x_{1j} ... x_{1M}
	. . .
	. . .
	. . .
i	x_{i1} ... x_{ij} ... x_{iM}
	. . .
	. . .
	. . .
N	x_{N1} ... x_{Nj} ... x_{NM}

TABLE 6.1 Statistical database with $N = 13$ students.

Name	Sex	Major	Class	SAT	GP
Allen	Female	CS	1980	600	3.4
Baker	Female	EE	1980	520	2.5
Cook	Male	EE	1978	630	3.5
Davis	Female	CS	1978	800	4.0
Evans	Male	Bio	1979	500	2.2
Frank	Male	EE	1981	580	3.0
Good	Male	CS	1978	700	3.8
Hall	Female	Psy	1979	580	2.8
Iles	Male	CS	1981	600	3.2
Jones	Female	Bio	1979	750	3.8
Kline	Female	Psy	1981	500	2.5
Lane	Male	EE	1978	600	3.0
Moore	Male	CS	1979	650	3.5

TABLE 6.2 Attribute values for Table 6.1.

Attribute A_j	Values	$|A_j|$
Sex	Male, Female	2
Major	Bio, CS, EE, Psy, ...	50
Class	1978, 1979, 1980, 1981	4
SAT	310, 320, 330, ..., 790, 800	50
GP	0.0, 0.1, 0.2, ..., 3.9, 4.0	41

statistics available. **Supplementary knowledge** is information that is not normally released by the database. This information may be confidential (e.g., a particular student's GP or SAT score) or nonconfidential (e.g., the student's sex).

6.1.2 Types of Statistics

Statistics are computed for subgroups of records having common attributes. A subgroup is specified by a **characteristic formula** C, which, informally, is any logical formula over the values of attributes using the operators "or" ($+$), "and" ($\bullet$), and "not" ($\sim$), where the operators are written in order of increasing priority. An example of a formula is

$$(Sex = Male) \bullet ((Major = CS) + (Major = EE)) \ ,$$

which specifies all male students majoring in either CS or EE. We shall omit attribute names where they are clear from context, e.g., "$Male \bullet (CS + EE)$". We shall also use relational operators in the specification of characteristics, since these are simply abbreviations for the "or" of several values; for example, "$GP > 3.7$" is equivalent to "$(GP = 3.8) + (GP = 3.9) + (GP = 4.0)$".

The set of records whose values match a characteristic formula C is called the **query set** of C. For example, the query set of $C = $ "$Female \bullet CS$" is $\{1, 4\}$, which consists of the records for Allen and Davis. We shall write "C" to denote both a formula and its query set, and $|C|$ to denote the number of records in C (i.e., the size of C). We denote by All a formula whose query set is the entire database; thus $C \subseteq All$ for any formula C, where "$\subseteq$" denotes query set inclusion.

Given $|A_j|$ values for each of the M attributes A_j ($j = 1, \ldots, M$), there are

$$E = \prod_{j=1}^{M} |A_j|$$

possible distinguishable records described by formulas of the form

$$(A_1 = a_1) \bullet \ldots \bullet (A_M = a_M) \ ,$$

where a_j is some value of attribute A_j. The query set corresponding to a formula of this form is called an **elementary set** because it cannot be further decomposed. The records in an elementary set (if any) are indistinguishable. Thus there are E elementary sets in the database, some of which may be empty. We let g denote the maximum size of all elementary sets; thus g is the maximum number of individuals having identical records, that is, the size of the largest indecomposable query set. If the number of records N satisfies $N \leq E$, then every individual may be identified by a unique elementary set, giving $g = 1$.

> *Example:*
> If we allow queries over all five attributes in Table 6.1, $E = (2)\,(50)\,(4)\,(50)\,(41) = 820{,}000$; $g = 1$ because each record is uniquely identifiable. If queries are restricted to the attributes *Sex*, *Major*, and *Class*, then $E = 400$; $g = 2$ because two students have the common characteristic "$Male \bullet EE \bullet 1978$". ■

Statistics are calculated over the values associated with a query set C. The simplest statistics are **counts (frequencies)** and **sums**:

$$\mathbf{count}(C) = |C|$$
$$\mathbf{sum}(C, A_j) = \sum_{i \in C} x_{ij} \ .$$

Example:
$\mathbf{count}(\textit{Female} \bullet \textit{CS}) = 2$, and $\mathbf{sum}(\textit{Female} \bullet \textit{CS}, \textit{SAT}) = 1400.$ ■

Note that sums apply only to numeric data (e.g., *GP*, and *SAT*). The responses from counts and sums are used to calculate **relative frequencies** and **averages** (**means**):

$$\mathbf{rfreq}(C) = \frac{\mathbf{count}(C)}{N} = \frac{|C|}{N}$$
$$\mathbf{avg}(C, A_j) = \frac{\mathbf{sum}(C, A_j)}{|C|}$$

Example:
$$\mathbf{avg}(\textit{Female} \bullet \textit{CS}, \textit{SAT}) = \frac{1400}{2} = 700. \ ■$$

More general types of statistics can be expressed as **finite moments** of the form:

$$q(C, e_1, \ldots, e_M) = \sum_{i \in C} x_{i1}^{e1} x_{i2}^{e2} \ldots x_{iM}^{eM} \ , \tag{6.1}$$

where the exponents $e_1, \ldots, e_M$ are nonnegative integers. Note that counts and sums can be expressed as moments:

$$\mathbf{count}(C) = q(C, 0, \ldots, 0)$$
$$\mathbf{sum}(C, A_j) = q(C, 0, \ldots, 0, 1, 0, \ldots, 0) \ ,$$

where the *j*th exponent for the **sum** is 1, and all other exponents are 0. Means, variances, covariances, and correlation coefficients can also be computed. For example, the **mean** and **variance** of attribute A_1 are given by:

$$\overline{A}_1 = \mathbf{avg}(C, A_1) = \frac{q(C, 1, 0, \ldots, 0)}{|C|}$$

$$\sigma_1^2 = \mathbf{var}(C, A_1) = \frac{q(C, 2, 0, \ldots, 0)}{|C| - 1} - (\overline{A}_1)^2 \ .$$

The **covariance** of attributes A_1 and A_2 is given by

$$\sigma_{12}^2 = \mathbf{covar}(C, A_1, A_2) = \frac{q(C, 1, 1, 0, \ldots, 0)}{|C| - 1} - \overline{A}_1 \overline{A}_2$$

and the **correlation coefficient** of A_1 and A_2 is

$$\rho_{12} = \mathbf{corcoef}(C, A_1, A_2) = \frac{\sigma_{12}^2}{\sigma_1 \sigma_2} \ .$$

By $q(C)$ we shall mean any statistic, or **query** for a statistic, of the form (6.1).

Another type of statistic selects some value (smallest, largest, median, etc.) from the query set. We shall write

median(C, A_j)

to denote the **median** or $\lceil |C|/2 \rceil$ largest value of attribute A_j in the query set C, where "$\lceil \ \rceil$" denotes the ceiling (round up to nearest integer). Note that when the query-set size is even, the median is the smaller of the two middle values, and not their average.

> *Example:*
> The set of *GP*s for all female students is {2.5, 2.5, 2.8, 3.4, 3.8, 4.0}; thus **median**(*Female, GP*) = 2.8. ■

Statistics derived from the values of m distinct attributes are called *m*-**order statistics**. The attributes can be specified by terms in the characteristic formula C, or by nonzero exponents e_j in Formula (6.1). There is a single 0-order statistic, namely **count**(*All*). Examples of 1-order statistics are **count**(*Male*) and **sum**(*All, GP*). Examples of 2-order statistics are **count**(*Male* • *CS*) and **sum**(*Male, GP*). Note that **count**(*EE* + *CS*) is a 1-order statistic because *CS* and *EE* are values of the same attribute.

6.1.3 Disclosure of Sensitive Statistics

A statistic is **sensitive** if it discloses too much confidential information about some individual (organization, company, etc.). A statistic computed from confidential information in a query set of size 1 is always sensitive.

> *Example:*
> The statistic
>
> **sum**(*EE* • *Female, GP*) = 2.5
>
> is sensitive, because it gives the exact grade-point of Baker, the only female student in *EE*. ■

A statistic computed from confidential information in a query set of size 2 may also be classified as sensitive, because a user with supplementary knowledge about one of the values may be able to deduce the other from the statistic. The exact criterion for sensitivity is determined by the policies of the system. One criterion used by the U.S. Census Bureau for sums of economic data is the *n*-**respondent**, *k*%-**dominance** rule, which defines a **sensitive** statistic to be one where n or fewer values contribute more than k% of the total [Cox80].

> *Example:*
> A statistic giving the sum of the exact earnings of IBM and all early music

stores in Indiana would be sensitive under a 1-respondent, 99%-dominance criterion; its release would disclose a considerable amount of information about IBM's earnings (namely the high-order digits), though it would disclose little about the early music stores (which would be hidden in the low-order digits). ∎

Clearly, all sensitive statistics must be restricted (i.e., not permitted). In addition, it may be necessary to restrict certain nonsensitive statistics if they could lead to disclosure of sensitive ones.

Example:
Suppose that the only statistics classified as sensitive in the sample database are those computed from query sets of size 1. Then neither **sum**(*EE, GP*) nor **sum**(*EE • Male, GP*) is sensitive. At least one of these statistics must be restricted, however, because if they are both released, Baker's grade-point is disclosed:

> **sum**(*EE • Female, GP*)
> $\quad$ = **sum**(*EE, GP*) − **sum**(*EE • Male, GP*)
> $\quad$ = $\quad$ 12.0 $\quad\quad$ − $\quad$ 9.5
> $\quad$ = $\quad\quad$ 2.5 . $\quad\quad$ ∎

Let R be a set of statistics released to a particular user, and let K denote the user's supplementary knowledge. **Statistical disclosure** [Haq75] occurs whenever the user can deduce from R and K something about a restricted statistic q; in terms of classical information theory (see Section 1.4),

$$H_{K,R}(q) < H_K(q) \; ,$$

where $H_K(q)$ is the equivocation (conditional entropy) of q given K, and $H_{K,R}(q)$ is the equivocation of q given K and R. Statistical disclosure of a sensitive statistic is sometimes called **residual** [Fell72] or **personal disclosure (compromise)** [Haq75]. If a disclosure occurs without supplementary knowledge, it is called **resultant disclosure**; if supplementary knowledge is necessary, it is called **external disclosure** [Haq75]. Supplementary knowledge is always required for personal disclosure to match the value disclosed with a particular individual.

Example:
Disclosure of **sum**(*EE • Female, GP*) can lead to personal disclosure of Baker's *GP* only if some user knows that Baker is a female student majoring in *EE*. The user must also know that Baker is the only female student in *EE*; this could be deduced from the statistic:

> **count**(*EE • Female*) = 1

or, if this statistic is restricted (because it isolates a single individual), from

> **count**(*EE*) − **count**(*EE • Male*) = 4 − 3 = 1 . ∎

The **amount of information** (in bits) that a set of statistics R discloses about a statistic q is measured by the reduction of entropy: $H_K(q) - H_{K,R}(q)$.

A disclosure may be either exact or approximate. **Exact disclosure** occurs when q is determined exactly; thus, $H_{K,R}(q) = 0$. For example, the preceding disclosure of Baker's grade-point is exact.

Approximate disclosure occurs when q is not determined exactly. Dalenius describes three types of approximate disclosure [Dale77]. First, a disclosure may reveal **bounds** L and U such that $L \leq q \leq U$.

Example:
If it is known only that **count**($EE \bullet$ *Female*) ≥ 1, then release of the statistic $R = $ **count**(EE) $= 4$ implies

$$1 \leq \textbf{count}(EE \bullet \textit{Female}) \leq 4 ,$$

thereby reducing the uncertainty about **count**($EE \bullet$ *Female*) to

$$H_{K,R}((\textbf{count}(EE \bullet \textbf{Female}))) = 2$$

bits of information (assuming all counts in the range [1, 4] are equally likely) . ∎

Example:
Release of the statistics

count(EE)	$= 4$
count($EE \bullet (GP \geq 3.0)$)	$= 3$
count($EE \bullet$ *Male*)	$= 3$
count($EE \bullet$ *Male* $\bullet (GP \geq 3.0)$)	$= 3$

reveals that

$$0 \leq \textbf{sum}(EE \bullet \textit{Female}, GP) < 3.0 . ∎$$

Second, a disclosure may be **negative** in the sense of revealing that $q \neq y$, for some value y. For example, a user may learn that **sum**($EE \bullet$ *Female*, GP) $\neq 3.5$.

Third, a disclosure may be **probabilistic** in the sense of disclosing information that is true only with some probability. An example is **interval estimation**, where it is learned that q falls in some interval $[L, U]$ with probability p; that is,

$$Pr[q \in [L, U]] = p .$$

The interval $[L, U]$ is called the **confidence interval** for q, and the probability p the **confidence level**.

Example:
Suppose an estimate $\hat{q}$ of q is a random variable drawn from a distribution approximately normal with standard deviation $\sigma_{\hat{q}}$. We then have:

$$Pr[q \in [\hat{q} \pm 1.645\sigma_{\hat{q}}]] \simeq .90$$
$$Pr[q \in [\hat{q} \pm 1.960\sigma_{\hat{q}}]] \simeq .95$$

$$Pr[q \epsilon [\hat{q} \pm 2.575\sigma_{\hat{q}}]] \simeq .99 .$$

The interval $[\hat{q} \pm 1.645\sigma_{\hat{q}}]$, for example, is called the 90% confidence interval of q because it is 90% certain that q lies in this interval. ∎

6.1.4 Perfect Secrecy and Protection

A statistical database provides **perfect secrecy** if and only if no sensitive statistic is disclosed. In practice, no statistical database can provide perfect secrecy, because any released statistic contains some information about the data used to compute it. Even the statistic **sum**(All, GP) contains some information about each student's grade-point, though it is difficult to extract a particular student's grade-point from it without additional statistics or supplementary information.

Our definition of perfect secrecy in statistical database systems is similar to the definition of perfect secrecy in cryptographic systems (see Section 1.4.2). But whereas it is a reasonable objective for cryptography, it is unreasonable for statistical databases—perfect secrecy would require that no information be released.

We are more interested in the difficulty of obtaining close approximations of confidential values. Given a sensitive statistic q, we say that q is **protected** from disclosure if and only if it is not possible to obtain an estimate $\hat{q}$ with confidence interval $[L_{\hat{q}}, U_{\hat{q}}]$ such that

$$Pr[q \epsilon [L_{\hat{q}}, U_{\hat{q}}]] \geq p \quad \text{where} \quad (U_{\hat{q}} - L_{\hat{q}}) \leq k \tag{6.2}$$

for probability p and interval length k (p and k can depend on q); otherwise, it is **compromisable**. Clearly, any statistic is compromisable for a sufficiently large interval or sufficiently small probability; therefore, we are only concerned about disclosure for relatively small k, and p near 1.0. Disclosure (compromise) occurs when an estimate $\hat{q}$ satisfying Eq. (6.2) can be obtained from a released set of statistics R. Note that this covers all forms of approximate disclosure except for negative disclosure. It also covers exact disclosure; here $p = 1.0$ and $k = 0$.

Example:
Let $q = $ **sum**($EE \bullet Female$, GP) $= 2.5$, $p = .95$, and $k = 1.0$. Then an estimate $\hat{q} = 2.0$ such that

$$Pr[q \epsilon [2.0 \pm 0.5]] \simeq .95$$

discloses q. Note that if a released set of statistics shows that q must lie in the interval $[2.0, 3.0]$, then q is disclosed because $[2.0, 3.0]$ is a 100% confidence interval for every estimate in the interval. ∎

6.1.5 Complexity of Disclosure

If a statistic q is not protected, we would like to know the difficulty of obtaining an estimate $\hat{q}$ satisfying Eq. (6.2). This will be measured by the number $N_{\hat{q}}$ of released statistics that a user with supplementary knowledge K needs to obtain $\hat{q}$.

Note that $N_{\hat{q}}$ is similar to the unicity distance of a cipher (see Section 1.4.3); it is the number of statistics needed to reduce the uncertainty about q to an unacceptable level.

Frank [Fran77] has investigated another way of applying information theory to disclosure. He defines the **disclosure set** D to be the set of individuals whose attributes are known. Personal disclosure occurs when the size of this set increases by at least 1. The uncertainty $H_K(D)$ of D is a function of the frequency distribution of the variables in the database and a user's supplementary knowledge. This uncertainty decreases by $H_K(D) - H_{K,R}(D)$ when a set R of frequency distributions is released.

6.2 INFERENCE CONTROL MECHANISMS

6.2.1 Security and Precision

An inference control mechanism must protect all sensitive statistics. Let S be the set of all statistics, P the subset of S classified as nonsensitive, and R the subset of S released. Let D be the set of statistics disclosed by R (including the statistics in R). The statistical database is **secure** if $D \subseteq P$; that is, no sensitive statistic is disclosed by R.

FIGURE 6.2 Security and precision.

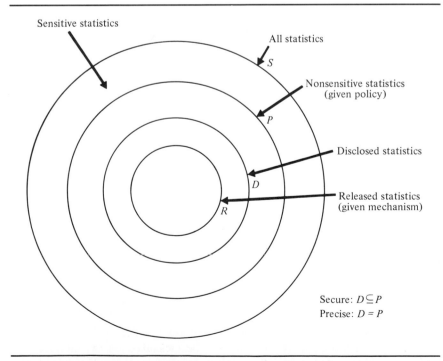

Sensitive statistics

All statistics

S

Nonsensitive statistics
(given policy)

P

Disclosed statistics

D

Released statistics
(given mechanism)

R

Secure: $D \subseteq P$
Precise: $D = P$

We would like the released set R to be complete in the sense that all nonsensitive statistics are in R or are computable from R (i.e., disclosed by R). A system in which $D = P$ is said to be **precise**. Whereas secrecy is required for privacy, precision is required for freedom of information. Figure 6.2 illustrates the requirements for security and precision; note the similarity of this figure with Figures 4.4 and 5.4.

The problem is that it can be extremely difficult to determine whether releasing a statistic will lead to disclosure of a sensitive statistic (violating security), or prevent the release of a complete set of statistics (violating precision). Most statistics lead to disclosure only when they are correlated with other statistics.

Example:
Although neither of the statistics **sum**(EE, GP) and **sum**($EE \cdot Male$, GP) is sensitive, if one is released, the other must be restricted to protect Baker's grade-point. Furthermore, it must be impossible to compute the restricted statistic from the set of released statistics. ■

This example shows that it is not generally possible to release a complete set of statistics; thus, any inference control mechanism must be imprecise. If we settle for releasing a maximal set of statistics, we find that the problem of determining a maximal set of statistics is **NP-complete** [Chin80].

Whether a statistic can lead to disclosure depends on a user's supplementary knowledge. Because it is not usually feasible to account for a particular user's supplementary knowledge, many mechanisms are based on a worst-case assumption about supplementary knowledge. A mechanism for the student record database, for example, might assume that a user knows the Sex, $Major$, and $Class$ of every student, and the GP and SAT of some of the students.

To avoid restricting too many statistics, many statistical databases add "noise" to the data or to released statistics. The objective is to add enough noise that most nonsensitive statistics can be released without endangering sensitive ones—but not so much that the released statistics become meaningless.

6.2.2 Methods of Release

Many of the mechanisms depend on the method in which statistics are released. Census bureaus and other agencies that conduct population surveys have traditionally released statistics in two formats: macrostatistics and microstatistics.

Macrostatistics.   These are collections of related statistics, usually presented in the form of 2-dimensional tables containing counts and sums.

Example:
Tables 6.3 and 6.4 show counts and total SAT scores for the student record database. The entries inside the tables give statistics for query sets defined by all possible values of Sex and $Class$. For example, the entry in row 1,

TABLE 6.3 Student counts by *Sex* and *Class*.

Sex	1978	1979	Class 1980	1981	Sum	
Female	1	2	2	1	6	
Male	3	2	0	2	7	
Sum	4	4	2	3	13	Total

TABLE 6.4 Total *SAT* scores by *Sex* and *Class*.

Sex	1978	1979	Class 1980	1981	Sum	
Female	800	1330	1120	500	3750	
Male	1930	1150	0	1180	4260	
Sum	2730	2480	1120	1680	8010	Total

column 3 gives the 2-order statistic **count**(*Female* • 1980) in Table 6.3, and the 3-order statistic **sum**(*Female* • 1980, *SAT*) in Table 6.4. The row sums give statistics for the query sets defined by *Sex*, and the column sums for the query sets defined by *Class*. For example, the sum for column 3 gives the 1-order statistic **count**(1980) in Table 6.3, and the 2-order statistic **sum** (1980, *SAT*) in Table 6.4. Finally, the total gives the 0-order statistic **count** (*All*) in Table 6.3 and the 1-order statistic **sum** (*All*, *SAT*) in Table 6.4. ■

Macrostatistics have the disadvantage of providing only a limited subset of all statistics. For example, it is not possible to compute correlations of *SAT* scores and grade-points from the data in Tables 6.3 and 6.4, or to compute higher-order statistics [e.g., **sum**(*Female* • *CS* • 1980, *SAT*)].

Because the set of released statistics is greatly restricted, macrostatistics provide a higher level of security than many other forms of release. Even so, it may be necessary to suppress certain cells from the tables or to add noise to the statistics.

Example:
Because Davis is the only female student in the class of 1978, the total *SAT* score shown in row 1, column 1 of Table 6.4 should be suppressed; otherwise, any user knowing that she is represented in the database can deduce her *SAT* score (the same holds for column 4, which represents Kline's *SAT* score). We shall return to this example and study the principles of cell suppression in Section 6.4.1. ■

Microstatistics.   These consist of individual data records having the format shown in Figure 6.1. The data is typically distributed on tape, and statistical evaluation programs are used to compute desired statistics. These programs have facilities for assembling (in main memory or on disk) query sets from the records on the tape, and for computing statistics over the assembled records. New query sets can be formed by taking a subset of the assembled records, or by assembling a new set from the tape.

Because no assumptions can be made about the programs that process the tapes, protection mechanisms must be applied at the time the tapes are created. Census bureaus control disclosure by

1.   removing names and other identifying information from the records,
2.   adding noise to the data (e.g., by rounding—see also discussion of privacy transformations in Section 3.5.2),
3.   suppressing highly sensitive data,
4.   removing records with extreme values,
5.   placing restrictions on the size of the population for which microdata can be released, and
6.   providing relatively small samples of the complete data.

The 1960 U.S. Census, for example, was distributed on tape as a random sample of 1 record out of 1000 with names, addresses, and exact geographical locations removed [Hans71]. A snooper would have at best a 1/1000 chance of associating a given sample record with the right individual.

Macrostatistics and microstatistics have been used for the one-time publication of data collected from surveys. Because they can be time-consuming and costly to produce, they are not well suited for the release of statistics in on-line database systems that are frequently modified.

Query-Processing Systems.   The development of on-line query-processing systems has made it possible to calculate statistics at the time they are requested; released statistics, therefore, reflect the current state of the system. These systems have powerful **query languages**, which make it easy to access arbitrary subsets of data for both statistical and nonstatistical purposes. The data is logically and physically organized for fast retrieval, so that query sets can be constructed much more rapidly than from sequential files of records stored on tape or disk.

Because all accesses to the data are restricted to the query-processing programs, mechanisms that enforce access, flow, or inference controls can be placed in these programs. The final decision whether to release a statistic or to grant direct access to data can be made at the time the query is made.

Many of the methods used to protect macrostatistics and microstatistics are not applicable to these systems. Techniques that add noise to the stored data generally cannot be used, because accuracy of the data may be essential for nonstatistical purposes. Techniques such as cell suppression that involve costly and time-consuming computations cannot be applied on a per-query basis. Sampling techniques that use relatively small subsets of the database may not give sufficiently accurate statistics in small to medium size systems.

Because we are primarily interested in controls for query-processing systems, most of the techniques discussed in this chapter are for these systems. A comprehensive discussion of the techniques used by government agencies to protect macrostatistics and microstatistics is given in [U.S.78].

We shall first study methods of attacking statistical databases, and then study techniques that reduce the threat of such attacks.

6.3 METHODS OF ATTACK

Before we can evaluate the effectiveness of existing and proposed inference controls, we must understand the threat. In this section, we shall examine several kinds of disclosure techniques. All the methods involve using released statistics and supplementary knowledge to solve a system of equations for some unknown.

6.3.1 Small and Large Query Set Attacks

Hoffman and Miller [Hoff70] showed that it is easy to compromise a database that releases statistics about small query sets. Suppose that a user knows an individual I who is represented in the database and who satisfies the characteristic formula C. If the user queries the database for the statistic **count**(C) and the system responds "1", then the user has identified I in the database and can learn whether I has an additional characteristic D by asking for the statistic **count**$(C \bullet D)$, where:

$$\textbf{count}(C \bullet D) = \begin{cases} 1 \text{ implies } I \text{ has } D \\ 0 \text{ implies } I \text{ does not have } D \end{cases}.$$

Similarly, the user can learn the value of attribute A for I by asking for the statistic **sum**(C, A).

> *Example:*
> Suppose a user knows Evans is represented in the student record database, and that Evans is a male biology student in the class of 1979. The statistic
>
> **count**$(Male \bullet Bio \bullet 1979) = 1$
>
> reveals Evans is the only such student. The statistic
>
> **count**$(Male \bullet Bio \bullet 1979 \bullet (Sat \geq 600)) = 0$
>
> reveals that his SAT score is under 600, and the statistic
>
> **sum**$(Male \bullet Bio \bullet 1979, SAT) = 500$
>
> reveals his exact SAT score. ■

This type of attack may work even when an individual cannot be uniquely identified. Suppose that an individual I is known to satisfy C and **count**$(C) > 1$. If

FIGURE 6.3 Query-set size control.

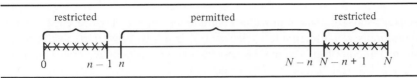

count($C \cdot D$) = count(C), then I must also satisfy D; however, if count($C \cdot D$) < count(C), then nothing can be concluded about whether I satisfies D. (See also Haq [Haq74,Haq75].)

To protect against this kind of attack, statistics based on small query sets must be restricted. Because these statistics are normally classified as sensitive, their restriction would be automatic. If the query language permits complementation, large query sets must also be restricted (even though they are not sensitive); otherwise, users could pose their queries relative to the complement $\sim C$ of the desired characteristic C. Suppose as before that C uniquely identifies an individual I in the database; thus count($\sim C$) = $N - 1$, where $N =$ count(All) is the size of the database. A user can determine whether C satisfies an additional characteristic D by posing the query count($\sim (C \cdot D)$), because

$$\mathbf{count}(\sim(C \cdot D)) = \begin{cases} N & \text{implies } I \text{ does not have } D \\ N-1 & \text{implies } I \text{ has } D \end{cases}.$$

The user can learn the value of an attribute A for I from

$$\mathbf{sum}(C, A) = \mathbf{sum}(All, A) - \mathbf{sum}(\sim C, A) .$$

In general, for any query $q(C)$ of the form (6.1),

$$q(C) = q(All) - q(\sim C) .$$

Query-Set-Size Control.   These results show that any statistical database needs at least a mechanism that restricts query sets having fewer than n or more than $N - n$ records, for some positive integer n:

> ***Query-Set-Size Control:***
> A statistic $q(C)$ is permitted only if
>
> $$n \le |C| \le N - n ,$$
>
> where $n \ge 0$ is a parameter of the database.   ■

(See Figure 6.3.) Note that $n \le N/2$ if any statistics at all are to be released. Note also that this restricts the statistics $q(All)$. In practice these statistics can be released; if they are restricted, they can be computed from $q(All) = q(C) + q(\sim C)$ for any C such that $n \le |C| \le N - n$.

6.3.2 Tracker Attacks

The query-set-size control provides a simple mechanism for preventing many trivial compromises. Unfortunately, the control is easily subverted. Schlörer [Schl75] showed that compromises may be possible even for n near $N/2$ by a simple snooping tool called the "tracker". The basic idea is to pad small query sets with enough extra records to put them in the allowable range, and then subtract out the effect of the padding. The following describes different types of trackers.

Individual Trackers.   Schlörer considered statistics for counts that are released only for query-set sizes in the range $[n, N - n]$, where $n > 1$. Suppose that a user knows an individual I who is uniquely characterized by a formula C, and that the user seeks to learn whether I also has the characteristic D. Because **count**$(C \cdot D)$ $\leq$ **count**$(C) = 1 < n$, the previous method cannot be used to determine whether I also has the characteristic D. If C can be divided in two parts, the user may be able to calculate **count**$(C \cdot D)$, however, from two answerable queries involving the parts.

Suppose that the formula C can be decomposed into the product $C = C1 \cdot C2$, such that **count**$(C1 \cdot \sim C2)$ and **count**$(C1)$ are both permitted:

$$n \leq \textbf{count}(C1 \cdot \sim C2) \leq \textbf{count}(C1) \leq N - n \ .$$

The pair of formulas $\{C1, C1 \cdot \sim C2\}$ is called the **individual tracker** (of I) because it helps the user to "track down" additional characteristics of I. The method of compromise is summarized as follows:

Individual Tracker Compromise:
Let $C = C1 \cdot C2$ be a formula uniquely identifying individual I, and let $T = C1 \cdot \sim C2$ [see Figure 6.4(a)]. Using the permitted statistics **count**(T) and **count**$(T + C1 \cdot D)$, compute:

$$\textbf{count}(C \cdot D) = \textbf{count}(T + C1 \cdot D) - \textbf{count}(T) \tag{6.3}$$

[see Figure 6.4(b)]. If **count**$(C \cdot D) = 0$, I does not have characteristic D. If **count**$(C \cdot D) = $ **count**(C), I has characteristic D. If **count**$(C) = 1$, Palme [Palm74] showed that the value of an attribute A of I can be computed from

$$\textbf{sum}(C, A) = \textbf{sum}(C1, A) - \textbf{sum}(T, A) \ .$$

In general, if $q(C)$ is any restricted query for a finite moment of the form (6.1), then $q(C)$ can be computed from

$$q(C) = q(C1) - q(T) \ . \tag{6.4}$$

[See Figure 6.4(a).] If it is not known whether the formula C uniquely identifies I, Eq. (6.4) can be used to determine whether **count**$(C) = 1$:

$$\textbf{count}(C) = \textbf{count}(C1) - \textbf{count}(T) \ . \quad \blacksquare$$

FIGURE 6.4 Individual tracker compromise.

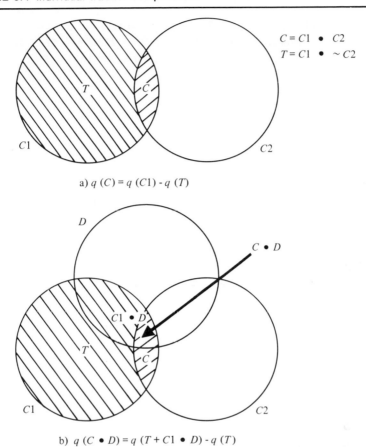

a) $q(C) = q(C1) - q(T)$

b) $q(C \bullet D) = q(T + C1 \bullet D) - q(T)$

Example:
Evans is identified by the formula

$$C = Male \bullet Bio \bullet 1979 \ .$$

Let $n = 3$, $C1 = Male$, and $C2 = Bio \bullet 1979$. Then

$$T = C1 \bullet {\sim}C2$$
$$= Male \bullet {\sim}(Bio \bullet 1979) \ .$$

We can determine whether Evans is uniquely identified by C and whether his SAT score is at least 600 by applying Eqs. (6.4) and (6.3), where $D = (SAT \geq 600)$:

count$(Male \bullet Bio \bullet 1979)$
    $= $ **count**$(Male) - $ **count**$(Male \bullet {\sim} (Bio \bullet 1979))$

$$= \quad 7 \qquad - \quad 6$$
$$= \quad 1$$

count$(Male \bullet Bio \bullet 1979 \bullet (SAT \geq 600))$
$= $ **count**$(Male \bullet \sim (Bio \bullet 1979) + Male \bullet (SAT \geq 600))$
$\quad - $ **count**$(Male \bullet \sim (Bio \bullet 1979))$
$$= \quad 6 \qquad - \quad 6$$
$$= \quad 0 \ .$$

His *GP* can be determined by applying Eq. (6.4):

sum$(Male \bullet Bio \bullet 1979, GP)$
$= $ **sum**$(Male, GP) - $ **sum**$(Male \bullet \sim (Bio \bullet 1979), GP)$
$$= \quad 22.2 \qquad - \quad 20.0$$
$$= \quad 2.2 \ . \quad \blacksquare$$

This type of compromise is not prevented by lack of a decomposition of *C* giving query sets *C1* and *T* in the range [*n*, *N* − *n*]. Schlörer pointed out that restricted sets *C1* and *T* can often be replaced with permitted sets *C1* + *CM* and *T* + *CM*, where **count**$(C1 \bullet CM) = 0$. The formula *CM*, called the "mask", serves only to pad the small query sets with enough (irrelevant) records to put them in the permitted range.

General Trackers.   The individual tracker is based on the concept of using categories known to describe a certain individual to determine other information about that individual. A new individual tracker must be found for each person. Schwartz [Schw77] and Denning, Denning, and Schwartz [Denn79] showed that this restriction could be removed with "general" and "double" trackers. A single general or double tracker can be used to compute the answer to every restricted statistic in the database. No prior knowledge about anyone in the database is required (though some supplementary knowledge is still required for personal disclosure).

A **general tracker** is any characteristic formula *T* such that

$$2n \leq |T| \leq N - 2n \ .$$

Notice that queries $q(T)$ are always answerable, because $|T|$ is well within the range [*n*, *N* − *n*] (see Figure 6.5).

Obviously, *n* must not exceed *N*/4 if a general tracker is to exist at all. Schlörer [Schl80] showed that if $g \leq N - 4n$, where *g* is the size of the largest elementary set (see Section 6.1.2), then the database must contain at least one general tracker.

FIGURE 6.5 General tracker.

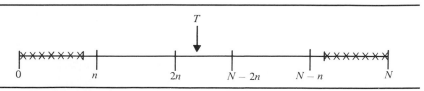

FIGURE 6.6 General tracker compromise.

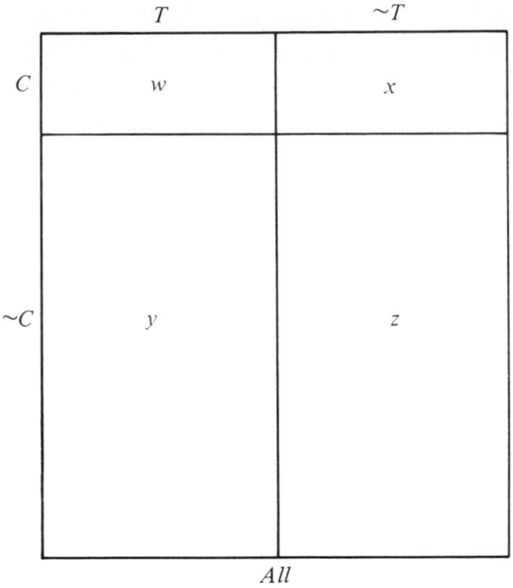

$$q\ (All) = q\ (T) + q\ (\sim T) = w + x + y + z$$

$$q\ (C)\ = q\ (C + T)\quad + q\ (C + \sim T)\ - q\ (All)$$

$$= (w + x + y)\ + (w + x + z)\ - (w + x + y + z)$$

$$= w + x$$

General Tracker Compromise:

Let T be a general tracker and let $q(C)$ be a restricted query for any finite moment of the form (6.1). First calculate

$$q(All) = q(T) + q(\sim T)\ .$$

If $|C| < n$, $q(C)$ can be computed from

$$q(C) = q(C + T) + q(C + \sim T) - q(All) \tag{6.5}$$

(see Figure 6.6), and if $|C| > N - n$, $q(C)$ can be computed from

$$q(C) = 2q(All) - q(\sim C + T) - q(\sim C + \sim T)\ . \tag{6.6}$$

If the user does not know whether the query set is too small or too large, Formula (6.5) can be tried first; if the queries on the right-hand side are permitted, the user can proceed; otherwise, Formula (6.6) can be used. Thus, $q(C)$ can be computed with at most five queries. ■

Example:

Let $n = 3$ in the student record database. To be answerable, a query set's size must fall in the range $[3, 10]$, but a general tracker's query-set size must fall in the subrange [6, 7]. Because $g = 1$ and $N - 4n = 13 - 12 = 1$, the database must contain at least one general tracker. The database actually contains several trackers; we shall use the tracker $T = Male$, where $|T| = 7$.

Suppose it is known that Jones satisfies the characteristic $C = Female \cdot Bio$, but it is not known whether C uniquely identifies her. The restricted statistic **count**(*Female* • *Bio*) can be computed from formula (6.5):

$$
\begin{aligned}
\textbf{count}(All) &= \textbf{count}(Male) + \textbf{count}(\sim Male) \\
&= \quad 7 \qquad\quad + \quad 6 \\
&= \quad 13
\end{aligned}
$$

$$
\begin{aligned}
\textbf{count}(Female \cdot Bio) & \\
&= \quad \textbf{count}(Female \cdot Bio + Male) \\
&\quad + \textbf{count}(Female \cdot Bio + \sim Male) - \textbf{count}(All) \\
&= \quad\quad 8 \quad + \quad 6 \quad - \quad 13 \\
&= \quad\quad 1 \ .
\end{aligned}
$$

Because Jones is uniquely identified by C, her GP can be deduced by computing the restricted statistic **sum**(*Female* • *Bio*, *GP*):

$$
\begin{aligned}
\textbf{sum}(All, GP) &= \textbf{sum}(Male, GP) + \textbf{sum}(\sim Male, GP) \\
&= \quad 22.2 \qquad\quad + \quad 19.0 \\
&= \quad 41.2
\end{aligned}
$$

$$
\begin{aligned}
\textbf{sum}(Female \cdot Bio, GP) & \\
&= \quad \textbf{sum}(Female \cdot Bio + Male, GP) \\
&\quad + \textbf{sum}(Female \cdot Bio + \sim Male, GP) - \textbf{sum}(All, GP) \\
&= \quad\quad 26.0 \quad + \quad 19.0 \quad - \quad 41.2 \\
&= \quad\quad 3.8 \ . \quad \blacksquare
\end{aligned}
$$

Once a tracker is found, any restricted statistic can be computed with just a few queries. We might hope that finding trackers would be difficult, but unfortunately this is not the case. Denning and Schlörer [Denn80a] constructed an algorithm that finds a tracker within $O(\log_2 E)$ queries, where E is the number of elementary sets. The algorithm begins by taking a formula $C1$ such that $|C1| < 2n$, and a formula $C2 = All$. Then $C1$ is padded and $C2$ reduced until either $|C1|$ or $|C2|$ falls inside the range $[2n, N - 2n]$. The padding and reducing is done using a binary search strategy, whence convergence is in logarithmic time. The results of an experiment performed on a medical database showed that a tracker could often be found with just one or two queries. Schlörer [Schl80] also showed that large proportions of the possible queries in most databases are general trackers; thus, a general tracker is apt to be discovered quickly simply by guessing.

Double Trackers.   We might hope to secure the database by restricting the range of allowable query sets even further. Because general trackers may exist for n near $N/4$, we must make $n > N/4$. Before we consider the security of such a strategy, let us examine its implications: $n = N/4$ already restricts half of all possible query-set sizes; even this is probably too large for most statistical applications. Any larger value of n is likely to seriously impair the utility of the database.

FIGURE 6.7 Double tracker compromise.

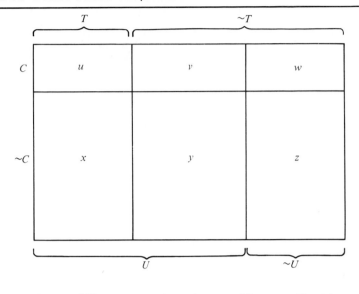

$$q(C) = q(U) \qquad + q(C + T) \qquad - q(T) \quad - q(\sim (C \cdot T) \cdot U)$$
$$= (u + v + x + y) + (u + v + w + x) - (u + x) - (v + x + y)$$
$$= u + v + w$$

Nevertheless, we found that trackers can circumvent much larger values of n. If $n \leq N/3$, compromise may be possible using a double tracker. A **double tracker** is a pair of characteristic formulas (T, U) for which

$T \subseteq U,$
$n \leq |T| \leq N - 2n$, and
$2n \leq |U| \leq N - n$.

Double Tracker Compromise:
Let $q(C)$ be a query for a restricted statistic, and let (T, U) be a double tracker. If $|C| < n$, $q(C)$ can be computed from

$$q(C) = q(U) + q(C + T) - q(T) - q(\sim(C \cdot T) \cdot U) \qquad (6.7)$$

(see Figure 6.7), and if $|C| > N - n$, $q(C)$ can be computed from

$$q(C) = q(\sim U) - q(\sim C + T) + q(T) + q(\sim(\sim C \cdot T) \cdot U) . \qquad (6.8)$$

Thus, $q(C)$ can be computed with at most seven queries. ■

Union Trackers. Schlörer generalized the concept of trackers to "union" trackers. Such trackers may exist even when n is near $N/2$, that is, when the only released statistics are those involving approximately half the population.

FIGURE 6.8 Union tracker compromise.

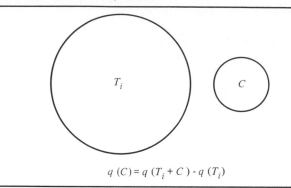

$$q\ (C) = q\ (T_i + C\ ) - q\ (T_i)$$

A **union tracker** is a set of $u \geq 2$ disjoint formulas $\{T_1, \ldots, T_u\}$ such that

$$n \leq |T_i| \leq N - n - g$$

for $i = 1, \ldots, u$, where g is the size of the largest elementary set. The formulas T_i can be used to compute any restricted statistic $q(C)$ when $n \leq N/2 - g$.

Union Tracker Compromise:
Let $q(C)$ be a restricted statistic, and let $\{T_1, \ldots, T_u\}$ be a union tracker. Split C into elementary sets $S_1, \ldots, S_t$ such that $C = S_1 + \ldots + S_t$. For each S_j, find a T_i such that $S_j \nsubseteq T_i$ (whence $S_j \cap T_i = \phi$), and compute

$$q(S_j) = q(T_i + S_j) - q(T_i) \ .$$

Because $|S_j| \leq g$, $q(T_i + S_j)$ is permitted for each j. Finally, compute

$$q(C) = q(S_1) + \cdots + q(S_t) \ .$$

Note that if C is a formula uniquely identifying some individual in the database, the preceding simplifies to

$$q(C) = q(T_i + C) - q(T_i) \ , \tag{6.9}$$

where $C \cap T_i = \phi$ (see Figure 6.8) . ∎

In general, the method is more difficult to apply than general or double trackers, especially for n near $N/2 - g$. Still, it demonstrates that controls restricting only the sizes of query sets are doomed to failure.

6.3.3 Linear System Attacks

Let $q_1, \ldots, q_m$ be a set of released statistics of the form $q_i = \textbf{sum}(C_i, A)$ $(1 \leq i \leq m)$. A **linear-system attack** involves solving a system of equations

$$H X = Q$$

for some x_j, where $X = (x_1, \ldots, x_N)$ and $Q = (q_1, \ldots, q_m)$ are column vectors, and $h_{ij} = 1$ if $j \in C_i$ and $h_{ij} = 0$ otherwise $(1 \leq i \leq m, 1 \leq j \leq N)$.

Example:
The queries $q_1 = $ **sum**(*Female, GP*) $= 19.0$ and $q_2 = $ **sum**(*Female + Male • CS • 1979, GP*) $= 22.5$ correspond to the linear system:

$$\begin{pmatrix} 1 & 1 & 0 & 1 & 0 & 0 & 0 & 1 & 0 & 1 & 1 & 0 & 0 \\ 1 & 1 & 0 & 1 & 0 & 0 & 0 & 1 & 0 & 1 & 1 & 0 & 1 \end{pmatrix} \begin{pmatrix} x_1 \\ x_2 \\ x_3 \\ x_4 \\ x_5 \\ x_6 \\ x_7 \\ x_8 \\ x_9 \\ x_{10} \\ x_{11} \\ x_{12} \\ x_{13} \end{pmatrix} = \begin{pmatrix} 19.0 \\ 22.5 \end{pmatrix}.$$

Moore's *GP* can be compromised by solving for $x_{13} = $ **sum**(*Male • CS • 1979, GP*) $= q_2 - q_1 = 22.5 - 19.0 = 3.5$. ∎

All the tracker attacks studied in the previous section are examples of linear-system attacks.

Key-Specified Queries. Dobkin, Jones, and Lipton [Dobk79] studied **key-specified queries** of the form **sum**(C, A), where C is specified by a set of k **keys** $\{i_1, \ldots, i_k\}$ identifying the records in the query set C. The value k is fixed for all queries, ruling out tracker attacks, which use different size query sets.
When disclosure is possible, the number of queries needed to achieve exact disclosure is no worse than linear in k.

Example:
Suppose $k = 3$ and consider the following queries:

$$\text{sum}(\{1, 2, 3\}, A) = x_1 + x_2 + x_3 = q_1$$
$$\text{sum}(\{1, 2, 4\}, A) = x_1 + x_2 + x_4 = q_2$$
$$\text{sum}(\{1, 3, 4\}, A) = x_1 + x_3 + x_4 = q_3$$
$$\text{sum}(\{2, 3, 4\}, A) = x_2 + x_3 + x_4 = q_4 .$$

These queries can be expressed as the following linear system:

$$\begin{pmatrix} 1 & 1 & 1 & 0 \\ 1 & 1 & 0 & 1 \\ 1 & 0 & 1 & 1 \\ 0 & 1 & 1 & 1 \end{pmatrix} \begin{pmatrix} x_1 \\ x_2 \\ x_3 \\ x_4 \end{pmatrix} = \begin{pmatrix} q_1 \\ q_2 \\ q_3 \\ q_4 \end{pmatrix}.$$

The value x_1 can be compromised by computing

$$x_1 = \frac{1}{3}(q_1 + q_2 + q_3 - 2q_4) \ . \quad \blacksquare$$

Schwartz, Denning, and Denning [Schw79,Schw77] extended these results to **weighted sums** of the form

$$\textbf{wsum}(\{i_1, \ldots, i_k\}, A) = \sum_{j=1}^{k} w_j x_{i_j} \ .$$

If the weights w_j are unknown, k of the x_i can be compromised within $k(k + 1)$ queries with supplementary knowledge of at least one x_j, and all x_i can be compromised within $N + k^2 - 1$ queries. Compromise is impossible, however, without supplementary knowledge, assuming none of the data values are zero [Schw79,Denn80b,Liu80].

Query-Set-Overlap Control.   Dobkin, Jones, and Lipton were primarily concerned with the complexity of linear systems when queries are not allowed to overlap by more than a few records. They observed that many compromises, including the one preceding, use query sets that have a large number of overlapping records. Such compromises could be prevented with a mechanism that restricts query sets having more than r records in common:

> *Query-Set-Overlap Control:*
> A statistic $q(C)$ is permitted only if $|C \bullet D| \le r$ for all $q(D)$ that have been released, where $r > 0$ is a parameter of the system. $\blacksquare$

Now, implementing such a control is probably infeasible: before releasing a statistic, the database would have to compare the latest query set with every previous one.

   The control would also seriously impair the usefulness of the database (i.e., it would be very imprecise), because statistics could not be released for both a set and its subsets (e.g., all males and all male biology majors). It would rule out publishing row and column sums in 2-dimensional tables of counts or aggregates.

   What is interesting and somewhat surprising is that the control does not prevent many attacks. Let $m(N, k, r)$ be the minimum number of key-specified queries for groups of size k needed to compromise a value x_i in a database of N elements having an overlap restriction with parameter r. Dobkin, Jones, and Lipton showed that without supplementary knowledge, compromise is impossible when

$$N < \frac{k^2 - 1}{2r} + \frac{k + 1}{2} \ .$$

For $r = 1$ (i.e., any pair of query sets can have at most one record in common), compromise is, therefore, impossible when $N < k(k + 1)/2$. They showed that compromise is possible for $r = 1$ when $N \ge k^2 - k + 1$; the number of queries needed is bounded by:

$$k < m(N, k, 1) \leq 2k - 1 .$$

The possibility of compromising when

$$\frac{k(k + 1)}{2} \leq N < k^2 - k + 1$$

was left open.

Example:
The following illustrates how x_7 can be compromised with five queries when $k = 3$ and $r = 1$:

$$
\begin{aligned}
q_1 &= x_1 + x_2 + x_3 \\
q_2 &= \qquad\qquad\quad x_4 + x_5 + x_6 \\
q_3 &= x_1 \qquad\quad + x_4 \qquad\quad + x_7 \\
q_4 &= \qquad x_2 \qquad\quad + x_5 \qquad + x_7 \\
q_5 &= \qquad\quad x_3 \qquad\qquad + x_6 + x_7 .
\end{aligned}
$$

Then $x_7 = (q_3 + q_4 + q_5 - q_1 - q_2)/3.$ ∎

In general, x_{k^2-k+1} can be determined from the $2k - 1$ queries:

$$q_i = \sum_{j=1}^{k} x_{k(i-1)+j} \qquad\qquad i = 1, \ldots, k - 1$$

$$q_{k+i-1} = \sum_{j=1}^{k-1} x_{k(j-1)+i} + x_{k^2-k+1} \qquad i = 1, \ldots, k .$$

Then

$$x_{k^2-k+1} = \frac{\sum_{i=1}^{k} q_{k+i-1} - \sum_{i=1}^{k-1} q_i}{k} .$$

Davida, Linton, Szelag, and Wells [Davi78] and Kam and Ullman [Kam77] have also shown that a minimum overlap control often can be subverted using key-specified queries.

Characteristic-Specified Queries. In on-line statistical database systems, users should not be allowed to specify groups of records by listing individual identifiers. Nevertheless, the preceding results give insight into the vulnerabilities of data-bases when groups of records are specified by characteristic formulas. On the one hand, we observe that if each record (individual) i in the database is uniquely identified by the characteristic C_i, then any key list $\{i_1, \ldots, i_k\}$ can be expressed as the characteristic formula $C_{i_1} + \ldots + C_{i_k}$. Therefore, if a database can be compromised with key-specified queries, it can be compromised with characteristic-specified queries. Caution must be taken in applying this result, however. Even though key-lists can be formulated as characteristics, it is not possible to do so without knowledge of the characteristics identifying the individuals named. Without this supplementary knowledge, it is not possible to precisely control the composition of query sets as for key-specified queries. Thus, achieving compromise with characteristics may be considerably more difficult than with keys. In practice, a database may be safe from this type of attack, especially if the attack must be done manually without the aid of a computer to formulate and pose queries.

On the other hand, the key model assumes all query sets are the same size k, ruling out simple attacks based on trackers. Because these attacks depend on highly overlapping query sets, we could eliminate tracker attacks with a query-set-overlap control. The preceding results are significant in that they show there are other methods of attack that do not use overlapping query sets. Because an overlap control would also seriously impair the usefulness of the database and be expensive to implement, we must search for other kinds of controls.

Fellegi [Fell72] and Chin and Ozsoyoglu [Chin80] show it is possible to determine whether the response to a query, when correlated with the responses to earlier queries, could result in exact disclosure. Chin and Ozsoyoglu do this by recording a complete history (audit trail) of all queries about some confidential attribute in a binary matrix H having N columns and at most N linearly independent rows. Each column represents one individual, and the rows represent a basis for the set of queries deducible from the previously answered queries (i.e., the set D in Figure 6.2); thus, each query that has been answered or could be deduced is expressed as a linear combination of the rows of H. When a new query is asked, the matrix is updated so that if the query would compromise the jth individual, updating the matrix introduces a row with all zeros except for a 1 in column j; thus, the potential compromise is easily detected. The matrix can be updated in $O(N^2)$ time, so the method is tractable for small databases.

6.3.4 Median Attacks

Another type of attack uses queries that select some value from the query set. In this section we consider queries for medians.

Example:
Suppose a user knows that Allen is the only student satisfying the formula (*Female* • *CS* • 1980). Consider these statistics:

median(*EE* • 1978 + *Female* • *CS* • 1980, *GP*) = 3.4
median(*BIO* + *Female* • *CS* • 1980, *GP*)   = 3.4

Because both query sets have the same median and each student in these sets has a different *GP*, the *GP* of 3.4 must correspond to a student in both query sets. Because Allen is the only student in both sets, this must be Allen's grade-point (see Figure 6.9). ■

This example further demonstrates the futility of a query-set-overlap control—indeed, the attack exploits the fact that Allen is the only student in both sets.

FIGURE 6.9 Compromise with medians.

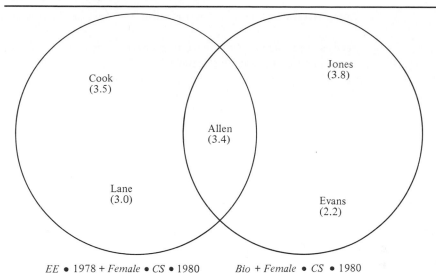

EE • 1978 + Female • CS • 1980   Bio + Female • CS • 1980

In general, let i be a record and C and D query sets such that:

1. $C \bullet D = \{i\}$,
2.   **median**$(C, A) = $ **median**(D, A), and
3. $x_j \neq x_{j'}$, for all $j, j' \in C \cup D, j \neq j'$.

Then $x_i = $ **median**(C, A).

To employ this attack, it is necessary to find two query sets that have the same median and a single common record. DeMillo, Dobkin, and Lipton [DeMi77] define $m(k)$ to be the number of queries of the form **median**$(\{i_1, \ldots, i_k\},$ $A)$ needed to find query sets satisfying Properties (1)–(3) under an overlap restriction of $r = 1$, assuming no two values are the same. They show that compromise of some x_i is always possible within

$$m(k) = \begin{cases} k^2 + 1 & \text{if } k \text{ is a prime power} \\ 4(k^2 + 1) & \text{otherwise} \end{cases}$$

queries if $N \geq m(k) - 1$.

A curious aspect of this result is that it applies to any type of selection query—including those that lie! As long as the database always returns some value in the query set, compromise is possible with any two queries satisfying only Properties (1)–(3).

Example:
Consider these queries:

   largest$(EE \bullet 1978 + Female \bullet CS \bullet 1980, GP) = 3.4$ (lying)

smallest($Bio + Female \bullet CS \bullet 1980, GP$)   = 3.4 (lying) .

By the same reasoning as before, the response 3.4 must be Allen's GP. ∎

Compromise is even easier when there is no overlap control. Reiss [Reis78] shows that some element can always be found within $O(\log^2 k)$ queries, and that a specific element can usually be found within $O(\log k)$ queries with supplementary knowledge and within $O(k)$ queries without supplementary knowledge if its value is not too extreme. DeMillo and Dobkin [DeMi78] show that at least $O(\log k)$ queries are required, so

$$O(\log k) \le m(k) \le O(\log^2 k) \ .$$

6.3.5 Insertion and Deletion Attacks

Dynamic databases that allow insertions and deletions of records are vulnerable to additional attacks. Hoffman [Hoff77] observed that a query-set-size restriction of n can be subverted if records can be added to the database. If $|C| < n$, then dummy records satisfying C are added to the database; if $|C| > N - n$, then dummy records satisfying $\sim C$ are added. Of course, this type of attack presupposes that the user has permission to add new records to the database; a user with statistical access only cannot use this technique.

A second type of attack involves compromising newly inserted records. Let i be a new record satisfying a formula C, and consider the following sequence of operations:

$q_1 = q(C)$
insert (i)
$q_2 = q(C)$.

Then $q(i) = q_2 - q_1$. Chin and Ozsoyoglu [Chin79] show this threat can be eliminated by processing insertions and deletions in pairs.

A third type of attack involves compromising an existing record i in a query set C by observing the changes to a statistic $q(C)$ when (pairs of) records are added to or deleted from C. If $|C|$ is odd, then i may be determined exactly (see exercises at end of chapter). Chin and Ozsoyoglu show that this threat can be eliminated by requiring that all query sets contain an even number of records (dummy records may be added to achieve this).

These attacks may not pose a serious threat if users with statistics-only access cannot insert and delete records, or otherwise control the changes being made to the database. Thus, many systems may not need controls that counter these attacks.

6.4 MECHANISMS THAT RESTRICT STATISTICS

We have studied two controls that restrict statistics that might lead to compromise: a query-set-size control and a query-set-overlap control. A size control, while

FIGURE 6.10 Identification of records in sample data.

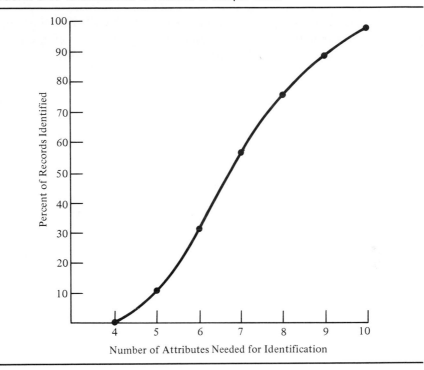

Number of Attributes Needed for Identification

Percent of Records Identified (y-axis)

extremely valuable and simple to implement, is insufficient. An overlap control is generally impractical, imprecise, and insufficient.

Another possibility is a **maximum-order control**, which restricts any statistic that employs too many attribute values. This would prevent compromises that require a large number of attributes to identify a particular individual. In a sample of 100 records drawn from a medical database containing over 30,000 records, Schlörer found that none of the records could be uniquely identified with fewer than 4 attributes, only 1 record could be identified with 4 attributes, about half of the records with 7 or fewer attributes, and nearly all with 10 attributes [Schl75] (see Figure 6.10). Thus, restricting queries to 3-order statistics might prevent most compromises in this database. Unfortunately, this can be overly restrictive because many of the higher-order statistics may be safe.

In the remainder of this section we examine three other possible controls aimed at restricting statistics that could lead to disclosure. The first is used by census bureaus to suppress statistics from tables of macrostatistics. While extremely effective, it is time-consuming and may not be suitable for on-line, dynamic databases. The second aims to decide at the time a query is posed whether release of the statistic could lead to compromise. The third partitions a database so that statistics computed over any partition are safe; queries about subsets of a partition are not permitted.

In [Denn82], we report on another restriction technique, called the $S_m/N -$

criterion.† The control, proposed by Schlörer [Schl76], restricts query sets over attributes that decompose the database into too many sets relative to the size N of the database (whence some of the sets are likely to be small). Formally, let C be a query set over attributes $A_1, \ldots, A_m$, and let $S_m = \prod_{i=1}^{m} |A_i|$ be the number of elementary sets over $A_1, \ldots, A_m$. A statistic $q(C)$ is restricted if

$$S_m/N > t$$

for some threshold t (e.g., $t = .1$). The control is extremely efficient and less restrictive than a maximum-order control. Although it does not guarantee security, it can be combined with a simple perturbation technique to provide a high level of security at low cost.

6.4.1 Cell Suppression

Cell suppression is one technique used by census bureaus to protect data published in the form of 2-dimensional tables of macrostatistics. It involves suppressing from the tables all sensitive statistics together with a sufficient number of nonsensitive ones, called **complementary suppressions**, to ensure that sensitive statistics cannot be derived from the published data. The sensitivity criterion for counts is typically a minimum query-set size. The sensitivity criterion for sums might be an n-respondent, $k\%$-dominance rule, where a sensitive statistic is one in which n or fewer values contribute more than $k\%$ of the total.

Example:
Let us now return to Table 6.4 in Section 6.2.2. Suppose we have a (n, k) sensitivity rule, where $n = 1$ and $k = 90$. Clearly the entries in row 1,

TABLE 6.5 Total *SAT* scores by *Sex* and *Class*.

Sex	1978	1979	Class 1980	1981	Sum	
Female	—	1330	1120	—	3750	
Male	1930	1150	0	1180	4260	
Sum	2730	2480	1120	1680	8010	Total

TABLE 6.6 Total *SAT* scores by *Sex* and *Class*.

Sex	1978	1979	Class 1980	1981	Sum	
Female	—	1330	1120	—	3750	
Male	—	1150	0	—	4260	
Sum	2730	2480	1120	1680	8010	Total

†Because the study was performed after the book had gone into production, it is not possible to give details here.

columns 1 and 4 must be suppressed; in both cases, one student contributed 100% of the total SAT score. Table 6.5 shows these changes. Note that none of the other statistics in the table is sensitive.

Now, suppressing only these entries is insufficient, because they can be computed by subtracting the entries in the corresponding columns of row 2 from the column sums. Therefore, it is necessary to suppress either the entries in row 2 or the column sums; Table 6.6 shows the result of the former approach. The table is now safe from exact disclosure (see exercises at end of chapter). ■

It is easy to determine whether a statistic is sensitive by itself. Consider the statistic $q = \mathbf{sum}(C, A)$, and let $d = \mathbf{sum}(C, A, n)$ denote the sum of the n largest (dominant) values used to compute q. Thus, if $|C| = m$ and

$$q = x_1 + \cdots + x_n + \cdots + x_m \,,$$

where

$$x_1 \geq \cdots \geq x_n \geq \cdots \geq x_m \,,$$

then

$$d = x_1 + \cdots + x_n \,.$$

The statistic q is sensitive if $d > (k/100)q$; that is, if $q < q^+$, where $q^+ = (100/k)d$ (see Figure 6.11). Note that it is actually d that requires protection.

It is considerably more difficult to determine whether a nonsensitive statistic can be used to derive—exactly or approximately—a sensitive statistic. Following Cox [Cox76,Cox78], we first discuss acceptable bounds on estimates of sensitive statistics.

Let $\hat{q}$ be an estimate of a sensitive statistic q. Now if $\hat{q} \geq q^+$, then $\hat{q}$ does not reveal any information about q that would not have been released if q were not sensitive [i.e., if $q \geq (100/k)d$ were true]. Thus, a lower bound on an **acceptable upper estimate** of q is given by

$$q^+ = \left(\frac{100}{k}\right)d \,. \tag{6.10}$$

To determine an acceptable lower estimate, we assume that n, k, and m are known, where $m = |C|$ (in practice, these values are not usually disclosed). Observe that $d \geq (n/m)q$, for any statistic q, sensitive or not. Suppose q is not sensitive; that is, d lies in the interval $[(n/m)q, (k/100)q]$. If q is right at the sensitivity threshold, that is, $q = (100/k)d$, this interval is $[(n/m)(100/k)d, d]$ (see Figure 6.12). Thus, $q_d^- = (n/m)(100/k)d$ is an acceptable lower estimate of d

FIGURE 6.11 Restricted statistic q.

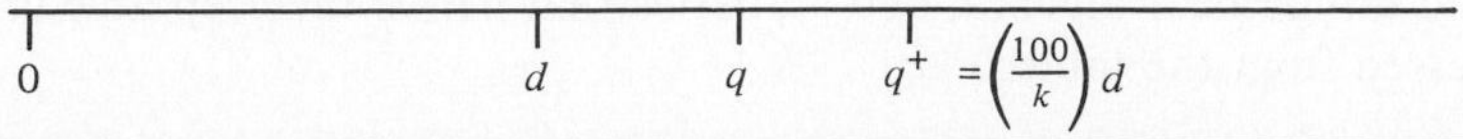

$$0 \qquad d \qquad q \qquad q^+ = \left(\frac{100}{k}\right)d$$

FIGURE 6.12 Interval for d at sensitivity threshold.

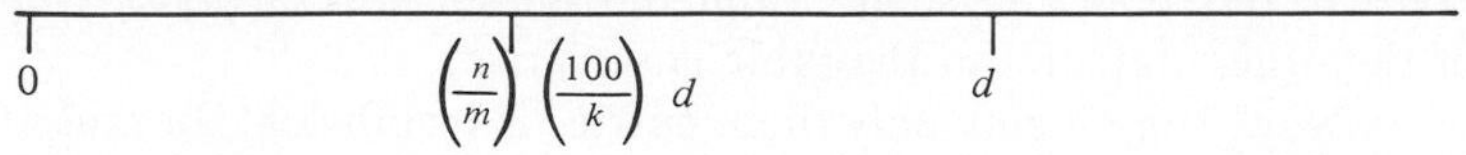

if q is sensitive, because q_d^- gives no more information about d than would be obtained if q were at the sensitivity threshold. Now, a lower estimate $L_{\hat{d}}$ of d can be obtained from a lower estimate $L_{\hat{q}}$ of q by

$$L_{\hat{d}} = \left(\frac{k}{100}\right) L_{\hat{q}} \ .$$

Therefore, an upper bound on an **acceptable lower estimate** of q is given by

$$q^- = \begin{cases} \left(\frac{n}{m}\right) \left(\frac{100}{k}\right)^2 d & \text{if } m > n \\ 0 & \text{if } m \le n \ . \end{cases} \tag{6.11}$$

Example:
Let $k = 90$, $n = 2$, $m = 10$, $q = 950$, and $d = 900$. Then q is sensitive, because $950 < (100/90)900$. An acceptable upper estimate of q is q^+ $= (100/90)900 = 1000$, because q would then have been released. Now, if q were at the sensitivity threshold $(100/90)900 = 1000$, we could conclude d falls in the interval $[(2/10) (100/90)900, 900] = [200, 900]$. An acceptable lower estimate of q is thus $q^- = (2/10) (100/90)^2 900 = 222.2$, which gives a lower bound of 200 for d. ∎

Cox explains it may be desirable to lower q^- so that q^+ and q^- are, respectively, subadditive and superadditive [Sand77]. The bound q^+ is **subadditive**, because the relation

$$q^+(C + D) \le q^+(C) + q^+(D)$$

holds, where $q^+(C)$ denotes the acceptable upper estimate for the cell corresponding to $q(C)$. The bound q^- is not **superadditive**, however, because the relation

$$q^-(C) + q^-(D) \le q^-(C + D)$$

does not hold (see exercises at end of chapter). Subadditivity and superadditivity reflect the principle that aggregation decreases the sensitivity of data; thus, we would expect the acceptable bounds to become tighter as data is aggregated.
    Given q^- and q^+, an interval estimate $I = [L_{\hat{q}}, U_{\hat{q}}]$ of q is acceptable if I falls below q^-, above q^+, or strictly contains the interval $[q^-, q^+]$. (In the latter case, I is too large to be of much value.) Interval estimates are obtained for each sensitive statistic using linear algebra, and statistics that derive unacceptable estimates are suppressed from the tables.

TABLE 6.7 Table with suppressed cells.

x_{11}	6	x_{13}	25
8	x_{22}	x_{23}	30
x_{31}	x_{32}	3	20
20	30	25	75

Example:

Consider Table 6.7, where the variables x_{ij} denote sensitive entries that have been suppressed. The six unknowns are related by the following equations:

$$x_{11} + x_{13} = 25 - 6 = 19 \tag{1}$$
$$x_{22} + x_{23} = 30 - 8 = 22 \tag{2}$$
$$x_{31} + x_{32} = 20 - 3 = 17 \tag{3}$$
$$x_{11} + x_{31} = 20 - 8 = 12 \tag{4}$$
$$x_{22} + x_{32} = 30 - 6 = 24 \tag{5}$$
$$x_{13} + x_{23} = 25 - 3 = 22 \ . \tag{6}$$

Equations (1)–(6) imply

$$0 \le x_{11} \le 12 \quad \text{(by 1 and 4)} \tag{7}$$
$$0 \le x_{13} \le 19 \quad \text{(by 1 and 6)} \tag{8}$$
$$0 \le x_{22} \le 22 \quad \text{(by 2 and 5)} \tag{9}$$
$$0 \le x_{23} \le 22 \quad \text{(by 2 and 6)} \tag{10}$$
$$0 \le x_{31} \le 12 \quad \text{(by 3 and 4)} \tag{11}$$
$$0 \le x_{32} \le 17 \quad \text{(by 3 and 5)} \ . \tag{12}$$

These interval estimates can then be used to derive tighter bounds for x_{13}, x_{22}, x_{23}, and x_{32}. By Eq. (3),

$$x_{32} = 17 - x_{31} \ .$$

Because x_{31} is at most 12 [by Eq. (11)], we have

$$5 \le x_{32} \le 17 \ . \tag{13}$$

The bounds on x_{32}, in turn, affect the interval estimate for x_{22}. By Eq. (5),

$$x_{22} = 24 - x_{32} \ ;$$

thus Eq. (13) implies

$$7 \le x_{22} \le 19 \ . \tag{14}$$

By Eq. (2),

$$x_{23} = 22 - x_{22} \ ,$$

so Eq. (14) implies

$$3 \le x_{23} \le 15 \ . \tag{15}$$

Similarly, by Eq. (6),

TABLE 6.8 Interval esti-
mates for Table 6.7.

0–12	6	7–19	25
8	7–19	3–15	30
0–12	5–17	3	20
20	30	25	75

$$x_{13} = 22 - x_{23} \, ,$$

so Eq. (15) implies

$$7 \le x_{13} \le 19 \, . \tag{16}$$

Equations (7), (11), and (13)–(16) give the best possible bounds on the unknowns (see Table 6.8). If any of the interval estimates is unacceptable, additional cells must be suppressed. ∎

Cox [Cox78] gives a linear analysis algorithm that determines interval estimates for suppressed internal cells in a 2-dimensional table. The algorithm is a modification of the simplex algorithm of linear programming (e.g., see [Dant63]). If the analysis uncovers unacceptable interval estimates, additional cells are suppressed (the complementary suppressions), and the analysis repeated until all estimates are acceptable. The method does not always determine the minimum set of complementary suppressions; this is an open problem. Sande [Sand77] has developed a similar interval analysis procedure.

Cell suppression is limited by the computational complexity of the analysis procedure. Whereas it has been successfully applied to 2- and 3-dimensional tables, whether it could be adapted to query-processing systems for general-purpose databases is an open problem. The set of all possible statistics for a database with 10 fields of data in each record corresponds to a 10-dimensional table. Applying cell suppression to a table of this size may not be tractable.

6.4.2 Implied Queries

Let us consider the possibility of dynamically applying a limited form of cell suppression in general-purpose databases when sensitivity is defined by a minimum query-set size. A statistic $q(C)$ is thus sensitive when $|C| < n$. For simplicity, we shall restrict attention to exact disclosure.

Let $q(C)$ be a sensitive statistic. Because $q(C)$ can be trivially computed from the relation $q(C) = q(All) - q(\sim C)$, it is necessary to suppress $q(\sim C)$ to protect $q(C)$ [we shall assume $q(All)$ is not restricted]. Because $|C| < n$ if and only if $|\sim C| > N - n$, we can prevent such trivial compromises by suppressing any statistic whose query-set size falls outside the range $[n, N - n]$; this is the same query-set-size restriction introduced in Section 6.3.1.

We observed earlier that sensitive statistics can often be derived from non-sensitive ones by means of trackers and linear-system attacks. Friedman and Hoff-

FIGURE 6.13 Partitioning over two attributes.

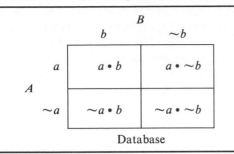

man [Frie80] show how some of these attacks can be prevented by suppressing nonsensitive statistics whose "implied query sets" fall outside the range $[n, N - n]$.

Let $q(C)$ be a 2-order statistic of the form $C = a \bullet b$ or $C = a + b$, where a and b are values of attributes A and B respectively. The following relations hold (see Figure 6.13):

$$q(\quad a \bullet \sim b) = q(a) - q(a \bullet b) \tag{1}$$
$$q(\sim a \bullet \quad b) = q(b) - q(a \bullet b) \tag{2}$$
$$q(\quad a \bullet \quad b) = q(a) + q(b) - q(a + b) \tag{3}$$
$$q(\sim a \bullet \sim b) = q(All) - q(a + b)$$
$$\qquad = q(All) - q(a) - q(b) + q(a \bullet b) \ . \tag{4}$$

Given $q(a \bullet b)$, Eqs. (1) and (2) can be used to derive $q(a \bullet \sim b)$ and $q(\sim a \bullet b)$, either of which could be sensitive even if $q(a \bullet b)$ is not. The formulas $(a \bullet \sim b)$ and $(\sim a \bullet b)$ are called the **implied query sets** of $(a \bullet b)$, and the statistic $q(a \bullet b)$ is restricted if either its query set or its implied query sets falls outside the range $[n, N - n]$. If $q(All)$ is permitted (even though $|All| > N - n$), the formula $q(\sim a \bullet \sim b)$ can be derived by Eq. (4), so that $(\sim a \bullet \sim b)$ is also implied by $(a \bullet b)$. Although $q(a + b)$ can also be derived from $q(a \bullet b)$ by Eq. (3), $q(a + b)$ cannot lead to disclosure if $q(\sim a \bullet \sim b)$ does not; therefore, it need not be explicitly checked.

Given $q(a + b)$, we can similarly derive $q(a \bullet b)$ by Eq. (3), and thereby also derive $q(a \bullet \sim b)$, $q(\sim a \bullet b)$, and $q(\sim a \bullet \sim b)$. Therefore, the statistic $q(a + b)$ is restricted if its query set or any of its other implied query sets $(a \bullet b)$,† $(a \bullet \sim b)$, $(\sim a \bullet b)$, and $(\sim a \bullet \sim b)$ fall outside the range $[n, N - n]$. Because $|\sim a \bullet \sim b| = N - |a + b|$, it is not necessary to explicitly check the size of both $(\sim a \bullet \sim b)$ and $(a + b)$.

To summarize: a query $q(a \bullet b)$ or $q(a + b)$ is permitted if and only if the sizes of the following query sets fall in the range $[n, N - n]$:

$$a \bullet b, \ a \bullet \sim b, \ \sim a \bullet b, \ \sim a \bullet \sim b \ .$$

---

† Friedman and Hoffman did not include $(a \bullet b)$ in their list of implied query sets for $(a + b)$; we have included it because $q(a \bullet b)$ can be sensitive even if $q(a + b)$ and its other implied queries are not.

By symmetry, the queries $q(\sim a \cdot b)$, $q(a \cdot \sim b)$, $q(\sim a \cdot \sim b)$, $q(\sim a + b)$, $q(a + \sim b)$, and $q(\sim a + \sim b)$ have the same four implied query sets. The four implied query sets partition the database as shown in Figure 6.13. The partitioning is such that given a statistic over any one of these areas (or over three of the four areas), then the same statistic can be computed over all the areas using only lower-order statistics [namely $q(a)$, $q(b)$, and $q(All)$].

Because the database is partitioned by the four query sets, it is not possible for one of the sets to be larger than $N - n$ unless some other set is smaller than n; therefore, it is not necessary to check upper bounds. It is necessary to check all four lower bounds, however, because any one of the four query sets could be sensitive even if the other three are not. We also observe that if the four 2-order query sets are not sensitive, then the 1-order statistics $q(a)$ and $q(b)$ cannot be sensitive. The converse, however, is not true.

Example:
We shall show how two attacks aimed at learning Baker's *GP* can be thwarted by checking implied query sets. Because Baker is the only *Female* student in *EE*, her *GP* could be derived using the following:

> **sum**(*Female* • *EE*, *GP*)
>   = **sum**(*Female*, *GP*) + **sum**(*EE*, *GP*) − **sum**(*Female* + *EE*, *GP*) .

Because the query set (*Female* + *EE*) has the implied query set (*Female* • *EE*) where $|Female \cdot EE| = 1$, the statistic **sum**(*Female* + *EE*, *GP*) would be suppressed, thwarting the attack.

Similarly, Baker's *GP* could be derived from:

> **sum**(*Female* • *EE*, *GP*)
>   = **sum**(*Female*, *GP*) − **sum**(*Female* • $\sim$*EE*, *GP*) .

Because the query set (*Female* • $\sim$*EE*) has the implied query set (*Female* • $\sim\sim$*EE*) = (*Female* • *EE*), the statistic **sum**(*Female* • $\sim$*EE*, *GP*) would similarly be suppressed, thwarting the attack. ■

The situation is considerably more complicated when the characteristic formula C of a query $q(C)$ is composed of more than two terms. We show in [Denn81] that given any m-order statistic q of the form $q(\alpha_1 \cdot \cdots \cdot \alpha_m)$ or $q(\alpha_1 + \cdots + \alpha_m)$, where $\alpha_i = a_i$ or $\sim a_i$ and a_i is the value of attribute A_i $(1 \le i \le m)$, the following 2^m statistics can be computed from q and lower-order statistics:

$$q(\quad a_1 \cdot \quad a_2 \cdot \cdots \cdot \quad a_m)$$
$$q(\quad a_1 \cdot \quad a_2 \cdot \cdots \cdot \sim a_m)$$
$$\cdot$$
$$\cdot$$
$$\cdot$$
$$q(\quad a_1 \cdot \sim a_2 \cdot \cdots \cdot \sim a_m)$$
$$q(\sim a_1 \cdot \quad a_2 \cdot \cdots \cdot \quad a_m)$$
$$q(\sim a_1 \cdot \quad a_2 \cdot \cdots \cdot \sim a_m)$$

FIGURE 6.14 Partitioning over three attributes.

$$B$$

	b	$\sim b$
a	$a \bullet b \bullet \quad c$	$a \bullet \sim b \bullet \quad c$
	$a \bullet b \bullet \sim c$	$a \bullet \sim b \bullet \sim c$
$\sim a$	$\sim a \bullet b \bullet \quad c$	$\sim a \bullet \sim b \bullet \quad c$
	$\sim a \bullet b \bullet \sim c$	$\sim a \bullet \sim b \bullet \sim c$

Database

$$\vdots$$

$$q(\sim a_1 \bullet \sim a_2 \bullet \cdots \bullet \sim a_m) \ .$$

We are thus led to the following control:

Implied-Queries Control:
An m-order statistic over attribute values $a_1, \ldots, a_m$ is permitted if and only if all 2^m implied query sets listed above have at least n records. ∎

Figure 6.14 shows the eight implied query sets for the case $m = 3$. The formulas relating a statistic q computed over one of the query sets to the remaining query sets are:

$$
\begin{aligned}
q(\quad a \bullet \quad b \bullet \sim c) &= q(a \bullet \quad b) - q(a \bullet b \bullet c) \\
q(\quad a \bullet \sim b \bullet \quad c) &= q(a \bullet \quad c) - q(a \bullet b \bullet c) \\
q(\sim a \bullet \quad b \bullet \quad c) &= q(b \bullet \quad c) - q(a \bullet b \bullet c) \\
q(\quad a \bullet \sim b \bullet \sim c) &= q(a \bullet \sim b) - q(a \bullet \sim b \bullet c) \\
&= q(a) - q(a \bullet b) - q(a \bullet c) + q(a \bullet b \bullet c) \\
q(\sim a \bullet \sim b \bullet \quad c) &= q(c) - q(a \bullet c) - q(b \bullet c) + q(a \bullet b \bullet c) \\
q(\sim a \bullet \quad b \bullet \sim c) &= q(b) - q(a \bullet b) - q(b \bullet c) + q(a \bullet b \bullet c) \\
q(\sim a \bullet \sim b \bullet \sim c) &= q(All) - q(a) - q(b) - q(c) \\
&\quad + q(a \bullet b) + q(a \bullet c) + q(b \bullet c) - q(a \bullet b \bullet c) \ .
\end{aligned}
$$

Because of the exponential growth of the number of implied queries, we conclude that an implied-queries control may become impractical for high-order

TABLE 6.9 Table with sensitive statistic $q(a_1 \cdot b_1)$.

		b_1	b_2	$\ldots$	b_t	
				B		
A	a_1	—	$q(a_1 \cdot b_2)$	$\ldots$	$q(a_1 \cdot b_t)$	$q(a_1)$
	a_2	$q(a_2 \cdot b_1)$	$q(a_2 \cdot b_2)$	$\ldots$	$q(a_2 \cdot b_t)$	$q(a_2)$
	.	.	.	.	.	.
	.	.	.	.	.	.
	.	.	.	.	.	.
	a_s	$q(a_s \cdot b_1)$	$q(a_s \cdot b_2)$	$\ldots$	$q(a_s \cdot b_t)$	$q(a_s)$
		$q(b_1)$	$q(b_2)$	$\ldots$	$q(b_t)$	$q(All)$

statistics. A 10-order statistic, for example, has 1024 implied queries.

Even if we examine all implied query sets, the control would not prevent deduction of sensitive statistics. To see why, suppose that attribute A has values a_1, $\ldots$, a_s, and that attribute B has values $b_1, \ldots, b_t$. Then the records of the database are partitioned into st groups, as shown in Table 6.9.

Suppose that the statistic $q(a_1 \cdot b_1)$ is sensitive, but that none of the remaining cells is sensitive. Then any attempt to deduce $q(a_1 \cdot b_1)$ from a statistic whose implied query sets include $(a_1 \cdot b_1)$ will be thwarted; for example, the following attack could not be used:

$$q(a_1 \cdot b_1) = q(b_1) - q(\sim a_1 \cdot b_1) .$$

Suppressing statistics that directly imply $q(a_1 \cdot b_1)$ does not, however, preclude deduction of $q(a_1 \cdot b_1)$ from queries about disjoint subsets of a_1 or b_1. For example,

$$q(a_1 \cdot b_1) = q(b_1) - [q(a_2 \cdot b_1) + \cdots + q(a_s \cdot b_1)].$$

This example suggests that for a given m-order statistic over attributes A_1, $\ldots$, A_m, it would be necessary to check all elementary sets defined by these attributes. If each attribute A_i has $|A_i|$ possible values, this would involve checking

$$\prod_{i=1}^{m} |A_i|$$

query sets.

It is more efficient to keep a history of previously asked queries for the purpose of determining whether each new query causes compromise (see Section 6.3.3) than it is to determine whether a query could potentially cause compromise. Moreover, the implied-queries approach is likely to be much less precise, because the additional queries needed to cause compromise may never be asked.

6.4.3 Partitioning

Yu and Chin [Yu77] and Chin and Ozsoyoglu [Chin79] have studied the feasibility of **partitioning** a dynamic database at the physical level into disjoint groups such that:

TABLE 6.10 Partitioned database.

Sex	Class			
	1978	1979	1980	1981
Female	4	2	2	0
Male		2	0	2

1. Each group G has $g = |G|$ records, where $g = 0$ or $g \geq n$, and g is even.
2. Records are added to or deleted from G in pairs.
3. Query sets must include entire groups. If the query set for a statistic includes one or more records from each of m groups $G_1, \ldots, G_m$, then $q(G_1 + \cdots + G_m)$ is released.

The first two conditions prevent attacks based on small query sets and insertion or deletions of records (see Section 6.3.5). The third condition prevents exact disclosure from attacks based on isolating a particular individual—for example, by using a tracker or a linear system of equations. Clever query sequences can at best disclose information about an entire group.

Example:
Table 6.10 gives counts for a possible partitioning of the student record database when $k = 1$. Because the database has an odd number of records, the record for Kline has been omitted. Because the query set "*Female •* 1978" contains a single record and the set "*Male •* 1978" contains an odd number of records (3) these sets have been merged (Olsson calls this "rolling up" [Olss75]). A query for a statistic **count**(*Male •* 1978) would thus return **count**(1978) $= 4$ (rather than 3), and a query **count**(*EE*) would return **count**(1978 + *Female •* 1980 + *Male •* 1981) $= 8$ (rather than 4) because there are *EE* majors in all three groups. ∎

Partitioning by 1-, 2-, or 3-order statistics is equivalent to releasing tables of macrostatistics as described in the previous section. Therefore, to control approximate disclosures (as by the *n*-respondent, *k*%-dominance rule) cell-suppression techniques must be applied; this may not be practical for dynamic databases. Using broad categories defined by 2- or 3-order statistics may also limit the usefulness of the database. Yet if we partition by higher-order statistics, cell suppression may be too costly.

Chin and Ozsoyoglu [Chin81] also consider the design of a complete database system that supports partitioning at the logical level. They describe their approach in terms of the Data Abstraction Model of Smith and Smith [Smit77]. The model partitions the individuals represented in the database into populations having common characteristics; populations can be decomposed into subpopulations, and populations that cannot be further decomposed are "atomic." The complete set of populations forms a hierarchy such that each nonatomic population is composed of disjoint atomic populations. Disjoint populations having a common parent may be grouped into "clusters".

FIGURE 6.15 Data abstraction model of student record database.

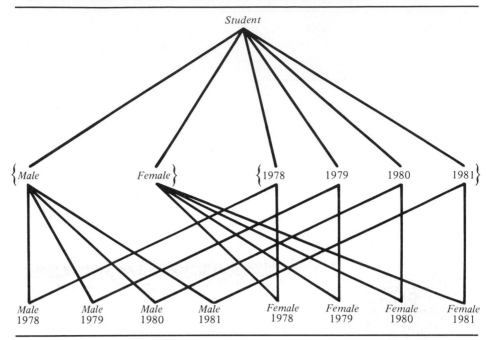

Example:

Figure 6.15 illustrates a partitioning of the student record database by *Sex* and *Class* similar to the partitioning in Table 6.10. The populations at the leaves of the hierarchy are atomic, and the populations at the middle level form two clusters: *Sex* = {*Male, Female*} and *Class* = {1978, 1979, 1980, 1981}. ∎

A **Population Definition Construct** (PDC) defines each population, the operations that can be performed over the population, and the security constraints of the population. The permitted statistics $q(P)$ for a population P must satisfy the constraints.

1. $q(P)$ is permitted if and only if $q(P')$ is permitted for every population P' in a cluster with P.
2. $q(P)$ is permitted if $q(S)$ is permitted for any subpopulation S of P.

If $P_1, \ldots, P_m$ are atomic populations in the same cluster, condition (1) says that if any P_i must be suppressed, then all P_i must be suppressed. This may be much more restrictive than necessary.

A **User Knowledge Construct** (UKC) defines groups of users and their supplementary knowledge about the database, the operations permitted to members of the group, and the security constraints of the group. Security information in both the PDCs and a UKC is used to determine whether a statistic should be released to a particular user.

Feige and Watts [Feig70] describe a variant of partitioning called **microaggregation:** individuals are grouped to create many synthetic "average individuals"; statistics are computed for these synthetic individuals rather than the real ones.

Partitioning may limit the free flow of statistical information if groups are excessively large or ill-conceived, or if only a limited set of statistics can be computed for each group. But if a rich set of statistical functions is available, large groups may not severely impact the practicality of some databases.

Dalenius and Denning [Dale79] considered the possibility of a single-partition database; that is, the only available statistics are those computed over the entire database. All released statistics would be finite moments of the form:

$$q(All, e_1, \ldots, e_M) = \sum_{i=1}^{N} x_{i1}^{e_1} x_{i2}^{e_2} \ldots x_{iM}^{e_M},$$

where

$$e_1 + e_2 + \cdots + e_M \leq e$$

for some given e. Because all statistics are computed over the entire database, disclosure is extremely difficult if not impossible. At the same time, it is possible for the statistician to compute correlations of attributes.

We considered the feasibility of releasing all moments for a given e as an alternative to releasing macrostatistics or microstatistics. This approach would provide a richer set of statistics than are provided by macrostatistics, but a higher level of protection than provided by microstatistics. The total number of moments increases rapidly with e and M, however, so it may not be feasible to compute and release more than a relatively small subset of all possible moments. The total number of moments over M variables is given by

$$m_e(M) = \binom{M + e}{e}.$$

Example:
If $M = 40$, then $m_2(40) = 861$ and $m_3(40) = 12{,}341.$ ∎

6.5 MECHANISMS THAT ADD NOISE

Restricting statistics that might lead to disclosure can be costly and imprecise, especially if we take into account users' supplementary knowledge. Consequently, there is considerable interest in simple mechanisms that control disclosure by adding noise to the statistics. These mechanisms are generally more efficient to apply, and allow the release of more nonsensitive statistics.

6.5.1 Response Perturbation (Rounding)

Response perturbation refers to any scheme which perturbs a statistic $q = q(C)$ by some function $r(q)$ before it is released. The perturbation usually involves some form of rounding—that is, q is rounded up or down to the nearest multiple of some base b.

There are two kinds of rounding: systematic rounding and random rounding. **Systematic rounding** always rounds q either up or down according to the following rule. Let $b' = \lfloor (b + 1)/2 \rfloor$ and $d = q \bmod b$. Then

$$r(q) = \begin{cases} q & \text{if } d = 0 \\ q - d & \text{if } d < b' \quad \text{(round down)} \\ q + (b - d) & \text{if } d \geq b' \quad \text{(round up)} \end{cases}$$

Given a rounded value $r(q)$, a user can deduce that q lies in the interval $[r(q) - b' + 1, r(q) + b' - 1]$. For example, if $b = 5$, then $r(q) = 25$ implies $q \in [23, 27]$.

Under certain conditions, it is possible to recover exact statistics from their rounded values. Let $C_1, \ldots, C_m$ be disjoint query sets, and let $C_{m+1} = C_1 \cup \ldots \cup C_m$; thus, $q_{m+1} = q_1 + \ldots + q_m$, where $q_i = \text{sum}(C_i, A)$ for some attribute A ($1 \leq i \leq m + 1$). Let $[L_i, U_i]$ be the interval estimates for each $r(q_i)$, and let $L = L_1 + \ldots + L_m$ and $U = U_1 + \ldots + U_m$. Achugbue and Chin [Achu79] show that it is possible to deduce the exact values of the q_i from the rounded values $r(q_i)$ when either:

(i) $U = L_{m+1}$, in which case

$$\begin{aligned} q_i &= U_i \quad (1 \leq i \leq m) \\ q_{m+1} &= L_{m+1}, \text{ or} \end{aligned}$$

(ii) $L = U_{m+1}$, in which case

$$\begin{aligned} q_i &= L_i \quad (1 \leq i \leq m) \\ q_{m+1} &= U_{m+1} . \end{aligned}$$

(See Figure 6.16.)

FIGURE 6.16 Disclosure from rounded values.

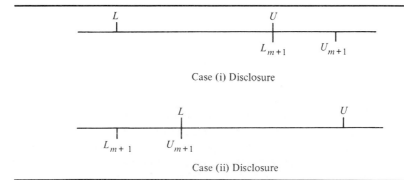

Case (i) Disclosure

Case (ii) Disclosure

TABLE 6.11 Disclosure under systematic rounding.

	$r(q_i)$	L_i	U_i
q_1	15	13	17
q_2	10	8	12
q_3	15	13	17
q_4	20	18	22
		52	68
q_{m+1}	70	68	72

Case (i) is illustrated in Table 6.11. Because $U = 68 = L_{m+1}$, each q_i $(1 \leq i \leq m)$ must achieve its maximum; otherwise q_{m+1} would be smaller, making $r(q_{m+1})$ and L_{m+1} smaller.

If neither Case (i) nor Case (ii) applies, then exact disclosure is not possible from $r(q_1)$, ..., $r(q_m)$. Nevertheless, if the overlap between $[L, U]$ and $[L_{m+1}, U_{m+1}]$, is not too large, it may be possible to reduce the interval estimates $[L_i, U_i]$. If other (rounded) statistics are available, the intervals may be further reduced. (Schlörer [Schl77] also investigated the vulnerabilities of systematic rounding to tracker attacks.)

Random rounding rounds a statistic q up or down according to the following rule:

$$r(q) = \begin{cases} q & \text{if } d = 0 \\ q - d & \text{with probability } 1 - p \quad \text{(round down)} \\ q + (b - d) & \text{with probability } \quad p \quad \text{(round up)} \end{cases}$$

When $p = d/b$, random rounding has the advantage of being unbiased.

Random rounding is subject to the same methods of error removal as systematic rounding.

Example:
Table 6.12 shows how exact values can be recovered from a 2-dimensional table of rounded sums, where the rounding base b is 5. Here the total must be at least 76, which is achievable only when the entries inside the table achieve their maximum possible values. ■

Random rounding is also vulnerable to another kind of attack in query-processing systems. If a query q is asked many times, its true value can be deduced by averaging the rounded values. (See also [Fell74,Narg72,Haq77,Palm74].)

Both systematic and random rounding have the drawback that the sum of the rounded statistics for disjoint query sets can differ from the rounded statistic for the union of the sets. As illustrated by Tables 6.11 and 6.12, this can often be exploited to obtain better estimates of the rounded values. **Controlled rounding** overcomes this deficiency by requiring the sum of rounded statistics to equal their rounded sum [Caus79,Cox81]; that is, if C_1, ..., C_m are disjoint query sets and C_{m+1} is the union $C_{m+1} = C_1 \cup ... \cup C_m$, then

TABLE 6.12 Disclosure under random rounding (adapted from [Schl77]).

10	20	35
10	20	40
25	50	80

(a)   Table of Rounded Values.

6–14	16–24	31–39
6–14	16–24	36–44
21–29	46–54	76–84

(b)   Table of Interval Estimates.

14	24	38
14	24	38
28	48	76

(c)   Table of Exact Values.

$$r(q_1) + \cdots + r(q_m) = r(q_{m+1}) \ .$$

Cox [Cox81] describes a method of achieving controlled rounding in 1- or 2-dimensional tables of macrostatistics. For a given integer $p \geq 1$, the method finds an **optimal controlled rounding** that minimizes the sum of the pth powers of the absolute values of the differences between the true statistics and their rounded values; that is, that minimizes the objective function

$$z_p = \sum_q |q - r(q)|^p$$

The problem of finding an optimal controlled rounding can be expressed as a capacity-constrained transportation problem [Dant63], and thereby solved using standard algorithms. The technique is particularly well-suited for protecting tables of relatively small frequency counts.

Other kinds of response perturbations are possible. For example, Schwartz [Schw77] studies functions $r(q)$ that return a pseudo-random value uniformly distributed over the interval $[q - d, q + d]$ for relatively small values of d. To prevent error removal by averaging, the same query must always return the same response.

6.5.2 Random-Sample Queries

We mentioned earlier that census agencies often protect microstatistics by releasing relatively small samples of the total number of records. In this section we shall describe the results of an ongoing research project aimed at applying sampling to query-processing systems.

Most inference controls are subverted by a single basic principle of compromise: because the user can control the composition of each query set, he can isolate a single record or value by intersecting query sets. Denning [Denn80c] introduced a new class of queries called **Random-Sample Queries** (RSQs) that deny the intruder precise control over the queried records. RSQs introduce enough uncertainty that users cannot isolate a confidential record but can get accurate statistics for groups of records.

This query-based control differs from the sampling controls employed in population surveys in two respects. First, it uses relatively large samples, say on the order of 80–90% of the total number of records in the database; thus, the released statistics are fairly accurate. Second, it uses a different sample to compute each statistic. It is this aspect of the strategy that radically departs from the traditional use of sampling and allows the use of large samples. But whereas this is economical to implement in query-processing systems, it would be expensive to use with microstatistics or macrostatistics. The control is defined as follows:

Random-Sample-Query Control:

Given a query $q(C)$, as the query processor examines each record i in C, it applies a selection function $f(C, i)$ that determines whether i is used to compute the statistic. The set of selected records forms a sampled query set

$$C^* = \{i \in C \mid f(C, i) = 1\} ,$$

from which the query processor returns $q^* = q(C^*)$. A parameter p specifies the sampling probability that a record is selected. ∎

The uncertainty introduced by this control is the same as the uncertainty in sampling the entire database, with a probability p of selecting a particular record for a sample. The expected size of a random sample over the entire database of size N is pN.

The control is easy to implement when $p = 1 - 1/2^k$. Let $r(i)$ be a function that maps the ith record into a random sequence of $m \geq k$ bits. Let $s(C)$ be a function that maps formula C into a random sequence of length m over the alphabet $\{0, 1, *\}$; this string includes exactly k bits and $m - k$ asterisks (asterisks denote "don't care"). The ith record is excluded from the sampled query set whenever $r(i)$ matches $s(C)$ [a "match" exists whenever each nonasterisk character of $s(C)$ is the same as the corresponding symbol of $r(i)$]. The selection function $f(C, i)$ is thus given by

$$f(C, i) = \begin{cases} 1 & \text{if } r(i) \text{ does not match } s(C) \\ 0 & \text{if } r(i) \text{ matches } s(C) \end{cases} .$$

This method applies for $p > 1/2$ (e.g., $p = .5, .75, .875,$ and $.9375$). For $p < 1/2$, use $p = 1/2^k$; the ith record is included in the sample if and only if $r(i)$ matches $s(C)$.

Example:

Let $p = 7/8$, $m = 8$, and $s(C) =$ "$*10*1***$". If $r(i) =$ "11011000" for some

i, that record would match $s(C)$ and be excluded from C^*. If r generates unique random bit sequences, then the expected size of C^* is $7/8$ that of C. ∎

Encryption algorithms are excellent candidates for the functions r and s, as they yield seemingly random bit sequences. If the database is encrypted anyway, the function r could simply select m bits from some invariant part of the record (e.g., the identifier field); this would avoid the computation of $r(i)$ during query processing. With a good encryption algorithm, two formulas C and D having almost identical query sets will map to quite different $s(C)$ and $s(D)$, thereby ensuring that C^* and D^* differ by as much as they would with pure random sampling.

Under RSQs, it is more natural to return relative frequencies and averages directly, since the statistics are not based on the entire database, and the users may not know what percentage of the records are included in the random sample. Recall that the true relative frequencies and averages are given by:

$$\mathbf{rfreq}(C) = \frac{|C|}{N}$$

$$\mathbf{avg}(C, A) = \frac{1}{|C|} \sum_{i \epsilon C} x_i .$$

The sampled relative frequencies and averages are:

$$\mathbf{rfreq}^*(C) = \frac{|C^*|}{pN}$$

$$\mathbf{avg}^*(C, A) = \frac{1}{|C^*|} \sum_{i \epsilon C^*} x_i .$$

Note the expected value of $|C^*|$ is $p|C|$; thus, the expected value of the sampled frequency is $|C|/N$, the true relative frequency.

The values of p and N may be published so users can judge the significance of the estimates returned. A user who knows p and N can then compute approximations for both the sampled and unsampled counts and sums.

A minimum query-set-size restriction is still needed with RSQs if the sampling probability is large. Otherwise, all records in a small query set would be included in a sample with high probability, making compromise possible.

Compromise is controlled by introducing small sampling errors into the statistics. For frequencies, the relative error between the sampled frequency and the true frequency is given by

$$f_C = \frac{\mathbf{rfreq}^*(C) - \mathbf{rfreq}(C)}{\mathbf{rfreq}(C)} .$$

The expected relative error is zero; thus, the sampled relative frequency is an unbiased estimator of the true relative frequency. The root-mean-squared relative error is

$$\hat{R}(f_C) = \sqrt{\frac{1-p}{|C|p}} \; .$$

Thus, for fixed p, the expected error decreases as the square root of the query-set size.

Figure 6.17 shows a graph of the error $\hat{R}(f_C)$ as a function of $|C|$ for several values of p. For $p > .5$, $|C| > 100$ gives less than a 10% error. For $p = .9375$, $|C| > 667$ gives less than a 1% error. For extremely small query sets, however, the relative errors may be unacceptably high. Absolute errors for counts are greater than those for relative frequencies by a factor of N; however, their relative errors are comparable. The same holds for sums as compared with averages.

The relative error between a sampled average and the true average is given by:

$$a_C = \frac{\mathbf{avg}^*(C,\, A) - \mathbf{avg}(C,\, A)}{\mathbf{avg}(C,\, A)} \; .$$

The sampled average is not unbiased, but its bias is negligible. The root-mean-square error depends on the distribution of the data values in the query set. For sufficiently large $|C|$, it is approximately

$$\hat{R}(a_C) \simeq \mathbf{cfv}(C,\, A)\hat{R}(f_C) \; ,$$

where $\mathbf{cfv}(C,\, A) = \mathbf{var}(C,\, A)^{1/2}/\mathbf{avg}(C,\, A)$ is the coefficient of variation for the distribution of data values of A in C. If the data values are uniformly distributed over a moderately large interval $[1,\, d]$ (e.g., $d > 10$), the root-mean-square error becomes

$$\hat{R}(a_C) \simeq 0.6\, \hat{R}(f_C) \; ,$$

showing that the relative errors in averages behave the same as in frequencies but are 40% smaller. These results were confirmed experimentally on a simulated database.

RSQs control compromise by reducing a questioner's ability to interrogate the desired query sets precisely. We have studied the extent to which the control may be circumvented by small query sets, general trackers, and error removal by averaging. Compromise may be possible with small query sets unless p is small or a minimum query-set-size restriction is imposed. Trackers, on the other hand, are no longer a useful tool for compromise.

RSQs appear to be most vulnerable to attacks based on error removal by averaging. Because the same query always returns the same response, it is necessary to pose different but "equivalent" queries to remove sampling errors. One method involves averaging the responses of equivalent queries that use different formulas to specify the same query set.

Example:
The statistic $q(Male \bullet 1978)$ could be estimated from the sampled statistics:

$q^*(Male \bullet 1978)$

FIGURE 6.17 Expected root mean squared relative error in frequency.

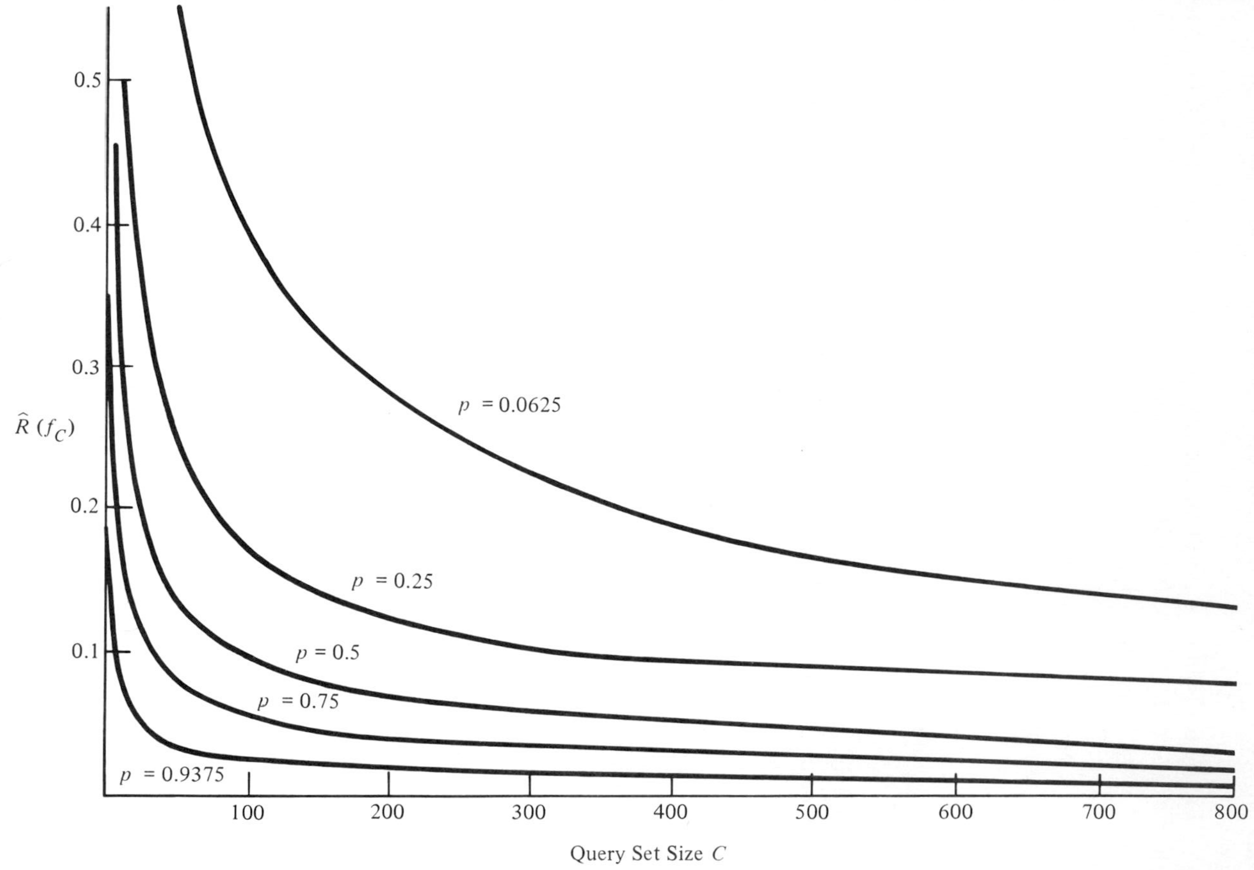

$q^*(\sim Female \bullet 1978)$
$q^*(Male \bullet \sim(1979 + 1980 + 1981))$
$q^*(Male \bullet (Bio \bullet 1978) + Male \bullet (\sim Bio \bullet 1978))$

.

.

.

■

Schlörer observed that this problem does not arise if $s(C)$ is a function of the query set C rather than the characteristic formula so that $s(C) = s(D)$ whenever formulas C and D are reducible to each other. Still, this would not prevent a second method of averaging that uses disjoint subsets of query sets.

Example:
The statistic $q(Male \bullet 1978)$ could be estimated from:

$q^*(Male \bullet 1978 \bullet Bio) + q^*(Male \bullet 1978 \bullet \sim Bio)$
$q^*(Male \bullet 1978 \bullet CS) + q^*(Male \bullet 1978 \bullet \sim CS)$
$q^*(Male \bullet 1978 \bullet EE) + q^*(Male \bullet 1978 \bullet \sim EE)$
$q^*(Male \bullet 1978 \bullet Psy) + q^*(Male \bullet 1978 \bullet \sim Psy)$

.

.

.

■

Let $q_1^*, \ldots, q_m^*$ be the responses from m independent queries that estimate $q = \mathbf{rfreq}(C)$, and let

$$\hat{q} = \frac{1}{m} \sum_{i=1}^{m} q_i^*$$

be an estimate of q. The mean and variance of $\hat{q}$ are:

$$E(\hat{q}) = \frac{|C|}{N}$$

$$Var(\hat{q}) = \frac{|C|(1 - p)}{m \, N^2 p} \, .$$

For large m ($m \geq 30$ should be sufficient when the distribution of possible responses for each q_i^* is symmetric), the distribution of $\hat{q}$ is approximately normal. Letting $\sigma_{\hat{q}} = [Var(\hat{q})]^{1/2}$, the confidence intervals for the true frequency q given $\hat{q}$ are:

$Pr[q \in [\hat{q} \pm 1.645\sigma_{\hat{q}}]] \simeq .90$
$Pr[q \in [\hat{q} \pm 1.960\sigma_{\hat{q}}]] \simeq .95$
$Pr[q \in [\hat{q} \pm 2.575\sigma_{\hat{q}}]] \simeq .99 \, .$

If we assume that a 95% confidence interval is required for disclosure, the length of this interval is given by

$$k = 3.92\sigma_{\hat{q}} = \frac{3.92}{N}\sqrt{\frac{(1-p)\,|C|}{p\,m}} \ .$$

Now, $k \le 1/N$ is required to estimate q to within one record (such accuracy is required, for example, to estimate relative frequencies for small query sets using trackers). The number of queries required to achieve this accuracy is

$$m \ge (3.92)^2 \left(\frac{1-p}{p}\right) |C| > 15\left(\frac{1-p}{p}\right) |C| \ .$$

For fixed p, the function grows linearly in $|C|$. For $p = .5$, over 450 queries are required to estimate frequencies for query sets of size 30; over 1500 queries are required to estimate frequencies for query sets of size 100. For $p = .9375$, 100 queries are required to estimate frequencies for query sets of size 100.

For averages taken over variables uniformly distributed over a range $[1, s]$,

$$m > 128\left(\frac{1-p}{p}\right) |C|$$

queries are required to obtain an estimate sufficiently accurate to enable personal disclosure by a simple tracker attack (more complex linear-system attacks would require even more queries). This is about an order of magnitude greater than for frequencies; whereas the relative errors in averages (for uniform distributions) are lower than in frequencies, more queries are required to obtain estimates accurate enough to compromise with averages than with frequencies. S. Kurzban observed, however, that compromise may be easier for skewed distributions, which would also have higher relative errors.

For large query sets, the number of queries required to obtain reliable estimates of confidential data under RSQs is large enough to protect against manual attacks. Nevertheless, a computer might be able to subvert the control by systematically generating the necessary queries. Threat monitoring (i.e., keeping a log or audit trail) is probably necessary to detect this type of systematic attack [Hoff70].

6.5.3 Data Perturbation

Noise can also be added to the data values directly—either by permanently modifying the data stored in the database, or by temporarily perturbing the data when it is used in the calculation of some statistic. The first approach is useful for protecting data published in the form of microstatistics, but it cannot be used in general-purpose databases where the accuracy of the data is essential for nonstatistical purposes. This section describes a temporary perturbation scheme for general-purpose systems. The next section describes data modification for published microstatistics.

Data perturbation involves perturbing each data value x_i used to compute a statistic $q(C)$ by some function $f(x_i)$, and then using $x_i' = f(x_i)$ in place of x_i in the computation. Beck [Beck80] showed how data perturbation could be integrated into a query-processing system for **count**, **sum**, and selection queries. We shall describe his approach for protecting data released as sums.

Consider the query

$$S = \mathbf{sum}(C, A) = \sum_{i \in C} x_i \ .$$

Rather than releasing **sum**(C, A), the system computes and releases

$$S' = \mathbf{sum'}(C, A) = \sum_{i \in C} x_i' \ , \tag{6.12}$$

where

$$x_i' = x_i + z1_i(x_i - \bar{x}_C) + z2_i \ ,$$

and $\bar{x}_C = \mathbf{avg}(C, A) = \mathbf{sum}(C, A)/|C|$ is the mean value taken over the query set C, and $z1_i$ and $z2_i$ are independent random variables, generated for each query, with expected value and variance:

$$E(z1_i) = 0 \quad \mathrm{Var}(z1_i) = 2a^2$$

$$E(z2_i) = 0 \quad \mathrm{Var}(z2_i) = \frac{2a^2}{|C|}(\bar{x}_C - \bar{x})^2 \ ,$$

where $\bar{x} = \mathbf{avg}(All, A)$ is the mean taken over the entire database, and the parameter a is constant for all queries. The expected value of S' is $E(S') = S$; thus, the perturbed statistic is an unbiased estimator of the true statistic.

The variance of S' is

$$\mathrm{Var}(S') = 2a^2\sigma_C^2|C| + 2a^2(\bar{x}_C - \bar{x})^2 \ , \tag{6.13}$$

where

$$\sigma_C^2 = \frac{1}{|C|} \sum_{i \in C} (x_i - \bar{x}_C)^2$$

is the sample variance over C. It is bounded below by

$$\mathrm{Var}(S') \geq a^2(x_i - \bar{x})^2 \tag{6.14}$$

for each x_i, which implies

$$\sigma_{S'} > a|x_i - \bar{x}| \ ,$$

where $\sigma_{S'}$ is the standard deviation of the estimate S'.

Beck defines a value x_i to be safe if it is not possible to obtain an estimate $\hat{x}_i$ of x_i such that

$$\sigma_{\hat{x}_i} < c|x_i - \bar{x}| \ ,$$

where c is a parameter of the system. The preceding result shows that it is not possible to compromise a value x_i using a single query if $a \geq c$.

Beck also shows that it takes a least $n = (a/c)^2$ queries to compromise a database using any kind of linear-system attack, including those based on error removal by averaging. Combining these two results, we see that compromise can be prevented by picking $a \gg c$.

Unfortunately, this has the undesirable side effect of introducing extremely large errors into the released statistics. Beck solves this problem by introducing a scheme for changing the $z1_i$ and $z2_i$ so that it is possible to achieve an exponential increase in the number of queries needed to compromise, with less than a linear increase in the standard deviation of the responses.

Rather than picking a completely new $z1_i$ and $z2_i$ for each record and each query, $z1_i$ and $z2_i$ are computed from the sum of m independent random variables:

$$z1_i = \sum_{j=1}^{m} z1_{ij} , \quad z2_i = \sum_{j=1}^{m} z2_{ij} ,$$

where:

$$E(z1_{ij}) = 0 \quad \text{Var}(z1_{ij}) = 2a^2$$

$$E(z2_{ij}) = 0 \quad \text{Var}(z2_{ij}) = \frac{2a^2}{|C|}(\bar{x}_C - \bar{x})^2$$

$(1 \leq j \leq m)$. Then

$$E(z1_i) = 0 \quad \text{Var}(z1_i) = 2ma^2$$

$$E(z2_i) = 0 \quad \text{Var}(z2_i) = \frac{2ma^2}{|C|}(\bar{x}_C - \bar{x})^2 .$$

This means that the response S' will have variance

$$\text{Var}(S') = 2ma^2\sigma_C^2|C| + 2ma^2(\bar{x}_C - \bar{x})^2 ,$$

so that the standard deviation will be bounded by

$$\sigma_{S'} > am^{1/2}|x_i - \bar{x}| .$$

Decomposing the $z1_i$ and $z2_i$ into m components therefore increases the standard deviation in the error by $m^{1/2}$.

Each $z1_i$ and $z2_i$ is changed for each query by changing at least one of the $z1_{ij}$ and $z2_{ij}$ $(1 \leq j \leq m)$. Beck shows that by changing only $z1_{i1}$ and $z2_{i1}$ after each query, compromise may be possible with $n = (a/c)^2$ queries as before. If in addition we change $z1_{i2}$ and $z2_{i2}$ after every $d = \lfloor (a/c)^2 \rfloor$ queries, then $n = d^2$ queries are required to compromise. If we continue in this way to change $z1_{ij}$ and $z2_{ij}$ after every d^{j-1} queries $(1 \leq j \leq m)$, then $n = d^m = \lfloor (a/c)^2 \rfloor^m$ queries are needed to compromise, whereas the standard deviation in the errors is proportional to only $am^{1/2}$. Beck shows that picking $a = 3^{1/2}c$ (i.e., $d = 3$) minimizes $am^{1/2}$ while holding $\lfloor (a/c)^2 \rfloor^m$ constant.

As m increases, the standard deviation of responses grows as $m^{1/2}$, while the difficulty of compromisng grows as 3^m. Using a simulated database, Beck confirmed his hypothesis that it was possible to protect against billions of queries and still provide reasonably accurate statistics.

Beck outlines a simple implementation that allows the released value S' to be computed with just a single pass over the data values. Let $r(i)$ be a function that maps the ith record into a pseudorandom bit pattern, as in the random-sample-queries control; similarly, let $r(S)$ be a pseudorandom bit pattern of the query S. We also associate $m - 1$ bit patterns $b_2, \ldots, b_m$ with the database, where each b_j is changed after every d^{j-1} queries. Then $z1_{i1}$ is generated using $r(i) \oplus r(S)$ as a seed to a random number generator (where $\oplus$ denotes exclusive-or); and for $j = 2, \ldots, m$, $z1_{ij}$ is generated using $r(i) \oplus b_j$ as the seed. Similarly, $z2^*_{ij}$ is generated, using a different random number generator, where $z2^*_{ij}$ is the same as $z2_{ij}$, except that $\text{Var}(z2^*_{ij}) = 1$ (thus it can be generated without knowing $\bar{x}_C$); therefore,

$$z2_{ij} = \left(\frac{2a^2(\bar{x}_C - \bar{x})^2}{|C|}\right)^{1/2} z2^*_{ij} .$$

To compute the released statistic in a single pass over the query set, we observe that

$$S' = \sum_{i \in C} x'_i = \sum_{i \in C} [x_i + z1_i(x_i - \bar{x}_C) + z2_i]$$

$$= S + S1 - \bar{x}_C Z1 + \left(\frac{2a^2(\bar{x}_C - \bar{x})^2}{|C|}\right)^{1/2} Z2^* ,$$

where:

$$S1 = \sum_{i \in C} z1_i x_i$$

$$Z1 = \sum_{i \in C} z1_i$$

$$Z2^* = \sum_{i \in C} z2^*_i .$$

6.5.4 Data Swapping

Schlörer [Schl77] suggested a data transformation scheme based on interchanging values in the records. The objective is to interchange (swap) enough values that nothing can be deduced from disclosure of individual records, but at the same time to preserve the accuracy of at least low-order statistics. The approach has subsequently been studied by Schlörer [Schl81] and by Dalenius and Reiss [Dale78], who introduced the term "data swapping".

Schlörer defines a database D to be **d-transformable** if there exists at least one other database D' such that

1. D and D' have the same k-order frequency counts for $k = 0, 1, \ldots, d$, and
2. D and D' have no records in common.

Example:
Table 6.13 shows a 2-transformable database D of student records containing the three fields *Sex*, *Major*, and *GP*. This database is 2-transformable

TABLE 6.13 A 2-transformable database.

Record	D			D'		
	Sex	Major	GP	Sex	Major	GP
1	*Female*	*Bio*	4.0	*Male*	*Bio*	4.0
2	*Female*	*CS*	3.0	*Male*	*CS*	3.0
3	*Female*	*EE*	3.0	*Male*	*EE*	3.0
4	*Female*	*Psy*	4.0	*Male*	*Psy*	4.0
5	*Male*	*Bio*	3.0	*Female*	*Bio*	3.0
6	*Male*	*CS*	4.0	*Female*	*CS*	4.0
7	*Male*	*EE*	4.0	*Female*	*EE*	4.0
8	*Male*	*Psy*	3.0	*Female*	*Psy*	3.0

because the database D' has the same 0-, 1-, and 2-order statistics. For example, **count**(*Female* • *CS*) = 1 in both D and D'. Note, however, that 3-order statistics are not preserved. For example,

$$\textbf{count}(\textit{Female} \bullet \textit{CS} \bullet 3.0) = \begin{cases} 1 & \text{in } D \\ 0 & \text{in } D' . \end{cases} \blacksquare$$

Because all 1-order counts must be preserved, D' must contain exactly the same set of values, and in the same quantities, as D. Thus, D' can be obtained from D by swapping the values among the records. If swapping is done on a single attribute A (as in Table 6.13), it suffices to check counts that involve the values of A to determine whether all low-order statistics are preserved.

Schlörer studied the conditions under which a database D is d-transformable; he proved that

1. D must have $M \geq d + 1$ attributes.
2. D must contain at least $N \geq (m/2)2^d$ records, where m is the maximum number of values $|A_j|$ for any attribute A_j $(1 \leq j \leq M)$.

He also showed that D must have a recursive structure. Consider each subdatabase D_1 of D consisting of all records having the same value for some attribute A (in D_1 the attribute A is omitted). If D is d-transformable, then D_1 must be $(d - 1)$-transformable over the remaining attributes.

Example:
Figure 6.18 illustrates the recursive structure of the database D of Table 6.13, where $A = Sex$. Note that the subdatabase D_1' is a 1-transformation of the subdatabase D_1, and vice-versa. $\blacksquare$

Data swapping could be used in two ways. One way would be to take a given database D, find a d-transformation on D for some suitable choice of d, and then release the transformed database D'. This method could be used with statistics-only databases and the publication of microstatistics; it could not be used with

FIGURE 6.18. Recursive structure of database.

D		
	D_1	
Female	Bio	4.0
Female	CS	3.0
Female	EE	3.0
Female	Psy	4.0
Male	Bio	3.0
Male	CS	4.0
Male	EE	4.0
Male	Psy	3.0
	D_1'	

general-purpose databases, where accuracy of the data is needed for nonstatistical purposes. Because k-order statistics for $k > d$ are not necessarily preserved, these statistics would not be computed from the released data.

If swapping is done over all confidential variables, the released data is protected from disclosure. Reiss [Reis79] has shown, however, that the problem of finding a general data swap is **NP**-complete. Thus, the method appears to be impractical.

To overcome these limitations, Reiss [Reis80] has studied the possibility of applying **approximate data swapping** to the release of microstatistics. Here a portion of the original database is replaced with a randomly generated database having approximately the same k-order statistics ($k = 0, \ldots, d$) as the original database. The released database is generated one record at a time, where the values chosen for each record are randomly drawn from a distribution defined by the k-order statistics of the original data. Reiss shows that it is possible to provide fairly accurate statistics while ensuring confidentiality.

Any scheme that modifies the data records cannot be used in general-purpose systems. There is, however, another way of applying data swapping that would be applicable to these systems. If we could simply show that a database D is d-transformable, we could safely release any k-order statistic ($k \leq d$), because such a statistic could have been derived from a different set of records. For example, there is no way of determining (without supplementary knowledge) a student's GP from the 0-, 1-, and 2-order statistics of the database shown in Table 6.13, even though each student is uniquely identifiable by *Sex* and *Major*. The problem with this approach is that there is no known efficient algorithm for testing a database for d-transformability. Even if an efficient algorithm could be found, security cannot be guaranteed if the users have supplementary knowledge about the database (see exercises at end of chapter).

Data released in the form of microstatistics may be perturbed in other ways—for example, by rounding or by swapping a random subset of values without regard to preserving more than 0 and 1-order statistics. Some of these techniques are discussed by Dalenius [Dale76] and by Campbell, Boruch, Schwartz, and Steinberg [Camp77].

6.5.5 Randomized Response (Inquiry)

Because many individuals fear invasion of their privacy, they do not respond truthfully to sensitive survey questions. For example, if an individual is asked "Have you ever taken drugs for depression?", the individual may lie and respond *No*, thereby biasing the results of the survey. Warner [Warn65] introduced a "randomized response" technique to deal with this problem. The technique is applied at the time the data is gathered—that is, at the time of inquiry.

The basic idea is that the individual is asked to draw a question at random from a set of questions, where some of the questions are sensitive and some are not. Then the individual is asked to respond to that question, but to not reveal the question answered.

Bourke and Dalenius [Bour75] and Dalenius [Dale76] discuss several strategies for doing this. Warner's original scheme is illustrated by the following sample questions:

1.   Were you born in August?
2.   Have you ever taken drugs for depression?

The objective of the survey is to determine the percentage of the population who have taken drugs for depression. The respondent picks one question at random (e.g., by tossing a coin), and then answers *Yes* or *No*. Assuming that the percentage of the population born in August is known, the percentage who have taken drugs for depression can be deduced from the number of *Yes* answers (see exercises at end of chapter).

Although it is not possible to determine whether an individual has taken drugs for depression from a *Yes* answer, a *Yes* answer might seem potentially more revealing than a *No* answer. This lack of symmetry may, therefore, bias the results, though the bias will be less than if the respondent is given no choice at all and asked Question 2 directly.

Bourke suggested a symmetric scheme to remove this bias. Here the respondent is asked to draw a card at random from a deck and respond with the number on the card that describes him. His approach is illustrated next:

Card 1:   (1)   I have taken drugs for depression.
          (2)   I have not taken drugs for depression.

Card 2:   (1)   I was born in August.
          (2)   I was not born in August.

Card 3:   (1)   I have not taken drugs for depression.
          (2)   I have taken drugs for depression.

Because a response of "1" (or "2") is linked to both having taken drugs and not having taken drugs, an individual might feel less threatened about responding truthfully to the survey.

Let p_i be the proportion of card (i) in the deck $(i = 1, 2, 3)$, let b be the probability that an individual is born in August. Suppose that N individuals are surveyed, and that N_1 of them respond "1". To determine the probability d that an individual has taken drugs for depression, we observe that the expected number of individuals responding "1" is given by

$$E(1) = [p_1 d + p_2 b + p_3(1 - d)]N .$$

If $p_1 \neq p_3$, we can solve for d, getting

$$d = \frac{\dfrac{E(1)}{N} - p_2 b - p_3}{p_1 - p_3} .$$

Because N_1 is an estimate of $E(1)$, we can estimate d with

$$\hat{d} = \frac{\dfrac{N_1}{N} - p_2 b - p_3}{p_1 - p_3} .$$

Example:
Let $N = 1000$, $p_1 = .4$, $p_2 = .3$, $p_3 = .3$, $b = .1$, and $N_1 = 350$. Then $d = .2$. ■

The randomized response technique can be viewed as an example of data perturbation, where each individual perturbs the data by a random selection. For obvious reasons, it is not applicable to general-purpose systems where accuracy of the data is essential (e.g., a hospital database or the student record database).

6.6 SUMMARY

Although it is not surprising that simple inference controls can be subverted, it is surprising that often only a few queries are required to do so. A query-set-size control, while necessary, is insufficient because it can be subverted with trackers. A query-set-overlap control is infeasible to implement, possible to subvert, and too restrictive to be of practical interest.

Controls that provide a high level of security by restricting statistics are not always practical for general-purpose database systems. Cell suppression may be too time-consuming to apply to on-line dynamic databases. Data swapping may be limited to the publication of microstatistics. Partitioning at the logical level is an attractive approach, but it could limit the free flow of statistical information if the partitions do not match the query sets needed by researchers, or if the set of available statistics are not sufficiently rich. If partitioning is used, it must be included in the initial design of the database; it cannot be added to an arbitrary database structure. The S_m / N–criterion is an alternative to partitioning that may be less restrictive and easier to integrate into an existing database system.

Controls that add noise to the statistics are an interesting alternative because they are efficient and allow the release of more nonsensitive statistics. They are also simple to implement and could be added to almost any existing database system. Two controls that look promising here are random-sample queries and data perturbation. These controls could augment simple restriction techniques such as a query-set-size control and the S_m / N–criterion.

EXERCISES

6.1 Show how Good's *GP* can be compromised under a query-set-size restriction of $n = 3$ using

a) An individual tracker attack [Eq. (6.4)], where $Cl = CS$ and $C2 = Male \bullet 1978$.
b) A general tracker attack [Eq. (6.5)], where $T = Male$.
c) A double tracker attack [Eq (6.7)], where $T = CS$ and $U = CS + EE$.
d) A union tracker attack [Eq. (6.9)], where $T_1 = Female$ and $T_2 = Male$.

6.2 Show Moore's *GP* can be compromised by a linear system attack under an overlap constraint of $r = 1$ using key-specified queries for sums, where the size of the key list is $k = 4$ (see Section 6.3.3).

6.3 Let $q_1, \ldots, q_m$ be key-specified queries of the form **median**$(\{i_1, \ldots, i_k\}, A)$, such that no two queries have more than one record in common and such that each query set consists of some subset of k records in the set $\{1, \ldots, m - 1\}$ (assume m is large enough that this is possible). Assuming all x_j are unique ($1 \le j \le m - 1$), show that some x_j can be determined from $q_1, \ldots, q_m$.

6.4 Let C be a formula with initial query set $\{1, 2, 3\}$. Suppose that records satisfying C can be added to or deleted from the database in pairs, and that the query **sum**(C, A) can be posed between such additions or deletions. Assuming a query-set-size restriction of $n = 3$, construct a minimal sequence of insertions, deletions, and queries that disclose x_1 when none of the x_i are known. Generalize your result to $C = \{1, 2, \ldots, s\}$ for any odd s and $n = s$.

6.5 Show the suppressed entries in Table 6.6 cannot be exactly determined from the remaining entries without supplementary knowledge by showing the four unknowns are related by only three linearly independent equations. Determine the best possible interval estimate for each unknown cell.

6.6 Prove the cell suppression bound $q^+(C)$ defined by Eq. (6.10) is subadditive by showing that

$$q^+(C + D) \le q^+(C) + q^+(D) .$$

6.7 Prove the cell suppression bound $q^-(C)$ defined by Eq. (6.11) is not superadditive by showing that the following may hold:

$$q^-(C) + q^-(D) > q^-(C + D).$$

6.8 Let $q = 100 + 5 + 5 + 5 + 5 = 120$. Show q is sensitive under a 1-respondent, 75%-dominance sensitivity criterion. Determine a lower bound on an acceptable upper estimate q^+ of q[Eq. (6.10)], and an upper bound on an acceptable lower estimate q^- of q[Eq. (6.11)].

6.9 Given the following table of rounded values, determine the exact values assuming that systematic rounding base 5 was used.

10	10	25
10	10	25
25	25	50

6.10 Karpinski showed it may be possible to subvert a systematic rounding control when records can be added to the database [Karp70]. As an example, suppose that **count**$(C) = 49$ and systematic rounding base 5 is used; thus, the system returns the value 50 in response to a query for **count**(C). Show how a user can determine the true value 49 by adding records that satisfy C to the database, and posing the query **count**(C) after each addition. Can this attack be successfully applied with random rounding?

6.11 Consider Beck's method of data perturbation. Show that S' as defined by Eq. (6.12) is an unbiased estimator of the true sum S. Derive Eqs. (6.13) and (6.14) for Var (S').

6.12 Consider the 2-transformable database D in Table 6.13 of Section 6.5.4. Suppose that a user knows Jane is represented in the database and that Jane is a CS major. Explain why it is not possible to deduce Jane's GP from 0-, 1-, and 2-order statistics without supplementary knowledge. Show that it is possible, however, to deduce Jane's GP if the user knows that her GP is not 4.0.

6.13 Consider the method of randomized response, and suppose that $N = 1000$ individuals participate in a population survey. Each individual is asked to toss a coin to determine which of the following questions to answer:

(1) Have you ever been to New York?
(2) Have you ever taken drugs for depression?

Suppose that 300 people respond *Yes*, and that it is known that roughly 40% of the population surveyed has visited New York. What is the expected percentage of the population surveyed who have taken drugs for depression? Now, suppose that it is learned that Smith answered *Yes* to the survey, but it is not known whether Smith has been to New York. What is the probability Smith answered Question (2)? What is the probability Smith has taken drugs for depression?

REFERENCES

Achu79. Achugbue, J. O. and Chin, F. Y., "The Effectiveness of Output Modification by Rounding for Protection of Statistical Databases," *INFOR* Vol. 17(3) pp. 209–218 (Mar. 1979).

Beck80. Beck, L. L., "A Security Mechanism for Statistical Databases," *ACM Trans. on Database Syst.* Vol. 5(3) pp. 316–338 (Sept. 1980).

Bour75. Bourke, P. D. and Dalenius, T., "Some New Ideas in the Realm of Randomized Inquiries," Confidentiality in Surveys, Report No. 5, Dept. of Statistics, Univ. of Stockholm, Stockholm, Sweden (Sept. 1975).

Camp77. Campbell, D. T., Boruch, R. F., Schwartz, R. D., and Steinberg, J., "Confidentiality-Preserving Modes of Access to Files and to Interfile Exchange for Useful Statistical Analysis," *Eval. Q.* Vol. 1(2) pp. 269–299 (May 1977).

Caus79. Causey, B., "Approaches to Statistical Disclosure," in *Proc. Amer. Stat. Assoc., Soc. Stat. Sec.* Washington, D.C. (1979).

Chin79. Chin., F. Y. and Ozsoyoglu, G., "Security in Partitioned Dynamic Statistical Databases," pp. 594–601 in *Proc. IEEE COMPSAC Conf.* (1979).

Chin80. Chin, F. Y. and Ozsoyoglu, G., "Auditing and Inference Control in Statistical Databases," Univ. of Calif., San Diego, Calif. (Dec. 1980).

Chin81. Chin, F. Y. and Ozsoyoglu, G., "Statistical Database Design," *ACM Trans. on Database Syst.* Vol. 6(1) pp. 113–139 (Mar. 1981).

Codd70. Codd, E. F., "A Relational Model for Large Shared Data Banks," *Comm. ACM* Vol. 13(6) pp. 377–387 (1970).

Codd79. Codd, E. F., "Extending the Database Relational Model to Capture More Meaning," *ACM Trans. on Database Syst.* Vol. 4(4) pp. 397–434 (Dec. 1979).

Cox76. Cox, L. H., "Statistical Disclosure in Publication Hierarchies," presented at the Amer. Stat. Assoc. Meeting, Stat. Comp. Sec. (1976).

Cox78. Cox, L. H., "Suppression Methodology and Statistical Disclosure Control," Confidentiality in Surveys, Report No. 26, Dept. of Statistics, Univ. of Stockholm, Stockholm, Sweden (Jan. 1978).

Cox80. Cox, L. H., "Suppression Methodology and Statistical Disclosure Control," *J. Amer. Stat. Assoc.* Vol. 75(370) pp. 377–385 (June 1980).

Cox81. Cox, L. H. and Ernst, L. R., "Controlled Rounding," U.S. Bureau of the Census, Washington, D.C. (Jan. 1981).

Dale76. Dalenius, T., "Confidentiality in Surveys," *J. Statistical Research* Vol. 10(1) pp. 15–41 (Jan. 1976).

Dale77. Dalenius, T., "Towards a Methodology for Statistical Disclosure Control," *Statistisk tidskrift* Vol. 15 pp. 429–444 (1977).

Dale78. Dalenius, T. and Reiss, S. P., "Data-Swapping—A Technique for Disclosure Control," Confidentiality in Surveys, Report No. 31, Dept. of Statistics, Univ. of Stockholm, Stockholm, Sweden (May 1978).

Dale79. Dalenius, T. and Denning, D., "A Hybrid Scheme for Statistical Release," Computer Sciences Dept., Purdue Univ., W. Lafayette, Ind. (Oct. 1979).

Dant63. Dantzig, G., *Linear Programming and Extensions,* Princeton Univ. Press, Princeton, N.J. (1963).

Davi78. Davida, G. I., Linton, D. J., Szelag, C. R., and Wells, D. L., "Data Base Security," *IEEE Trans. on Software Eng.* Vol. SE-4(6) pp. 531–533 (Nov. 1978).

DeMi77. DeMillo, R. A., Dobkin, D. P., and Lipton, R. J., "Even Databases That Lie Can Be Compromised," *IEEE Trans. on Software Eng.* Vol. SE-4(1) pp. 73–75 (Jan. 1977).

DeMi78. DeMillo, R. A. and Dobkin, D. P., "Combinatorial Inference," pp. 27–35 in *Foundations of Secure Computation,* Academic Press, New York (1978).

Denn79. Denning, D. E., Denning, P. J., and Schwartz, M. D., "The Tracker: A Threat to Statistical Database Security," *ACM Trans. on Database Syst.* Vol. 4(1) pp. 76–96 (March 1979).

Denn80a. Denning, D. E. and Schlörer, J., "A Fast Procedure for Finding a Tracker in a Statistical Database," *ACM Trans. on Database Syst.* Vol. 5(1) pp. 88–102 (Mar. 1980).

Denn80b. Denning, D. E., "Corrigenda: Linear Queries in Statistical Databases," *ACM Trans. on Database Syst.* Vol. 5(3) p. 383 (Sept. 1980).

Denn80c. Denning, D. E., "Secure Statistical Databases Under Random Sample Queries," *ACM Trans. on Database Syst.* Vol. 5(3) pp. 291–315 (Sept. 1980).

Denn81. Denning, D. E., "Restricting Queries That Might Lead to Compromise," in *Proc. 1981 Symp. on Security and Privacy,* IEEE Computer Society (Apr. 1981).

Denn82. Denning, D. E., Schlörer, J., and Wehrle, E., "Memoryless Inference Controls for Statistical Databases," manuscript in preparation (1982).

Dobk79. Dobkin, D., Jones, A. K., and Lipton, R. J., "Secure Databases: Protection Against User Inference," *ACM Trans. on Database Syst.* Vol. 4(1) pp. 97–106 (Mar. 1979).

Feig70. Feige, E. L. and Watts, H. W., "Protection of Privacy Through Microaggregation," in *Databases, Computers, and the Social Sciences,* ed. R. L. Bisco, Wiley-Interscience, New York (1970).

Fell72. Fellegi, I. P., "On the Question of Statistical Confidentiality," *J. Amer. Stat. Assoc.* Vol. 67(337) pp. 7–18 (Mar. 1972).

Fell74. Fellegi, I. P. and Phillips, J. L., "Statistical Confidentiality: Some Theory and Applications to Data Dissemination," *Annals Econ. Soc'l Measurement* Vol. 3(2) pp. 399–409 (Apr. 1974).

Fran77. Frank, O., "An Application of Information Theory to the Problem of Statistical Disclosure," Confidentiality in Surveys, Report No. 20, Dept. of Statistics, Univ. of Stockholm, Stockholm, Sweden (Feb. 1977).

Frie80. Friedman, A. D. and Hoffman, L. J., "Towards a Fail-Safe Approach to Secure Databases," pp. 18–21 in *Proc. 1980 Symp. on Security and Privacy,* IEEE Computer Society (Apr. 1980).

Hans71. Hansen, M. H., "Insuring Confidentiality of Individual Records in Data Storage and Retrieval for Statistical Purposes," *Proc. Fall Jt. Computer Conf.,* Vol. 39, pp. 579–585 AFIPS Press, Montvale, N.J. (1971).

Haq74. Haq, M. I., "Security in a Statistical Data Base," *Proc. Amer. Soc. Info. Sci.* Vol. 11 pp. 33–39 (1974).

Haq75. Haq, M. I., "Insuring Individual's Privacy from Statistical Data Base Users," pp. 941–946 in *Proc. NCC,* Vol. 44, AFIPS Press, Montvale, N.J. (1975).

Haq77. Haq, M. I., "On Safeguarding Statistical Disclosure by Giving Approximate Answers to Queries," *Int. Computing Symp.,* North-Holland, New York (1977).

Hoff70. Hoffman, L. J. and Miller, W. F., "Getting a Personal Dossier from a Statistical Data Bank," *Datamation* Vol. 16(5) pp. 74–75 (May 1970).

Hoff77. Hoffman, L. J., *Modern Methods for Computer Security and Privacy,* Prentice-Hall, Englewood Cliffs, N.J. (1977).

Kam77. Kam, J. B. and Ullman, J. D., "A Model of Statistical Databases and their Security," *ACM Trans. on Database Syst.* Vol. 2(1) pp. 1–10 (Mar. 1977).

Karp70. Karpinski, R. H., "Reply to Hoffman and Shaw," *Datamation* Vol. 16(10) p. 11 (Oct. 1970).

Liu80. Liu, L., "On Linear Queries in Statistical Databases," The MITRE Corp., Bedford, Mass. (1980).

Narg72. Nargundkar, M. S. and Saveland, W., "Random Rounding to Prevent Statistical Disclosure," *Proc. Amer. Stat. Assoc., Soc. Stat. Sec.,* pp. 382–385 (1972).

Olss75. Olsson, L., "Protection of Output and Stored Data in Statistical Databases," ADB-Information, 4, Statistika Centralbyrän, Stockholm, Sweden (1975).

Palm74. Palme, J., "Software Security," *Datamation* Vol. 20(1) pp. 51–55 (Jan. 1974).

Reis78. Reiss, S. B., "Medians and Database Security," pp. 57–92 in *Foundations of Secure Computation,* ed. R. A. DeMillo et al., Academic Press, New York (1978).

Reis79. Reiss, S. B., "The Practicality of Data Swapping," Technical Report No. CS-48, Dept. of Computer Science, Brown Univ., Providence, R.I. (1979).

Reis80. Reiss, S. B., "Practical Data-Swapping: The First Steps," pp. 38–45 in *Proc. 1980 Symp. on Security and Privacy,* IEEE Computer Society (Apr. 1980).

Sand77. Sande, G., "Towards Automated Disclosure Analysis for Establishment Based Statistics," Statistics Canada (1977).

Schl75. Schlörer, J., "Identification and Retrieval of Personal Records from a Statistical Data Bank," *Methods Inf. Med.* Vol. 14(1) pp. 7–13 (Jan. 1975).

Schl76. Schlörer, J., "Confidentiality of Statistical Records: A Threat Monitoring Scheme for On-Line Dialogue," *Meth. Inf. Med.,* Vol. 15(1), pp. 36–42 (1976).

Schl77. Schlörer, J., "Confidentiality and Security in Statistical Data Banks," pp. 101–123 in *Data Documentation: Some Principles and Applications in Science and Industry; Proc. Workshop on Data Documentation,* ed. W. Guas and R. Henzler, Verlag Dokumentation, Munich, Germany (1977).

Schl80. Schlörer, J., "Disclosure from Statistical Databases: Quantitative Aspects of Trackers," *ACM Trans. on Database Syst.* Vol. 5(4) pp. 467–492 (Dec. 1980).

Schl81. Schlörer, J., "Security of Statistical Databases: Multidimensional Transformation," *ACM Trans. on Database Syst.* Vol. 6(1) pp. 95–112 (Mar. 1981).

Schw77. Schwartz, M. D., "Inference from Statistical Data Bases," Ph.D. Thesis, Computer Sciences Dept., Purdue Univ., W. Lafayette, Ind. (Aug. 1977).

Schw79. Schwartz, M. D., Denning, D. E., and Denning, P. J., "Linear Queries in Statistical Databases," *ACM Trans. on Database Syst.* Vol. 4(1) pp. 476–482 (Mar. 1979).

Smit77. Smith, J. M. and Smith, D. C. P., "Database Abstractions: Aggregation and Generalization," *ACM Trans. on Database Syst.* Vol. 2(2) pp. 105–133 (June 1977).

U.S.78. U.S. Dept. of Commerce, "Report on Statistical Disclosure and Disclosure-Avoidance Techniques," U.S. Government Printing Office, Washington, D.C. (1978).

Warn65. Warner, S. L., "Randomized Response: A Technique for Eliminating Evasive Answer Bias," *J. Amer. Stat. Assoc.* Vol. 60 pp. 63–69 (1965).

Yu77. Yu, C. T. and Chin, F. Y., "A Study on the Protection of Statistical Databases," *Proc. ACM SIGMOD Int. Conf. Management of Data,* pp. 169–181 (1977).

Index